Computer Misuse

Computer Misuse
Response, regulation and the law

Stefan Fafinski

WILLAN
PUBLISHING

Published by

Willan Publishing
Culmcott House
Mill Street, Uffculme
Cullompton, Devon
EX15 3AT, UK
Tel: +44(0)1884 840337
Fax: +44(0)1884 840251
e-mail: info@willanpublishing.co.uk
Website: www.willanpublishing.co.uk

Published simultaneously in the USA and Canada by

Willan Publishing
c/o ISBS, 920 NE 58th Ave, Suite 300
Portland, Oregon 97213-3644, USA
Tel: +001(0)503 287 3093
Fax: +001(0)503 280 8832
e-mail: info@isbs.com
Website: www.isbs.com

© Stefan Fafinski 2009

First published 2009

ISBN 978-1-84392-379-4 paperback
      978-1-84392-380-0 hardback

British Library Cataloguing-in-Publication Data

A catalogue record for this book is available from the British Library

Mixed Sources
Product group from well-managed
forests and other controlled sources
Cert no. SGS-COC-2482
www.fsc.org
© 1996 Forest Stewardship Council

Project management by Deer Park Productions, Tavistock, Devon
Typeset by GCS, Leighton Buzzard, Beds
Printed and bound by T.J. International, Padstow, Cornwall

Contents

List of abbreviations

ACLU	American Civil Liberties Union
APCERT	Asia Pacific Computer Emergency Response Team
APIG	All Party Internet Group
ARPANET	Advanced Research Projects Agency Network
BCS	British Computer Society
BITNET	Because It's There Network
BSE	Bovine Spongiform Encephalopathy
CEENet	Central and Eastern European Networking Association
CERN	Conseil Européen pour la Recherche Nucléaire (European Council for Nuclear Research)
CERT	Computer Emergency Response Team
CFSP	Common Foreign and Security Policy
CIRCA	Computer Incident Response Co-ordination Austria
CJD	Creutzfeldt-Jakob disease
CMA	Computer Misuse Act 1990
CoE	Council of Europe
CPNI	Centre for the Protection of the National Infrastructure
CPS	Crown Prosecution Service
CSIRT	Computer Security Incident Response Team
D&G	Domestic & General
DARPA	Defence Advanced Research Projects Agency
ECSC	European Coal and Steel Community
EGC	European Government CSIRTs group
EJN	European Judicial Network

ENIAC	Electronic Numerical Integrator and Computer
ENISA	European Network and Information Security Agency
EURATOM	European Atomic Energy Community
EURIM	European Information Society Group (formerly European Information Management Group)
FCC	Federal Communications Commission
FIRST	Forum of Incident Response and Security Teams
FSA	Financial Services Authority
FSISAC	Financial Services Information Sharing and Analysis Centre
G8	Group of Eight
INTERPOL	International Criminal Police Organisation
IP	Internet Protocol
ISP	Internet Service Provider
ITC	Information Technologists' Company
JANET	Joint Academic Network
JHA	Justice and Home Affairs
NASA	National Aeronautics and Space Administration
NCFTA	National Cyber Forensic Training Alliance
OECD	Organisation for Economic Cooperation and Development
PGP	Pretty Good Privacy
PJCC	Police and Judicial Cooperation in Criminal Matters
RAYNET	Radio Amateurs' Emergency Network
SIRC	Social Issues Research Centre
SIS	Schengen Information System
SOCA	Serious Organised Crime Agency
TERENA	Trans-European Research and Education Networking Association
TF-CSIRT	Task Force of Computer Security and Incident Response Teams
TI	Trusted Introducer
UK-ILGRA	United Kingdom Interdepartmental Liaison Group on Risk Assessment
UKERNA	United Kingdom Education and Research Network Association (now JANET)
UNIVAC	Universal Automatic Computer
US-CERT	United States Computer Emergency Readiness Team
WANK	Worms Against Nuclear Killers
WARP	Warning, Advice and Reporting Point

List of figures and tables

Figures

Tables

Table of cases

Court of Justice of the European Communities and Court of First Instance

United States of America

Hong Kong

European Union

Treaties and agreements

Treaty establishing the European Economic Community (Treaty of Rome) 1957/CEE 1 188

Treaty of Amsterdam amending the Treaty on European Union, the Treaties Establishing the European Communities and Related Acts [1997] OJ C340/1 195, 198

The 1985 Agreement between the Governments of the States of the Benelux Economic Union, the Federal Republic of Germany and the French Republic on the gradual abolition of checks at their common borders [2000] OJ L239/13 198

The 1990 Convention implementing the Schengen Agreement of 14 June 1985 between the Governments of the States of the Benelux Economic Union, the Federal Republic of Germany and the French Republic on the gradual abolition of checks at their common borders [2000] OJ L239/19 198

Treaty on European Union (as amended) [2002] OJ C325/5 189, 194, 198, 203

Treaty establishing the European Community (as amended) [2002] OJ C325/33 188, 194, 198

Treaty of Lisbon amending the Treaty on European Union and the Treaty establishing the European Community [2007] OJ C306/1 196, 197, 199

Computer Misuse

Regulations

Council Regulation (EC) 460/2004 of 10 March 2004 establishing the European Network and Information Security Agency [2004] OJ L 77/1 254

Directives

Council Directive (EC) 76/207/EEC of 9 February 1976 on the implementation of the principle of equal treatment for men and women as regards access to employment, vocational training and promotion, and working conditions [1976] OJ L39/40 240

Council Directive (EC) 80/181/EEC of 20 December 1979 on the approximation of the laws of the Member States relating to units of measurement and on the repeal of Directive 71/354/EEC [1980] OJ L39/40 208

Council Directive (EC) 2000/31 of 23 November 1995 on the protection of individuals with regard to the processing of personal data and of the free movement of such data [1995] OJ L281/31 85

Council Directive (EC) 2000/31 of 8 June 2000 on certain legal aspects of information society services, in particular electronic commerce, in the Internal Market (e-commerce Directive) [2000] OJ L178/1 221

Council Directive (EC) 2001/29 of 22 May 2001 on the harmonisation of certain aspects of copyright and related rights in the information society [2001] OJ L167/10 102

Council Directive (EC) 2005/35 of 7 September 2005 on ship-source pollution and on the introduction of penalties for infringements [2005] OJ L255/11 193

Framework Decisions

Council Framework Decision (EU) 2003/80/JHA of 17 January 2003 on the protection of the environment through criminal law [2003] OJ L29/55 191

Council Framework Decision (EU) 2005/222/JHA of 24 February 2005 on attacks against information systems [2005] OJ L69/67 72, 203, 204, 205

Council Framework Decision (EU) 2005/667/JHA of 12 July 2005 to strengthen the criminal law framework for the enforcement of the law against ship-source pollution [2005] OJ L255/164 193

Council Decisions

Council Decision (EC) 1999/435 concerning the definition of the Schengen acquis for the purpose of determining, in conformity with the relevant provisions of the Treaty establishing the European

United Kingdom

Acts of Parliament

Computer Misuse

Communications Decency Act 47 USC §223 216
Constitution of the United States of America (as amended) (25 July 2007) 216
Counterfeit Access Device and Computer Fraud and Abuse Act 18 USC § 1030 37
Model Penal Code and Commentaries (Official Draft and Revised Comments) (1985) 100
Telecommunications Act 1996 USC §551 242

Hong Kong

Theft Ordinance, Cap 210 24

Council of Europe

Council of Europe Convention for the Protection of Human Rights and Fundamental Freedoms (signed 4 November 1950) ETS 005 99
Council of Europe Convention for the Protection of Individuals with Regard to Automatic Processing of Personal Data (signed 28 January 1981) ETS 108 85
Council of Europe Committee of Ministers Recommendation R(89) 9 'On Computer-Related Crime', 13 September 1989 209
Council of Europe Committee of Ministers Recommendation R(95) 13 'Concerning Problems of Criminal Procedural Law Connected with Information Technology', 11 September 1995 209
Council of Europe Convention on Cybercrime (signed 23 November 2001) ETS 185 38, 66, 75
Council of Europe Explanatory Report to the Convention on Cybercrime ETS 185 210
Council of Europe Additional Protocol to the Convention on cybercrime, concerning the criminalisation of acts of a racist and xenophobic nature committed through computer systems (signed 28 January 2003) ETS 189 215

United Nations

United Nations General Assembly Resolution A/RES/45/121 (14 December 1990) 228
United Nations General Assembly Resolution A/RES/55/63 (22 January 2001) 229

Acknowledgements

This book is the result of a research study which was funded by the Centre for Criminal Justice Studies at the University of Leeds from 2005 to 2008. I therefore owe the University of Leeds a considerable debt of gratitude not only for its financial support, but also, and more importantly, for the many people at Leeds who have supported me throughout this project. Professor Clive Walker provided meticulous and thorough guidance as well as thought-provoking and robust comments on many parts of the work in progress. He has also enlightened me in other areas, particularly the trials and tribulations of Hartlepool United FC and the resurgence of punk rock through Rancid and the Dropkick Murphys. I also wish to thank Professor David S. Wall (despite his allegiance to Aston Villa) for his insight, particularly in the more socio-legal areas of the book and the previews of his excellent book *Cybercrime: The Transformation of Crime in the Information Age*. My very grateful thanks also go to Karin Houkes and Sarah Wallace at Leeds for their ever-entertaining views of the world, their readiness to put the kettle on and the surreal enterprise involving the road-safety hedgehog.

Living in the Royal County of Berkshire, as I do, the University of Leeds is some 210 miles from home. There has therefore been an inordinate amount of travel between Reading and Leeds over the past three years which has been both facilitated and hindered in equal measure by GNER/Virgin Trains (at the start) and National Express/CrossCountry (at the end). Abolishing the direct train from Reading to Leeds was not a help. Wakefield Westgate station became a landmark, its slightly shabby (but not yet derelict) 1960s edifice, beloved of bashers, denoting that I was either 'nearly there' or 'a long way from home'. The loneliness of the long-distance commuter was, however, made bearable at worst and positively enjoyable at best by my virtual travelling companion, Johnno, whose stream of textually deviant inanity and profanity brightened my journeys when services over the points were far from punctual and alternative entertainment was sparse. Johnno, I thank you. Obligatory.

As well as Johnno, there are many other friends who have been neglected to a greater or lesser extent during this project. Sorry. It's done now.

Christmas 2008 is approaching as I write these final few words and I am minded to thank those who contributed to my learning thus far and yet will not be able to read this book: my father, the original Stefan Fafinski, my grandfather, Fred, along with Sylvia, Win and George. My mother, Rita, is still here to be proud and I am sure she will.

Finally, my love and thanks go to my wife, Emily, who has lived second-hand the inevitable lows of research and writing without failing to glow with love and support. She is with me to share the highs of completion which are as much hers as mine. As well as this, her inspiration, perception and diligent proof-reading have made this book better. I love her immeasurably and am very lucky to be with her.

SF
Wokingham
December 2008

Preface

This book is concerned with the nature of computer misuse and the legal and extra-legal responses to it. It explores what is meant by the term 'computer misuse' and charts its emergence as a problem as well as its expansion in parallel with the continued progression in computing power, networking, reach and accessibility. In doing so, it surveys the attempts of the domestic criminal law to deal with some early manifestations of computer misuse and the consequent legislative passage of the Computer Misuse Act 1990. Having outlined the new criminal offences introduced by the 1990 Act, the book examines the extent to which the 1990 Act has been effective in controlling computer misuse, taking both prosecution rates and issues of judicial interpretation into account. It further examines the amendments made to the 1990 Act by the Police and Justice Act 2006 and their potential ramifications which have recently come into force. Having considered the position at domestic criminal law, the book turns to assess whether the solution to the effective regulation of computer misuse requires more than just the domestic criminal law. It explores the characteristics and purpose of the criminal law in the context of computer misuse and examines whether the domestic criminal law has limitations.

The book then introduces theories of risk from realist, cultural and symbolic, 'risk society' and governmentality perspectives before considering the idea of a governance network as a means of responding to risk. It examines computer misuse and the role of the domestic criminal law in the light of these theories. Having established the theoretical governance framework, the book then explores the role of the law in general within this framework, examining potential new nodes of governance from the European Union, Council of Europe, Commonwealth, United Nations and Group of Eight. It considers whether there might be advantages in moving beyond the domestic criminal law in the response to computer misuse. The book then broadens the discussion of potential means of governance beyond the law to encompass extra-legal initiatives. It establishes a typology of these extra-legal initiatives and examines the contribution made by each to the governance of computer misuse.

Finally, the book concludes with an examination of the complex governance network. It establishes and considers whether the regulation of computer misuse is only viable in a global networked society by a networked response combining nodes of both legal and extra-legal governance.

The law stated in this book is correct as at 1 October 2008. Any errors are the author's own.

Chapter 1

Introduction

I do not fear computers. I fear the lack of them.

Isaac Asimov (1920–92)

In 1990, Tim Berners-Lee, working with Robert Cailliau at CERN, proposed a 'hypertext' system which provided one of the building blocks of the Internet as we understand it today; Microsoft released Windows 3.0 and the first commercial Internet dialup access provider, 'The World', came online. By comparison, as of July 2008, it is estimated that in excess of 1.4 billion people are online throughout the world.[1] Over the last twenty years, computers have become an increasingly unremarkable part of contemporary western society. Computer technology is no longer just concerned with specialist scientific, engineering or military applications. It pervades many aspects of everyday life and underpins both state and commercial enterprises as well as the routine activities of many individuals.

Although computers have been used for unauthorised or illegitimate purposes since the earliest days of their existence, the proliferation of networked technology which transcends traditional state boundaries is generating, in turn, a greatly expanding realm of potential computer misuse and its victims. It follows that, as everyday life and computer technology converge, the misuse of that technology has the capacity greatly to disrupt many facets of global society. As such, computer misuse is both a prevalent and contemporary issue and it is the purpose of this book to explore the range of possible

---

1 <http://www.internetworldstats.com/stats.html> accessed 25 September 2008.

1

legal and extra-legal responses by which computer misuse might be regulated.

This chapter seeks to set the overall framework for the remainder of the book. It will describe the central hypothesis which will be examined and provide an overview of the structure of the main body of the work in the context of the research questions to be answered before concluding with a discussion of the concept and definition of computer misuse which will be used throughout the book. The main narrative of this book draws upon a range of different sources and is founded on documentary research supported by findings from fieldwork which was designed to provide an insight into the views of experts on the efficacy of various forms of regulation and their practices and attitudes towards the issue of computer misuse. An outline of the research methodology used is provided in the Appendix.

Principal research questions and chapter structure

The central hypothesis which is explored by this book is as follows:

There are a number of incompatibilities between the nature of computer misuse and the nature of the criminal law. This means that computer misuse cannot be regulated effectively by the criminal law alone. Such regulation requires a reflexive and cohesive approach which is only viable in a global networked society by a networked response combining nodes of both legal and extra-legal governance.

The book breaks down into three discrete but interrelated parts. The first part explores whether computer misuse has presented problems for the law. This requires an examination of the nature and purpose of both computer misuse and the domestic criminal law. The second part considers the application of a multi-tiered governance approach as a response to the types of risk posed by computer misuse. In doing so, it expands upon the discussion in the first part to encompass the use of the law in general and extra-legal governance mechanisms. The final part concludes with an examination of the central hypothesis.

Within the confines of this hypothesis, this book seeks to answer six principal research questions in the forthcoming chapters.

- *What is computer misuse and did it present a problem for the domestic law? If so, how did the law respond?*

Chapter 2 considers both the evolution of computer technology and computer use and misuse up until the enactment of the Computer Misuse Act 1990. It explores whether there were any shortcomings in the application of domestic law to computer misuse before charting the legislative history, genesis and purpose of the 1990 Act in more detail.

- *Was the Computer Misuse Act 1990 an effective response to computer misuse and has it stood the test of time?*

Chapter 3 continues the coverage of the two parallel evolutionary strands begun in Chapter 2 from 1990 to the present. It discusses the continued progression in computing power, reach and accessibility and the consequent expansion of manifestations of computer misuse. Following on from Chapter 2, it will examine whether or not the 1990 Act has been effective in controlling the problems inherent in computer misuse considering both prosecution rates and judicial interpretation. It will also discuss any proposed updates and amendments to the 1990 Act, with particular focus on the Police and Justice Act 2006 and its possible ramifications.

- *Does the effective regulation of computer misuse require more than just a response in domestic criminal law?*

Having considered the evolution of computing, computer misuse and the Computer Misuse Act 1990 in Chapters 2 and 3, Chapter 4 reflects upon the question of whether the solution to the effective regulation of computer misuse requires more than just the domestic criminal law. It considers the characteristics and purpose of the criminal law from a range of theoretical perspectives and its application to the problem of computer misuse in particular. This facilitates an examination of whether the domestic criminal law has limitations and, if so, whether those limitations arise from the nature of computer misuse or the nature of the criminal law itself.

- *How do theories of risk and governance apply to computer misuse and the domestic criminal law?*

Chapter 5 introduces the theoretical framework upon which the second part of the book is based. It explores theories relating to risk from realist, cultural and symbolic, 'risk society' and governmentality perspectives before considering the idea of a governance network as a means of responding to risk. It concludes with an examination of computer misuse and the role of the domestic criminal law in the light of these theories.

- *What is the role of the law in the governance of computer misuse?*

Chapter 6 builds upon the discussion from Chapter 5 by evaluating the role of the law in general within the governance framework. It broadens the analysis beyond the domestic criminal law to introduce new nodes of governance at the European Union, Council of Europe, Commonwealth, United Nations and G8 levels in order to explore whether there may be advantages in moving beyond the domestic criminal law in the response to computer misuse.

- *Can extra-legal approaches provide an effective response to computer misuse?*

Chapter 7 widens the discussion of the role of the law in relation to computer misuse covered in Chapter 6 to include potential extra-legal responses. It will establish a typology of extra-legal governance initiatives and will examine the contribution made by each of these to the regulation of computer misuse.

Chapter 8 summarises the findings of the preceding chapters by way of conclusion and provides a final critical examination of the central hypothesis.

Terminology

'Computer misuse' has been defined as 'unethical or unauthorised behaviour in relation to the use of computers, programs, or data'.[2]. Defined in this way, a wide variety of computer misuse issues can be considered to determine the most appropriate means of response to them.

---

2   Wasik, M., *Crime and the Computer* (Clarendon Press, Oxford, 1991) 3.

Computer misuse is a different concept to 'computer crime' or 'cybercrime'. It is important to differentiate between these terms. Computer crime is usually defined by reference both to the use of a computer as the principal tool to perpetrate criminal offences and by threats to the computer or system itself.[3] In essence, a computer crime is one in which a computer has either been the object, subject or instrument of a crime. For example, by this definition, 'phishing'[4] is a computer crime, since it would fall within the boundaries of section 1 of the Fraud Act 2006 which criminalises fraud by false representation. This is satisfied by the dishonest false representation that the phishing website is legitimate, with the intention of making a gain or causing the victim to suffer loss. The use of the computer here could be considered peripheral to the offence itself. Fraud by false representation can be committed without a computer by, for example, dishonestly using a stolen credit card or selling fake designer goods. Similarly, physical threats to the computer or system itself such as the theft of hardware or software are manifestations of familiar property offences. They are not 'special' simply because a computer is the target of the attack. As Ingraham comments:

Striking a watchman with a disk pack should remain the battery that it is, and not be elevated to the status of a computer crime. There are enough red herrings in our courts already.[5]

Whether computer crimes should have particular status is immaterial for the purposes of this discussion. It is sufficient to say that they are crimes falling within the parameters of the criminal law and, as such, there is some legal basis for their definition.

By contrast to computer crime, cybercrime is not a legal term of art. As such, it carries with it a certain degree of contextual mutability, including 'cyberspace crime'[6] and 'the transformation of criminal

3   Mandell, S., *Computers, Data Processing and the Law* (West Publishing, St Paul, MN, 1984) 155.
4   The use of counterfeit websites designed to trick users who have been lured there by fake e-mail messages into divulging financial data such as credit card numbers, account usernames and passwords.
5   Ingraham, D., 'On charging computer crime' (1980) 2 *Computer and Law Journal* 429, 438.
6   'Cyberspace' being a term coined by William Gibson; see Gibson, W., 'Burning chrome' *Omni Magazine* (July 1982), reproduced in Gibson, W., *Burning Chrome* (Arbor, New York, 1986). It was popularised in Gibson, W., *Neuromancer* (HarperCollins, London, 1984).

or harmful behaviour by networked technology'.[7] Cybercrime can therefore encompass the use of computers to assist 'traditional' offending, either within particular systems or across global networks (such as the phishing example discussed in conjunction with the Fraud Act 2006). It can also include crimes that are wholly mediated by technology – so-called 'third-generation' cybercrimes.[8] Such cybercrimes, such as spam e-mail for example, are solely the product of the Internet and could not exist without it. However, many of the so-called cybercrimes that have caused concern over the past decade are not necessarily crimes in the criminal law.[9] In essence, the suffix of 'crime' is attached to behaviours which do not readily fall within the boundaries of the criminal law. There is, therefore, not always a legal basis for certain so-called cybercrimes. As Wall comments, these include the more controversial harms which 'fall outside the jurisdiction and experience of the criminal justice process'[10] such as cyber-rape[11] and the virtual vandalism of virtual worlds.[12]

In order to avoid the 'considerable linguistic agency'[13] associated with the term cybercrime, particularly the use of the word 'crime' in relation to something which might not lie entirely within the boundaries of the criminal law, this book focuses on computer *misuse* rather than computer crime or cybercrime. Indeed, the legalistic use of the word 'crime' implies an action accompanied by the requisite state of mind which properly attracts the attention of the criminal law. It therefore follows that, since certain forms of behaviour involving the misuse of a computer fall outside the boundaries of the criminal law, then computer crime is but a subset of computer misuse. Computer misuse considers these particular behaviours to determine whether or not they fall within the criminal law and, if not, whether they should be dealt with via legal means or otherwise. Therefore some instances of computer misuse, such as spam, might also be a cybercrime (since

7   Wall, D.S., *Cybercrime: The Transformation of Crime in the Digital Age* (Polity Press, Cambridge, 2007) 10.
8   Ibid., 47.
9   Ibid., 10.
10 Ibid., 48.
11 MacKinnon, R., 'Virtual rape' (1997) 2(4) *Journal of Computer Mediated Communication* <http://jcmc.indiana.edu/vol2/issue4/mackinnon.html> accessed 25 September 2008.
12 Williams, M., *Virtually Criminal* (Routledge, Abingdon, 2006).
13 Wall, D.S., *Cybercrime: The Transformation of Crime in the Digital Age* (Polity Press, Cambridge, 2007) 10.

spam is a product of the Internet) and a computer crime.[14] However, a denial-of-service attack is an instance of computer misuse which could be classified as a cybercrime but which poses some difficulties for the criminal law.[15] Given that this book considers computer misuse, a precise definition of computer crime or cybercrime is not required. As Nimmer helpfully summarises:

Although aspects of computer use in society create vulnerabilities or opportunities for abuse these are not always qualitatively different from vulnerabilities that exist independently of computers. In many cases, however, the degree of risk and the nature of conduct are sufficiently different to raise questions about basic social decisions concerning levels of criminality for computer-related actions and the ability to discover and prosecute them under current law. Whether these are discussed under the heading of computer crime or merely as general criminal law problems is not important.[16]

The burgeoning ubiquity of computer technology and the spread of networked technology has generated an expanded realm of computer misuse. Various forms of computer misuse are increasingly prevalent within the media.[17] This media exposure, in conjunction with society's mixed experience with new technologies, has stemmed a range of notions of risk. Such risks include the spread of computer viruses,[18] the threat of hackers, the accessibility of online child pornography[19] and the virtual shadow of cyberterrorism.[20] These risks form part of the increasing culture of risk evident within contemporary western society.

---

14   Privacy and Electronic Communications (EC Directive) Regulations 2003, r. 22, 23.

15   See the discussion on *Lennon* in Chapter 3, for example.

16   Nimmer, R., *The Law of Computer Technology* (Wiley, New York, 1985) 9.

17   For example, de Bruxelles, S., 'Hackers force mass website closures', *The Times* (6 December 2007); Harvey, M. and Henderson, M., 'Hackers claim there's a black hole in the atom smashers' computer network', *The Times* (13 September 2008); Denby, K., 'Dissident websites crippled by Burma on anniversary of revolt', *The Times* (22 September 2008).

18   For example, Frith, H., 'Stowaway computer virus sent into orbit', *The Times* (28 August 2008).

19   For example, Hines, N., '"Philip Thompson admits he is child porn "librarian"', *The Times* (18 August 2008).

20   For example, Richards, J., 'Thousands of cyber attacks each day on key utilities', *The Times* (23 August 2008).

It can be argued that technology itself has no bearing on behaviour and that it is simply the intention of the user (or misuser) of that technology which makes it good or bad. However, it can also be argued that the very existence of the technology itself makes its misuse inevitable and therefore that technology is far from being a neutral force in society. Those who fear the risks associated with new technology may be concerned at the release of increasingly powerful tools into the hands of individuals, businesses and the state. They may be uncomfortable in a world in which services are accessed, goods purchased and transactions in general are increasingly mediated via the use of technology. Those who are wholly ignorant of technological risk cannot fear its consequences, yet they become potential victims since they are equally ignorant of the need to guard against that risk. It may also be true that those who understand the technology are fearful, as they understand more about the potential weaknesses in a system and the consequent risks associated with its abuse. The National Identity Register[21] is a case in point. Much public hostility towards the introduction of identity cards is driven from a civil liberties perspective[22] with less consideration given to the technical feasibility of implementation, although recent high-profile losses of personal data[23] have highlighted some of the potential technological and human flaws in large state-controlled systems. In the report commissioned by HM Treasury concerning the loss of child benefit data in November 2007, contributory factors included:

... the prioritisation by HMRC staff of other considerations above information security risk concerns [and] inadequate awareness, communication and training in information security.[24]

Even where there was awareness of information security risks, staff 'failed to manage those risks in an appropriate manner'.[25]

21 Established by the Identity Cards Act 2006, s. 1.
22 For instance the NO2ID campaign at <http://www.no2id.net> accessed 25 September 2008.
23 Webster, P., O'Neill, S. and Blakely, R., '25 million exposed to risk of ID fraud', *The Times* (21 November 2007); Webster, P., 'Millions more ID records go missing', *The Times* (18 December 2007); Evans, E., 'Personal data of 600,000 on lost laptop', *The Times* (19 January 2008); O'Neill, S. and Ford, R., 'Thousands of criminal files lost in data fiasco', *The Times* (22 August 2008).
24 Poynter, K., *Review of Information Security at HM Revenue and Customs: Final Report* (HMSO, London, 2008) 7.
25 Ibid., 23.

In light of the increasing realisation of the criminogenic potential of computer technology and the risks associated with it, then it seems desirable that these risks are met with an effective response. The response has hitherto been based on legislation, of which the primary piece controlling criminal computer misuse is the Computer Misuse Act 1990. Indeed, there is often an instinctive reaction to criminalise any perceived social problem without exploration of viable alternatives. For example, the UK was swift to criminalise the ownership of dangerous dogs[26] in response to a spate of vicious attacks on young children and to extend the use of banning orders in response to football violence overseas.[27] This demonstrates a tendency for the UK to rely upon the criminal law as a panacea for social ills. However, this book considers whether the approach of using the criminal law alone is the most appropriate response to computer misuse or whether alternative mechanisms might be preferable or complementary.

The next chapter will begin this consideration by examining the origins of computer misuse and its regulation by the domestic criminal law.

---

26 Dangerous Dogs Act 1991.
27 Football (Disorder) Act 2000.

Part I

Constructing the problem of computer misuse

Chapter 2

The emergence of the problem of computer misuse

Everything that can be invented has already been invented.
Charles H. Duell, director of the US Patent Office (1899)

This chapter will examine the emergence of the problem of computer misuse, covering the period up to 1990 when the primary piece of legislation controlling criminal computer misuse – the Computer Misuse Act 1990 – was enacted. It will consider two parallel strands. First, the evolution of computer technology itself, and, second, the evolution of the scope of their legitimate use and consequently their misuse. Having looked at the emergence of computer misuse up until 1990, the chapter will turn to consider the attempted means of legal regulation of computer misuse at the time and examine whether or not computer misuse proved to be challenging for the criminal law. It will conclude with a discussion of the legislative history, genesis and intent of the 1990 Act and a detailed examination of the offences that it created.

A brief history of computing

This section will provide a brief history of computing, focusing on the key advances in computing power and accessibility and the emergence and growth of computer networks.

Key advances in computing

In the sense that a computer is viewed as a 'calculating machine', computers have existed in various forms since the abacus was used by the Babylonians around 500 BC. Other mechanical calculators included Schickard's 'calculating clock' of 1623, Oughtred's slide-rule from 1625 and the difference engine, first theorised by Mueller in 1786 and built by Babbage in 1832.[1] In 1834, Babbage conceived, and began to design, his 'analytical engine' which combined many of the elements familiar in modern computer technology. The engine would run programs which were stored in read-only memory, specifically in the form of punch cards.

An early indication of the impact that computing technology could have on society was demonstrated by the US census of 1890. The 1880 census took seven years to complete by hand. However, the increasing population suggested that, by the 1890 census, the data processing would take longer to complete than the ten years before the next scheduled census. A competition was held to try to find a more efficient data-processing method. This was won by a Census Department employee, Herman Hollerith, who used Babbage's idea of using punch cards for the data storage. The 1890 census data was processed in six weeks.[2] The Second World War proved to be an influential driving force behind technological development. In April 1943, the Bletchley Park team completed the 'Heath Robinson'. This was a specialised machine for cipher-breaking as opposed to a general-purpose calculator or computer. This machine was the forerunner of the earliest programmable electronic computer, Colossus, built in December 1943. Colossus was used to crack the German cipher used by the enemy 'Enigma' machines and was able to translate 5,000 characters per second input on punched tape.[3]

The ENIAC[4] was developed between 1943 and 1946 at the US Ballistic Research Laboratory by J. Presper Eckert and John W. Mauchly. It was one of the first totally electronic, valve-driven, digital computers. It weighed 30 tonnes, contained 18,000 electronic valves and consumed around 25kW of electrical power (roughly equivalent

---

1 Ifrah, G., *The Universal History of Computing: From the Abacus to the Quantum Computer* (Wiley, New York, 2007).
2 Austrian, G.D., *Herman Hollerith: The Forgotten Giant of Information Processing* (Columbia University Press, New York, 1982).
3 Copeland, B.J., *Colossus: The Secrets of Bletchley Park's Code-breaking Computers* (Oxford University Press, Oxford, 2006).
4 Electronic Numerical Integrator and Computer.

to that consumed by 15 electric convector heaters). It is widely recognised as the first universal electronic computer. The ENIAC was further developed into the UNIVAC[5] through the 1950s. By 1954 20 UNIVACs had been installed at a cost of one million dollars each. They were used for private and commercial functions such as logistical and budgeting problems, payroll and accounting, as well as for military purposes. The UNIVAC was closely followed by IBM 701 and IBM 650. In essence, the 1950s 'inaugurated the era of commercial stored-program computing'.[6] The machines at this time were vast in size and existed as discrete installations in isolation. They were the province of the specialist and limited in their processing capability.

The reach of computer technology expanded greatly throughout the 1960s. The minicomputer opened further areas of application. While still a stand-alone system, the minicomputer introduced larger groups of people to direct interaction with computer technology. These were originally engineers and scientists and subsequently 'data processing' workers. Therefore, although computer technology was in existence long before the 1970s, it was not truly 'personal'. Users were homogeneous and the computer worked on its tasks in series. However, the DEC PDP-10 offered a 'time-sharing' system. This created an illusion that each user had access to the full resources that the system had to offer. Moreover it provided a random-access disk system allowing users access to their personal files and the ability to spool these files onto tape which was portable enough to be carried around in a briefcase.[7]

Advances in semiconductor technology could be also seen in the spread of electronic calculators. In 1970, a calculator cost around $400; in 1971, $250; in 1976, $50. The increased accessibility of computing technology sparked an interest for programming for many. However, these machines were sold as commodities; as such the manufacturers could not afford to educate the purchasers on their full range of capabilities, leading those who wanted to know more to congregate together, giving rise to user groups and clubs with a range of publications.[8]

5 Universal Automatic Computer.
6 Ceruzzi, P., *A History of Modern Computing* (2nd edn, MIT Press, Cambridge, MA, 2003) 45.
7 Bell, C., Mudge, J. and McNamara, E., *Computer Engineering: A DEC View of Hardware Systems Design* (Digital, Bedford, 1979).
8 Ceruzzi, P., *A History of Modern Computing* (2nd edn, MIT Press, Cambridge, MA, 2003) 213.

The new microprocessors and memory chips which came out of the semiconductor laboratories converged with the increasing desire for personal computing in 1974. The microprocessor-based MITS Altair 8800 sparked an immense period of activity in personal computing, even though it had significant shortcomings in terms of complexity and unreliability.[9] In 1980, Sinclair Research set out to build a simple to use personal computer, running BASIC and capable of breaking the psychological price barrier of £100. It succeeded with the ZX80, the computer which started the home computer revolution in the UK. Before production ceased in August 1981, the ZX80 sold over 100,000 units. It was also one of the first aimed at the home user as opposed to the hobbyist or professional.[10] It marked the arrival of personal computing.

A range of new personal computers – and accompanying software applications – was introduced throughout the 1980s. The IBM PC was announced in August 1981 along with a suite of accounting and games software.[11] The Apple Macintosh was released in January 1984. It had a new 3.5 inch disk drive, a mouse and a graphical user interface which Microsoft tried later to copy with Windows. This interface was driven by a desire to make computing technology more accessible to a wider range of individuals without requiring them to understand the workings of DOS, by hiding much of the underlying technology beneath a readily acceptable metaphor.[12] The development of interfaces designed to circumvent lack of technical knowledge could, in turn, propagate a greater lack of in-depth knowledge by shielding the non-specialist user from increasingly complex knowledge underlying technology.

The growth of networked computing

The ARPANET[13] was the first transcontinental, high-speed computer network. It grew out of a 1969 experiment in digital communications by the US Department of Defense to link universities, defence contractors and research laboratories. It provides an example of technological catalysis at work: a technological collaboration and

---

9 Levy, S., *Hackers* (Anchor Doubleday, New York, 1984) 191.
10 Dale, R., *The Sinclair Story* (Duckworth, London, 1985).
11 Pugh, E., *Building IBM: Shaping an Industry and Its Technology* (MIT Press, Cambridge, MA, 1995).
12 Linzmayer, O., *Apple Confidential 2.0: The Real Story of Apple Computer, Inc.* (2nd edn, No Starch Press, San Francisco, CA, 2004).
13 Advanced Research Projects Agency Network.

productivity tool which consequently increased both the pace and intensity of technological advance.[14]

Ethernet technology was invented in 1973, yet it was not until the proliferation of personal computers in the 1980s that it found its mass-market role. The nature of personal computers meant that employees, particularly those who had acquired skills, software or both on a home machine, were free to install whatever software they liked on their computers, leading to a loss of corporate control. As User 1[15] commented:

In the early days, disks were flying everywhere. We had no idea who was running what, whether it had a licence – it usually didn't – or whether it was infected with something horrible.

One of the driving forces behind local area networking was to give some control back to the corporations, storing files and applications on a central server rather than on individual PCs. This removed much of the 'personal' from personal computing, at least in the workplace, although the users maintained more autonomy and independence that their predecessors with dumb mainframe terminals.[16] This was echoed by users:

I didn't like the idea of the LAN at first. Although it was easier to share things around – even things we probably shouldn't have – the idea of a technologically-challenged boss looking at my code wasn't appealing at all.[17]

LANs were great for management, but they stifled our creativity at first.[18]

Academic networks also formed. BITNET[19] was a cooperative US university network founded in 1981 between the City University of New York and Yale University. At its peak around 1990, BITNET

---

14 Salus, P (ed.), *The ARPANET Sourcebook: The Unpublished Foundations of the Internet* (Peer-to-Peer Communications, Charlottesville, VA, 2008).
15 See Appendix for further details of the participants interviewed in connection with the study.
16 Spurgeon, C., *Ethernet: The Definitive Guide* (O'Reilly, Sebastopol, CA, 2000).
17 User 7.
18 User 4.
19 Because It's There Network.

extended to almost 500 organisations with 3,000 network nodes, all within educational institutions.[20]

Knowledge gap

It can be seen that the principal advancements which occurred during this period were in capacity, user-friendliness and net-working. Capacity increased both in terms of storage capability and in processing speed. User-friendliness advanced from textual commands requiring syntactic rigour to the graphical user interfaces offered by the Apple Macintosh and Microsoft Windows. Networking increased both socially in the user communities arising in the 1970s and technologically in the rise of local area networking in the 1980s. As a result of these advances, new applications were possible and computer technology became more readily accessible, at first in the workplace and then in the home. Technology had moved from the realm of the specialist and the scientist to increasingly widespread public availability and consequently into the public consciousness. The level of understanding needed of how systems operated at the lowest level, which was a necessary and expert skill in the earlier days of computing, became a lesser requirement. The user opening a file on the Apple Macintosh by clicking a picture certainly did not need to know, or care, where the underlying data was distributed on its hard disk.

However, the collective diminution in general computing skill levels gave rise to a knowledge gap between the expert and non-expert user. As Technician 2 commented:

We were quite scornful of anyone who had to use pictures to do their jobs. 'Real' computer engineers wrote in text which the general public had no right to understand. They thought they knew how it all worked, but it was just smoke and mirrors to sell more kit.

The exploitation of this knowledge gap could be a potential driver and facilitator of susceptibility to computer misuse and computer crime: unless the criminal law was able to deter and punish such activity or the technology itself was able to include safeguards as well as introduce vulnerabilities.

---

20 Clough, B. and Mungo, P., *Approaching Zero: Data Crime and the Criminal Underworld* (Faber and Faber, London, 1992) 101.

Having established the technological and social landscapes, it is next necessary to chart some of the early manifestations of computer misuse before discussing the response of the criminal law.

Manifestations of computer misuse

According to Levy, the emergence of the hacker culture began in 1961 when MIT acquired the first PDP-1. The Signals and Power Committee of MIT's Tech Model Railroad Club invented programming tools, slang and a new subculture, elements of which remain recognisable.[21] This group also seems to have been the first to adopt the term 'hacker'. The social impact of the ARPANET also came to bear. It brought together hackers all over the US in a critical mass. Instead of remaining in isolated small groups with their own developing ephemeral local cultures, the hackers formed themselves as a networked 'tribe' of experts and enthusiasts.[22] The facilities for electronic mailing lists that had been used to foster cooperation among continent-wide special-interest groups were increasingly also used for more social and recreational purposes. DARPA[23] deliberately turned a blind eye to all the technically 'unauthorised' activity; it understood that the extra overhead was 'a small price to pay for attracting an entire generation of bright young people into the computing field'.[24] In the early days of computing technology, the terms 'hacker' and 'hacking' had a meaning distinct from that of today:

The term can signify the free-wheeling intellectual exploration of the highest and deepest potential of computer systems. Hacking can describe the determination to make access to computers as free and as open as possible. Hacking can involve the heartfelt conviction that beauty can be found in computers, that the fine aesthetic in a perfect program can liberate the mind and spirit.[25]

---

21 Levy, S., *Hackers* (Anchor Doubleday, New York, 1984) 20–2.
22 Raymond, E., *A Brief History of Hackerdom* (May 2000) <http://catb.org/~esr/writings/hacker-history/hacker-history.html> accessed 25 September 2008.
23 Defence Advanced Research Projects Agency.
24 Raymond, E., *A Brief History of Hackerdom* (May 2000) <http://catb.org/~esr/writings/hacker-history/hacker-history.html> accessed 25 September 2008.
25 Sterling, B., *The Hacker Crackdown* (Bantam Books, New York, 1992) 54.

Hacking has also been described as a 'recreational and educational sport' in which the intellectual challenge of gaining access is paramount:

In the vast majority of cases, the process of 'getting in' is much more satisfying than what is discovered in the protected computer files.[26]

In the late 1970s and early 1980s the most direct precursors to modern computer misusers appeared – the so-called 'phone phreaks'. The phreaks used a 'black box' which mimicked the signal used by the phone systems and gave the phreak unlimited long-distance access.[27] It was generally agreed that phreaking as an intellectual game and a form of exploration was semi-respectable, but that the widescale 'theft' of services was not. However, as Hafner comments:

When the personal computer was invented and mated with the modem, phreaking took on a whole new dimension and the modern age of the hacker was born.[28]

The emerging networks of the 1980s were places in which information was plentiful, and security was almost non-existent. Hackers were able to exploit this disparity between information richness and security weakness. For example, Hans Hubner, a German hacker known as 'Pengo',[29] used simple guest user accounts to steal sensitive government data and sell it to the Eastern Bloc.[30] The first computer virus to appear outside the place in which it was written was *Elk Cloner* written for the Apple DOS in 1982. This spread by floppy disk and simply displayed a poem about itself every fiftieth time that the contents of the disk were run. The first PC virus was arguably ©*Brain* which appeared in 1986[31] and was designed to deter pirated copies

26 Cornwall, H., *The Hacker's Handbook* (Century, London, 1985) 1.
27 Clough, B. and Mungo, P., *Approaching Zero: Data Crime and the Criminal Underworld* (Faber & Faber, London, 1992) 10.
28 Hafner, K. and Markoff, J., CYBERPUNK: *Outlaws and Hackers on the Computer Frontier* (Touchstone, New York, 1995).
29 Clough, B. and Mungo, P., *Approaching Zero: Data Crime and the Criminal Underworld* (Faber & Faber, London, 1992) 168.
30 Stoll, C., *The Cuckoo's Egg: Tracking a Spy Through the Maze of Computer Espionage* (Pocket Books, New York, 1990).
31 The *Ashar* virus, a variant of ©*Brain*, may have possibly predated ©*Brain* based on the code within the virus.

of software legitimately written and distributed by the creators of the virus itself.[32] Before computer networks became widespread, most viruses spread on removable media, particularly floppy disks. In the early days of personal computers, many users regularly exchanged information and programs on disk. Some viruses, such as *Elk Cloner*, spread by infecting programs stored on these disks, while others, such as ©*Brain* installed themselves into the disk boot sector, ensuring that they would be run when the user booted the computer from the disk.[33]

By the end of the 1980s certain types of computer misuse, particularly hacking and virus writing, were occurring increasingly frequently. Most users interviewed recalled experiencing several virus attacks:

We had SEX, so to speak, Data Crime and Fu Manchu. Great names, but intensely irritating. Data Crime formatted part of our hard disks, as I recall.[34]

Cascade was a good one. Characters used to fall off the screen. I think there was a nastier version which formatted disks too, but we were lucky.[35]

The spread of the hacker culture via the burgeoning networks had disseminated the tools and techniques of misuse to a wider audience, many of whom saw, and acted upon, the potential to use this information with their own technical knowledge to misuse technology for their own gain – whether this be purely intellectual satisfaction or something more insidious. Moreover, many misusers began to realise the distinction between the physical world of criminal behaviour and the relative safety of their actions, mediated by distance and technology. As a result, public concern over hacking and viruses also began to grow during the 1980s. The next section will examine the extent to which this public concern could be addressed by the application of the criminal law at the time.

32 Fites, P., Johnston, P. and Kratz, M., *The Computer Virus Crisis* (Van Nostrand Reinhold, New York, 1989) 30.
33 Hruska, J., *Computer Viruses and Anti-Virus Warfare* (Ellis Horwood, Chichester, 1990) 33.
34 User 3.
35 User 5.

Pre-1990 regulation

It is true to say that the criminal law was able to deal with some of the problems resulting from computer misuse before the Computer Misuse Act 1990 came into being.[36] For instance, case law tended to suggest that erasing computer data held on a magnetic disk would fall within the ambit of section 1(1) of the Criminal Damage Act 1971:

> A person who without lawful excuse destroys or damages any physical property belonging to another, intending to destroy or damage such property or being reckless as to whether any such property would be destroyed or damaged shall be guilty of an offence.

This was so despite the fact that this could be done without causing physical damage to property 'of a tangible nature' as required by the Act.[37] This required a certain degree of creativity in the interpretation of tangible property in relation to the facts of the case.

In *R v. Talboys*,[38] the defendant was convicted of charges brought under the Criminal Damage Act 1971 after a programming prank went wrong. Talboys reprogrammed his employer's computer to display a farewell message every time his colleagues entered his leaving date. Unfortunately, no message was displayed: instead, the screens were entirely blanked. As a result of Talboys's guilty plea no legal argument was heard; he was given a conditional discharge and ordered to reimburse his employer £1,000 to cover the costs of investigating and rectifying the problem.

The similar case of *Cox v. Riley*[39] did lead to a judicial view. Here, the defendant deliberately erased all computer programs from the plastic circuit card of a computerised saw which relied upon it for its operation, each program corresponding to a window-frame profile of a different design.[40] This rendered the saw inoperable, apart from limited manual operation, which would cause production to be slowed dramatically. At first instance, the defendant was convicted under section 1(1) of the Criminal Damage Act 1971, the magistrates

---

36 Tapper, C., 'Computer crime: Scotch mist?' [1987] *Criminal Law Review* 4.
37 Criminal Damage Act 1971, s. 10(1).
38 *R v. Talboys*, *The Times* 29 May 1986.
39 *Cox v. Riley* (1986) 83 Cr App R 54 (DC).
40 Wasik, M., 'Criminal damage and the computerised saw' (1986) 136 *New Law Journal* 763.

reasoning that since the printed circuit card was tangible it was 'property' within the meaning of section 10(1) and that damage was caused to the card since it would no longer operate the computerised saw until it had been reprogrammed.[41] The defendant appealed on the basis that the programs erased were not tangible property within the Criminal Damage Act 1971. Unfortunately the defendant had been charged with damage *to the card*, which the court viewed as 'undoubtedly ... property of a tangible nature', rather than damage to the program. The Divisional Court concluded with the opinion:

[We] would answer the question posed by the justices 'Can the erasing of a program from a printed circuit *card* which is used to operate a computerised saw constitute damage within the meaning of the Criminal Damage Act 1971?' with the emphatic answer yes.[42] (emphasis added)

Stephen Brown LJ commented that:

It seems to me to be quite untenable to argue that what this appellant did on this occasion did not amount to causing damage to property.[43]

Indeed this was a view initially shared by the Law Commission. In its subsequent Working Paper on Computer Misuse it stated that:

In essence, any interference with the operation of a computer or its software which causes loss or inconvenience to its legitimate users can probably now be charged as criminal damage ... The law of criminal damage now seems to extend to persons who damage a computer system, without the need for any further reform of the law.[44]

R v. *Whiteley*[45] concerned an 18-year-old hacker who had gained unauthorised access to the JANET[46] computer network. He deleted

---

41 R v. *Fisher* (1865) LR 1 CCR 7 established that temporarily rendering a machine useless with intent can be damage; this case involved ramming a stick up the water feed of a steam engine.
42 *Cox v. Riley* (1986) 83 Cr App R 54 (DC) 58 (Stephen Brown LJ).
43 Ibid.
44 Law Commission, *Computer Misuse* (Working Paper No. 110, 1988) [3.35], [3.68].
45 R v. *Whiteley* (1991) 93 Cr App R 25 (CA).
46 The Joint Academic Network.

and replaced files with messages of 'schoolboy humour' that taunted and insulted the computer centre staff. It was held that he had been properly convicted of criminal damage since the deletion of various files and their replacements caused an alteration of the state of the magnetic particles on the computer disks. The disks and the particles were considered to be a single entity capable of being damaged and their usefulness had been impaired. The defendant argued that only the intangible information had been damaged and that there should be a distinction drawn between the physical disc itself and the information thereon. This argument failed and Whiteley was sentenced to twelve months' imprisonment, eight of which were suspended.

Despite the issues surrounding tangibility, criminal damage seemed to be a potential route to the imposition of criminal liability. A further, although somewhat more creative, possibility lay in the offence of abstraction of electricity contrary to section 13 of the Theft Act 1968 which provides that:

A person who dishonestly uses without due authority, or dishonestly causes to be wasted or diverted, any electricity shall on conviction be liable to imprisonment for a term not exceeding five years.

Therefore, even though the offence is primarily aimed at the dishonest bypassing of an electricity meter,[47] a person who dishonestly uses another's computer without due authority may also commit the offence on the basis of the unauthorised use of electricity that is an inevitable result of its use.[48] Perhaps unsurprisingly, there is little authority on this point in England and Wales, although in *Sui-Tak Chee*[49] a Hong Kong case, the defendant was charged with, and found guilty of, abstracting electricity under section 15 of the Theft Ordinance[50] (which is worded identically to section 13 of the Theft Act 1968) after accidentally discovering passwords, and thereafter accessing (allegedly out of curiosity rather than motivation for gain), a Cable & Wireless plc e-mail system. The defendant received an absolute discharge from the magistrate, who ordered that no conviction should

---

47 *Boggeln v. Williams* [1978] 2 All ER 1061 (DC).
48 This could prove to be even more complex in the case of a battery-powered computer.
49 *Sui-Tak Chee* (Hong Kong, unreported) August 1984, in Wasik, M., *Crime and the Computer* (Clarendon Press, Oxford, 1991) 88 (n. 15).
50 Cap 210, Theft Ordinance.

be imposed and that, in his opinion, the prosecution should never have been brought, the value of the electricity abstracted having been proved at around one-eighth of a Hong Kong cent, or approximately one-thousandth of a British penny. As Wasik suggests, the mischief that the offence seeks to counter is quite different from the substance of the offence when applied to computer misuse.[51] It is perhaps interesting to note that the argument of mismatch of mischief to circumstances was not employed when considering the prosecutions for computer misuse under the criminal damage legislation in *Cox v. Riley* and *Whiteley*; this probably lies in the fact that 'damage' is a term more readily understood and employed in this context whereas stretching the ambit of abstraction of electricity to cover the miniscule cost of powering a few cycles on a misused computer chip seemed to be a little too extreme. The magistrate in *Sui-Tak Chee* clearly considered that a *de minimis* approach would be sensible and appropriate. However, Bainbridge argued that the abstraction of even the tiniest amount of electricity should attract liability, stating that:

The very art of hacking will result in the host computer ... performing work ... . If the information is kept on magnetic disks, the disk drive heads will physically move, tracking across the disks, locating then reading the information which will then be moved into the computer's volatile memory by means of tiny electrical impulses. More electricity will be used in transmitting the information to the hacker's computer terminal.[52]

This analysis led Bainbridge to the inevitable conclusion that:

Every hacker is committing [the offence of abstracting electricity] regardless of the nature of his actions.[53]

Despite this view, relying on abstracting electricity as a means to counter computer misuse seems convoluted, especially when considering the miniscule amounts of electricity involved and the mischief at which the offence was aimed. Abstracting electricity fails to encapsulate the wrongness of the defendant's conduct and takes no heed of his actions in potentially disrupting the computer system

---

51 Wasik, M., *Crime and the Computer* (Clarendon Press, Oxford, 1991) 88–9.
52 Bainbridge, D., 'Hacking – the unauthorised access of computer systems: the legal implications' (1989) 52 *Modern Law Review* 236, 240
53 Ibid.

or corrupting or destroying valuable data: the situation is analogous to charging someone who had stolen a car with the theft of petrol.

It is not only the existing criminal damage and abstraction of electricity legislation that has been used in an attempt to impose criminal liability for computer misuse: the Forgery and Counterfeiting Act 1981 has also been employed. In *R v. Gold and Schifreen*,[54] the defendants gained access to the British Telecom Prestel[55] computer network by using the Customer Identification Number '22222222' and password '1234'. This gave them access to a test computer, thence the password of the British Telecom system manager and ultimately the passwords of everyone on the Prestel system. As Schifreen described in a 2003 interview:

I stumbled upon a correct password that wasn't mine ... [t]he BT Prestel system recognised me as a legitimate customer and suddenly I found the door was open for me into one of the biggest computer systems in the world.[56]

The defendants altered files on the system and (in)famously accessed Prince Philip's private mailbox, seeing the message 'Good evening, HRH Duke of Edinburgh'; they then left a message for the real system manager saying 'I do so enjoy puzzles and games. Ta ta. Pip pip! HRH Royal Hacker'. Schifreen decided to inform Prestel although they were reluctant to believe him:

Why would they? Someone ... tells them that they used a £400 computer to circumvent their inbuilt security and penetrate a mainframe system worth millions? It had to be a hoax.[57]

The defendants were ultimately believed after amending the word 'Index' on the first page to read 'Idnex': this alerted Prestel to the fact that their security had indeed been breached. It notified all customers to change their passwords, changed the system manager codes to block the defendants and called in the police. As Schifreen said 'Everything went nuclear after that'.[58]

---

54 *R v. Gold and Schifreen* [1987] 1 QB 1116 (CA), aff'd [1988] AC 1063 (HL).
55 Prestel was a viewdata (teletext) service originally developed by the British Post Office in the early 1970s.
56 Higney, F., 'Interview: Robert Schifreen', *Legal IT Forum Bulletin* (16 October 2003).
57 Ibid.
58 Ibid.

The defendants were convicted at first instance on nine counts of forgery contrary to section 1(1) of the Forgery and Counterfeiting Act 1981 which provides that:

A person is guilty of forgery if he makes a false instrument, with the intention that he or another shall use it to induce somebody to accept it as genuine, and by reason of so accepting it to do or not to do some act to his own or any other person's prejudice.

In the usual realm of the offence, a false instrument is usually a tangible item. However, here the 'false instrument' was argued to have been 'made' by entering a genuine Customer Information Number and password into the system with the intention that the system accepted it as genuine to the prejudice of British Telecom who were induced to provide Prestel services to the value of £379 without charge. At first instance, the defendants were convicted on all counts, fined and ordered to pay costs.

However, on appeal, the central issue revolved around the definition of 'false instrument', an instrument being defined by section 8(1) of the 1981 Act as:

(a) any document, whether of a formal or informal character;
(b) any stamp issued or sold by the Post Office;
(c) any Inland Revenue stamp; and
(d) any disc, tape, sound track or other device on or in which information is recorded or stored by mechanical, electronic or other means.

The Court of Appeal first considered, presumably using the *noscitur a sociis* rule of statutory interpretation, that the electronic impulses generated by physically entering the Customer Information Number and password into the Prestel system could not constitute the false instrument, since all the examples provided in the Act were tangible and the impulses were not. The prosecution argued that 'user segment' of the computer momentarily became a false instrument once the Customer Information Number and password were entered into it for the purposes of user authentication. However, this argument failed. The court considered that the signals that caused the user segment to verify them as authorised users were never 'recorded or stored' with any degree of continuity within section 8(1)(d) of the 1981 Act since they appeared only momentarily on a screen before

27

immediately being deleted. The House of Lords concurred, Lord Brandon of Oakbrook commenting that:

We have accordingly come to the conclusion that the language of the Act was not intended to apply to the situation which was shown to exist in this case ... It is a conclusion that we reach without regret. The Procrustean attempt to force these facts into the language of an Act not designed to fit them produced grave difficulties for both judge and jury which we would not wish to see repeated.[59]

It is clear, then, at this stage, there were cracks appearing in the ability of the existing criminal law to deal with some manifestations of computer misuse, in particular those resulting from the intangible nature of the subject matter. Despite this increasingly apparent inadequacy, there were still conflicting views on whether Parliament should intervene with specific legislation to counter such activity. For instance, Bainbridge argued that the existing body of criminal law was adequate, claiming that Gold and Schifreen 'should have been charged with abstraction of electricity and criminal damage'[60] since the messages left were 'a form of graffiti',[61] whereas Lloyd's opposing view was that 'legislative action should not be long delayed'.[62]

The genesis of the Computer Misuse Act 1990

The legislative action desired by Lloyd and opposed by Bainbridge had already been under investigation by both the Scottish Law Commission and that of England and Wales.

The Scottish Law Commission

The first substantial consideration of computer misuse by a reform body was undertaken by the Scottish Law Commission in March

---

59 R v. Gold and Schifreen [1988] AC 1063 (HL), 1069.
60 Bainbridge, D., 'Hacking – the unauthorised access of computer systems: the legal implications' (1989) 52 Modern Law Review 236, 245.
61 Ibid.
62 Lloyd, I., 'Computer abuse and the law' (1988) 104 Law Quarterly Review 202, 207.

1986 in its Consultative Memorandum *Computer Crime*.[63] This was issued in response to a July 1984 proposal from the Law Society of Scotland:

> To consider the applicability and effectiveness of the criminal law in Scotland in relation to the use and abuse of computers, computer systems and other data storing, data processing and telecommunications systems ...[64]

This provided an eight-fold categorisation of the different kinds of computer misuse perceived at the time to be:

• erasure or falsification of data or programs so as to obtain a pecuniary or other advantage;
• obtaining unauthorised access to a computer;
• eavesdropping on a computer;
• taking of information without physical removal;
• unauthorised borrowing of computer discs or tapes;
• making unauthorised use of computer time or facilities;
• malicious or reckless corruption or erasure of data or programs;
• denial of access to authorised users.[65]

Following a period of consultation with a range of individuals, academic and commercial organisations and professional bodies, the resulting 1987 *Report on Computer Crime*[66] was published. This made it clear that the Scottish Law Commission remained doubtful that there existed 'sufficient hard evidence as to the scale ... of computer misuse which would of itself suggest an impending crisis of a kind that demanded prompt legislative action'[67] and considered that caution should be taken 'not to over-dramatise the scale and extent of computer misuse at present'.[68] However, despite this uncertainty regarding the nature and extent of the risk arising from a failure to criminalise computer misuse, it recommended the creation of an offence directed at obtaining unauthorised access to a computer[69]

63 Scottish Law Commission, *Computer Crime* (Consultative Memorandum No. 68, 1986).
64 Ibid. [1.1].
65 Ibid. [2.29].
66 Scottish Law Commission, *Report on Computer Crime* (Cm 174, July 1987).
67 Ibid. [3.4].
68 Ibid. [3.5].
69 Ibid. [3.7].

where there was specific ulterior intent to obtain an advantage for the defendant (or another) or to damage another's interests or where, following unauthorised access, another's interests had actually been damaged by the reckless modification or erasure of programs or data.[70]

The accompanying draft Computer Crime (Scotland) Bill[71] proposed these offences as follows:

1. (1) A person commits an offence if, not having authority to obtain access to a program or data stored in a computer, or to a part of such program or data, he obtains such unauthorised access in order to inspect or otherwise to acquire knowledge of the program or data or to add to, erase or otherwise alter the program or the data with the intention –

    (a) of procuring an advantage for himself or another person;

    (b) of damaging another person's interests.

    (2) A person commits an offence if, not having authority to obtain access to a program or data stored in a computer, or to a part of such program or data, he obtains such unauthorised access and damages another person's interests by recklessly adding to, erasing or otherwise altering the program or data ...[72]

The Scottish Law Commission did not consider it necessary to propose legislation specifically aimed at any of the other categories of misuse identified in its consultative typology,[73] neither did it propose criminalising unauthorised access per se.

The Law Commission of England and Wales

A Private Member's Bill sponsored by Emma Nicholson MP was introduced in April 1989 shortly after the findings of the Scottish Law Commission were published. The Bill's proposals ran along similar lines to those of the Scottish Law Commission. However, this

---

70 Ibid. [4.12].
71 Ibid., Appendix A.
72 Ibid., 30.
73 Ibid. [3.20].

Bill was promptly withdrawn in August 1989 when the government undertook to legislate on the matter in the light of the forthcoming Report of the Law Commission of England and Wales.[74] This was published in October 1989 and followed on from its 1988 Working Paper on Computer Misuse.[75]

Unlike its Scottish counterpart, the England and Wales Law Commission did not provide a draft Bill to accompany its report, although it concluded with the recommendation that three new offences of computer misuse be created: unauthorised access to a computer; unauthorised access to a computer with intent to commit or facilitate the commission of a serious crime; and unauthorised modification of computer material.[76]

The government did not manage to introduce a Bill to implement these proposals. Instead, the late Michael Colvin MP sponsored a Bill[77] which followed the approach of the Law Commission of England and Wales.

The passage of the Computer Misuse Act 1990

Michael Colvin's Computer Misuse Bill received its second reading in the House of Commons on 9 February 1990. A large part of the debate was based around a number of key issues: the impact of computer misuse on industry and commerce; the inadequacy of the pre-existing criminal law; and the prevailing media reporting of the dangers posed by hackers at the time.

At the time, the government was 'seeking to encourage the greater use of information technology to create wealth ... [with] a single Europe in mind'[78] and could not underestimate the potential impact on industry. Accordingly, the sponsor of the Bill reported that:

Computer misuse probably costs the United Kingdom between £400 million – the CBI's[79] figure – and perhaps as much as £2 billion a year, in terms of damage to systems.[80]

---

74 Law Commission, *Criminal Law – Computer Misuse* (Law Com. No. 186, Cm 819, 1989).

75 Law Commission, *Computer Misuse* (Working Paper No. 110, 1988).

76 Law Commission, *Criminal Law – Computer Misuse* (Law Com. No. 186, Cm 819, 1989) [5.1].

77 Computer Misuse HC Bill (1989–90) [18].

78 Hansard HC vol. 166 col. 1135 (9 February 1990).

79 Confederation of British Industry.

80 Hansard HC vol. 166 col. 1134 (9 February 1990).

Moreover, the costs associated with 'cleaning up such a network can amount to hundreds of thousands of pounds'.[81] The source of the extra £1.6 billion of commercial risk over and above the CBI's estimate or the six-figure cost of rectification is, however, unclear and was not challenged in debate.

Aside from the legislative and interpretative difficulties with the pre-existing law which have already been identified, attention was also drawn to the practical difficulties associated with prosecuting computer misuse:

It is significant, for example, that of 270 cases that have been verified by the Department of Trade and Industry as involving computer misuse over the past five years, only six were brought to court for prosecution and only three of those were successfully prosecuted ...[82]

It was therefore envisaged that the new Bill would ease the difficulties associated with bringing a successful prosecution for computer misuse. Its success in this regard will be further considered in Chapter 3.

Perhaps the most disquieting facet of the debate was the MPs' perception of computer misusers. They were considered not to be 'some sort of Raffles of the microchip'[83] but rather belonging to 'the twisted culture that the Bill is trying to stamp out',[84] living a drug-fuelled lifestyle, because:

... hackers are very clever. They will find a way round protection that one buys or creates. That is what they are there for. They make a great deal of money out of it and the German hackers, at any rate, support a drug-based lifestyle on their activities ... Because drugs are expensive, hackers need to make a great deal of money to support their lifestyle.[85]

Not content with labelling all computer misusers as twisted drug-addicts, MPs moved on to consider their sexual adequacy and personality profile:

---

81 Ibid.
82 Ibid.
83 Hansard HC vol. 166 col. 1142 (9 February 1990).
84 Hansard HC vol. 166 col. 1137 (9 February 1990).
85 Hansard HC vol. 166 col. 1154 (9 February 1990).

The motives for malice are very complex ... They are similar to people who make obscene telephone calls or misuse short-wave radio .... I believe that a profound sexual inadequacy is often related to such behaviour.[86]

[Hackers] may well be unemployed because they spend all night hacking, and lose their job because of poor performance or bad time-keeping, or they may have been sacked for hacking whilst at work ... consequently they are often poor ... They either go in for fraud or become security consultants ....[87]

The consistent theme in the debate was that the expansion of technology into the realm of the non-specialist was the root cause of the misuse problem:

At one time, computers were used by only a few professors and very disciplined professionals, but the tremendous growth in microcomputing has meant the entry into the arena of the unspeakable.[88]

Examples of the risks associated with computer misuse which were put forward during debate could be argued to be somewhat sensationalist, including the posting of pornography on bulletin boards used by an international club of disabled children,[89] hacking into NASA and CERN,[90] the blackmail of AIDS victims,[91] the remote turning-off of a life-support system in a hospital intensive-care unit[92] and a factory worker almost killed by a hacked robot.[93]

The Bill was not universally welcomed and a large number of amendments were proposed at the Standing Committee stage, most notably by Harry Cohen MP. In particular, Cohen wished to amend the Bill such that it would be a defence to the basic hacking offence to prove that 'such care as in all the circumstances, was reasonably required to prevent the access or intended access in question, was not

---

86 Hansard HC vol. 166 col. 1156 (9 February 1990).
87 Hansard HC vol. 166 col. 1177 (9 February 1990).
88 Hansard HC vol. 166 col. 1151 (9 February 1990).
89 Ibid.
90 Hansard HC vol. 166 col. 1152 (9 February 1990).
91 Hansard HC vol. 166 col. 1153 (9 February 1990).
92 Hansard HC vol. 166 col. 1161 (9 February 1990).
93 Hansard HC vol. 166 col. 1179 (9 February 1990).

taken'.[94] This was argued to be in line with data protection principles and modelled on section 23(3) of the Data Protection Act 1984 which provides a defence to data loss if the defendant exercised reasonable care in all the circumstances to prevent it. Cohen argued that the amendment would encourage users to make their systems secure since the criminalisation of computer misuse would mean that individuals might feel less compelled to take care of the security of their own systems. In other words, the presence of a criminal offence could be seen as adequate protection. This amendment was withdrawn on the basis that it would 'introduce into English law the novel principle of contributory negligence as a defence in a criminal case'.[95] However, it does demonstrate that there was some feeling even at the time of debating the Bill that criminal legislation as the only means of regulation might be in some way insufficient. The Bill received Royal Assent on 29 June 1990.

The Computer Misuse Act 1990[96]

The Computer Misuse Act 1990 describes itself as:

An Act to make provision for securing computer material against unauthorised access or modification; and for connected purposes.[97]

As such it created three main offences: unauthorised access to computer material,[98] unauthorised access to computer material with intent to commit or facilitate further offences[99] and unauthorised modification of computer material.[100]

---

94 Standing Committee C, *Computer Misuse Bill* HC (1989–90) col. 15 (14 March 1990).
95 Standing Committee C, *Computer Misuse Bill* HC (1989–90) col. 17 (14 March 1990).
96 The Computer Misuse Act 1990 was amended by the Police and Justice Act 2006. The underlying reasons for these amendments and their implications are discussed further in Chapter 3; however, since this chapter sets out the legal and technological position to 1990, the remainder of this section will consider the offences as originally enacted in 1990.
97 Computer Misuse Act 1990, Long Title.
98 Computer Misuse Act 1990, s. 1.
99 Computer Misuse Act 1990, s. 2.
100 Computer Misuse Act 1990, s. 3.

Although there was some disparity between the Scottish Law Commission's recommendations and those of the Law Commission of England and Wales, the Act extended to Scotland and Northern Ireland.[101] Before considering how the Act was applied, it is necessary to provide a brief overview of the details of each of the offences it created.

Section 1 – Unauthorised access to computer material

Section 1 of the Act provides that:

(1) A person is guilty of an offence if –

    (a) he causes a computer to perform any function with intent to secure access to any program or data held in any computer;

    (b) the access he intends to secure is unauthorised; and

    (c) he knows at the time when he causes the computer to perform the function that that is the case.

(2) The intent a person has to have to commit an offence under this section need not be directed at –

    (a) any particular program or data;

    (b) a program or data of any particular kind; or

    (c) a program or data held in any particular computer.

The section 1 offence is a summary offence which carries a penalty on summary conviction of imprisonment for a term not exceeding six months or to a fine not exceeding level 5 on the standard scale or to both.[102]

'Securing access' is defined within section 17(2) of the Act as altering or erasing a program or data; copying or moving it to a different location on its storage medium or to a new storage medium; using it; or, having it output from the computer in which it is held. Section 17(5) deals with 'unauthorised' access. Access is unauthorised if the person gaining access is not entitled to control access to the program or data and does not have the consent to access the program or data from someone who is so entitled.

It is perhaps interesting to note that section 17 does not define either 'computer' or 'misuse'. With respect to the definition of 'computer' the Scottish Law Commission was of the view that it:

---

101 Computer Misuse Act 1990, s. 13 (Scotland) and s. 16 (Northern Ireland).
102 Computer Misuse Act 1990, s. 1(3).

... might be preferable not to offer any definition of that word on the basis that, since computer technology is advancing so fast, any definition, even if expressed in terms of function rather than construction, would rapidly become obsolete.[103]

It also noted that the relatively new (at the time) computer evidence provisions within the Police and Criminal Evidence Act 1984[104] did not seek to provide a definition. Moreover, the Law Commission of England and Wales considered that attempting to define 'computer' would have been wrong since any attempt would be necessarily complex, potentially flawed and susceptible to the creeping inaccuracy introduced by technological advances:

[It] would be unnecessary, and indeed might be foolish, to attempt to define computer ... In view of the nature of the proposed hacking offence ... we cannot think that there will ever be serious grounds for arguments based on the ordinary meaning of the term 'computer'. By contrast, all the attempted definitions that we have seen are so complex, in an endeavour to be all-embracing, that they are likely to produce extensive arguments, and thus confusion for magistrates, juries and judges ...[105]

In *DPP* v. *McKeown; DPP* v. *Jones*,[106] Lord Hoffman defined a computer simply as 'a device for storing, processing and retrieving information'.[107]

Indeed, attempts at a legislative definition of 'computer' from other jurisdictions are often cumbersome. For instance, the United States Code defines a 'computer' as:

... an electronic, magnetic, optical, electrochemical, or other high speed data processing device performing logical, arithmetic, or storage functions, and includes any data storage facility or communications facility directly related to or operating in conjunction with such device, but such term does not include

---

103 Scottish Law Commission, *Report on Computer Crime* (Cm 174, July 1987) [4.17].
104 Police and Criminal Evidence Act 1984, ss. 69, 70.
105 Law Commission, *Criminal Law – Computer Misuse* (Law Com. No. 186, Cm 819, 1989) [3.39].
106 *DPP* v. *McKeown; DPP* v. *Jones* [1997] 1 WLR 295 (HL).
107 Ibid., 302.

an automated typewriter or typesetter, a portable hand-held calculator, or other similar device.[108]

As the Law Commission speculated, such a complex definition has been open to much discussion in the United States.[109]

The view of the Law Commission that no definition was necessary was largely echoed throughout the debate on the Computer Misuse Bill, although in Standing Committee, Harry Cohen MP attempted, without success, to amend the Bill to provide a definition as follows:

(1A)   A computer means equipment which can, in the form of one or more continuous variables, accept data, store data or programs in a storage medium, process data by means of a program and provide for the output of data.

(1B)   Where a computer is embedded within other equipment, the computer shall form a unit which can be: (a) identified as being a distinct part of the equipment and (b) routinely accessed in order to allow modifications to programs or data to be made.[110]

This definition is expressed in terms of functionality and not devices. In this sense, it is similar to the definition of 'data' provided in the Data Protection Act 1998 which expresses itself in terms of processing and not devices.[111]

The *Oxford English Dictionary* defines a computer as:

An electronic device which is capable of receiving information (data) and performing a sequence of logical operations in accordance with a predetermined but variable set of procedural instructions (program) to produce a result in the form of information or signals.[112]

---

108   Counterfeit Access Device and Computer Fraud and Abuse Act 18 USC § 1030(e)(1)

109   Tompkins, J. and Mar, L., 'The 1984 Federal Computer Crime Statute: a partial answer to a pervasive problem' (1985) 6 *Computer and Law Journal* 459; Kutz, R., 'Computer crime in Virginia' (1986) 27 *William and Mary Law Review* 783.

110   Standing Committee C, *Computer Misuse Bill* HC (1989–90) col. 81 (28 March 1990).

111   Data Protection Act 1998, s. 1(1).

112   <http://www.oed.com> accessed 25 September 2008.

This establishes the defining characteristics as data storage and retrieval and the ability to process information within an electronic device. An alternative definition, albeit for 'computer systems' rather than 'computer' per se, can be found in the Council of Europe Convention on Cybercrime which defines such 'computer systems' as:

Any device or group of interconnected or related devices, one or more of which, pursuant to a program, performs automatic processing of data.[113]

These definitions also neatly illustrate the difficulties facing the draftsman: although computers are now electronic, Babbage's 'analytical engine' designed in 1822 is surely also a computer despite its being mechanical.[114] Moreover, a microwave oven which calculates cooking time based on the weight and type of the food placed within it could be said to fall within both the dictionary definition and the Council of Europe definition, since it undeniably makes decisions on the basis of information received and is therefore processing data, even though this is secondary to the attainment of its primary purpose of cooking food. Moreover, it could potentially fall within the wording of Cohen's proposed amendment to the Bill, since the computing part of a microwave oven, where instructions are input, could be said to be clearly distinct from its cooking part where the food rotates on its platter. However, it would be patently absurd to refer to such a device as a 'computer' and even less a 'computer system' in the normal everyday meaning of the terms.

Despite the seeming difficulties with the definition of 'computer', an All Party Parliamentary Internet Group (APIG) study in 2004 considered that there had been no difficulties resulting from the lack of statutory definition. Moreover, the Home Office reported that they had 'never come across a case' where the courts had failed to use a 'broad definition' of the term, concluding that:

We recommend that the Government resist calls for words such as 'computer' to be defined on the face of the Computer Misuse Act and continue with the scheme whereby they will be

---

113 Council of Europe Convention on Cybercrime (signed 23 November 2001) ETS 185, art. 1a.
114 Ormerod, D., *Smith and Hogan Criminal Law* (11th edn, Oxford University Press, Oxford, 2004) 926 (n. 15).

understood by the courts to have the appropriate contemporary meaning.[115]

What constitutes a computer therefore remains for the court to decide.

Having considered the meaning of computer, the second element of the *actus reus* of the section 1 offence is 'causing a computer to perform any function'. This encompasses those who use the computer but are denied access as well as the more successful hacker. Merely switching the computer on or using a non-open access computer without permission[116] is sufficient to satisfy the *actus reus*. The section 1 offence is a summary offence[117] and, since there is no express provision to the contrary, there can be no liability for attempting to commit it.[118] Therefore, if the *actus reus* was defined in terms of 'unauthorised access' alone, it would fail to extend to the unsuccessful hacker who had merely attempted to make an unauthorised access, hence the broadening of the *actus reus* to cover 'any function'.

The *mens rea* of the section 1 offence is twofold: the defendant must know that his intended access was unauthorised and he must intend to secure access to any program or data held in the computer. Reckless access is insufficient.[119]

Section 2 – Unauthorised access with intent to commit or facilitate further offences

Section 2 of the Act provides that:

(1) A person is guilty of an offence under this section if he commits an offence under section 1 ... with intent –

(a) to commit an offence to which this section applies [generally arrestable offences],[120] or

(b) to facilitate the commission of such an offence (whether by himself or by any other person);

---

115 All Party Internet Group, *Revision of the Computer Misuse Act: Report of an Inquiry by the All Party Internet Group* (June 2004) [15].

116 *Ellis* v. *DPP* [2001] EWHC Admin 362.

117 Computer Misuse Act 1990, s. 1(3).

118 Criminal Attempts Act 1981, s. 1(4).

119 Although this was proposed under Emma Nicholson's Private Member's Bill, cl. 1(1)(b).

120 Police and Criminal Evidence Act 1984, s. 24, as substituted by the Serious Organised Crime and Police Act 2005, s. 110.

39

and the offence he intends to commit or facilitate is referred to ... as the further offence.

This is a more serious offence than the basic section 1 offence and, as such, carries a maximum penalty on conviction on indictment to five years' imprisonment, a fine or both. As with section 1, this offence is defined in terms of preparatory conduct: it is not necessary to prove that the intended further offence has been committed; moreover, the further offence need not be committed by computer or at the same time as the unauthorised access.[121] In this sense, it is analogous to burglary under section 9(1)(a) of the Theft Act 1968: an initial unauthorised entry with the requisite intent to commit a further offence.[122]

Section 3 – Unauthorised modification of computer material

Section 3 of the Act provides that:

(1) A person is guilty of an offence if –
(a) he does any act which causes an unauthorised modification of the contents of any computer; and
(b) at the time when he does the act he has the requisite intent and the requisite knowledge.

(2) For the purposes of subsection (1)(b) above the requisite intent is an intent to cause a modification of the contents of any computer and by so doing –
(a) to impair the operation of any computer
(b) to prevent or hinder access to any program or data held in any computer; or
(c) to impair the operation of any such program or the reliability of any such data.

(3) The intent need not be directed at –
(a) any particular computer;
(b) any particular program or data or a program or data of any particular kind; or
(c) any particular modification or a modification of any particular kind.

---

121 Computer Misuse Act 1990, s. 2(3).
122 For burglary, these are listed in s. 9(2) of the Theft Act 1968: the list is much narrower than that under s. 2 of the Computer Misuse Act 1990.

(4) For the purposes of subsection (1)(b) above, the requisite knowledge is knowledge that any modification he intends to cause is unauthorised.

Sections 17(7) and 17(8) of the 1990 Act provide the statutory definition of an 'unauthorised modification' of the contents of a computer. A 'modification' takes place if any program or data held in the computer concerned is added to, altered or erased. An unauthorised modification is one where the person causing it is not entitled to determine whether it should be made and does not have the consent of a person who is entitled to determine whether or not the modification should be made.

The section 3 offence is designed to encompass activities involving computer viruses,[123] 'Trojan horses'[124] and worms[125] as well as interference with websites[126] or accessing subscription cable television channels without paying the subscription.[127] This is a different mischief to that tackled by sections 1 and 2. Here, the offence is concerned with forms of electronic sabotage which may be carried out without the unauthorised access required in the other offences. Moreover, it deals with the potential for overlapping liability with the criminal damage charges arising from *Cox* v. *Riley* and *Whiteley* by introducing section 3(6) which provides that:

For the purposes of the Criminal Damage Act 1971, a modification of the contents of a computer shall not be regarded as damaging any computer or computer storage medium unless its effect on that computer or computer storage medium impairs its physical condition.

By effectively reversing *Cox* v. *Riley*, the Act partitions electronic vandalism from physical vandalism, although it should be noted that

---

123 A small program written to alter the way a computer operates without the permission of the user. It must execute and replicate itself. (Symantec, Norton AntiVirus Knowledge Base version 7.0, 30 March 2005.)

124 A file that claims to be something desirable but is, in fact, malicious. Unlike true viruses, Trojan horse programs do not replicate themselves. (Symantec, Norton AntiVirus Knowledge Base version 7.0, 30 March 2005.)

125 Programs that replicate themselves from system to system without the use of a host file, in contrast to viruses which require the spreading of an infected host file. (Symantec, Norton AntiVirus Knowledge Base version 7.0, 30 March 2005.)

126 *R* v. *Lindesay* [2002] 1 Cr App R (S) 370 (CA).

127 *R* v. *Parr-Moore* [2003] 1 Cr App R (S) 425 (CA).

the maximum penalties following conviction on indictment for the offences are different: five years' imprisonment under the Computer Misuse Act and ten years under the Criminal Damage Act. Many would contend, particularly systems administrators, that the levels of damage and consequent expenditure of highly skilled labour required after an electronic attack are at least comparable to a physical attack. For the purposes of section 3(2), a computer's reliability is impaired if it is used to record information as deriving from a particular person when it is, in fact, derived from someone else.[128]

Jurisdiction

The Law Commission recognised that the nature of computer misuse often transcended national boundaries:

A hacker, with or without dishonest intentions, may for instance sit in London and, through an international telephone system, enter or try to enter a computer in New York or vice versa. More complex 'chains', involving computer systems in a number of countries before the 'target' computer is accessed are entirely possible.[129]

The 1990 Act gives jurisdiction to prosecute all offences where there is at least one significant link with domestic jurisdiction in the circumstances of the case.[130] Such a link is defined as either that the accused was in the 'home country'[131] at the time that he did the act which caused the computer to perform the function[132] or that the computer to which the accused secured (or intended to secure) access was in the home country at that time.[133] Therefore the courts have jurisdiction where the misuse originates in the home country or is directed at a computer within it. However, this jurisdiction is subject to dual criminality, such that where a section 2 offence is committed within the home country but the further offence is to take place outside the national boundaries, the courts only have jurisdiction if

128 *Zezev v. Governor of HM Prison Brixton* [2002] EWHC 589 (Admin).
129 Law Commission, *Criminal Law – Computer Misuse* (Law Com. No. 186, Cm 819, 1989) [4.1].
130 Computer Misuse Act 1990, s. 4(2).
131 England and Wales, Scotland or Northern Ireland; Computer Misuse Act 1990, s. 4(6).
132 Computer Misuse Act 1990, s. 5(2)(a).
133 Computer Misuse Act 1990, s. 5(2)(b).

the further offence is also a criminal offence in the target country as well as in the home country.[134] The Court of Appeal has taken this approach in relation to obscene articles, holding that website content hosted abroad falls within domestic jurisdiction when downloaded in the United Kingdom.[135]

Conclusion

In the period up until 1990, computer technology advanced in terms of storage capacity, processing power, user-friendliness and accessibility. It also became progressively cheaper to produce and therefore more widely available in the commercial and private marketplace. Computer technology moved from the realm of the specialist and the scientist into private industry and the home. Computers also gave rise to networks, not only the early networks of interconnected computers such as ARPANET and BITNET but also the social networks organised by user communities and enthusiasts.

In parallel with the technological advancements, computers also began to be used for unauthorised purposes. Initially this unauthorised activity, pursued by enthusiastic insiders keen to understand and engage further with the new possibilities offered by computing, was ignored. Indeed, in some instances it was encouraged as a means of attracting talented operatives. However, via the phone phreaks, a hacker culture emerged. While the activities of the hacker were often predominantly led by the intellectual challenge of gaining unauthorised access to a system, fears around data security and public safety increasingly became matters of public concern. Malicious hacking began to become more prevalent during the 1980s, at which time the first computer viruses also came into circulation.

The domestic criminal law which existed at the time had some success in dealing with unauthorised access and unauthorised modification of data. Prosecutions were often brought on the basis of the Criminal Damage Act 1971. However, the failure of the Forgery and Counterfeiting Act 1981 to deal with the 'Prestel hack' by Gold and Schifreen helped to give impetus to the proposals put forward by the Law Commissions of Scotland and, later, England and Wales. The Computer Misuse Act 1990 created three new criminal offences: unauthorised access to computer material, unauthorised access to

---

134 Computer Misuse Act 1990, ss. 4(4), 8(1).
135 *R v. Waddon* (6 April 2000) (CA); *R v. Perrin* [2002] EWCA Crim 747.

computer material with the intent to commit or facilitate further offences and unauthorised modification of computer material. It also gave jurisdiction to prosecute offences where there is a significant link with domestic jurisdiction.

Having charted the technological and legal landscape up to the enactment of the 1990 Act, the next chapter will explore technological developments since its enactment, survey how the Act has been used in practice and consider recent proposals for its reform.

Chapter 3

The evolution of the problem of computer misuse

Humanity is acquiring all the right technology for all the wrong reasons.

R. Buckminster Fuller, developer of the geodesic dome
(1895–1983)

The previous chapter charted the evolution of computers and computer misuse up to the enactment of the Computer Misuse Act 1990. This chapter will continue those two parallel evolutionary strands: the continued progression in computing power, reach and accessibility post-1990 and the consequent expansion of the types of computer misuse. Following on from the conclusion of the last chapter which discussed the offences created by the 1990 Act, this chapter will examine whether or not the Act was effective in controlling the problem together with any potential reasons for any ineffectiveness. It will consider both prosecution rates and judicial interpretation. This chapter will conclude with a survey of the various attempts that have been made to update the 1990 Act, discussing the driving forces behind these attempts and their outcomes, analysing the amendments to the 1990 Act made by the Police and Justice Act 2006 and considering the possible ramifications of those amendments.

The evolution of computing and computer misuse post-1990

Computing and networking

As discussed in Chapter 2, local networking of hitherto stand-alone 'personal' computers had become commonplace in the office environment at the time of the 1990 Act. However, the underlying technology which facilitated local networking also enabled the development of the Internet.

The Internet evolved from the ARPANET, although there are key differences between the two. The Internet is not a single network. It comprises a 'network of networks' spread across the globe, with a number of these networks allowing public access, rather than restricting access to a particular community. On a technical level, the Internet allows communications between these networks using a single common protocol known as TCP/IP[1], whereas ARPANET was originally based on a communications technology called NCP.[2] NCP, however, could not enable communications between separate networks and the ARPANET migrated to use the prevailing TCP/IP protocol in January 1983.

The growth of the Internet was driven by a combination of both social and technological factors. State financial and administrative support was moved away from ARPA on to the National Science Foundation in the 1980s and in the 1990s to organisations which allowed Internet access to anyone, including commercial concerns. By 1995 commercial users (the 'dot coms') vastly outnumbered the Internet's original governmental, military and educational users. In addition, the enabling TCP/IP protocol was supported by ARPA and thus became widely available in academic institutions. The fact that this protocol was not proprietary to IBM or DEC enabled its swift propagation throughout the development community. The increasing prevalence of local area networks also enabled increasingly large numbers of people to access the Internet without each individual computer requiring a direct connection.

The World Wide Web is distinct from the Internet in that it is a system of interlinked, hypertext documents that runs *over* the Internet. In other words, the Internet itself is the enabling technology that allows the World Wide Web to function. The original prototype for the Web was developed in 1990 by Sir Tim Berners-Lee at CERN, the European particle physics laboratory. He later stated that:

---

1 Transmission control protocol/Internet protocol.
2 Network control protocol.

The Web's major goal was to be a shared information space through which people and machines could communicate. This space was to be inclusive, rather than exclusive.[3]

The design of the Internet has allowed it to scale enormously without severe disruption. In parallel with this networked expansion, the processing and storage capabilities of computers have continued to grow while their price has fallen. The increasing commoditisation of computer technology coupled with the scalability and accessibility of the Internet has resulted in over one billion people worldwide (16.6 per cent of the total global population) becoming Internet users. The growth in world internet usage is illustrated in Figure 3.1.[4]

It can be seen that extent of Internet usage has grown dramatically since the enactment of the 1990 Act. This expansion of networked technology has also given rise to a much greater number of potential targets for computer misuse which may be accessed remotely via the network.

The expansion of computer misuse

The number of incidents of computer misuse grew in parallel with the increased availability of networked technologies. The Computer

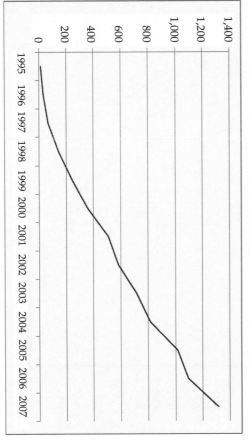

Figure 3.1 World Internet usage (millions) 1995–2007

3 Berners-Lee, T., 'WWW: past, present and future' (1996) 29 IEE Computer 69, 70.
4 Miniwatts Marketing Group, World Internet Usage Statistics <http://www.internetworldstats.com/stats.htm> accessed 25 September 2008.

Emergency Response Team (CERT)[5] collects statistical information on security vulnerabilities which may render computers susceptible as targets of misuse. These vulnerability statistics are compiled from reliable public sources and incidents notified to the CERT directly. While these statistics may not encapsulate the entire spectrum of potential vulnerabilities, they do allow some insight into the increasing trend in their number over the past 13 years, as shown in Figure 3.2.[6]

The CERT also collected statistics relating to the number of incident reports received up until 2003. By this time, the prevalence of automated attack tools used against Internet-connected systems had become so commonplace that counts of the number of incidents reported provide little information with regard to assessing the scope and impact of attacks. However, it can be clearly seen in Figure 3.3[7] that the number of incidents had increased greatly until the point that data collection was discontinued.

In summary, there has been a vast expansion in the prevalence of networked computer technology since 1990 which has been mirrored by a corresponding increase in the numbers of potential vulnerabilities to computer misuse and the numbers of incidents reported. Given this, it is next necessary to explore whether the 1990 Act has produced a corresponding rise in prosecution rates.

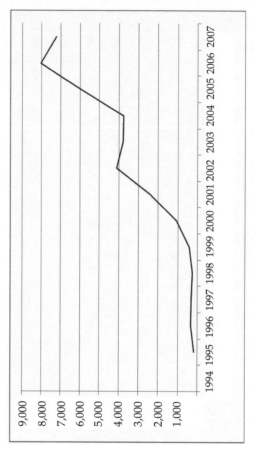

Figure 3.2 Vulnerabilities catalogued by CERT 1994–2007

5 See Chapter 7 for a detailed discussion of the role of CERTs.
6 <http://www.cert.org/stats/fullstats.html> accessed 25 September 2008.

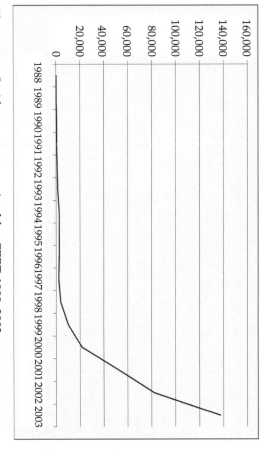

Figure 3.3 Incident reports received by CERT 1988–2003

Prosecutions under the Computer Misuse Act 1990

At the time that the 1990 Act was enacted, it was lamented that only six cases in the preceding five years had been brought to court and, of those, only three were successfully prosecuted. It was hoped that the 1990 Act would alleviate these difficulties; however, official statistics tend to suggest otherwise (see Tables 3.1 and 3.2).[8]

These figures are, perhaps, surprisingly low. There are a number of potential explanations for this.[9] In particular, major organisations believed that they would not benefit from bringing a prosecution under the 1990 Act, instead relying on internal disciplinary matters in the case of misuse committed by employees.[10] According to the DTI:

Companies were generally good at taking disciplinary action against staff when policies were breached. However, very few took any form of legal action. For virus infections, there was

---

7 Ibid.
8 Akdeniz, Y., 'CyberCrime', in Stokes, S. and Carolina, R. (eds) *E-Commerce Law and Regulation Encyclopedia* (Sweet & Maxwell, London, 2003) 15–18.
9 Ibid., 15–21.
10 For example, *Denco Ltd* v. *Joinson* [1992] 1 All ER 463 (EAT) which involved unauthorised access to data on an employer's computer system via a colleague's password.

Table 3.1 Number of persons cautioned by the police for principal offences under the Computer Misuse Act 1990 (England and Wales) 1991–2001

	Section 1	Section 2	Section 3
1991	–	–	–
1992	–	–	–
1993	–	1	1
1994	–	–	–
1995	–	–	2
1996	–	–	6
1997	–	–	1
1998	–	–	–
1999	9	2	7
2000	4	5	15
2001	10	–	10
Total (1991–2001)	**23**	**8**	**42**

Table 3.2 Number of persons proceeded against for principal offences under the Computer Misuse Act 1990 (England and Wales) 1991–2002

	Section 1	Section 2	Section 3
1991	–	–	4
1992	–	1	6
1993	–	1	7
1994	–	1	3
1995	–	1	5
1996	–	2	2
1997	–	–	7
1998	6	6	4
1999	6	3	4
2000	8	3	8
2001	9	4	12
2002	4	6	8
Total (1991–2002)	**33**	**28**	**70**

a general perception that no-one had broken the law. There was little appetite to pursue the virus writers. When staff caused breaches, internal disciplinary measures were normally considered sufficient.[11]

This may be because there is no prospect of restitutionary damages or compensation for loss in a criminal prosecution under the 1990 Act. For most organisations, the prospect of adverse publicity resulting from a security breach seems to outweigh the benefit of prosecution. As User 8 said:

If someone got into our data, the last thing we'd want is for it to be all over the courts and the papers. Software is our business. Do you really think we'd want our customers to hear we'd been caught out? That would be commercial suicide.

Moreover, there are concerns that the police will not have the resources or expertise to assist. This was a common theme in the interviews with both police officers and technology users alike:

If someone came up to my desk and told me that they had a virus, I'd tell them to go to their doctor. It would be different if they'd had their car nicked, I suppose, but we can't go looking for things that don't exist, can we?[12]

We just haven't got the time. We can't handle burglaries, let alone all these computer attacks. I'm not saying that we shouldn't. We just can't.[13]

What would be the point in going to the police? They're not going to recover our data. Even if there's a miracle and they do catch whoever's done it, we'll still be out of pocket. Locking someone up won't help us.[14]

It seems therefore that the 1990 Act has not been greatly exercised in comparison to the growth of the problem of computer misuse. In

11 DTI, *Information Security Breaches Survey 2004* <http://www.pwc.com/images/gx/eng/about/svcs/grms/2004Technical_Report.pdf> accessed 25 September 2008.
12 Police Officer 2.
13 Police Officer 1.
14 User 3.

order to explore why this might be the case, the next section will consider the ways in which it is has been applied and examine whether the Act presents particular interpretative challenges for the court.

Interpretation of the Computer Misuse Act 1990[15]

Section 1 – The basic hacking offence

Early judicial interpretation of this section was somewhat curious. In *R v. Cropp*,[16] the defendant visited his former employer and obtained a 70 per cent discount on goods by entering the discount on the computerised till part way through a transaction, while the sales assistant was absent in the storeroom checking details of the serial number of the goods in question. This resulted in an invoice for £204.60 plus VAT instead of the correct sum of £710.96 plus VAT. Cropp was charged under section 2(1) of the 1990 Act, allegedly having secured unauthorised access to a computer in contravention of section 1(1) of the 1990 Act with intent to commit the further offence of false accounting.[17] However, at first instance, it was held that section 1(1) did not apply to the facts of this case, since, in order to contravene the section, it was necessary to establish that the defendant had used one computer with intent to secure unauthorised access into another computer. Aglionby J held:

It seems to me, doing the best that I can in elucidating the meaning of section 1(1)(a), that a second computer must be involved. It seems to me to be straining language to say that only one computer is necessary when one looks to see the actual wording of the subsection: 'Causing a computer to perform any function with intent to secure access to any program or data held in any computer'.

15 See also Fafinski, S., 'Access denied: computer misuse in an era of technological change' (2006) 70 *Journal of Criminal Law* 424.

16 *R v. Cropp* (unreported) 4 July 1990, in Teichner, F., 'Regulating cyberspace', 15th BILETA Conference (14 April 2000) <http://www.bileta.ac.uk/Document%20Library/1/Regulating%20Cyberspace.pdf> accessed 25 September 2008.

17 Theft Act 1968, s. 17(1)(a).

This decision seemed incongruous with the purpose that the Act declared in its own long title: securing computer material against unauthorised access. If *Cropp* was to be followed, this would have the effect of limiting the scope of the Act to networked systems alone; while this would not seem to be too problematic in the modern networked society, it is particularly surprising in the context of the time when many more computers were stand-alone. The prospect of excluding computer material on stand-alone machines from the protection of the Act led to the swift intervention of the Attorney-General and consideration by the Court of Appeal who ruled that Aglionby J had erred in law. Lord Taylor of Gosforth CJ commented:

[Counsel for the Attorney-General] pointed to the surprising, and indeed unlikely lacunae which this Act would have left in the field of interference with computers if the construction for which [counsel for the respondent] contends were correct … [The] kind of activity of going straight to the in-house computer and extracting confidential information from it could be committed with impunity so far as the three offences in this Act are concerned.[18]

In effect, the Court of Appeal implied the words 'including itself' at the end of the section 1(1)(a), closed the door that Aglionby J opened in *Cropp*.

However, it is interesting to note that an amendment to the Bill was moved during the Standing Committee which would have had precisely the same effect as the decision in *Cropp*:

[The amendment] ensures that at least two computers are involved in a clause 1 offence: the computer used by the hacker and the target computer that is misused.[19]

This amendment was unsuccessful, although its existence demonstrates that there was at least some Parliamentary support for Aglionby J.

---

18 *Attorney-General's Reference (No. 1 of 1991)* [1993] QB 94 (CA) 100.
19 Standing Committee C, 'Computer Misuse Bill' HC (1989–90) (14 March 1990).

In *Bedworth*[20] it was alleged that the defendant and two others modified code within the *Financial Times* share index database and disrupted research work at the European Organisation for the Research and Treatment of Cancer. Bedworth was charged *inter alia* with two counts of conspiracy under the Act relating to both the section 1 and section 3 offences. However, Bedworth argued that he had developed an addiction to computer use, calling expert witnesses to corroborate his claim to suffering from 'computer tendency syndrome' and as a result was unable to form the requisite intent. The jury accepted this argument and Bedworth was acquitted, a decision 'described by some as a "licence to hack"'.[21]

DPP v. Bignell[22] imposed a significant limitation on the ambit of the Act. This case concerned a husband and wife who were both officers in the Metropolitan police force. They instructed police computer operators to extract the registration and ownership details of two cars parked outside the house of the husband's ex-wife from the Police National Computer. They were convicted on six counts of the section 1 unauthorised access offence by a district judge (magistrates' court) and fined. The defendants appealed on the basis that their access was not unlawful; their access had been with authority, even though the authority was used for an unauthorised purpose: this was upheld, but the prosecution appealed by way of case stated. This prosecution appeal was unsuccessful, with Astill J considering that:

[T]he starting point is to consider the purpose of the Computer Misuse Act 1990. It is common ground that it was enacted to criminalise the breaking into or 'hacking' of computer systems.[23]

Therefore, the police officers involved had not acted unlawfully, since they were authorised to access the system:

A person who is authorised to secure access to a program or data does not commit an offence under s. 1 of the Computer

---

20 *R v. Bedworth* (unreported) 1991 in Akdeniz, Y., 'Section 3 of the Computer Misuse Act 1990: an antidote for computer viruses!' [1996] 3 *Web Journal of Current Legal Issues* <http://webjcli.ncl.ac.uk/1996/issue3/akdeniz3.html> accessed 25 September 2008.
21 Charlesworth, A., 'Addiction and hacking' (1993) 143 *New Law Journal* 540.
22 *DPP v. Bignell* [1998] 1 Cr App R 1 (DC).
23 Ibid, 12.

Misuse Act 1990 if he accesses the computer at the authorised level.[24]

Wasik commented that this decision was 'inconvenient and ... open to criticism' since:

... on ordinary construction of language, authorising a person's access for one (legitimate) purpose ought not to be regarded as authorising his access for another (non-legitimate) purpose.[25]

The decision is also at odds with the situation in relation to burglary in the physical world. In *R v. Jones and Smith*,[26] the Court of Appeal held that a general permission to enter a property did not encompass permission with intention to steal. However, *Bignell* effectively confined the concept of unauthorised access to 'outside' hackers who have no authority to access a particular computer system. It is particularly noteworthy given that much misuse was, and still is, committed by 'insiders' and that many of the computers subject to misuse have been stand-alone. Examples of this include the computerised saw in *Cox v. Riley* and the electronic cash register in *Cropp*.

However, Astill J's dicta were disapproved by the House of Lords in *R v. Bow Street Metropolitan Stipendiary Magistrate and Allison, ex parte Government of the United States of America*.[27] This case involved the attempted extradition from England to the United States of an individual who had allegedly obtained 189 sets of account information from a credit analyst employed by American Express and used that information to forge credit cards and subsequently withdraw around US$1,000,000 from automatic teller machines. The extradition order specified *inter alia* two proposed charges of conspiring with the employee to commit the section 2(1) offence; specifically that of securing unauthorised access to the American Express computer system contrary to section 1(1) of the 1990 Act with the further intent to commit forgery and theft. This set of facts seemed analogous to those in *Bignell*, both cases involving the misuse of information obtained by a person authorised to secure access to that information.

---

24 Ibid., 13.
25 Wasik, M., 'Computer misuse and misconduct in public office' (2008) 22 *International Review of Law, Computers and Technology* 135, 137.
26 *R v. Jones and Smith* [1976] 1 WLR 672 (CA).
27 *R v. Bow Street Metropolitan Stipendiary Magistrate and Allison, ex parte Government of the United States of America* [2000] 2 AC 216 (HL).

The magistrate refused to commit the defendant on these charges, holding a view consistent with *Bignell* that 'unauthorised access' did not extend to an authorised user who misused the information obtained. The US Government sought judicial review of the decision not to extradite.

In considering whether the defendant had committed an offence under section 1(1) of the 1990 Act (and thereby potentially having conspired to commit the section 2(1) offence, a sufficient crime for extradition to the US to be granted), the Divisional Court upheld the decision at first instance.[28] On further appeal, the House of Lords considered that the court in *Bignell*, and indeed the Divisional Court, had confused the concept of being entitled to access a particular computer or network with that of being entitled to access programs and data on a machine:

[The decision of the Divisional Court in *Bignell*] seems to derive from … confusion between kinds of access and kinds of data. Nor is section 1 of the Act concerned with authority to access kinds of data. It is concerned with authority to access the actual data involved. Because section 1(1) creates an offence which can be committed as a result of having an intent to secure unauthorised access without … actually succeeding, section 1(2) does not require that the relevant intent relate to any specific data. But that does not mean that access to the data in question does not have to be authorised.

Therefore, any ambiguity regarding the definition of 'unauthorised' was resolved: the term relates to the specific data accessed rather than the same 'kind of data' suggested by Astill J in *Bignell*. However, Lord Hobhouse also considered that *Bignell* was probably decided correctly, in that the defendants had 'merely requested' another to obtain the information, and that the operator had not exceeded the authority permitting him to access data in response to requests made to him in proper form by a police officer. This has been criticised by J.C. Smith as a 'rather narrow view of the activity of the defendants',[29] the operators seemingly acting as innocent agents:

---

28 *R v. Bow Street Metropolitan Stipendiary Magistrate and Allison, ex parte Government of the United States of America* [1999] QB 847 (DC).

29 Smith, J.C., 'R v. Bow Street Metropolitan Stipendiary Magistrate and Another, ex parte Government of the United States of America' (case note) [1999] *Criminal Law Review* 970, 971.

Were they any different from a janitor who is instructed to unlock the door of a cell? Was it not really the defendants who were accessing data on the computer? ... [It] may be that they were authorised to access the data in question in the way that they did.[30]

The decision in *Allison* also made it clear that the Act's application extended to employees, meaning that, if an employee is subject to a limitation on their authorisation to access data on a computer and that authorisation is exceeded, this activity may fall within the ambit of the 1990 Act. This decision was welcomed 'signalling that the Act, after seeing little use in its first decade, has come of age and will now be a useful tool for prosecuting authorities'.[31]

However, the 1990 Act was not used in *R v. Hardy*.[32] This involved similar facts to *Bignell*. In *Hardy*, the defendant had used the Police National Computer to download information on three people. He passed this information to his co-defendant, Jolley, a known criminal with previous convictions for offences of violence, in order that Jolley could deal with those whom he believed to have committed offences against himself and his partner. Hardy was charged with, and pleaded guilty to, misconduct in public office[33] rather than the section 1 offence. Section 4(1) of the Official Secrets Act 1989 might also have been used as the offender was a Crown servant[34] who disclosed information obtained by virtue of his position without lawful authority which would be likely to result in the commission of an offence,[35] however, this would have applied to the consequences of the disclosure rather than the acquisition of the information in its own right. When questioned as to why Hardy was not charged under the 1990 Act following *Allison* and *Bignell*, counsel for the Attorney-General commented that the answer was threefold.

---

30 Ibid., 972.
31 Stein, K., '"Unauthorised access" and the UK Computer Misuse Act 1990: House of Lords "leaves no room" for ambiguity (2000) 6 *Computer and Telecommunications Law Review* 63.
32 *R v. Hardy (Attorney-General's Reference (No. 1 of 2007))* [2007] EWCA Crim 760.
33 *R v. Dytham* [1979] QB 722 (CA) deals with the offence in relation to the failure of a police officer in his duty to preserve the Queen's peace; the offence is now defined in *Attorney General's Reference (No. 3 of 2003)* [2004] EWCA Crim 868 [30], such that the defendant must be subjectively aware of the duty and subjectively reckless in its fulfilment.
34 This includes police officers: Official Secrets Act 1989, s. 12(1)(e).
35 Official Secrets Act 1989, s. 4(2)(b).

The first possibility was through ignorance, in that 'most criminal lawyers are unfamiliar with and wary of "computer" offences, as they expect them to hold hidden dangers for all but the über-geek'.[36] The second was that the 'gravamen of the misconduct was not really the misuse of the computer but the abuse of the officer's position of trust'.[37] The final option was that the person selecting the charge was 'ignorant of [*Allison and Bignell*] (as was I) or at least did not have it in mind at the relevant time'.[38] This provides an interesting insight into the reluctance of the prosecuting authorities to use the 1990 Act, preferring instead to rely upon a relatively unusual common law offence. However, as Wasik comments, the offence of misconduct in public office has been used successfully against police officers in a very wide range of factual circumstances. It has been used relatively frequently in relation to police misuse of police computers.[39] It remains a convenient recourse for prosecutors because, as a common law offence, it carries a penalty of up to life imprisonment and is therefore more appropriate for use in the more serious cases where the conduct merits a penalty well in excess of that available under statute. Being loosely defined, it also avoids many of the definitional problems already identified within the 1990 Act.[40] Moreover, there may have been an alternative (but less attractive) basis for prosecution under section 55 of the Data Protection Act 1998 as will be examined further later in this chapter.

Section 2 – Unauthorised access with intent to commit or facilitate further offences

An illustration of the section 2 offence can be found in *R v. Delamare (Ian)*.[41] Here, the defendant worked in the Poole branch of Barclays Bank and was approached by an old school acquaintance who asked him to disclose the details of two bank account holders for £50 each and in discharge of a favour he owed this acquaintance as a result of events during their schooldays. This led to an attempt

---

36 Statement by Adrian Darbishire (personal e-mail correspondence, 17 April 2007).

37 Ibid.

38 Ibid.

39 See *R v. O'Leary* [2007] EWCA Crim 186; *R v. Kassim* [2006] EWCA Crim 1020; *R v. Keyte* [1998] 2 Cr App R (S) 165 (CA): in Wasik, M., 'Computer misuse and misconduct in public office' (2008) 22 *International Review of Law, Computers and Technology* 135, 138–40.

40 Ibid., 140–1.

41 *R v. Delamare (Ian)* [2003] EWCA Crim 424.

to impersonate one of the account holders and obtain £10,000 from the bank. Delamare was convicted (after pleading guilty) on two counts of the section 2(1) offence and sentenced to 18 months in a young offender institution, reduced to four months on appeal. This illustrates how using the bank's computer to access information with a view to facilitating, in this case, a fraud falls squarely within the ambit of section 2(1), Jackson J commented:

Bank customers must be able to open accounts and to carry on their affairs in full confidence that their private details will not be disclosed to outsiders. It must be clearly understood that breaches of trust by bank officials of the kind which occurred in this case are likely to attract prison sentences.[42]

This further demonstrates the increased severity with which the courts view the section 2 offence, just as burglary is a broader and more serious offence than simple theft.

Section 3 – Unauthorised modification

The 1990 Act did prove somewhat more successful in addressing misuse relating to viruses. In *R v. Pile*,[43] the first case in which the author of computer viruses was prosecuted in England and Wales, the defendant was charged with five counts of the section 1 offence for gaining unauthorised access to computers, five counts of the section 3 offence for making unauthorised modifications and one count of incitement after encouraging others to spread the viruses he had written, two 'vicious and very dangerous viruses named *Pathogen* and *Queeg*'.[44] This fell squarely within the sort of mischief that the 1990 Act was designed to address. Pile, also known as the 'Black Baron', was sentenced to 18 months' imprisonment after pleading guilty.

Notwithstanding this success (albeit following a guilty plea), the interpretation of the 1990 Act continues to be problematic. Two contrasting cases provide an illustration of the reluctance of the courts to be flexible in the application of the Act, even when faced

---

42 Ibid. [8].
43 R v. *Pile* (unreported) 15 November 1995, in Akdeniz, Y., 'Section 3 of the Computer Misuse Act 1990: an antidote for computer viruses!' [1996] 3 *Web Journal of Current Legal Issues* <http://webjcli.ncl.ac.uk/1996/issue3/akdeniz3.html> accessed 25 September 2008.
44 Ibid.

with novel circumstances arising from technological advances and despite the fact that unusual decisions might result.[45]

R v. Cuthbert

In *R* v. *Cuthbert*,[46] a computer consultant was fined £400 with £600 costs after being convicted under section 1 of the Act for gaining unauthorised access to the Disasters Emergency Committee fundraising website. This site was collecting donations for victims of the 2004 Asian tsunami. At the time of the offence, Cuthbert was employed as a security system penetration tester. He had donated £30 to the tsunami appeal but became concerned that he might have fallen foul of a 'phishing' scam[47] after receiving no final confirmation page from a website which he considered to have suspiciously slow response times and poor graphics. He therefore checked the security of the site and satisfied himself that the site was safe, receiving no error messages in response to his tests nor warnings that he had accessed an unauthorised area.

However, the tests set off alarms in an intrusion detection system and Cuthbert was traced extremely easily, having just entered his name, address and credit card details and having had his IP address[48] captured. In his defence, Cuthbert argued that he had merely 'knocked on the door' of the site, pointing out that he had the skills to break into it if he wanted. However, the court took a literal interpretation of the section 1 offence of making unauthorised access, there being no burden on the prosecution to prove that the defendant had intended to cause any damage. Indeed, Purdy J accepted that Cuthbert had not intended to cause any damage and considered it a matter of 'deep regret that he was finding him guilty', lamenting the fact that there was 'almost no case law in this area'.

45 Detailed technical accounts of the two cases can be found in Sommer, P., *Computer Misuse Prosecutions* (Society for Computers and Law, 2005) <http://www.scl.org.uk/services/default.asp?p=154&c=-9999&cID=1140001017&ctID=12>, accessed 25 September 2008.

46 *R* v. *Cuthbert* (Horseferry magistrates' court, unreported) 29 September 2005.

47 Defined by the Anti-Phishing Working Group as an attack using 'both social engineering and technical subterfuge to steal consumers' personal identity data and financial account credentials. Social-engineering schemes use "spoofed" e-mails to lead consumers to counterfeit websites designed to trick recipients into divulging financial data such as credit card numbers, account usernames, passwords and social security numbers.' <http://www.antiphishing.org> accessed 25 September 2008.

48 A unique number that devices use in order to identify and communicate with each other on a network.

DPP v. Lennon[49]

A case heard at Wimbledon magistrates' court the following month found that a teenager had no case to answer after admitting that he used a mail-bomber program to flood the e-mail system of his former employer with over five million e-mails.

David Lennon was dismissed by Domestic and General Group plc (D&G) after failing to complete a timesheet. He was 16 years of age at the time. One Friday evening, Lennon started sending e-mails to D&G using a mail-bombing program (*Avalanche* v. 3.6) which he had downloaded via the Internet. Mail-bombing is characterised by the repeated sending of e-mail messages to a particular e-mail address (or addresses) within an organisation. In many instances, these messages are large and constructed from meaningless data in an effort to consume additional system and network resources. This is an example of a 'denial-of-service' attack, defined by APIG as occurring:

> when a deliberate attempt is made to stop a machine from performing its usual activities by having another computer create large volumes of specious traffic. The traffic may be valid requests made in an overwhelming volume or specially crafted protocol fragments that cause the serving machine to tie up significant resources to no useful purpose.[50]

The *Avalanche* program was set to 'mail until stopped'. In other words, e-mail would be sent to D&G automatically and continuously until stopped by some sort of manual intervention. The e-mails sent appeared to be from Betty Rhodes, personnel manager at D&G, rather than from Lennon. Each e-mail sent was also copied to a list of other D&G employees, thereby increasing the overall number of messages needing to be handled by D&G's network and e-mail servers. Toward the end of the mail-bombing, different addresses were used in an attempt to circumvent any measures that might be put in place by D&G to block their arrival. The last message said 'It won't stop' and was addressed to Ms Rhodes.

Over the course of the weekend it was estimated that approximately five million e-mails had been received by D&G's servers which were

---

49 *DPP* v. *Lennon* (Wimbledon magistrates' court, unreported) 2 November 2005; Fafinski, S., 'Computer misuse: denial-of-service attacks' (2006) 70 *Journal of Criminal Law* 474.

50 All Party Internet Group, *Revision of the Computer Misuse Act: Report of an Inquiry by the All-Party Internet Group* (June 2004) [56].

consequently overwhelmed and taken out of service along with the corporate website. The attack was subsequently neutralised. Lennon was arrested. He admitted to sending the e-mails purporting to be from Betty Rhodes with the intention of causing a 'bit of a mess up' within D&G. However, he did not believe that what he had done was criminal, neither did he realise the impact of his actions, nor the intention to cause the damage that was in fact sustained by D&G, estimated at around £18,000.

He did, however, state that he could have carried out a 'ping' attack. 'Ping' is a simple computer network tool which determines whether a particular computer is reachable over a network. The test computer sends an 'echo request' message to the target, which, if reached, sends back an 'echo reply'. In other words 'are you there?' receives 'yes' or silence. In a ping attack the target system is overwhelmed with echo request messages requiring vast numbers of echo replies to be sent in return. This consumes both incoming and outgoing network resources. However, ping flooding is a relatively unsophisticated means of launching a denial-of-service attack and its effects are often mitigated by a simple firewall. Lennon recognised this, saying that the reason that he did not instigate a ping flood was that it would only have slowed D&G's network for a few hours. In doing so he therefore acknowledged that he at least considered the relative potential for disruption of two courses of action and chose the one more likely to cause difficulties for D&G.

Lennon was charged under section 3(1) of the 1990 Act. At first instance[51] the prosecution submitted that Lennon had satisfied the elements of the section 3(1) offence since he had caused a 'modification' of the contents of D&G's e-mail servers by adding the data associated with the five million e-mails to their contents. He had the requisite intent to impair their operation by admitting that he wanted to cause 'a bit of a mess up' and the requisite knowledge that the modifications effected by sending the e-mails was unauthorised. However, the case turned on the matter of 'authorisation'. The defendant argued that since the function of an e-mail server was to receive e-mail, D&G consented to receive e-mails on its servers. This consent amounted to authorisation to potential senders of e-mails to modify the contents of the receiving computer by adding to the data already stored therein. Therefore, by virtue of section 17(8)(b) of the 1990 Act, Lennon, as a potential sender of e-mail to D&G's e-mail system, *did* have consent to the modification from D&G.

---

51 *DPP v. Lennon* (Wimbledon magistrates' court, unreported) 2 November 2005.

The prosecution countered this on four potential grounds. The first ground was that there can only be consent to *bona fide* e-mails and Lennon's were not. The second was that, in any event, the e-mails were unauthorised from the moment that *Avalanche* was instructed to send them. Alternatively, even if there was a number of e-mails that were impliedly authorised, there was a threshold at which their number transgressed into being unauthorised. The final possibility was that all the e-mails were unauthorised since they came from Lennon rather than the purported sender, Ms Rhodes.

District Judge Grant, sitting as a youth court, held that there was no case to answer since the purpose of section 3 was to deal with the sending of malicious material such as viruses, worms and Trojan horses which modify data, and not to deal with the sending of e-mail. Moreover, considering each e-mail sent by Lennon on an individual basis, the implied consent to each resulted in implied consent collectively and therefore the modifications made were authorised. Charges against Lennon were dismissed. As with *Cuthbert*, the court ignored pleas to consider the wider mischief beyond the strict wording of the 1990 Act, accepting the defence argument in a written ruling:

> In this case, the individual e-mails each caused a modification which was in each case an 'authorised' modification. Although they were sent in bulk resulting in the overwhelming of the server, the effect on the server is not a modification addressed by section 3.

The Director of Public Prosecutions appealed against the decision by way of case stated, asking whether the magistrate was right to find that there was no case to answer. The Divisional Court allowed the appeal[52] and remitted the case back to the magistrates to continue the hearing. They considered that the district judge had 'rather missed' the 'reality of the situation' by wrongly finding that there was no case to answer. The court considered whether the addition of data was unauthorised within the meaning of section 17(8) of the Act. The first limb of the test was unproblematic, since Lennon was not himself in a position to determine whether or not such modification should

Judge Grant also echoed the words of Judge Purdy in *Cuthbert* by stating that 'the computer world has considerably changed since the 1990 Act' and that there is little legal precedent to which to refer.

be made. With regard to the issue of consent, the court considered that the implied consent of a computer owner to receive e-mails is not without limit and is withdrawn where e-mails are sent 'for the purpose of interrupting the proper operation and use of his system': as such it is not necessary to 'define the limits of the consent'. The conduct should be considered as a whole and not on an e-mail-by-e-mail basis.

The deliberate and informed act of bringing down computer systems under a barrage of e-mail, or indeed any other manifestation of a denial-of-service attack, instinctively feels like the sort of behaviour that should fall within the criminal law particularly when it results in loss, such as the financial loss suffered by D&G. As such, the finding of no case to answer at first instance seems surprising, a view echoed in the professional media at the time.[53]

The Divisional Court drew reference to a number of analogies when considering the issue of consent in this case. For example, they stated that 'the householder does not consent to having his letterbox choked with rubbish'. It does, however, appear that the Divisional Court has continued with its approach to a threshold of implied consent that is seen in other areas of both criminal and civil law. For instance, in *The Calgarth*,[54] Scrutton LJ famously remarked 'when you invite a person into your house to use the staircase, you do not invite him to slide down the banisters': an analogy that could have been restated as 'when you allow someone to send you an e-mail, you do not invite him to overwhelm your systems'. In relation to battery, there is implied consent to physical contact with one's person resulting from the exigencies of everyday life, such as jostling on a crowded train or physical contact within certain sports. However, such consent may not be implied where there is an element of persistence in the contact or where it has gone beyond generally acceptable standards.[55] Therefore the court considered that there is implied consent to ordinary unsolicited e-mail of the sort that is incidental to using a computer, but not to an unacceptable mass delivery.

As an aside, the Divisional Court also drew a distinction between unwanted e-mail which does not harm the server – low-volume 'spam' e-mail – and bulk e-mail which does overwhelm it. Keen LJ *obiter* speculated, in respect of spam, that the recipient may be taken

---

53 Neal, D., 'Judge says law allows denial-of-service attacks', *IT Week* (7 November 2005) <http://www.itweek.co.uk/itweek/news/2145679/judge-law-allows-dos-attacks> accessed 25 September 2008.

54 *The Calgarth* [1927] P 93, 110 (CA).

55 *Collins v. Wilcock* [1984] 1 WLR 1172 (DC); *R v. Barnes* [2004] EWCA Crim 3246.

to have consented to its receipt if 'he does not configure the server so as to exclude [it]'. This is perhaps a tacit acknowledgement that the courts may look less favourably on claimants who have failed to take adequate precautions for the security of their own systems. It is not a new idea, having already formed the basis for an amendment to the Computer Misuse Bill. Keen LJ's *dicta* that a lack of security might imply consent to receive unwanted or malicious traffic is not dissimilar, albeit veiled in terms of consent rather than (contributory) negligence. However, there is no analogous defence of 'failing to install an alarm' which negates liability for burglary, although failure to do so may invalidate an insurance policy.

At the continued hearing at Wimbledon magistrates' court, Lennon entered a plea of guilty and was sentenced to a two-month curfew order (between the hours of 00:30 and 07:30 during the week and 00:30 and 10:30 at weekends) enforced by electronic tagging.

The *actus reus* of the section 3(1) offence is committing any act which causes an addition to the contents of any program or data without consent which in turn causes permanent or temporary impairment of the operation of that computer. The *mens rea* is twofold: the intention of committing the *actus reus* and knowledge that the modification has been undertaken without consent. The Divisional Court focused on the *mens rea*. In particular, their 'guidance' given to the district judge suggested that he consider the answer 'which Mr Lennon would have expected had he asked D&G whether he might start *Avalanche*' suggested that, in their opinion, since Lennon knew that D&G would not consent to him sending five million e-mails then this would render his act non-consensual and thereby satisfy the contentious element of the *actus reus*. In other words, knowledge that D&G would not consent meant that it did not, in fact, consent.

However, the Divisional Court failed to address the point relating to implied consent to the receipt of e-mail. Moreover, there was no consideration as to whether the *actus reus* is taken to be a composite act (launching *Avalanche* as a single action which precipitated the sending of five million e-mails without further intervention) or as a series of individual acts (considering one e-mail at a time). If instructing *Avalanche* to begin bombardment without further intervention satisfies the *actus reus*, then a loophole immediately arises. If Lennon had manually sent the e-mails individually or via a number of discrete *Avalanche* attacks none of which would have in isolation brought down D&G's system, then there could be no impairment of their computer's operation – hence no *actus reus* and no offence, irrespective of actual or implied consent. There is no notion within the 1990 Act of embarking on a course of conduct. In cases where a system does not suffer total breakdown, further difficulties arise in measuring and determining the threshold at which its performance crosses the threshold between 'slow' and criminally 'impaired'.

In *Lennon*, the Divisional Court attempted to find a construction of the 1990 Act which suited the notion of wrongdoing encapsulated in Lennon's actions. It is perhaps unfortunate that his guilty plea denied the opportunity for further legal argument. However, the issues raised by *Lennon* formed much of the discussion surrounding the amendments to the 1990 Act which must now be considered.

Limitations and proposals for reform

The 1990 Act has produced relatively low prosecution rates and some interpretative challenges for the courts. It is particularly interesting to note that it came into being from the pre-existing law's difficulties in being stretched to encompass hitherto unencountered mischief resulting from technological advances and yet, 16 years on, it had begun to suffer itself from similar problems of scope. This situation is perhaps unsurprising. The 1990 Act was drafted without foresight of the immense advances in technology during its lifetime and their potential to cause harm. Moreover, it was based on an amalgam of existing property offences rather than being specific to any particular technological situation.

In the same way that the 1990 Act was brought into existence as a response to the public concern following *Gold and Schifreen*, the new millennium saw increasing pressure to amend the existing legislation in response to public concern around denial-of-service attacks, such as those encountered in *Lennon*,[56] lobbying by the All-Party Internet Group (APIG)[57] and the UK's obligations as a signatory to the Council of Europe Convention on Cybercrime.[58]

In April 2005, Derek Wyatt MP, chair of APIG, introduced the Computer Misuse Act 1990 (Amendment) Bill[59] which sought to enact the amendments proposed by APIG by inserting new sections

---

56 Richards, J., 'Georgia accuses Russia of waging "cyber-war"', *The Times* (11 August 2008).

57 All Party Internet Group, *Revision of the Computer Misuse Act: Report of an Inquiry by the All-Party Internet Group* (June 2004).

58 Council of Europe Convention on Cybercrime (signed 23 November 2001) ETS 185.

59 Computer Misuse Act 1990 Amendment HC Bill (2004–05) [102].

specifically to address denial-of-service attacks and to increase the maximum penalty for the basic section 1 offence to two years' imprisonment. Increasing the penalty to two years would have the joint effect of bringing the domestic legislation in line with Convention requirements and making the offence extraditable. Making it an indictable offence would also allow prosecutions for attempted commission.[60] This was the second attempt to tack a denial-of-service extension onto the 1990 Act. The first was a Private Member's Bill introduced by the Earl of Northesk in 2002. Both these attempts failed for lack of Parliamentary time.

In July 2005, Tom Harris MP introduced another ten-minute rule Bill along similar lines. This prompted swift response from the Home Office who stated the following week that 'changes will be proposed as soon as the parliamentary diary will allow'.[61] The parliamentary diary became free in January 2006, with the introduction of the Police and Justice Bill[62] which received Royal Assent to become the Police and Justice Act 2006 on 8 November 2006.

The Police and Justice Act 2006[63]

The Police and Justice Act 2006 introduced three amendments to the 1990 Act which came into force on 1 October 2008.[64] The section 1 offence relating to the unauthorised access to computer material is broadened and attracts an increased tariff.[65] The section 3 offence covering the unauthorised modification of computer material is replaced by a new provision concerning unauthorised acts with intent to impair the operation of a computer.[66] A new section 3A offence is also introduced which criminalises making, supplying or obtaining articles for use in computer misuse offences.[67] This section will consider the rationale behind the 2006 Act before considering the legislative passage and potential impact of each of the new provisions in turn.

60 Criminal Attempts Act 1981, s. 1(1).

61 Thomas, D., 'Home Office seeks to increase jail terms for hackers' *Computing* (20 July 2005).

62 Police and Justice HC Bill (2005–06) [119].

63 See also Fafinski, S., 'Computer misuse: the implications of the Police and Justice Act 2006' (2008) 72 *Journal of Criminal Law* 53 (reproduced in Appendix B).

64 Police and Justice Act 2006 (Commencement No. 9) Order 2008 SI 2008/2503.

65 Police and Justice Act 2006, s. 35.

66 Police and Justice Act 2006, s. 36.

67 Police and Justice Act 2006, s. 37.

Computer Misuse

The rationale behind the 2006 Act

The 2006 Act is predominantly concerned, as its name suggests, with various policing reforms and, as such, the amendments it proposed to the 1990 Act were largely peripheral to the main debate. Indeed, when the Home Secretary, Charles Clarke MP, introduced the Second Reading of the Police and Justice Bill in the House of Commons, he made no mention of the computer misuse amendments, stressing instead that:

The central objective of the Bill is to help build safer communities ... by taking forward our agenda for delivering real, sustained and lasting reforms to the police service [and] ... by helping to create a modern culture of respect based on the needs, rights and responsibilities of the law-abiding majority.[68]

Clarke eventually gave some insight into the rationale behind the seemingly incongruous inclusion of computer law into an Act predominantly concerning policing reforms by stating that:

We must recognise that in an increasingly interdependent world, work with international partners to tackle terrorism and serious organised crime will be increasingly important. We have therefore included a number of measures to strengthen policing at international level. Computer misuse – the continued threat posed by computer hacking and denial-of-service attacks – is one of the growing new threats that can be tackled only through extensive international co-operation. To that end, the Bill takes up a private Member's Bill tabled by my hon. Friend the Member for Glasgow, South (Mr. Harris) to amend the Computer Misuse Act 1990. I am grateful to my hon. Friend for his initiative.[69]

It is perhaps interesting to note that the 1990 Act was introduced to counter the risks posed by hacking and virus propagation and the amendments to counter the 'continued threat posed by computer hacking and denial-of-service attacks'. This could be taken as tacit government acknowledgement that the 1990 Act had been ineffective at controlling the hacker threat: an acknowledgement that is supported, as shown previously by the low prosecution and conviction statistics for the original section 1 offence.

---

68 Hansard HC vol. 443 col. 608 (6 March 2006).
69 Hansard HC vol. 443 col. 618 (6 March 2006).

In a five-hour debate, the Second Reading offered little further insight into the proposed amendments, other than general support for the hacking initiative. For Lynne Featherstone MP the changes were a necessary counter to the risks associated with the security of the proposed national identity register database:

… we support the Government in their attempt to tackle better the problems caused by computer hacking. Given their penchant for creating surveillance databases, whether on national identity[70] or DNA, the security of those databases is paramount.[71]

A greater perceived risk was introduced by Mark Pritchard MP, parliamentary vice-chairman of the Conservative technology forum, that to the critical national infrastructure:

… al-Qaeda suspects have admitted that cyber crime and cyber terrorism were one of their key objectives. They have admitted trying to infiltrate critical British infrastructures for the intelligence agencies and, allegedly, our nuclear and energy infrastructures.[72]

The Second Reading of the Police and Justice Bill echoed the 1990 debate, with the exception that the original threat posed by hackers was related to the cost to industry (of great public interest in late-Thatcherite Britain), whereas the new threat – from the same conduct – was connected with the post-September 11 concerns of terrorism and national security. However, outside the House, the commercial cost argument still prevailed. At the time that the Bill was introduced, a Home Office spokeswoman said:

The estimated cost to UK business from these sorts of electronic attacks and denial-of-service is estimated to be over £3 billion and they continue to grow in sophistication … The Bill will increase penalties for hacking, viruses and other cybercrimes to reflect their severity … In addition we are looking to amend section 3 of the Computer Misuse Act to clarify that all means of interference to a computer system are criminalised.[73]

70 Identity Cards Act 2006, s. 1(1).
71 Hansard HC vol. 443 col. 631 (6 March 2006).
72 Hansard HC vol. 443 col. 657 (6 March 2006).
73 Thomas, D., 'New bill to beef up e-crime law: Home Office proposes tougher sentences for hackers and virus writers', *Computing* (25 January 2006).

Moreover, as will be seen later in this chapter, technological attacks on critical security systems may already fall within the reach of the Terrorism Act 2000. In general, use of the anti-terrorism legislation should be reserved for that which is properly terrorist.

This examination of the broad rationale behind the amendments within the 2006 Act will now be expanded with a more detailed consideration of the debate surrounding each of the new provisions and their ramifications.

Unauthorised access to computer material

Clause 33 of the Bill[74] proposed an increase in the penalty for the section 1 offence of unauthorised access to computer systems or data (the basic hacking offence). The offence was made indictable and the maximum penalty increased from six months' to twelve months' imprisonment on summary conviction or to two years on conviction on indictment.[75] The clause passed through the Commons without discussion.

During the Committee stage in the Lords, a government amendment proposed further changes to the wording of the section 1 offence such that the basic hacking offence would be complete if a person caused a computer to perform any function with intent to secure *or enable to be secured* knowingly unauthorised access to a program or data on any computer. The broadening of the offence to encompass enabling access to be gained without authority criminalised the act of 'opening the door' to unauthorised access without stepping through it and attracted little further debate of consequence.[76] As such, the clause became section 35 of the 2006 Act.

This provision was subsequently amended by the Serious Crime Act 2007 such that the 'enabling' provisions in section 35(2) of the 2006 Act were omitted. The enabling offences are covered by the new general offence of intentionally encouraging or assisting an offence or believing that such an offence will be committed.[77]

---

74 As introduced into the House of Commons.
75 Note, however, that the proposed increase in the maximum sentencing powers of the magistrates' courts from six to twelve months' imprisonment (Criminal Justice Act 2003, s. 154(1)) is not yet in force. The maximum prison sentence within the magistrates' courts' powers therefore remains six months (Powers of Criminal Courts (Sentencing) Act 2000, s. 78(1)).
76 Hansard HL vol. 684 col. 604 (11 July 2006).
77 Serious Crime Act 2007, ss. 44, 45.

The increase in tariff for the section 1 offence is a clear indication that the law recognises the serious consequences that can result from unauthorised access to systems and has the effect of making the offence extraditable. This is desirable given the cross-border nature of many hacking attacks. The increase in tariff may also have an increased deterrent effect, although whether the potential for a longer jail sentence proves to discourage the committed computer misuser remains to be seen. Its classification as an indictable offence also enables prosecution for attempted commission.[78]

Unauthorised acts with intent to impair operation of computer

Clause 34 of the Bill[79] proposed a replacement for section 3 of the 1990 Act which previously dealt with the unauthorised modification of computer material as follows:

34 Unauthorised acts with intent to impair operation of computer, etc.

For section 3 of the 1990 Act (unauthorised modification of computer material) there is substituted –

'3 Unauthorised acts with intent to impair operation of computer, etc.

(1) A person is guilty of an offence if –
(a) he does any unauthorised act in relation to a computer; and
(b) at the time when he does the act he has the requisite intent and the requisite knowledge.

(2) For the purposes of subsection (1)(b) above the requisite intent is an intent to do the act in question and by so doing –
(a) to impair the operation of any computer,
(b) to prevent or hinder access to any program or data held in any computer, or
(c) to impair the operation of any such program or the reliability of any such data, whether permanently or temporarily.

78 Criminal Attempts Act 1981, s. 1(1).
79 As introduced into the House of Commons.

(3) The intent need not be directed at –
   (a) any particular computer;
   (b) any particular program or data; or
   (c) a program or data of any particular kind.

(4) For the purposes of subsection (1)(b) above the requisite knowledge is knowledge that the act in question is unauthorised.

(5) In this section –
   (a) a reference to doing an act includes a reference to causing an act to be done;
   (b) "act" includes a series of acts ...'

This new clause attempts to ensure that denial-of-service attacks are criminalised by broadening the *actus reus* of the offence from 'any act which causes an unauthorised modification of the contents of any computer' to 'any unauthorised act in relation to a computer'. Moreover, it expressly states that an 'act' includes a 'series of acts'. It also increases the maximum tariff for this offence from five years' to ten years' imprisonment following conviction on indictment.[80] Despite the view of the Home Office and the National Hi-Tech Crime Unit[81] that the pre-existing Act covered the relatively recent phenomenon of denial-of-service attacks this was not a view shared within the industry or indeed by APIG even though it was seemingly approved by the Divisional Court in *Lennon*. The new wording of section 3, being wider in scope, removed the 'modification' requirement and thus seemed to address these shared concerns. Moreover, the amendment satisfies the requirement imposed by the EU Council Framework Decision on attacks against information systems to legislate against illegal system interference by 16 March 2007.[82] This clause also passed through the Commons without discussion to meet amendment in the Lords.

The concept of recklessness was introduced to the offence in a government amendment and was agreed without debate.[83] It

80 Police and Justice HC Bill (2005–06) [119] cl. 34(6).
81 Now part of the Serious Organised Crime Agency (SOCA); Serious Organised Crime and Police Act 2006, s. 1(1).
82 Council Framework Decision (EU) 2005/222/JHA of 24 February 2005 on attacks against information systems [2005] OJ L69/67, art. 3.
83 Hansard HL vol. 684 col. 610 (11 July 2006).

therefore remains to be seen whether the courts will adopt the approach to recklessness from *R v. Cunningham*[84] or from *R v. G*[85] in relation to this clause. *Cunningham* recklessness requires that the defendant had foreseen that the particular kind of harm might be done and yet had gone on to take the risk of it. The test (in relation to criminal damage) from *R v. G* is based upon clause 18(c) of the Draft Criminal Code,[86] providing that the defendant is reckless where he is aware of a risk that a circumstance exists or will exist, or aware of a risk that a result will occur and it is, in the circumstances known to him, unreasonable to take that risk. Although *R v. G* explicitly applies to criminal damage, the Court of Appeal emphasised that it laid down a 'general principle'.[87] Therefore its subsequent application to computer misuse should not be ruled out. Indeed, the objective standard from *Metropolitan Police Commissioner v. Caldwell*[88] has been held to be applicable to data protection law.[89] The introduction of recklessness into the *mens rea* of the offence would have meant that, in *Lennon*, even a realisation that there was a possibility that the unauthorised e-mail bombardment might impair the operation of the target computer would suffice. However, the problems relating to implied consent (and therefore authorisation) to the receipt of e-mail identified in *Lennon* still remain.

The second amendment was moved by Lord Bassam of Brighton such that the requisite intent included that of enabling any of the forms of impairment to be done.[90] This was agreed without further debate.

The final amendment came from the Earl of Northesk who wished to clarify that 'a reference to impairing, preventing or hindering something includes a reference to doing so temporarily'.[91] This was also agreed without debate. Northesk's amendment ensures that transient effects of attacks are sufficient to attract criminal liability without the requirement for erasure or modification of data, thereby acknowledging the real-time nature of modern data processing.

---

84 *R v. Cunningham* [1957] 2 QB 396 (CA).
85 *R v. G* [2003] UKHL 50.
86 Law Commission, *Criminal Code for England and Wales* (Law Com. No. 177, Cm 299, 1989).
87 *Attorney-General's Reference (No. 3 of 2003)* [2004] EWCA Crim 868 [12].
88 *Metropolitan Police Commissioner v. Caldwell* [1982] AC 341 (HL).
89 *Data Protection Registrar v. Amnesty International (British Section)* (unreported) 8 November 1994 (DC).
90 Hansard HL vol. 684 col. 609 (11 July 2006).
91 Hansard HL vol. 684 col. 610 (11 July 2006).

With these amendments, the clause became section 36 of the 2006 Act. As it stands, the section 3 offence now hinges on 'impairment', which is, unfortunately, an entirely undefined concept. To complicate matters further, this impairment need only be temporary. The previous section 3 offence concerned the unauthorised modification of computer material. While modification of data was relatively straightforward to establish, the threshold at which a transient decline in system performance crosses the boundary into 'temporary impairment' is likely to trouble the courts when considering offences under the new section. The *Oxford English Dictionary* definition of 'impairment' is of little assistance:

Rendered worse; injured in amount, quality, or value; deteriorated, weakened, damaged.[92]

Perhaps a meaningful legal definition of impairment in this instance might be 'deterioration in performance that is noticeable to the senses': setting the threshold of the offence sufficiently high such that an impairment measured in microseconds would be unlikely to attract liability, since it would most likely go unnoticed and cause no harm. Once a system is fixed and running normally, it may also be problematic to prove system impairment: the CPS would have to present evidence that demonstrated sufficient temporary impairment at the appropriate time and link it to the unauthorised act. Although processor usage logs might assist, it remains to be seen how the courts will set the threshold. This may prove to be less than straightforward.

This provision was also amended by the Serious Crime Act 2007[93] to remove the 'enabling' provision in section 36(2)(d) of the 2006 Act in favour of the new inchoate offences within the 2007 Act.[94]

Making, supplying or obtaining articles for use in computer misuse offences

Clause 35 of the Bill[95] proposed the insertion of a new section 3A into the 1990 Act. This section introduces an offence of making, supplying or offering to supply articles for use in computer misuse offences, or obtaining such tools with the intention to use them to facilitate the commission of such an offence as follows:

---

92 *Oxford English Dictionary Online* <www.oed.com> accessed 16 August 2007.
93 Serious Crime Act 2007, s. 61(3).
94 Serious Crime Act 2007, ss. 44, 45.
95 As introduced into the House of Commons.

35 Making, supplying or obtaining articles for use in computer misuse offences

After section 3 of the 1990 Act insert –

'3A Making, supplying or obtaining articles for use in offence under section 1 or 3

(1) A person is guilty of an offence if he makes, adapts, supplies or offers to supply any article –
  (a) knowing that it is designed or adapted for use in the course of or in connection with an offence under section 1 or 3; or
  (b) intending it to be used to commit, or to assist in the commission of, an offence under section 1 or 3.

(2) A person is guilty of an offence if he obtains any article with a view to its being supplied for use to commit, or to assist in the commission of, an offence under section 1 or 3.

(3) In this section "article" includes any program or data held in electronic form ...'

This provision makes it quite clear that 'articles' include software.[96] This offence carries a maximum two-year prison sentence following conviction on indictment. The new clause 3A was designed to satisfy the requirement of the Council of Europe Convention on Cybercrime to criminalise 'the production, sale, procurement for use, import, distribution or otherwise making available of ... a computer password, access code, or similar data by which the whole or any part of a computer system is capable of being accessed' when 'committed intentionally and without right'[97] for the purposes of committing illegal access,[98] interception[99] or data[100] or system interference[101] offences – in other words, the ulterior intent to commit a further section 1 or 3 offence.

96 Police and Justice HC Bill (2005–06) [119] cl. 35(3).
97 Council of Europe Convention on Cybercrime (signed 23 November 2001) ETS 185, art. 6.
98 Ibid., art. 2.
99 Ibid., art. 3.
100 Ibid., art. 4.

The new section 3A offence sought to criminalise the creation, supply or application of 'hacker tools' for use in computer misuse offences. However, the clause as originally drafted attracted widespread criticism from within the software industry amid fears that it 'could effectively criminalise IT professionals who use penetration testing – also known as ethical hacking – to identify security weaknesses'.[102] Technician 2 commented that:

That's the end for penetration testing then. Why would I risk ending up in jail for doing my job? It's madness. It takes away the incentive for making systems secure and plays right into the hands of the criminals.

However, Policy-Maker 3 offered a less alarmed, if potentially misguided, view:

I can't imagine that the courts would throw someone into jail for doing the right thing.

The fears of Technician 2 were supported by the fact that the existing Act had been shown in *Lennon* and *Cuthbert* to make no distinction between malicious and benign intentions.

Many of the tools which are used by systems administrators and computer forensics investigators are commercially available products used in the course of load, penetration and network and resilience testing. The distinction between the lawful and unlawful use of such tools is a fine one. For instance, software tools such as *Nmap*[103] can be used to examine the security of computers and to discover services or servers on a computer network as well as to find insecurities to exploit. In the extreme, it has been suggested that even web browsers, such as Internet Explorer, could fall foul of the new offence since they can be used to gain unauthorised access to insecure systems.

Analogies may be drawn between software tools and everyday physical articles. For example, the offence of 'going equipped for stealing, etc.' is committed if a person 'when not at his place of abode … has with him any article for use in the course of or in connection

---

101 Ibid., art. 5.
102 Goodwin, W., 'Computer Misuse Act amendment could criminalise tools used by IT professionals', *Computer Weekly* (21 February 2006).
103 *Nmap* ('Network Mapper') is a free open-source software utility that can be used for network exploration or security auditing.

with any burglary, theft or cheat'.[104] This wording was not able to be immediately transferred verbatim into the new section 3A such that test tools only become hacker tools outside the user's place of abode. With a network connection and suitable hardware and software, all manner of computer misuse can be carried out from home. A parallel may also be drawn with aggravated burglary which covers the situation in which a burglary is committed by a person who has with him, *inter alia*, a 'weapon of offence'.[105] A weapon of offence is any article made or adapted for causing injury or incapacitation or intended for such use.[106] Here, the offence turns on the article itself or the intention behind the use to which it may be put. There are therefore some items which are inherently weapons of offence, but there are other innocuous articles commonly used for legitimate purposes which only become weapons of offence due to the intention of the defendant to use them in a particular unlawful way.

It was suggested by EURIM that a similar technology-appropriate form of words be found in order to 'disrupt the growing "trade" in producing and distributing tools that have limited legitimate use and are more commonly intended to support computer-assisted extortion and fraud'.[107] Interestingly, the analogous provisions in the Council of Europe Convention on Cybercrime draw specific reference to the fact that articles produced for the authorised testing or protection of a computer system are produced for legitimate purposes and that their use is considered to be 'with right'.

The additional difficulty presented by the clause as originally drafted was that of proving the requisite degree of intention. Given the dual-usability of many security software tools, it would always be open to the defendant to claim that the prohibited result was not his aim, purpose or goal, or that he did not know that the result was a virtually certain consequence of his actions. *CBS Songs Ltd v. Amstrad Consumer Electronics plc*[108] concerned a dual-cassette recorder capable of duplicating cassettes. The owners of copyright in the music claimed *inter alia* that the respondents had incited the making of infringing copies of protected works contrary to section 21(3) of the Copyright Act 1956. However, the House of Lords held that although the machines were capable of both lawful and unlawful use, the

104 Theft Act 1968, s. 25(1), as amended by the Fraud Act 2006, sch. 1, para. 8(a).
105 Theft Act 1968, s. 10(1).
106 Theft Act 1968, s. 10(1)(b).
107 EURIM, Newsletter (March 2006). Software tools used to support fraud would now fall within the Fraud Act 2006.
108 *CBS Songs Ltd v. Amstrad Consumer Electronics plc* [1988] AC 1013 (HL).

respondents had no control over the use once the machine had been sold and could not therefore be held liable. Similar reasoning has also been used in the United States.[109]

The clause was first amended during the Commons Committee Stage: Lynne Featherstone MP simply suggested changing the 'or' to 'and', thereby requiring both knowledge that an article was designed or adapted for use in an offence under section 1 or 3 *and* the intention that it be so used; this would ensure

> ... that an offence is committed only when there is possession and intent to use the programs for the purposes of hacking, and so a security consultant using them legitimately to check that a system is secure would not be caught by the drafting.[110]

However, this was rejected on the basis that it set 'too stringent a test'[111] in favour of a late government amendment which removed the 'knowledge' limb of the offence altogether, replacing it with a belief 'that it is likely to be so used'.[112] The offence therefore became:

(1) A person is guilty of an offence if he makes, adapts, supplies or offers to supply any article –
  (a) intending it to be used to commit, or to assist in the commission of, an offence under section 1 or 3; or
  (b) believing that it is likely to be so used.

Therefore the amendment proposed by Featherstone would have set a higher threshold of wrongdoing to attract liability than before; the government's amendment lowered it. The offence is therefore more akin to that of aggravated burglary which requires either possession of an injurious article *or* (rather than *and*) the intention that an article be used to injure or incapacitate. The government amendment was passed in Committee, although concern was expressed regarding the interpretation of 'likely', James Brokenshire MP asking:

What proof would be required to show that somebody thought that the article was likely to be used to commit an offence?

109 *Sony Corporation of America v. Universal City Studios Inc* 464 US 417 (USSC 1984).
110 Hansard HC (Standing Committee D) col. 260 (28 March 2006).
111 Hansard HC (Standing Committee D) col. 266 (28 March 2006).
112 Hansard HC (Standing Committee D) col. 259 (28 March 2006).

What test would the prosecutors adopt? We need clarity on the extent and ambit of the provision to ensure that it catches those people who are reckless with the coding or other tools that they create to facilitate the perpetration of cybercrime ...[113]

The government's response to these questions was vague at best, with the Minister for Policing, Security and Community Safety, Hazel Blears MP, simply stating that '[t]he word "likely" is pretty well known in our legal system ... it is a matter for the courts to decide'.[114] Considering the difficulties that the courts had in discerning a meaning for the everyday words 'intention'[115] and 'recklessness'[116] in the criminal law involving decades of argument, this may have been overly dismissive. As Lord Edmund Davies stated in *Metropolitan Police Commissioner* v. *Caldwell* (dissenting):

The law in action compiles its own dictionary. In time what was originally the common coinage of speech acquires a different value in the pocket of the lawyer than when in the layman's purse.[117]

Moreover, despite the Minister's assertion, 'likely' has a range of definitions in law. For example, it has been held to mean more than a bare possibility but less than probable,[118] more probable than not but with no requirement of foreseeability,[119] more than 51 per cent probable;[120] a 'real prospect',[121] excluding only that which would fairly be described as highly unlikely,[122] or 'probable' or 'more probable

113 Hansard HC (Standing-262 (28 March 2006).
114 Hansard HC (Standing Committee D) col. 267 (28 March 2006).
115 See *Hyam* v. *DPP* [1975] AC 55 (HL); *R* v. *Moloney* [1985] AC 905 (HL); *R* v. *Hancock and Shankland* [1986] AC 455 (HL); *R* v. *Nedrick* [1986] 1 WLR 1025 (CA); *R* v. *Woollin* [1999] 1 AC 82 (HL).
116 See *R* v. *Cunningham* [1957] 2 QB 396 (CA); *Metropolitan Police Commissioner* v. *Caldwell* [1982] AC 341 (HL); *R* v. *G* [2003] UKHL 50.
117 *Metropolitan Police Commissioner* v. *Caldwell* [1982] AC 341 (HL) 357.
118 *Bennington* v. *Peter* [1984] RTR 383 (DC) interpreting the Heavy Goods Vehicle (Drivers' Licences) Regulations 1977 SI 1977/1309, r. 4.
119 *Bailey* v. *Rolls Royce (1971) Ltd* [1984] ICR 688 (CA) interpreting the Factories Act 1961, s. 72(1) 'likely to cause injury'.
120 *Taplin* v. *Shippam* [1978] ICR 1068 (EAT) interpreting the Employment Protection Act 1975, s. 78(5).
121 *Re SCL Building Services* (1989) 5 BCC 746 (DC); *Re Primlaks (UK) Ltd* [1989] BCLC 734 (DC) interpreting the Insolvency Act 1986, s. 8(1)(b).
122 *R* v. *Wills* [1990] Crim LR 714 (CA) interpreting the Children and Young Persons Act 1933, s. 1 'likely to cause ... suffering or injury'.

than not' but could mean an event 'such as might well happen'.[123] The Commons did not further concern itself with the 1990 Act amendments in the Third Reading, other than with a passing reference to the nature of computer hacking as a '21st century crime',[124] the previous thirty years having seemingly gone unnoticed.

The Committee Stage in the House of Lords continued the debate on the wording of the proposed new section 3A. The Earl of Northesk, one of the proponents of an earlier Bill to amend the 1990 Act, moved an amendment to remove paragraph (b) altogether, describing it as 'unnecessarily and dangerously broad'[125] in debate, and having previously referred to it outside the House as 'pure idiocy' and 'absolute madness'.[126] He also shed some light on the Home Office view on the probable judicial interpretation of 'likely' which had previously been raised in the Commons. A Home Office letter stated that it:

... boils down to the court deciding whether it is more likely than not each individual instance of the article will be used to commit an offence, i.e. the offence is only committed if it will be used criminally more than legally.[127]

This resurrected the issue of how a court would measure such 'percentages of usage' which had been first raised by Brokenshire. The Earl of Erroll concurred with Northesk, fearing that the use of 'likely' may lead to 'very clever barristers [using] very clever verbal gymnastics to twist the meaning of the word "likely" to suit their case'.[128] He proposed alternatives such as 'primarily', 'largely intended for' or 'principally'. However, Lord Bassam of Brighton maintained that the government was 'satisfied' that it had 'struck the right balance between protecting those who develop or supply tools for legitimate use and criminalising those who deliberately ... develop or supply them for criminal use'.[129] Here, Bassam drew reference to

---

123 *Smith v. Ainger, The Times* 5 June 1990 (CA).
124 Hansard HC vol. 446 col. 431 (10 May 2006).
125 Hansard HL vol. 684 col. 611 (11 July 2006).
126 Espiner, T., 'Lord vows to fight cybercrime laws' (25 May 2006) <http://news. zdnet.co.uk/security/0,1000000189,39271086,00.htm> accessed 25 September 2008.
127 Hansard HL vol. 684 col. 612 (11 July 2006).
128 Hansard HL vol. 684 col. 613 (11 July 2006).
129 Hansard HL vol. 684 col. 616 (11 July 2006).

'deliberate' development or supply of tools, even though the new provision did not make explicit reference to deliberate activity.

The proposed amendments were withdrawn, despite Northesk stating that:

The Minister has not clarified the issue for me one iota.[130]

At the subsequent report stage, Baroness Anelay of St Johns revisited the point yet again,[131] claiming that the provision would not prove a deterrent to 'script kiddies'[132] or 'code monkeys'[133] (since legal regulation against hacking per se had not deterred the committed hacker) and that alleged offences under the new section 3A could not be adequately investigated or prosecuted successfully in practice.[134] The Earl of Erroll concurred, stating:

Will it work? It will not, I am afraid. It is one of those things that sounds good but will do nothing.[135]

The threshold of 'likelihood' was debated further, with a further alternative wording being proffered in the form of 'more likely than not'.[136] Again, these amendments proved to be unsuccessful and were withdrawn. Lord Bassam of Brighton did, however, provide some further illumination of the meaning of 'likely' when he stated that:

[I]n our view, 'likely' reflects a belief that there is a strong possibility that the articles will be used for Computer Misuse Act offences.[137]

This 'strong possibility' represented a higher threshold than the Home Office view of 'more likely than not' and demonstrated the malleability of the terminology used. Despite the degree of discomfort

---

130 Ibid.
131 On behalf of the Earl of Northesk who was not present.
132 A derogatory term used within the hacker community for inexperienced hackers who use scripts and programs developed by others without knowing what they are or how they work for the purpose of compromising computer accounts and files and for launching attacks on whole computer systems.
133 A derogatory term for an amateur (or low-level professional) software developer.
134 Hansard HL vol. 685 col. 213 (10 October 2006).
135 Hansard HL vol. 685 col. 214 (10 October 2006).
136 Hansard HL vol. 685 col. 215 (10 October 2006).
137 Hansard HL vol. 685 col. 216 (10 October 2006).

felt by many of the Lords that the clause has gone 'much further than this House should be comfortable with'[138] since any piece of security testing software can be used for hacking and thus 'the word "likely" means that everyone is prosecutable by the courts',[139] the likelihood test remained in the final wording of the clause, which became section 37 of the 2006 Act as follows:

37 Making, supplying or obtaining articles for use in computer misuse offences

After section 3 of the 1990 Act there is inserted –

'3A Making, supplying or obtaining articles for use in offence under section 1 or 3

(1) A person is guilty of an offence if he makes, adapts, supplies or offers to supply any article intending it to be used to commit, or to assist in the commission of, an offence under section 1 or 3.

(2) A person is guilty of an offence if he supplies or offers to supply any article believing that it is likely to be used to commit, or to assist in the commission of, an offence under section 1 or 3.

(3) A person is guilty of an offence if he obtains any article with a view to its being supplied for use to commit, or to assist in the commission of, an offence under section 1 or 3.

(4) In this section "article" includes any program or data held in electronic form …

The broad term 'any article' could also potentially include information alerting users to known security vulnerabilities in pieces of software. The threshold of belief that an article is likely to be used to commit an offence is also unclear and untested; however, the section does appear to put the onus on manufacturers and distributors to decide whether they are supplying to legitimate users or likely criminals. Publicly-available security alerts may need to be carefully

138 Hansard HL vol. 685 col. 218 (10 October 2006) (Lord Lawson of Blaby).
139 Hansard HL vol. 685 col. 219 (10 October 2006) (Earl of Erroll).

drafted so as not to give away too much information, so that vendors may claim that they did not believe that they were likely to be used to commit an offence. Equally, posting password details to a security bulletin board such as *Bugtraq*,[140] believing that those details likely to be used to commit a computer misuse offence, could also fall within the section 3A offence. Moreover, it is unclear where liability will lie in the supply chain. Since supplying a tool with belief that it is likely be used in the commission of a Computer Misuse Act offence would itself become an offence, then liability could attach to manufacturer, wholesaler and retailer. It could be problematic for a supplier to establish that it was confident in its belief that the purchaser's intentions were honourable. So-called spyware could also be rendered illegal.[141] Since spyware can be used to track activity on a computer system (ostensibly for advertising or marketing purposes), then if it is supplied in the belief that it is likely to harvest information that could be used to hack into or impair the performance of a system then this could be sufficient to make out a section 3A offence.

The Crown Prosecution Service subsequently issued guidance on the new provisions within the 1990 Act.[142] This advises prosecutors to consider the functionality of the article and what thought the suspect gave to who would use it. It also gives a list of factors which a prosecutor should consider in determining the likelihood of an article being misused to commit a criminal offence:

- Has the article been developed primarily, deliberately and for the sole purpose of committing a CMA offence (i.e. unauthorised access to computer material)?
- Is the article available on a widescale commercial basis and sold through legitimate channels?
- Is the article widely used for legitimate purposes?
- Does it have a substantial installation base?
- What was the context in which the article was used to commit the offence compared with its original indented purpose?[143]

The guidance also points out that if the article was supplied in connection with fraud, then there may also be liability under sections

140 Available at <http://www.securityfocus.com> accessed 25 September 2008.
141 Computer software that collects personal information about users without their informed consent.
142 Crown Prosecution Service, *Computer Misuse Act 1990* <http://www.cps.gov.uk/legal/section12/chapter_s.shtml> accessed 25 September 2008.
143 Ibid, 6.

6 or 7 of the Fraud Act 2006 which criminalise the possession, making and supply of articles for use in frauds.

It is clear, then, that despite the amendments made during its legislative passage, the new section 3A remains beset with problematic drafting. Despite these potential flaws, the Bill, as introduced, was 'welcomed by businesses and politicians'[144] as a means of reducing the impact on UK businesses resulting from computer misuse. Policy-Maker 1 commented that:

It seems like a sensible way of bringing the [1990] Act up to date at last. It should certainly catch denial-of-service attacks. We need to do all we can to protect our businesses and this law couldn't have come quickly enough.

This justification harked back to the economic risks put forward as a justification for the original 1990 Act rather than the contemporary concerns of national security and terrorist threat.

Alternative domestic criminal legislation

This chapter has shown that the 1990 Act has not been used in large numbers of prosecutions and has suffered from some potential defects of drafting and judicial interpretation. Although the numbers of prosecutions and the instances of problematic interpretation are potentially disappointing, it does not necessarily follow that the 1990 Act itself is without merit. It may, for instance, have had a deterrent effect. This notion will be returned to in Chapter 4. However, it does suggest that there may be more important, or at least more *familiar*, avenues within the law that are more frequently exercised in situations where the 1990 Act might be applied. The use of the common law offence of misconduct in a public office has already been discussed. This section will explore other potential sources of domestic legislation that might potentially be relevant to the problems posed by computer misuse.

Theft Act 1968

'Ransomware' is a form of malicious code which encrypts or threatens

144 Thomas, D., 'Clamping down on the cyber criminals', *Computing* (2 February 2006).

to delete a number of files on the victim's computer.[145] It leaves behind a ransom note for the victim, demanding payment of a sum in return for the decryption key with which the affected 'kidnapped' files may be recovered. While this will naturally fall within section 3(1) of the 1990 Act[146] it may also amount to blackmail for the purposes of section 21 of the Theft Act 1968 which provides that:

(1) A person is guilty of blackmail if, with a view to gain ... or with intent to cause loss ..., he makes any unwarranted demand with menaces ...

Menaces need not be physical: 'any action detrimental to or unpleasant to the person addressed' will suffice.[147] Therefore, given the likely detriment of data loss or the unpleasant inconvenience of data encryption, it is possible that ransomware may adequately be dealt with by the existing blackmail legislation, although this point remains untested by the courts.

Data Protection Act 1998

The Data Protection Act 1998 repealed the earlier Data Protection Act 1984.[148] The 1984 Act implemented the Council of Europe's Convention for the Protection of Individuals with Regard to Automatic Processing of Personal Data[149] which was signed by the UK in 1981 and ratified in 1987. This established the Data Protection Registrar and the Data Protection Tribunal to 'represent the interests' of data users and of data subjects.[150] The 1998 Act implements Council Directive 95/46/EC on the protection of individuals with regard to the processing of personal data and of the free movement of such data.[151] It also expanded the remit of the enforcement agency and renamed the Data

145 In March 2006, the Zippo Trojan horse demanded US$300 from victims for the safe return of their encrypted data. The Ransom-A Trojan horse threatened to delete compromised files one-by-one until extortion demands were met.
146 Also possibly within s. 1, depending on how the ransomware was introduced to the computer.
147 *Thorne v. Motor Trade Association* [1937] AC 797 (HL) 817 (Lord Wright).
148 Data Protection Act 1998, sch. 16(l) para. 1.
149 Council of Europe Convention for the Protection of Individuals with Regard to Automatic Processing of Personal Data (signed 28 January 1981) ETS 108.
150 Data Protection Act 1984, s. 3.
151 Council Directive (EC) 2000/31 of 23 November 1995 on the protection of individuals with regard to the processing of personal data and of the free movement of such data [1995] OJ L281/31.

Protection Registrar and Tribunal as the Information Commissioner and Information Tribunal respectively.[152] The Act itself does not make extensive use of the criminal law, although it does create a number of criminal offences. The Act contains offences concerning enforced subject access notification,[153] information and enforcement notices[154] and obstructing certain lawful inspections[155] but these deal with transgressions of a more administrative nature. Those relating to obtaining, disclosing and procuring personal data have the greatest degree of potential overlap with the 1990 Act.[156]

The Data Protection Act 1984 was amended by the Criminal Justice and Public Order Act 1994.[157] This inserted provisions relating to procuring the disclosure and selling (or offering to sell) computer-held personal information. This is now dealt with by section 55 of the 1998 Act. This provides that:

(1) A person must not knowingly or recklessly, without the consent of the data controller –
  (a) obtain or disclose personal data or the information contained in personal data; or
  (b) procure the disclosure to another person of the information contained in personal data.

...

(3) A person who contravenes subsection (1) is guilty of an offence.

Selling[158] or offering to sell[159] personal data obtained in contravention of section 55(1) are also offences.

---

152 Data Protection Act 1998, s. 6.
153 Data Protection Act 1998, s. 56(5). This is partly in force from 7 July 2008 under limited circumstances relating only to 'vulnerable groups'; Data Protection Act 1998 (Commencement No. 2) Order 2008 SI 2008/1592, art. 2.
154 Data Protection Act 1998, ss. 21, 22, 24, 47.
155 Data Protection Act 1998, s. 54A (inserted by the Crime (International Cooperation) Act 2003, s. 81).
156 Wasik, M., 'Dealing in the information market: procuring, selling and offering to sell personal data' (1995) 9 International Yearbook of Law, Computers and Technology 193.
157 Criminal Justice and Public Order Act 1994, s. 161
158 Data Protection Act 1998, s. 55(4).
159 Data Protection Act 1998, s. 55(5); including via advertisement, s. 55(6).

There are exceptions relating to prevention and detection of crime,[160] where disclosure is authorised by law,[161] where disclosure is in the public interest,[162] and where there was reasonable belief that the data was being obtained, disclosed, disclosed or procured lawfully,[163] or that the data controller would have consented if he had known of the circumstances of the disclosure.[164]

This offence historically carried a maximum penalty of a fine of up to £5,000 in the magistrates' court and an unlimited fine in the Crown Court. This maximum penalty may be increased by order of the Secretary of State (following proposals from the Information Commissioner[165] and subsequent public consultation)[166] to six months' imprisonment in the magistrates' courts and two years' imprisonment in the Crown Court.[167] The Information Commissioner commented that this increase was to discourage the 'unlawful trade' in personal information:

This can be achieved only by increasing the penalty in a way that underlines the seriousness of the offence and makes reputable businesses and individuals reflect on the possible consequences of their actions: by introducing the possibility of a custodial sentence for convictions obtained in the Crown Court and the Magistrates' Courts.[168]

As well as unlawful trade, the section 55 offences could potentially cover the situation where official information is misused (particularly by police officers) for private purposes. This would amount to the obtaining or disclosure of personal information without the consent of the data controller, since it is presumed that the data controller would not consent to disclosure of personal data for an unauthorised purpose. Walden comments that the criminal provisions focus more

---

160   Data Protection Act 1998, s. 55(2)(a)(i).
161   Data Protection Act 1998, s. 55(2)(a)(ii).
162   Data Protection Act 1998, s. 55(2)(d).
163   Data Protection Act 1998, s. 55(2)(b).
164   Data Protection Act 1998, s. 55(2)(c).
165   Information Commissioner, *What Price Privacy? The Unlawful Trade in Confidential Personal Information* (The Stationery Office, London, 10 May 2006) [7.8].
166   Department for Constitutional Affairs, *Increasing Penalties for Deliberate and Wilful Misuse of Personal Data*, Consultation Paper CP 9/06 (24 July 2006).
167   Criminal Justice and Immigration Act 2008, s. 77.
168   Information Commissioner, *What Price Privacy? The Unlawful Trade in Confidential Personal Information* (The Stationery Office, London, 10 May 2006) [7.6].

on the commercial value of data as an information asset rather than as an element of the data subject's private life.[169]

There are, however, limitations to the usefulness of the use of section 55 to such circumstances. As Wasik comments, the 'relatively low' penalties before the increase in tariff may make the 1998 Act offences less useful to a prosecutor.[170] The Information Commissioner reported that:

Prosecutions brought under the Act have generally resulted in low penalties: either minimal fines or conditional discharges. Between November 2002 and January 2006, only two out of 22 cases produced total fines amounting to more than £5,000. Other investigations led to frustrating outcomes, despite the detriment caused to individuals and to public confidence generally.[171]

Moreover, in *R v. Brown*,[172] the House of Lords held that mere browsing of data did not constitute its use. However, such browsing could fall within section 1 of the 1990 Act provided that the access was knowingly unauthorised. In this instance though, the facts of *Brown* took place before the 1990 Act was in force. A prosecution (on three counts from eleven of the section 55(1) offence) was successful in *R v. Rooney*.[173] Here, a personnel administrator accessed personal information held on a database of employees relating to the address of her sister's ex-fiancé. Her sister then sent unwanted mail to the new partner of her ex-fiancé. However, following *Allison* this could potentially have fallen within section 1 of the 1990 Act, or conceivably section 2 if the persistent sending of unwanted mail constituted a further offence.[174]

The common law offence of misconduct in public office may therefore have provided a more satisfactory alternative to prosecuting

---

169 Walden, I., *Computer Crimes and Digital Investigations* (Oxford University Press, Oxford, 2007) 104.

170 Wasik, M., 'Computer misuse and misconduct in public office' (2008) 22 *International Review of Law, Computers and Technology* 135, 137.

171 Information Commissioner, *What Price Privacy? The Unlawful Trade in Confidential Personal Information* (The Stationery Office, London, 10 May 2006) [1.12].

172 *R v. Brown* [1996] 2 Cr App R 72 (HL).

173 *R v. Rooney* [2006] EWCA Crim 1841.

174 For example, the Malicious Communications Act 1988, s. 1(1) establishes the offence of sending letters with intent to cause distress or anxiety. Liability could also potentially arise under the Protection from Harassment Act 1997, s. 2.

certain cases rather that the 1990 Act or the 1998 Act. However, as Wasik concludes,[175] now that the maximum penalties have been increased, the CPS will have to reconsider its guidance in respect of the use of misconduct in public office as a basis for prosecution.

Regulation of Investigatory Powers Act 2000

In R v. Stanford,[176] the defendant was charged, inter alia, with the unlawful and unauthorised interception of electronic mail communications to a public company, contrary to section 1(2) of the Regulation of Investigatory Powers Act 2000:

(2) It shall be an offence for a person –
    (a) intentionally and without lawful authority ...
    to intercept, at any place in the United Kingdom, any communication in the course of its transmission by means of a private telecommunication system.

The defendant had been deputy chairman of the company. After his resignation, he authorised an employee with an administrator username and password to set up an e-mail rule to mirror e-mail messages sent to a former colleague to another account which he then accessed. He wanted to use the material to oust the chairman of the company and take control of it for himself. Following the judge's ruling that the defendant had no defence in law, the defendant pleaded guilty. There is therefore potential overlap with the concept of using authorised access for an unauthorised purpose within section 1 of the 1990 Act as previously discussed in relation to Allison.

Malicious Communications Act 1988 (as amended)

Section 1 of the Malicious Communications Act 1988 introduced an offence of sending letters with intent to cause distress or anxiety. It was amended by the Criminal Justice and Police Act 2001[177] to include electronic communications:

---

175 Wasik, M., 'Computer misuse and misconduct in public office' (2008) 22 International Review of Law, Computers and Technology 135, 141.
176 R v. Stanford [2006] EWCA Crim 258.
177 Criminal Justice and Police Act 2001, s. 43(1)(a).

(1) Any person who sends to another person –

  (a) a [letter, electronic communication or article of any description] which conveys –

    (i)   a message which is indecent or grossly offensive;

    (ii) a threat; or

    (iii) information which is false and known or believed to be false by the sender; or

  (b) any [article or electronic communication] which is, in whole or part, of an indecent or grossly offensive nature,

is guilty of an offence if his purpose, or one of his purposes, in sending it is that it should, so far as falling within paragraph (a) or (b) above, cause distress or anxiety to the recipient or to any other person to whom he intends that it or its contents or nature should be communicated.

Therefore indecent, grossly offensive, threatening or false e-mail messages sent knowingly and with intent to cause distress or anxiety could fall within section 1. There are currently no reported cases on this point. However, it is conceivable that this could have been stretched in an attempt to encapsulate the wrongdoing in *Lennon*. The e-mails sent contained knowingly false information in that they purported to come from a person other than their actual sender and Lennon knew this to be the case, having set up *Avalanche* accordingly. Lennon's purpose could also have been argued to have caused anxiety to Ms Rhodes since, to the casual observer, it would appear that it was her actions that had caused D&G's loss, not those of Lennon. Perhaps the addition of 'loss' to 'distress and anxiety' would remove the necessity for any strained construction.

Communications Act 2003

The Communications Act 2003 may also have provided an alternative means of prosecuting denial-of-service attacks which took place over the public network. Section 127(2)(c) of the Communications Act 2003 provides that:

A person is guilty of an offence if, for the purpose of causing annoyance, inconvenience or needless anxiety to another, he ... persistently makes use of a public electronic communications network.

This could be construed as encompassing the mass sending of e-mail, although interpretation may turn on the meaning of 'persistently' and whether one action in causing a mail-bombing program to run would be a persistent use or a single usage of the network. There are currently no reported cases on this point. Section 127 has been judicially considered in the context of nuisance[178] or grossly offensive material,[179] but not persistent misuse or data bombardment. However, this is a summary offence which carries a maximum penalty of six months' imprisonment. This is considerably less than the five-year (ten-year following amendment) tariff associated with section 3 of the 1990 Act.

Terrorism Act 2000 (as amended in 2006)

Some manifestations of computer misuse may also fall within the Terrorism Act 2000. Section 1(1) of the Act (as amended by the Terrorism Act 2006)[180] defines 'terrorism' as:

[T]he use or threat of action where –
(a) the action falls within subsection (2);
(b) the use or threat is designed to influence the government or an international governmental organisation or to intimidate the public or a section of the public, and;
(c) the use or threat is made for the purpose of advancing a political, religious or ideological cause.

The list of proscribed actions is provided by section 1(2) which includes, under section 1(2)(e), those 'designed seriously to interfere with or seriously to disrupt an electronic system'. The accompanying Explanatory Notes[181] make it clear that the Act is designed to cover

… actions which might not be violent in themselves but which can, in a modern society, have a devastating impact. These could include interfering with the supply of water or power where life, health or safety may be put at risk. *Subsection (2)(e)* covers the disrupting of key computer systems.[182]

---

178 *R v. Rimmington* [2005] UKHL 63.
179 *DPP v. Collins* [2006] UKHL 40.
180 The Terrorism Act 2006, s. 34 inserted 'or an international governmental organisation' into s. 1(1) of the Terrorism Act 2000.
181 Terrorism Act 2000, Explanatory Note.
182 Ibid. [10].

Therefore it is clear that a cyber attack on a key system within the critical national infrastructure[183] may well fall within the Terrorism Act 2000 if used – or threatened to be used – in the furtherance of a political, religious or ideological cause. Such attacks would also give rise to a corresponding increase in police powers to investigate.[184]

Attacking such systems could therefore give rise to highly serious offences under the Terrorism Act 2000 even though they may not fall within the 1990 Act. However, even where the two pieces of legislation overlap it is, as Walker suggests, only the 'truly terrorising' that should require a special legal response'[185] and that only threats to the well-being of an individual, rather than a machine, should fall within the Terrorism Act 2000:

… activities such as defacing, corrupting or denying are unlikely to have the same impact on the lives of individuals, even if the potential disruption to the capacities of state agencies remains large and of increasing significance … We should hesitate to demonise [such activities] with the title 'terrorism' even if they infringe such elements of the criminal law as the Computer Misuse Act 1990 or the Criminal Damage Act 1971.[186]

Legal technicalities aside, the Terrorism Act 2000 should therefore be reserved for that which is 'properly' terrorist. This leaves the rest of the law to deal with the more mundane instances of computer misuse, many of which in this context are better labelled as political activism rather than terrorism.

Fraud Act 2006

The application of the deception offences within the Theft Act 1968 to situations involving the use of computers often proved to be problematic since case law suggested that it was not possible to deceive a machine:

---

183 Those assets, services and systems that support the economic, political and social life of the UK whose importance is such that any entire or partial loss or compromise could cause large-scale loss of life, have a serious impact on the national economy, have other grave social consequences for the community, or be of immediate concern to the national government.

184 Terrorism Act 2000, ss. 114–16.

185 Walker, C., 'Cyber-terrorism: legal principle and law in the United Kingdom' (2006) 110 *Penn State Law Review* 625, 642.

186 Ibid, 643.

For a deception to take place there must be some person or persons who will have been deceived.[187]

Similarly, the offence of obtaining services by deception in section 1 of the Theft Act 1978 provides that:

[a] person who by any deception obtains services *from another* shall be guilty of an offence. (emphasis added.)

In *Re Holmes* the court also stated that:

We ... accept that 'The prevailing opinion is that it is not possible in law to deceive a machine'.[188]

However, the Fraud Act 2006 repealed all the deception offences in the Theft Acts 1968 and 1978 and replaced them with a single offence of fraud (section 1) which can be committed by false representation (section 2), failure to disclose information when there is a legal duty to do so (section 3) and abuse of position (section 4). Of these, the offence of fraud by false representation is the most interesting in relation to computer misuse. The *actus reus* is making a false representation. The *mens rea* requires dishonesty, knowledge that the representation is false and intention to make a gain or cause a loss. The intention may be expressed or implied.[189] Most importantly, section 2(5) provides that:

a representation may be regarded as made if it (or anything implying it) is submitted in any form to any system or device designed to receive, convey or respond to communications (with or without human intervention).[190]

Therefore, fraud can be committed by a false electronic representation. Moreover, sections 6 and 7 criminalise the possession, making or supply of articles for use in frauds, including 'any program or data held in electronic form.'[191] There is a degree of overlap here with possessing, making or supplying articles for use in computer misuse offences.

187 *DPP v. Ray* [1974] AC 370 (HL) 384.
188 *Re Holmes* [2004] EWHC 2020 (Admin); [2005] 1 WLR 1857, 1863.
189 Fraud Act 2006, s. 2(4).
190 Fraud Act 2006, s. 2(5).
191 Fraud Act 2006, s. 8(1).

Conclusion

While the availability of networked technology and instances of computer misuse have increased greatly since 1990, the Computer Misuse Act 1990 has produced relatively low prosecution rates. It has also given rise to some interpretative difficulties, particularly in relation to new manifestations of computer misuse. As Holder comments, specific legislation will only provide protection to those situations envisaged at the time,[192] yet the nature of technological advance is such that its use (or misuse) may give rise to unenvisaged situations. This concept will be returned to in the discussion of manufactured uncertainty in the risk society in Chapter 5.

The Police and Justice Act 2006 has introduced some amendments to the 1990 Act in a bid to remedy some of the interpretational difficulties and to facilitate the application of the Act to more recent forms of computer misuse, particularly denial-of-service attacks. However, it has been seen that even the recent provisions may give rise to interpretational challenges for the courts. As the Earl of Northesk commented during the debate on the 2006 Act:

I am unconvinced that the insertion of these few odd confused clauses at the tail end of a portmanteau Bill demonstrates either adequate understanding of the complexities of the issues or firm resolve to attend to the whole corpus of internet crime … To be blunt, I fear that ultimately these clauses will create more problems than they solve.[193]

It has also been seen that 'old' legal principles and criminal offences remain relevant in the new technological age. The common law offence of misconduct in public office has been used in preference to the 1990 Act and there are a range of possible statutory alternatives which might be employed in circumstances where computer technology has been misused in some way. As Wasik comments:

Despite the existence of the more specialist [computer misuse] offences … it has always been clear that the majority of cases

---

192 Holder, C., 'Staying one step ahead of the criminals' (2002) 10(3) *IT Law Today* 17.

193 Hansard HL vol. 684 col. 607 (11 July 2006).

involving misuse of information technology will continue to be prosecuted under more traditional ... offences.[194]

Computer misuse remains a current issue. This is not to say that the domestic criminal law has no part to play in its control or that it has been ineffective to date. Indeed, the 1990 Act has stood the test of time reasonably well, only requiring statutory amendment after 16 years. However, the majority of instances of computer misuse are not reported which gives the law no opportunity to prove its worth. It is therefore necessary to explore the extent to which computer misuse is amenable to governance by the domestic criminal law alone or whether alternative or additional modes of regulation might also form an appropriate response.

---

194 Wasik, M., 'Hacking, viruses and fraud', in Akdeniz, Y., Walker, C. and Wall, D.S. (eds) *The Internet, Law and Society* (Pearson Education, Harlow, 2000).

Chapter 4

Computer misuse and the criminal law

Technology ... is a queer thing. It brings you great gifts with one hand, and it stabs you in the back with the other.
C.P. Snow, scientist and novelist, *New York Times*
(15 March 1971)

The previous two chapters have considered the parallel evolutionary strands of computer technology and computer misuse together with the attempts of the domestic criminal law to regulate that misuse. Chapter 2 considered the emergence of the problem of computer misuse, the challenges which it presented for the domestic criminal law and the genesis of the Computer Misuse Act 1990 which introduced three new specific offences aimed at computer misuse. The efficacy of the 1990 Act was considered in Chapter 3. This showed that the 1990 Act produced a relatively low number of prosecutions. Moreover, the application of the 1990 Act seemed to be inconsistent, with the courts struggling at times to interpret the Act in a way which furthered its general purpose to prevent computer misuse. Some of these difficulties arose as a result of technological advances. Just as the pre-existing criminal law had been stretched in an attempt to accommodate unforeseen mischief resulting from technologies emerging in the 1980s, so the 1990 Act began itself to suffer during its first 16 years. The Police and Justice Act 2006 introduced some amendments to the 1990 Act in an attempt to bring the legislation in line with technological capability. While the effect of these amendments remains to be seen, it is undoubtedly clear that the domestic criminal law is still seen to have a role to play in the regulation of computer misuse.

It is, however, necessary to consider whether the regulation of computer misuse requires *more* than just the domestic criminal law. Therefore, this chapter will explore the nature and purpose of the criminal law both in the abstract and in the context of the problems arising from computer misuse established in Chapters 2 and 3, thereby facilitating a discussion of the interplay between computer misuse and the domestic criminal law.

Theories of criminal law

The two main approaches which may be taken to provide a philosophical theory of the criminal law are analytical and normative.[1] Analytical theorists attempt to provide an account of what the criminal law 'is'[2] along with explanations of closely-related concepts such as crime itself. By comparison, normative theorists go beyond seeking what the criminal law is to consider both what it 'ought' to be and, indeed, whether the criminal law ought to exist only as a last resort[3] or, indeed, *at all*. The distinction between descriptive ('is') and prescriptive ('ought') statements was considered by Hume, who proposed that norms cannot be properly inferred from facts and, as such, normative theories are distinct from analytical theories.[4] Hume's proposition was made in the context of a major philosophical debate surrounding the fundamental notions of natural law and natural justice and, as such, served much wider purposes than that of the philosophical basis of the criminal law alone. The deduction of an 'ought' from an 'is' (in other words, the attempted definition of a moral norm in terms of a fact) were condemned by Moore as the 'naturalistic fallacy'.[5] This is/ought dichotomy was also considered by Kant:

For whereas, so far as nature is concerned, experience supplies the rules and is the source of truth, in respect of the moral laws

1 Husak, D.N., *Philosophy of Criminal Law* (Rowman & Littlefield, Totowa, NJ, 1987) 20–6.
2 Duff, R.A., 'Theorizing criminal law: a 25th anniversary essay' (2005) 25 *Oxford Journal of Legal Studies* 353, 354.
3 Husak, D.N., 'The criminal law as last resort' (2004) 24 *Oxford Journal of Legal Studies* 207.
4 Hume, D. (1777) *A Treatise of Human Nature*, in Freeman, M.D.A., *Lloyd's Introduction to Jurisprudence* (6th edn, Sweet & Maxwell, London, 1994) 34.
5 Moore, G.E., *Principia Ethica* (Cambridge University Press, Cambridge, 1903).

it is, alas, the mother of illusion! Nothing is more reprehensible than to derive the laws prescribing what ought to be done from what is done ... [6]

As Milton comments: 'For Kant the distinction between *is* and *ought* was not something reluctantly conceded; it was indispensible'.[7]

The predominant analytical theory building upon this position is that of legal positivism. Within positivist theory, the law is separate from morality, even though that law may well correspond to contemporary moral standards and be influenced by moral considerations. By contrast, normative theories consider the moral character of law: a system of morality being the body of requirements to which an action must conform in order to be right or virtuous. This is in contrast with positive laws, the obligation of which depends solely on the fact that they have been imposed by a rightful authority.

Fuller contends that the purpose of law is to 'subject human conduct to the governance of rules'[8] and that a system of governance must necessarily contain certain desirable attributes, such as clarity, consistency and stability, in order to have legitimacy. These principles reflect the internal morality of law. Therefore, although in reality all systems of law must make compromises, the more closely a system is able to adhere to Fuller's key procedural principles, the more likely that substantively just laws will result. This procedural naturalism was criticised by Hart.[9] Not only did Hart consider Fuller's principles merely to be ones of efficacy rather than morality but he also viewed Fuller's philosophy as confusing purposive activity and morality. For Hart, *all* actions, virtuous or otherwise, have their own internal standards of efficacy which are distinct from moral standards, thus concluding that, although Fuller's principles are existence conditions for a legal system, they do not conceptually connect law with morality.[10] However, Hart's analysis overlooks the fact that most of Fuller's principles represent moral ideals of fairness. For Fuller, the

---

6 Kant, I., *Critique of Pure Reason* (1781) trans. Kemp Smith, N. <http://www.hkbu. edu.hk/~ppp/cpr/toc.html> accessed 25 September 2008.

7 Milton, P., 'David Hume and the eighteenth-century conception of natural law' [1982] *Legal Studies* 14, 32.

8 Fuller, L.L., *The Morality of Law* (Yale University Press, New Haven, CT, 1964) 106.

9 Hart, H.L.A., 'Book review of *The Morality of Law*' (1965) 78 *Harvard Law Review* 1281.

10 Ibid., 1285–6.

purpose and nature of law is mixed: some 'legal' purposes do not necessarily comply with an inner morality. Divergences from Fuller's internal morality or Hart's principles of efficacy, such as divergences from certainty, only become inconsistent with a system of governance when they are so great that they render the system incapable of guiding behaviour. Fuller's position is vindicated by article 6 of the European Convention on Human Rights[11] which requires due process in determining civil rights and obligations and criminal charges. The way in which the law operates requires a moral foundation as well as efficacy.

Whether analytical or normative, Duff suggests that philosophical theories of criminal law cannot subsist in isolation but must have some regard to the empirical actualities of that which they theorise.[12] Therefore the theories which follow will be discussed in the context of computer misuse relating to emerging technologies within a global networked society. Within this context, the criminal law may be conceptualised as an instrumentalist or moralistic construct. Here the instrumentalist view represents the 'is' being influenced by the 'ought' whereas the moralistic construct focuses predominantly on the 'ought'.

The instrumentalist construction of the criminal law

The instrumentalist construction views the criminal law as an instrument or a technique which may serve several ends. It cannot, however, be said that the purpose of the criminal law is simply that of an instrument of crime prevention or deterrence. Adopting a strictly legalistic definition that a crime is 'an intentional act in violation of the criminal law',[13] then without the criminal law there would be no crime since no conduct would be criminal. This is a circular argument. Indeed, as Michael and Adler contend:

---

11 Council of Europe Convention for the Protection of Human Rights and Fundamental Freedoms (signed 4 November 1950) ETS 005.

12 Duff, R.A., 'Theories of criminal law' *Stanford Encyclopedia of Philosophy* <http://plato.stanford.edu/entries/criminal-law/> accessed 25 September 2008.

13 Tappan, P.W., 'Who is the criminal?' (1947) 12 *American Sociological Review* 96, 100.

If crime is merely an instance of conduct that is proscribed by the criminal code, it follows that the criminal law is the cause of crime.[14]

Therefore, in this sense, the traditional perception of criminal law as establishing prohibitive norms that proscribe certain conduct[15] or creating disciplinary norms that bound acceptable behaviour[16] is unhelpful. In order to achieve a clear understanding of the nature of crime and reasons for criminalisation, the social setting in which the conduct occurs should be considered. As Packer states:

Crime is a socio-political artefact, not a natural phenomenon. We can have as much or as little crime as we please, depending on what we choose to count as criminal.[17]

The instrumentalist purpose of the criminal law can therefore be considered to be the protection of a particular set of public or private interests. For example, the American Model Penal Code[18] provides that:

The general purposes of the provisions governing the definition of offenses are:
(a) to forbid and prevent conduct that unjustifiably and inexcusably inflicts or threatens substantial harm to individual or public interests ...[19]

Therefore, given a set of interests warranting protection from substantial harm, instrumentalists such as Devlin take the pragmatic view that the criminal law should uphold the 'smooth functioning of society and the preservation of order'.[20] However, it is worth noting the instrumentalist view typically limits the ambit of the criminal law

---

14 Michael, J. and Adler, M., *Crime, Law and Social Science* (Harcourt Brace Jovanovich, New York, 1933) 5.
15 Quinney, R., *The Social Reality of Crime* (Little, Brown, Boston, MA, 1970).
16 Foucault, M., *Discipline and Punish: the Birth of the Prison* (Allen Lane, London, 1977).
17 Packer, H.L., *The Limits of the Criminal Sanction* (Stanford University Press, Stanford, CA, 1968) 364.
18 As adopted at the 1962 Annual Meeting of the American Law Institute.
19 Model Penal Code and Commentaries (Official Draft and Revised Comments) (1985), §1.01(1).
20 Devlin, P., *The Enforcement of Morals* (Oxford University Press, Oxford, 1965) 5.

to substantial harms. It is questionable whether the harm resulting from computer misuse is as substantial as those harms that have traditionally fallen within the instrumentalist view: for instance, non-consensual harm to others resulting from the acts of rape, criminal damage or burglary. These acts are historically linked in the social conscience as harmful since they result in violation of personal interests widely recognised as legitimate and demanding respect from other individuals and from the state. Whether the state labels these interests as rights is a separate issue. It is possible to conceive of harms of a similar nature being the product of computer misuse, albeit with less immediate physicality. Unauthorised access to a computer system or data represents a violation of the boundary of that system. Unauthorised access with intent to commit or facilitate the commission of a further offence is akin to the harmful trespass in burglary. Impairing the performance, operation or reliability of a system is damaging to that system as a whole. Therefore it is possible that the instrumentalist view of substantial harm could be applied to computer misuse by analogy. However, the consequences of misuse tend to be viewed as less substantial than the more tangible and familiar results typically constructed as harm.

This is similar to the position regarding the infringement of copyright, which is widespread, especially among younger Internet users who do not consider downloading copyright material to be illegal. Twenty-six per cent of all 10- to 25-year-old Internet users reported that they had illegally downloaded software, music or films in 2004.[21] Although the Copyright, Designs and Patents Act 1988[22] provides a number of criminal offences in relation to making or dealing with articles that have infringed copyright, it primarily provides *civil* remedies such as damages or injunction to those whose copyright has been infringed.[23] From April 2007, enforcement of the criminal offences was primarily delegated to local weights and measures authorities rather than to the police.[24] This transition of police responsibility to local enforcement authorities reflects the

21   Wilson, D. and others, *Fraud and Technology Crimes: Findings from the 2003/04 British Crime Survey, the 2004 Offending, Crime and Justice Survey and Administrative Sources*, Home Office Online Report 09/06 <http://www.homeoffice.gov.uk/rds/pdfs06/rdsolr0906.pdf> (20 May 2007).
22   Copyright, Designs and Patents Act 1988, s. 107.
23   Copyright, Designs and Patents Act 1988, ss. 96–106.
24   Copyright, Designs and Patents Act 1988, s. 107A, added by the Criminal Justice and Public Order Act 1994, s. 165.

construction of much of the criminal harm caused by copyright infringement as insubstantial. The Gowers Review of Intellectual Property[25] acknowledges the link between harm and criminal sanction, stating that 'IP crime must carry penalties *proportionate to the harm caused* and the risk of being caught'[26] (emphasis added). Copyright infringement carries different maximum sentences depending upon whether the offence was committed online or in the physical world.[27] Online offences carry a maximum of two years' imprisonment; real-world offences have a maximum of ten years'.[28] It therefore follows that online offences are considered less culpable and thus attract a lower sentence.

The possible reasons behind this perception of the consequences of computer misuse as being a relatively trifling harm are threefold. First, the harm cannot be easily proved: it is often secret, latent or hidden. For instance, key logging software or other spyware is not always detected. Malicious software may contain a payload set to activate at some future time. Cookies used for authenticating, tracking and maintaining specific information about users may be considered a harm to privacy, but are often either unnoticed or even considered to be useful, since they enable repeat visits to favourite websites. In this sense, computer misuse is analogous to white-collar crime where, similarly, harm is not always conceptualised or identified as such. White-collar crime usually targets a substantial number of victims who are often unaware of their victimisation. Even where this is not the case, as in organisations subject to fraud, there is often unwillingness to admit to vulnerability.[29] The same reluctance to risk attracting adverse publicity has already been seen in relation to the low number of prosecutions brought under the 1990 Act.

Second, the victim may not understand that they have been harmed at all. This may be a consequence of the 'invisible' nature of some types of computer misuse previously discussed, or as a consequence of the victim's own lack of technical knowledge. As User 6 illustrated:

---

25 Supplementary report to HM Treasury, *Investing in Britain's Potential: Building Our Long-term Future* (Cm 6984, 2006).
26 Ibid. [3.11].
27 Following implementation of Council Directive (EC) 2001/29 of 22 May 2001 on the harmonisation of certain aspects of copyright and related rights in the information society [2001] OJ L167/10.
28 Copyright, Designs and Patents Act 1998, ss. 107(2A), 198(1A).
29 Levi, M. and Pithouse, A., 'Victims of fraud', in Downes, D. (ed.) *Unravelling Criminal Justice* (Macmillan, London, 1992).

We had spyware on our machines for weeks before we found it. We had no idea that it was there – or what information we'd lost while it was there.

As previously discussed, the collective diminution in general computing skill levels as technology became more widely available gave rise to a knowledge gap between the expert and non-expert user. Therefore, not only does this gap become a potential driver and facilitator of computer misuse, but it may also lead to a general perception that it is not a source of serious harm and therefore not worthy of criminal sanction.

The final reason lies in the fact that certain manifestations of computer misuse may not be considered harmful at all. Peer-to-peer file sharing networks, such as *eDonkey* and *Kazaa*, which facilitate copyright infringement, or the plethora of websites offering activation codes for software by Microsoft or Adobe (many of which also host a variety of malicious software) are considered by some to be legitimate in that they allow true freedom of information. Boyle criticises the current regime of intellectual property rights, arguing that, *inter alia*, software should not be subject to copyright or patent law since it may tend to concentrate market power in the hands of a small number of companies, such as Microsoft.[30] He considers that the system of grants of exclusivity is in tension with the development of a public domain of information: in other words, that 'information wants to be free'.[31] This theme is also picked up by Rheingold[32] who considers how 'virtual homesteading' gives rise to virtual communities supported by free information propagated via online knowledge-sharing infrastructures. Wagner challenges Boyle's stance, considering that control

may in many cases actually increase open information or the public domain … Furthermore, control offers both flexibility in information-sharing or transfer arrangements and better

30   Boyle, J., *Shamans, Software, and Spleens: Law and the Construction of the Information Society* (Harvard University Press, Cambridge, MA, 1996).

31   Boyle, J., *Foucault In Cyberspace: Surveillance, Sovereignty, and Hard-Wired Censors* (1997) <http://www.law.duke.edu/boylesite/foucault.htm> accessed 25 September 2008.

32   Rheingold, H., *The Virtual Community: Homesteading on the Electronic Frontier* (MIT Press, London, 2000).

coordination of activities that both produce and disseminate open information, to society's benefit.[33]

Nevertheless, it remains true that, for some, that which is criminalised is not considered harmful.

Consideration of the notion of harm leads naturally to the consensus view of crime which proposes that behaviours which are defined as criminal (in other words, the boundaries of criminality) are determined by reference to those which deviate from the norms which are commonly agreed to be acceptable among the majority of people within a particular society. Therefore conduct that is defined as criminal naturally reflects the values, beliefs and opinions of the social majority. The consensus approach reflects the utilitarian view encapsulated by John Stuart Mill, who believed that the state is only justified in regulating the behaviour of its citizens in the interests of the prevention of harm either to others or to society as a whole:

[T]he sole end for which mankind are warranted, individually or collectively, in interfering with the liberty of action of any of their number, is self-protection. [...] The only purpose for which power can be rightfully exercised over a member of a civilised community, against his will, is to prevent harm to others. His own good, either physical or moral, is not a sufficient warrant.[34]

Therefore, according to Mill, and later Hart, who applied Mill's principle to the limits of the criminal law,[35] if an individual's behaviour is likely to harm others, then his individual liberty to behave as he wishes should be sacrificed in the interests of society in general. It is clear from this that the consensus view makes a strong link between prohibited conduct and morality: conduct is prohibited because it is harmful or 'wrong'. While this is in accord with the instrumentalist prohibition on crimes which are *mala in se*[36] such as murder or rape, the consensus view has greater difficulty in justifying the criminalisation of less substantially harmful conduct, or conduct which is *mala*

---

33 Wagner, R.P., 'Information wants to be free: intellectual property and the mythologies of control' (2003) 103 *Columbia Law Review* 995, 1034.
34 Mill, J.S., *On Liberty and Other Essays* (revd edn, Oxford University Press, Oxford, 1991) 14.
35 Hart, H.L.A., *Law, Liberty and Morality* (Oxford University Press, Oxford, 1963).
36 Conduct which is wrong in itself.

prohibita,[37] that is prohibited for the protection of society, not because it is morally wrong'.[38] Examples of *mala prohibita* conduct are driving without a licence and illegal tax evasion. Consensus theorists argue that since the aim of the criminal law is to protect individuals and society from harm, it must necessarily cover an immense spectrum of harms. As such, it is injurious to both individuals and society that unlicensed drivers are on the roads and that revenues due are not being paid. While individuals might not agree with the minutiae of these laws, in particular their application to themselves, there remains a general agreement with their overarching principles in that there should be some controls over driving behaviour in the interests of public safety and that people should contribute to the cost of providing free services such as state healthcare and education. In some respects, it is true to say that social harm is the factor that distinguishes *deviant* behaviour, that is any conduct that departs from the norms of society, and *criminal* behaviour. The liberal basis of the consensus view, based upon the idea of maximising freedom, autonomy and choice, would not see the criminalisation of deviant behaviour as justified unless it crossed the threshold of seriousness that rendered it harmful to others or to society.

It is therefore necessary to examine whether computer misuse crosses the threshold of seriousness justifying its criminalisation on the basis of its harm to another or to society as a whole. The harm to society – in the form of harm to the national economy – was the view put forward by the proponents of the Computer Misuse Bill, in particular Michael Colvin MP, who quoted the cost of computer misuse to the UK as between £400 million and £2 billion annually during debate.[39] Moreover, general media-led public concern over hacking and viruses also began to grow during the 1980s, giving weight to a general public consensus that such misuse was harmful in a general sense.

Therefore, while the utilitarian instrumentalist conception of the criminal law may provide a deterrent to *substantial* harm, it has not provided a deterrent to the harm perceived as resulting from computer misuse. Wall describes this as the '*de minimis* trap': computer misuse (as a subset of what Wall defines as cybercrime)

---

37 Conduct which is wrong *because* it is prohibited.
38 Lacey, N., Wells, C. and Meure, D., *Reconstructing Criminal Law: Critical Social Perspectives on Crime and the Criminal Process* (Weidenfeld & Nicolson, London, 1990).
39 Hansard HC vol. 166 col. 1134 (9 February 1990).

often involves bulk, but low-harm, victimisation and consequently that the use of finite police resources for individual instances of harm would be often hard to justify in the public interest.[40] Similarly, the DTI found that 'for virus infections, there was a general perception that no-one had broken the law'.[41] From a consensus perspective, there is no agreement that computer misuse is harmful enough to be treated invariably as criminal. This supports the proposition that, save for those breaches that pose a threat to safety or national security, computer misuse is *mala prohibita*. Since people are more inclined to obey laws which prohibit behaviour that is *mala in se*, the proliferation of computer misuse strongly suggests that the criminal law may be an ineffective instrument of control. Therefore, if computer misuse does not seem to be *mala in se*, it should be examined in terms of its moral content to consider why this might be the case. However, the relationship between the criminal law and morality is uncertain in the instrumentalist view. As Duff comments:

[A]n instrumentalist approach to the justification of criminal law seems to leave it as something of an open question whether the law should criminalise only immoral conduct, or should subject only morally culpable agents to criminal liability.[42]

It is therefore necessary to consider computer misuse within a construction of the criminal law which centres on immorality and moral culpability.

The moralistic construction of the criminal law

Sir James Stephen infamously argued that criminal law is in 'the nature of a persecution of the grosser forms of vice' and that these

have in fact been forbidden and subjected to punishment not only because they are dangerous to society, and so ought to

---

40 Wall, D.S., *Cybercrime: The Transformation of Crime in the Digital Age* (Polity Press, Cambridge, 2007) 161–2.

41 DTI, *Information Security Breaches Survey 2004* <http://www.pwc.com/images/gx/eng/about/svcs/grms/2004Technical_Report.pdf> accessed 25 September 2008.

42 Duff, R.A., 'Theories of criminal law', *Stanford Encyclopedia of Philosophy* <http://plato.stanford.edu/entries/criminal-law/> accessed 25 September 2008.

be prevented, but also for the sake of gratifying the feeling of hatred – call it revenge, resentment, or what you will – which the contemplation of such conduct excites in healthily constituted minds.[43]

To Stephen, the criminal law exists to regulate conduct which is repugnant to the healthily constituted mind (that is, the mind of the right-thinking members of society) and, in doing so, serves an (indirectly) instrumentalist purpose of satisfying the collective social feelings of hatred towards gross forms of vice, a response which Stephen considered to be appropriate and natural. For Cohen, conduct such as pornography, prostitution and that involving abhorrent sexual practices should be criminalised because:

It is one of the functions of the criminal law to give expression to the collective feeling of revulsion toward certain acts, even when they are not very dangerous.[44]

This moralistic construction of avoiding collective revulsion is echoed by Moore who stated that the function of the criminal law is to punish

all and only those who are morally culpable in the doing of some morally wrongful action.[45]

The moralist arguments of Stephen, Cohen and Moore are encapsulated by Devlin in a classic statement on the function of morality within the law:

Without shared ideas on politics, morals and ethics, no society can exist ... If men and women try to create a society in which there is no fundamental agreement about good and evil, they will fail; if having based it on common agreement, the agreement goes, the society will disintegrate. For society is not something that is kept together physically; it is held by the invisible bonds

---

43 Stephen, J.F., *Liberty, Equality, Fraternity* (1873), reprinted in White, J. (ed.), *Liberty, Equality, Fraternity* (Cambridge University Press, Cambridge, 1967) 148–9.
44 Cohen, M.R., 'Moral aspects of the criminal law' (1940) 49 *The Yale Law Journal* 987, 991.
45 Moore, M.S., *Placing Blame: A Theory of Criminal Law* (Oxford University Press, Oxford, 1997) 35.

of common thought. If the bonds were too far relaxed, the members would drift apart. A common morality is part of the bondage. The bondage is the price of society; and mankind, which needs society must pay its price.[46]

Devlin therefore contended that there is a common public morality that must be protected by the criminal law and that to remove the regulation of morality from the reach of the criminal law would inevitably lead to the spread of immoral behaviour and the disintegration of society. It followed that conduct which was viewed as immoral by the majority at the time, such as homosexuality, needed to be suppressed in the interests of society.

The doctrine that it is justifiable to make some kinds of conduct punishable by the criminal law simply because the conduct in question is commonly held to be immoral, irrespective of whether it does any harm, was criticised by Hart.[47] This gave rise to the Hart–Devlin debate which followed the publication of the Wolfenden report.[48] This report made recommendations which led to the decriminalisation of consensual homosexual activity between adult males in private. These were based on Mill's libertarian view that legal power can only be exercised for the purpose of preventing harm to others and that no such harm was being done. Devlin was highly critical of both the decriminalisation of homosexuality and Hart's view that the criminal law had no role to play in the enforcement of morality. Hart disagreed with Devlin over the existence of a common morality, preferring instead the idea of a 'number of mutually tolerant moralities'[49] and that the use of law to reflect a snapshot of the dominant morality of the time was, as Zedner comments, 'conservative and potentially harmful',[50] particularly in the contemporary multicultural, multi-ethnic, multi-faith society.[51] Hart believed that the prohibition of conduct on the basis of a moral consensus was an unjustifiable interference with individual autonomy. Therefore legislation designed to enforce moral standards can have a flawed basis due to the difficulties of defining

---

46 Devlin, P., *The Enforcement of Morals* (Oxford University Press, Oxford, 1965) 26.
47 Hart, H.L.A., *Law, Liberty and Morality* (Oxford University Press, Oxford, 1963).
48 Committee on Homosexual Offences and Prostitution, *Report of the Committee on Homosexual Offences and Prostitution* (HMSO, London 1957).
49 Hart, H.L.A., *Law, Liberty and Morality* (Oxford University Press, Oxford, 1963) 62–3.
50 Zedner, L., *Criminal Justice* (Oxford University Press, Oxford, 2004) 49.
51 Ibid.

morality and delineating between that which is immoral and that which is not. However, Hart did concede a role for the criminal law in the *maintenance* of morality, but only where necessary to protect those who would engage in such immoral activities. Hart's reluctance to treat law as a moral issue was later criticised by Dworkin who considered that law could never be entirely divorced from morality.[52] Similarly, Mitchell argued that law might be used to protect a utilitarian morality, that is to reinforce it rather than enforce it.[53]

In relation to computer misuse, it has been suggested by Spafford[54] and Denning[55] that the moral boundaries relating to technology are at odds with the moral standards of the physical world. In essence, the novelty of the technological realm suggests that the ethical considerations relating to personal property and privacy in the physical world do not apply in the electronic world. This allows people to engage in deviant behaviour involving computer misuse whereas they would be less likely to engage in the analogous physical world mischief. This view was consistently echoed across all categories of interview participant:

Online criminals do things from the safety of their own homes that they wouldn't dream of doing in the High Street. They will quite happily commit fraud and theft online, but you'd never see them in Lloyd's with a mask on.[56]

The world within the computer is different in almost every respect. You become disassociated from what you're doing. And the consequences of what you're doing, I suppose.[57]

We must accept that online behaviour is different to everyday behaviour and deal with it accordingly.[58]

52 Dworkin, R., *Law's Empire* (Belknap Press, Cambridge, MA, 1986).
53 Mitchell, B., *Law, Morality and Religion in a Secular Society* (Oxford University Press, London, 1967) 75.
54 Spafford, E., 'Are hacker break-ins ethical?', in Ermann, M., Williams, M. and Shauf, M. (eds) *Computers, Ethics, and Society* (Oxford University Press, New York, 1997) 77.
55 Denning, D., *Information Warfare and Security* (Addison-Wesley, Harlow, 1998).
56 Police Officer 2.
57 Technician 6.
58 Policy-Maker 4.

Moreover, as Rogers et al.[59] established, computer misusers tend not to consider their actions as immoral. Technician 3 comments further:

I used to hack. So what? As long as I didn't cause any havoc while I was in there, then I don't see that I was really doing anything wrong. You couldn't call it immoral. Not unless I put loads of porn in someone's account or something like that. Of course, I never did.

Suler links this lack of virtual moral consensus to 'toxic disinhibition', arising from the very nature of the interaction of the individual with the technology.[60]

Therefore it seems that there is little support for a theory which bases the criminalisation of computer misuse on moralistic grounds. It is therefore necessary to consider alternative theories of structural conflict and interactionism which may provide greater insight.

The structural conflict theory of criminal law

The consensus view of crime largely prevailed unchallenged until the 1960s and the advent of critical criminology. One of the key counter theories is the structural conflict view of crime. This builds upon the work of Marx, who outlined the fundamentals of the conflict approach as follows:

In the social production of their life, men enter into definite relations that are indispensable and independent of their will, relations of production which correspond to a definite stage of development of their material productive forces. The sum total of these relations … constitutes the economic structure of society, the real foundation, on which rises a legal and political super-structure and to which correspond definite forms of social consciousness. The mode of production of material life conditions the social, political and intellectual life process in general. It is not the consciousness of men that determines their

59 Rogers, M.K., Siegfried, K. and Tidke, K., 'Self-reported computer criminal behavior: a psychological analysis' [2006] Digital Investigation 116.
60 Suler, J., The Psychology of Cyberspace <http://www.rider.edu/~suler/psycyber/psycyber.html> accessed 25 September 2008.

being, but, on the contrary, their social being that determines their consciousness.[61]

It is, however, important to note that Marx wrote about the social organisation of society and did not theorise about crime. However, his ideas have formed the basis for the development of theories about crime put forward by others. Bonger attempted to explain crime from a Marxist perspective in a crudely deterministic fashion that over-predicted the prevalence of crime occurring under capitalism resulting from a social structure which alienated the lower social classes.[62] Sellin further argued that in a homogenous society, the norms – or rules of behaviour – which emerge from within a culture are embedded in its members and become laws where enforcement is necessary to preserve that unitary culture.[63] However, where separate cultures diverge, the laws which represent the norms, values and interests of the dominant cultural group may produce conflict. This idea was further developed by Vold who contended that the social group which proves most efficient in the control of political processes obtains the power to enact laws that limit the behaviour of other groups and, in some cases, prevent the fulfilment of minority group needs.[64] Turk builds on this position, and the work of Dahrendorf[65] to conclude that social control is exercised by the 'control of legal images';.[66] the inherent discretion in the way in which formal laws are exercised allows the powerful to manipulate the legal system to protect their position while still appearing objectively impartial. The notion of social classes as the most significant relations of production are not defined explicitly by Marx, but Giddens infers that:

Classes are constituted by the relationship of groupings of individuals to the ownership of private property in the means of production. This yields a model of class relations which is basically dichotomous: all class societies are built around a primary line of division between two antagonistic classes, one

---

61 Marx, K., *A Contribution to the Critique of Political Economy* (trans. Progress, Moscow, 1970) 1. Originally published in German in 1859.

62 Bonger, W., *Criminality and Economic Conditions* (reissued edn, Indiana University Press, Bloomington, IN, 1969).

63 Sellin, T., *Culture, Conflict and Crime* (Social Research Council, New York, 1938).

64 Vold, G., *Theoretical Criminology* (Oxford University Press, Oxford, 1958).

65 Dahrendorf, R., *Class and Class Conflict in Industrial Society* (Stanford University Press, Stanford, CA, 1959).

66 Turk, A.T., *Criminality and the Social Order* (Rand-McNally, Chicago, IL, 1969).

dominant and the other subordinate. In Marx's usage, class of necessity involves a conflict relation.[67]

In summary, then, Marxist theorists do not see society as built upon consensus but as characterised by conflict between diverse groups who compete for power. Those who hold power have the ability to influence the content of the law and therefore may exercise their power to protect their own interests and to advance their own social and economic position. As such, the criminal law reflects and protects established economic, racial, gender and political power groups and thus reinforces and perpetuates the power conflict in society.

Conflict theorists see the interests of the powerful reflected not only in the content of the law but in the relative severity with which the crimes of the powerful and the powerless are viewed. For example, crimes against property committed by the lower classes, such as robbery and burglary, are viewed as significantly more serious than the so-called white collar crimes, such as insider dealing and security violations, despite the fact that the latter are likely to involve significantly greater sums of money and have the potential to create more widespread social harm.[68] Therefore, according to the conflict view, the definition of crime is controlled by those who possess power, wealth and position who have an interest in preserving their preferential status in society. Crime is shaped by the values of the ruling class and not by an objective moral consensus that reflects the needs of all people. Crime, according to this perspective, can be defined as a political concept designed to protect the power and position of the upper classes at the expense of the poor. This view sees even crimes such as murder and rape as having political overtones as the prohibition of violent acts ensures domestic tranquillity and guarantees that the anger of the poor and disenfranchised will not be directed towards their wealthy capitalist exploiters.

The criminalisation of computer misuse can be conceptualised within the framework of conflict theory. The predominant political argument advanced during the House of Commons debate centred on the cost to the UK economy. Moreover, the preceding Law Commission report recommended that hacking should be criminalised 'because of the

67 Giddens, A., *Capitalism and Modern Social Theory: An Analysis of the Writings of Marx, Durkheim and Max Weber* (Cambridge University Press, Cambridge, 1973).
68 Levi, M. and Pithouse, A., 'Victims of fraud', in Downes, D. (ed.), *Unravelling Criminal Justice* (Macmillan, London, 1992).

general importance of computer systems'[69] which had 'created radical alterations in the methods and conditions of information storage'[70] deemed to be 'strongly in the public interest'[71] in order to 'reduce the incidence of costs'.[72] The resulting criminal offences that were created by the 1990 Act can be seen to have their roots in the protection of the capitalist state, and hence the protection of those with political power. Although it is perhaps less immediately apparent how this exercise in political power was achieved at the expense of the poor, it is worth remembering the comments of the MPs at the time of the debate, in particular that computer misusers were considered to be 'often poor'[73] and living in a 'twisted [sub]culture that the Bill is trying to stamp out'.[74] These comments provide a clear illustration of those with political and economic power protecting their interests by criminalising the activities which threatened those interests, perpetrated by a class viewed as poor and twisted. Moreover, the largest global software corporation, Microsoft, is criticised by advocates of free software for its embedded approach to Digital Rights Management technology and regularly vilified for alleged unfair and anticompetitive commercial practices. These include the abuse of monopoly power in operating system and web browser sales in the United States[75] and breach of European competition law in relation to Windows Media Player.[76] Microsoft products have also been characterised as being unstable and prone to overall system insecurity which can be exploited by computer misusers. This can also be viewed in terms of a class struggle as the dispossessed fight back against their oppressor. However, Microsoft also has a role to play in terms of technological governance, as will be discussed further in Chapter 7.

Therefore, the use of the criminal law as one means of regulating computer misuse may be firmly situated within the bounds of structural conflict. However, if the criminal law protects the interests of the powerful, it is questionable why the criminal law has not been used more to protect those interests. Despite the support by trade and industry bodies seen in Chapters 2 and 3 to both the original 1990

---

69 Law Commission, 'Computer Misuse' (Law Com. No. 186, Cm 819, 1989) [2.13].
70 Ibid. [2.12].
71 Ibid. [2.12].
72 Ibid. [2.24].
73 Hansard HC vol. 166 col. 1177 (9 February 1990) (Arbuthnot, J).
74 Hansard HC vol. 166 col. 1137 (9 February 1990) (Colvin, M).
75 *United States v. Microsoft* 87 F. Supp. 2d 30 (DDC 2000).
76 Case T-201/04 *Microsoft v. Commission* [2004] ECR II-463 (CFI).

Act and the amendments which were introduced by the Police and Justice Act 2006, companies generally tend to favour taking internal measures over legal action where possible. It is therefore reasonable to conclude that for the majority of incidents in the majority of organisations, companies consider that their interests in preventing and addressing the problem of computer misuse are better served by alternative means to the criminal law. Organisations perceive a lack of police manpower available to deal with such incidents. This is demonstrated by an increased focus on national rather than private security, particularly since the terrorist attacks of 11 September 2001. For instance, the National Hi-Tech Crime Unit was formed in 2001 but was subsumed into the e-crime unit of the Serious Organised Crime Agency on 1 April 2006. The incorporation of a dedicated Internet crime unit into a general organised crime agency demonstrated a drift in policing focus away from technology crime. This view was borne out by comments from users and the police at interview:

Unless someone hacks into the air traffic control system or tries to start a 'fire sale' like in *Die Hard 4.0* then the policing agencies won't want to know.[77]

The police have limited resources. If we had a choice between protecting the public at large from the consequences of a major security breach, or using the same resources to deal with someone who'd just lost their holiday photos from their hard disk, then common sense would have to prevail.[78]

We can't deal with every incident where a computer is involved. We'd be swamped.[79]

Therefore, organisations are less likely to complain, believing that the police involvement would not be as effective as seeking a private remedy – or no remedy at all.

The interactionist theory of criminal law

The interactionist theory of criminal law is derived from the symbolic

---

77 Technician 7.
78 Police Officer 3.
79 Police Officer 4.

114

interactionism school of sociology that is associated with Mead,[80] Cooley[81] and Thomas,[82] which analyses the way in which individuals conceptualise themselves and others with whom they interact. Symbolic interactionists consider that meanings emerge out of the social processes of interpretation by which definitions of objects are created and used.[83] There is a three-stage process by which people ascribe meaning. People act in accordance with their own view of reality based upon the meaning that they give to things. They then observe how others react to these things, whether positively or negatively. The final stage is that they re-examine and interpret their own behaviour according to the meaning that they have learned from others. As Thomas stated:

It is not important whether or not the interpretation is correct – if men define situations as real, they are real in their consequences.[84]

Therefore, according to this perspective, there is no objective reality. People, institutions and events are neither good nor bad in themselves but come to be viewed as such according to the subjective interpretation of the observer. For interactionists, the definition of crime reflects the preferences and opinions of people who hold social power within a particular legal jurisdiction: the property of 'deviance' is *attributed* to certain forms of conduct by an audience rather than being intrinsic to them. Those with social power use their influence to impose their definition of right and wrong on the rest of the population. For many, the acceptance of the legitimate authority of those in power leads them unquestioningly to internalise those rules and consequently to adopt their views of right and wrong. Conversely, criminals are people who society has chosen to label as outcasts or deviants because they have violated social rules. This position was famously summarised by Becker:

Social groups create deviance by making the rules whose infraction constitutes deviance and by applying those rules to

---

80 Mead, G., *Mind, Self and Society* (University of Chicago Press, Chicago, IL, 1934).
81 Cooley, C.H., *Sociological Theory and Social Research* (Henry Holt, New York, 1930).
82 Thomas, W.I. and Thomas, D.S., *The Child in America: Behavior Problems and Programs* (Knopf, New York, 1928).
83 Plummer, K., *Sexual Stigma* (Routledge & Kegan Paul, London, 1975).
84 Ibid.

particular people and labelling them as outsiders. From this point of view ... the deviant is one to whom the label has successfully been applied; deviant behaviour is behaviour people so label.[85]

Therefore crimes are regarded as wrong because society has labelled them as wrong not because there is anything inherently wrong or evil about them.

The interactionist view of crime coincides with the conflict view to the extent that both regard criminal laws as being made by the powerful to protect their interests and which are enforced on those without power. However, unlike the conflict view, the interactionists do not attribute economic and political motivations to the process of defining crime. Instead, they see the criminal law as conforming to the beliefs of moral entrepreneurs who use their influence to create rules for the benefit of the less fortunate in accordance with their views and beliefs. Laws against pornography, prostitution and drug use are illustrative of this view as they can be seen to be the result of successful moral crusades rather than originating from capitalist sensibilities.

Moreover, interactionists are interested in the shifting boundaries of the criminal law and their relationship with changes in the conventional morality of society, what Lacey refers to as the contingent nature of the boundaries of criminality.[86] Crime is historically and culturally relative: the content of the criminal law is not universal and static but varies both over time within a single culture and across different cultures. Of course, changes in the boundaries of criminality over time are not solely dictated by changes in attitudes towards the acceptability of the conduct involved. It may be the case that new situations arise that are deemed to require the intervention of the criminal law. Technological change affects the opportunities for crime, the forms of crime that are prevalent and patterns of crime.[87] As Heidensohn comments:

[C]riminality does take novel forms from time to time, reflecting technological development: no-one could hijack an aeroplane until powered flight was possible.[88]

85 Becker, H., *Outsiders: Studies in the Sociology of Deviance* (Free Press, New York, 1963) 4.

86 Lacey, N., 'Contingency and criminalisation', in Loveland, I. (ed.) *Frontiers of Criminality* (Sweet & Maxwell, London, 1995).

87 Croall, H., *Crime and Society in Britain* (Longman, Harlow, 1998).

88 Heidensohn, F., *Crime and Society* (Macmillan, Basingstoke, 1989) 9.

As previously discussed, the amendments to the 1990 Act within the Police and Justice Act 2006 also resulted from new manifestations of computer misuse made possible by technological advances.

However, it is worth remembering that the conduct criminalised by the 1990 Act was not new. As has already been seen, DARPA deliberately turned a blind eye to all the unauthorised activity on its computer systems in the 1970s. It understood that the extra overhead was 'a small price to pay for attracting an entire generation of bright young people into the computing field'[89] and therefore did not have a position of power to protect. On the contrary, it sought to *gain* power by allowing unauthorised activity as a means of growing its intellectual capital. As the central research and development organisation for the United States Department of Defense, it follows that its success was also inextricably linked with the political power inherently underlying the work of a state department. Therefore non-criminalisation supported growth of both economic[90] and political power. As time moved on, the social reaction to the conduct changed while the conduct itself was constant. As Young states:

> Crime … is not an objective 'thing' out there, but a product of socially created definitions; deviance is not inherent in an item of behaviour, it is a quality bestowed upon it by human evaluation.[91]

It therefore follows that, since criminal law is based upon norms of social conduct, then it manifestly has to change to reflect social changes.[92]

Interactionist theory also considers that the boundaries of criminality will move as more information becomes available about the effects of particular conduct. In light of this information, the conduct may then be reclassified from deviant to criminal or criminal to deviant. As such, the content of the criminal law is contingent on the level of harm that is attached to any particular form of conduct. For those who wish to criminalise or decriminalise a particular form of conduct,

---

89 Raymond, E., *A Brief History of Hackerdom* (May 2000) <http://catb.org/~esr/writings/hacker-history/hacker-history.html> accessed 25 September 2008.

90 In the sense that intellectual capital is an economic intangible: see Stewart, T.A., *Intellectual Capital: The New Wealth of Organizations* (Currency/Doubleday, New York, 1999).

91 Young, J., *The Exclusive Society* (Sage, London, 1999).

92 Heidensohn, F., *Crime and Society* (Macmillan, Basingstoke, 1989) 4.

the key objective is to demonstrate that it causes harm (or that it does not cause any harm) to individuals or to society. This theory has been applied to a diverse range of conduct including marijuana use,[93] juvenile delinquency,[94] domestic violence[95] and stalking.[96]

Interactionist theory can be applied to support the criminalisation of computer misuse. In the same way that conflict theory suggested that its criminalisation was an exercise of power (albeit political and economic power) to suppress the harmful conduct of the subservient classes, interactionist theory can also draw reference to an exercise of power. However, to the interactionist, this power is that of the moral entrepreneurs who constructed the problem as a criminal matter. This social power was held by corporations and institutions whose influence was exercised upon the Law Commission in their responses to the original Working Paper;[97] these included representatives from academia,[98] industry,[99] the criminal justice system[100] and learned societies.[101] The collective construction of computer misuse as a wrong deserving of criminal sanction was therefore imposed as a reflection of the conventional morality of those involved, most of whom had by 1990, to a greater or lesser degree, a position to protect. As User 2 commented:

The early 90s was the time when we started making serious money. We didn't want a load of spotty hackers coming along and spoiling the party.

---

93 Becker, H., *Outsiders: Studies in the Sociology of Deviance* (Free Press, New York, 1963).

94 Platt, A.M., *The Child Savers: The Invention of Delinquency* (University of Chicago Press, Chicago, IL, 1969).

95 Tierney, K., 'The battered women movement and the creation of the wife beating problem' [1982] 2 *Social Problems* 207.

96 Finch, E., *The Criminalisation of Stalking: Constructing the Problem and Evaluating the Solution* (Cavendish, London, 2001).

97 Law Commission, *Computer Misuse* (Working Paper No. 110, 1988).

98 For example, the Universities and Research Councils Computer Board, the Society of Public Teachers of Law, the University of London Computer Centre and the Centre for Criminal Justice Studies, University of Leeds.

99 For example, Cray Research (UK) Ltd, IBM UK, ICL, British Telecom, BP International Ltd and Prudential Corporation plc.

100 For example, the Association of Chief Police Officers, the General Council of the Bar, the Law Society, the Magistrates' Association and the Crown Prosecution Service.

101 For example, the British Computer Society, the Confederation of British Industry, the Society for Computers and Law and the Computing Services Association.

Moreover, the constructionist approach also offers an explanation as to why computer misuse is not seen as a criminal problem for private individuals. The media is the main source of public knowledge about crime, yet computer misuse is not usually presented as a criminal problem. This distinction between the public and private spheres must be considered further, in order to consider where the criminal law should and can regulate and whether there is any inconsistency between the nature of computer misuse and the nature of the criminal law.

Computer misuse as a public or private wrong

Most legal systems distinguish criminal from civil wrongdoing. Criminal wrongs result in a prosecution and imposition of penalty by the state. The state decides whether a charge will be brought and, if so, what charge. On the other hand, civil wrongs are generally treated as private matters, in the sense that it is for the victim to investigate and instigate proceedings if they so choose. Civil remedies typically lie in damages to compensate for injury or loss or injunction to compel a party to desist from or to pursue some course of action. These differences serve to distinguish a civil or private paradigm in which causation of, and remedy for, harm is paramount and a criminal or public paradigm which focuses on public wrongdoing and the identification of who should be punished for that wrong.

To the pure legal moralist, the criminal law exists to protect morality and thus any kind of immorality justifies criminalisation. However, there is conduct that is considered to be immoral that does not attract the attention of the criminal law: many would consider it immoral to commit adultery, yet adultery is not a criminal offence in England and Wales.[102] This is representative of a class of private immorality that does not concern the intervention of the criminal law. At the other extreme, the utilitarian view is that the state may only regulate behaviour to prevent harm and therefore immorality of itself never provides sufficient reason for criminalisation. It has already been seen that there is little support for an argument to criminalise computer misuse on purely moral grounds. Therefore, even if computer use

---

102 Adultery is a criminal offence in other jurisdictions, such as India, Egypt, Nigeria and the Sudan. It has also been so in some US states; for example, North Carolina criminalised lewd and lascivious associations between any man and woman, not being married to each other (GS §14-184).

is immoral, it is of a private immorality which is inconsistent with categorisation as a public wrong. Moreover, it is typified by bulk *de minimis* harms which, in isolation, could be viewed as too trivial to warrant public regulation.

The criminal law is, therefore, traditionally reluctant to interfere within the private sphere. However, the conceptualisation of crimes as public wrongs which harm 'the public' as a collective body is inconsistent with certain conduct which is clearly harmful to individuals. For example, a husband who forced his wife to have sexual intercourse without consent was not guilty of rape until *R v. R (Rape: Marital Exemption)*[103] in 1991. Prior to that, sexual conduct within marriage was viewed as a domestic matter. A similar situation existed in relation to domestic violence. Although giving rise to criminal offences, the police were often reluctant to take domestic disputes seriously, even those of a violent nature.[104] Moreover, where an arrest is made, the CPS only brings around ten per cent of domestic violence cases to trial,[105] often as a result of the victim withdrawing their support for prosecution.[106] A combination of victims not wishing to purse criminal prosecutions and the reluctance of the police and CPS to press for such prosecutions results in a low conviction rate.[107] Marital rape and domestic violence are therefore examples of conduct which do not *harm* the public, but which properly *concern* the public and are therefore public wrongs.[108]

In the same way that the boundary of the criminal law is historically relative, so the public or private nature of a wrong may also vary over time. For instance, homosexuality has transitioned from being a criminal offence which was actively policed as a matter of public concern from the late nineteenth century to the 1950s to a largely

---

103 *R v. R (Rape: Marital Exemption)* [1992] 1 AC 599 (HL). This decision was put into statutory form in the Criminal Justice and Public Order Act 1994, s. 142, now covered by Sexual Offences Act 2003, s. 1.

104 Edwards, S., *Sex and Gender in the Legal Process* (Blackstone, London, 1996) 196–8. In some jurisdictions police have adopted 'pro-arrest' or 'mandatory arrest' policies in relation to domestic violence: Ellison, L., 'Prosecuting domestic violence without victim participation' (2002) 65 *Modern Law Review* 834.

105 Cretney, S. and Davis, G, 'Prosecuting "domestic" assault' [1996] *Criminal Law Review* 162.

106 Crown Prosecution Service Inspectorate, *The Inspectorate's Report on Cases Involving Domestic Violence* (Crown Prosecution Service Inspectorate, London, 1998).

107 Cretney, S. and Davis, G., 'Prosecuting "domestic" assault' [1996] *Criminal Law Review* 162.

108 Marshall, S.E. and Duff, R.A., 'Criminalisation and sharing wrongs' (1998) 11 *Canadian Journal of Law and Jurisprudence* 7.

private matter today. It is not only decriminalised, but now enjoys private rights in relation to prohibition of discrimination on the grounds of sexual orientation[109] and full legal recognition for same-sex civil partnerships.[110] By contrast, domestic violence was once considered a private matter but is increasingly attracting more public concern. A 1990 Home Office Circular[111] recommended that police should approach domestic violence with a presumption in favour of arrest, later strengthened by further guidance that, in the absence of exceptional circumstances, there should be an arrest in *all* domestic violence cases.[112] There are many factors that may influence this dynamic. These include the nature of the harm caused, the degree of harm, the moral consensus in relation to the conduct and the presence or absence of consent or coercion. The prevention of harm to people is self-evidently in the public interest, even in situations where those people themselves have consented to the infliction of physical harm.[113] Equally, it is plain that conduct causing substantial harm is of greater public concern than that causing lesser or *de minimis* harm. Conduct which involves coercing an individual to do something against their will or causes them to suffer an outcome to which they have not consented is instinctively that which will concern this public. In relation to consensual homosexuality where there is little physical harm caused[114] and a prevailing social acceptance of the morality of the act, it is unsurprising that it has become a private matter. Similarly, domestic violence can cause significant physical harm to a victim and is inflicted without consent. As equality in relationships has become the prevailing social attitude so has the view that domestic violence is morally unacceptable. This supports the trend towards the view of domestic violence as a public wrong.

Computer misuse lies somewhere between homosexuality and domestic violence on the public/private continuum. As shown,

109 The Equality Act 2006, s. 81 enables delegated legislation to make provision about discrimination or harassment on grounds of sexual orientation; the Equality Act (Sexual Orientation) Regulations 2007 SI 2007/1063, r. 4 prohibits discrimination in relation to the supply of goods, facilities and services on the grounds of sexual orientation.
110 Civil Partnership Act 2004.
111 Home Office Circular 60/1990.
112 Home Office Circular 19/2000.
113 *R v. Brown* [1994] 1 AC 212 (HL) considered the consensual infliction of offences against the person within a group of sado-masochistic homosexuals. The law will intervene in cases where extreme physical harm (such as genital torture) is inflicted, even where this is done with consent.
114 Ibid.

there is no agreement from the consensus perspective that computer misuse is particularly harmful, with the exception of those acts of computer misuse that pose a threat to safety or national security. Furthermore, the harm done is more likely to affect property rather than individuals. Neither is computer misuse considered to be especially immoral. Victims of computer misuse have not, however, given consent to the harmful conduct.[115] Therefore, computer misuse is better constructed as a private wrong, comprised in many instances of *de minimis* harms and with insufficient public interest on the whole to justify its regulation by the criminal law alone, except where the computer misuse results in a level of substantial public harm such as a threat to the critical national infrastructure. This has already been seen to be covered within the Terrorism Act 2000 which addressed the collectively shared public concern of national security.

This view of computer misuse as a private wrong is supported by the fact that victims of computer misuse are more likely to seek either a private remedy or no remedy at all rather than involve the police. Victims of computer misuse need their computer systems to be rectified if damaged and, assuming a perpetrator can be found, would more likely seek damages for the costs of repair than seek to press criminal charges, even if the police were amenable to proceeding.

Computer misuse and jurisdiction

The criminal law must be workable and viable. It is traditionally associated with sovereignty. For Hart,[116] law was simply an aspect of sovereignty such that the necessary and sufficient conditions for the truth of a proposition of law were simply that the law was internally logical and consistent and that state power was being exercised responsibly. This view was rejected by Dworkin[117] who argued it is a fundamental political right of the individual to the equal respect and concern of the state. Dworkin proposed a theory of compliance, deference and enforcement to identify legitimacy. The link between criminal law and sovereignty is reflected in the fact that, until recently, countries have not taken an interest in criminal activity beyond their borders.

---

115 See the decision of the Divisional Court in *DPP v. Lennon* [2006] EWHC 1201 which considered the role of consent in relation to a denial-of-service attack.

116 Hart, H.L.A., *The Concept of Law* (Oxford University Press, Oxford, 1961).

117 Dworkin, R., *Taking Rights Seriously* (Harvard University Press, Cambridge, MA, 2005).

The inherent problem with jurisdiction in relation to computer misuse is summarised by Johnson and Post:

The rise of an electronic medium that disregards geographical boundaries throws the law into disarray by creating entirely new phenomena that need to become the subject of clear legal rules but that cannot be governed, satisfactorily, by any current territorially based sovereign.[118]

The Computer Misuse Act 1990 gives the domestic courts jurisdiction where the misuse originates in the home country or is directed at a computer within it (subject to the principle of dual criminality).[119] While the rise in organised crime has provided more legislative means of expediting and facilitating international law enforcement, such as the European arrest warrant system under the Extradition Act 2003, it remains the case that this is not widely used in practice. In 2007, there were 9,313 warrants issued by 27 member states, an average of 345 per state. Of these, 2,658 resulted in an arrest.[120] Therefore, given the global nature of the Internet and the fact that over 95 per cent of malicious activity originates outside the UK,[121] it follows that the international nature of computer misuse renders the use of domestic criminal law cumbersome and unattractive as a means of control. The exception here is, as it is with public wrongs, that extra-territorial criminal law will only tend to be employed where there is a threat to national security. For example, in *McKinnon v. USA*,[122] the House of Lords upheld the decision of the Secretary of State under Part 2 of the Extradition Act 2003 to extradite Gary McKinnon to the USA following his alleged unauthorised access to 97 computers belonging to and used by the US Army, Navy and NASA from his own computer in London. Similarly, Babar Ahmad is awaiting extradition to the USA after allegedly running websites supporting

118 Johnson, D. and Post, D., 'Law and borders – the rise of law in cyberspace' (1996) 48 *Stanford Law Review* 1367, 1375.

119 Computer Misuse Act 1990, ss. 4(4), 8(1).

120 Council of the European Union, *Replies to Questionnaire on Quantitative Information on the Practical Operation of the European Arrest Warrant – Year 2007*, COPEN 116 EJN 44 EUROJUST 58 (Brussels, 11 June 2008).

121 The UK accounted for 4 per cent of malicious activity globally between July and December 2006: *Symantec Internet Security Threat Report: Trends for July – December 06*, Vol. XI (March 2007) Symantec Corporation <http://eval.symantec.com/mktginfo/enterprise/white_papers/ent-whitepaper_internet_security_threat_report_xi_03_2007.en-us.pdf> accessed 25 September 2008.

122 *McKinnon v. USA* [2008] UKHL 59.

terror and urging Muslims to fight a holy war,[123] and Younes Tsouli was convicted to ten years' imprisonment[124] under the Terrorism Act 2000 after conducting a similar online campaign.[125] These are, however, isolated and extreme manifestations of criminal computer misuse. It is unlikely that the majority of instances would trigger such a reaction. As Police Officer 2 commented:

> Do you seriously think we'd try and get someone extradited unless they'd done something very bad indeed?

Therefore, with the exception of serious computer misuse, the domestic criminal law may encounter practical difficulties where the misuse operates beyond the national borders.

Conclusion

This chapter has considered a number of different theoretical standpoints in relation to the criminal law in general and its application to the problem of computer misuse in particular. Many of these theories struggle with the notion of harm arising from computer misuse, the consequences of which are viewed as less substantial than those arising from other more tangible and familiar criminalised conduct. This perception of generally insubstantial harm is, in part, a consequence of the nature of many manifestations of computer misuse. The harm is often secret, latent or hidden. It may not be understood as harmful by the victim. It may also be considered to be non-criminal.

Therefore the instrumentalist standpoint, in which the criminal law serves as the means of protecting a set of individual or public interests from substantial harm, is not generally applicable to computer misuse where the harm is often insubstantial. Moreover, a liberal consensus view would not see the criminalisation of deviant behaviour as justified unless it crossed the threshold of seriousness that rendered it harmful to others or to society. Given that computer misuse generally comprises non-serious, or *de minimis*, harms, then its criminalisation cannot be justified from a consensus perspective, save for those instances that pose a threat to safety or national security.

---

123 *Ahmad and another v. United States of America* [2006] EWHC 2927 (Admin).
124 Later increased to 16 years' imprisonment.
125 *R v. Tsouli and others, The Times* 6 July 2007 (Woolwich Crown Court).

There is also little support for the criminalisation of computer misuse on moralistic grounds, since computer misuse is not generally considered to be especially immoral. This viewpoint may arise from the relationship between the individual and the technology, within which conventional moral rules and norms do not apply.

Structural conflict theory may, however, provide an explanation in terms of protection of political and economic power. This was certainly the primary justification behind the enactment of the 1990 Act and was more recently cited in support of the amendments to the 1990 Act introduced by the Police and Justice Act 2006. However, if this is the case, it must still be questioned why the criminal law has not been used more to protect the interests of the powerful. While organisations consider that their interests in preventing and addressing the problem of computer misuse are better served by alternative means to the criminal law, then conflict theory alone will not provide an explanation. From the interactionist standpoint, it can be seen that the social reaction to the same sort of conduct has changed over time. That which was initially seen as harmless had, by the mid-1980s, become seen as positively harmful. Social pressure for criminalisation was been brought to bear by actors with less overtly political positions to protect, although the protection of commercial interests could also be considered by conflict theory as the protection of political capitalism.

While there are some apparent explanations for the criminal law having some role to play in the regulation of computer misuse, each theoretical position taken suffers from inadequacies to a greater or lesser extent. It is therefore difficult to propose a single coherent theoretical basis upon which to justify its criminalisation. Despite this difficulty, the domestic criminal law is still seen as an appropriate vehicle for effective regulation. This has been demonstrated in the expansion and amendment of the 1990 Act in response to technological advances. However, it has been amply demonstrated that the pre-existing criminal law was not particularly vigorously exercised during its first 16 years. This does not necessarily mean that the lack of prosecutions under the 1990 Act means that the criminal law is not required at all. Indeed, at the very least, the symbolic role of the law in setting standards of behaviour remains a positive reason for its existence. As Wasik[126] comments:

126 Wasik, M., *The Role of the Criminal Law in the Control of Misuse of Information Technology* (University of Manchester Working Paper No. 8, July 1991) 13.

While the criminal law undoubtedly has a role to play in this general area [of computer misuse], its purpose and proper scope is problematic and its routine overuse must be avoided.

If the criminal law is little used and there is no firm theoretical basis for its use, then it must be considered whether there is something in the nature of computer misuse or the criminal law itself that renders its use problematic. The law generally demands certainty. The European Convention on Human Rights only allows interference with certain fundamental rights 'in accordance with law'.[127] It therefore follows that the law must be certain, published and accessible in order for individuals to ensure those rights are not unnecessarily infringed. Moreover, the House of Lords has long acknowledged the 'special need for certainty in the criminal law'[128] and has stated that judges should not change the law unless they can achieve finality and certainty.[129] This echoes a key principle of both Fuller's internal morality and Hart's principles of efficacy. It therefore follows that the criminal law may have particular difficulty in dealing with uncertain material.

Computer misuse suffers from an inherent ill-definition. Its possible manifestations have evolved as technology has advanced and will continue to do so. However, that is not to say that if an offence cannot be easily defined, it should not be an offence. There is little doubt that murder should be a criminal offence, but the common law definition of murder has not been constant, particularly with regard to its *mens rea*.[130] However, in relation to computer misuse, this ill-definition renders its boundaries uncertain. Moreover, unlike police powers or sentencing, for example, computer misuse is not the type of criminal law that is high priority, either for the government or for

127 Articles 8 (the right to respect for private life), 9 (the right to freedom of conscience, thought and religion), 10 (the right to freedom of expression) and 11 (the right to freedom of assembly and association) all permit restrictions which are in accordance with law and 'necessary in a democratic society'.

128 *Practice Statement: Judicial Precedent* [1966] 1 WLR 1234 (HL).

129 *C (a minor) v. DPP* [1996] AC 1 (HL). Despite the overriding quest for certainty, the House of Lords has itself occasionally changed its decisions in relatively short order: on the *mens rea* of murder in *R v. Moloney* [1985] AC 905 (HL) and *R v. Hancock and Shankland* [1986] AC 455 (HL) and on impossibility in attempted crimes in *Anderton v. Ryan* [1985] AC 560 (HL) and *R v. Shivpuri* [1987] 1 AC 1 (HL).

130 *Moloney and Hancock and Shankland* (see note 129); also *R v. Nedrick* [1986] 3 All ER 1 (CA); *R v. Woollin* [1999] AC 82 (HL).

the general public. As demonstrated in Chapter 3, it took 16 years for the original 1990 Act to be amended to enable it to cope more effectively with new forms of misuse that had evolved over time.

As has also been seen, computer misuse is better constructed as a private rather than a public wrong. This is consistent with the consensus view of it as being of low harm and not particularly immoral. It is therefore unworthy of public concern unless a particular incident poses a particular threat to public safety. This is reflected in the paucity of extradition proceedings for the more mundane instances of computer misuse which cross traditional jurisdictional boundaries, notwithstanding the provisions within the 1990 Act which extend domestic jurisdiction for extra-territorial offences.

In summary, various aspects of computer misuse and the criminal law can be listed side by side as shown in Table 4.1. It is apparent that there is a clear mismatch between the features of computer misuse and the criminal law.

Table 4.1 Correspondence between features of computer misuse and the domestic criminal law

Computer misuse	Criminal law	Match?
Potential to cause serious or financial loss or threat to national security	Deals with significant issues of public concern	✓
Can be entirely within jurisdiction	Focuses on domestic jurisdiction	✓
Often crosses jurisdictional boundaries	Focuses on domestic jurisdiction	✗
Commonly causes bulk de minimis harms	Concerned with substantial harms	✗
Uncertain in definition	Requires certainty	✗
Commonly fleeting and uncertain	Requires certainty	✗
Generally viewed as a private wrong	Predominantly concerned with public wrong	✗
Not considered to be immoral	Concerned with upholding public morality	✗

Therefore, when considering computer misuse in terms of its mechanics, it suffers from ill-definition and fluidity; when considering it in terms of its substance, it is not generally particularly harmful. Since the use of the criminal law has difficulty in dealing with uncertainty and struggles to justify dealing with *de minimis* harms, it is doubtful that it is the sort of problem with which the domestic criminal law is entirely capable of dealing. It follows, therefore, that:

There are a number of incompatibilities between the nature of computer misuse and the nature of the criminal law. This means that computer misuse cannot be regulated effectively by the criminal law alone.

Part 2

The governance of computer misuse

Chapter 5

The risk of computer misuse and its governance

Often a certain abdication of prudence and foresight is an element of success.

Ralph Waldo Emerson (1803–82)

The first part of this book charted the evolution of both computer technology and computer misuse and surveyed the attempts of the domestic criminal law to control computer misuse. In doing so, it situated the problem within the framework of the existing criminal law and concluded that there are a number of incompatibilities between the nature of computer misuse and the nature of the domestic criminal law. These incompatibilities suggested that the domestic criminal law is only a partial means of control. This part of the book will build upon this conclusion by exploring the risks associated with computer misuse and evaluating the possibility of a multi-tiered governance approach as a potential solution to the problematised issues identified in the first part.

This chapter will introduce the theoretical framework upon which this part of the book will be based. It will begin by considering theories relating to risk from various perspectives. This will begin with a consideration of risk from a realist perspective, exploring the interrelationship between risk and insurance and examining the role of the state and the influence of moral hazard upon risk. The chapter will further consider risk from cultural and symbolic positions before introducing the concept of the 'risk society', its relationship with technology and its reflexive nature. This analysis of the risk society will lead into a consideration of risk from the governmentality standpoint. Having introduced these theories of risk, the chapter will move on to consider the idea of a governance network as a means of managing risk before concluding with an examination of the domestic criminal law discussed in the first part of the book in the light of these theories.

Risk

The first part of this book considered computer misuse in the context of a variety of offences established by the domestic criminal law, particularly those arising from the Computer Misuse Act 1990. Society is naturally concerned about the risk of crime and looks to the state to provide public assurance that the risk of crime is being controlled. However, risk itself is a much broader concept than that of crime. It encompasses pandemic risks; that is, risks that are global and which may be difficult to eradicate. Such risks include risks to health and risks to the environment, both of which figure prominently in the public discourse of contemporary western societies. Therefore it is necessary to consider what is meant by the concept of risk before surveying a range of theoretical perspectives within the 'continuum of epistemological approaches'[1] which have arisen on the topic.

The concept of risk

The concept of risk is not new. Ewald, for example, contends that the idea arose in the Middle Ages:

At that time, risk designated the possibility of an objective danger, an Act of God, a *force majeure*, a tempest or other peril of the sea that could not be imputed to wrongful conduct.[2]

This view sees risk as arising from ungovernable sources beyond human control and therefore as something unpreventable. It did not countenance the possibility of any human fault or responsibility and, as Walker and Broderick comment, represented 'pre-modern social attempts to understand catastrophes and hazards'.[3] A definition of

---

1 Lupton, D., *Risk* (Routledge, Abingdon, 1999) 35.
2 Ewald, F, in Luhmann, N., *Risk: A Sociological Theory* (Aldine de Gruyter, New York, 1993) 120.
3 Walker, C. and Broderick, J., *The Civil Contingencies Act 2004: Risk, Resilience and the Law in the United Kingdom* (Oxford University Press, Oxford, 2006) 2.

risk which is equally blame-free but broader than that which simply includes risks of nature is offered by Steele. This categorises risk as a simple state of affairs:

... we are faced with a situation of 'risk' when circumstances may (or importantly, may not) turn out in a way that we do not wish for.[4]

This concept of risk is characterised by a lack of human control and hence no attribution of blame.

However, the notion of risk evolved to include some element of measurement. A pervasive idea during the Industrial Revolution of the late eighteenth and early nineteenth centuries was that rationalised counting and ordering would control disorder.[5] Throughout the Industrial Revolution and into modernity,[6] the meaning and usage of risk changed to encompass a more scientific approach to quantifying and measuring events. Its boundaries were, as with Steele's definition, also extended beyond the natural world to 'human beings, in their conduct, in their liberty, in the relations between them, in the fact of their association, in society'.[7] This modern conception of risk as including things that were amenable to control therefore recognised that unanticipated outcomes may be the consequence of human action rather than 'expressing the hidden meanings of nature or ineffable intentions of the Deity'.[8] As a result, this notion of risk included an element of human responsibility and consequently the opportunity to attribute blame.

The everyday notion of risk is that of hazard, danger, exposure to mischance or peril. Here, the idea of 'mischance' incorporates the ideas of scientific probability, quantification and measurement first postulated during the Industrial Revolution. However, there is a range of theoretical positions that can be taken over and above this

4 Steele, J., *Risks and Legal Theory* (Hart, Oxford, 2004) 6.
5 Hacking, I., *The Taming of Chance* (Cambridge University Press, Cambridge, 1990).
6 The 'institutions and modes of behaviour established first of all in post-feudal Europe, but which in the twentieth century increasingly have become world-historical in their impact': Giddens, A., *Modernity and Self-Identity* (Polity Press, Cambridge, 1991) 14–15.
7 Ewald, F., 'Two infinities of risk', in Burchell, G., Gordon, C. and Miller, P. (eds) *The Politics of Everyday Fear* (University of Minnesota Press, Minneapolis, MN, 1993) 221, 226.
8 Giddens, A., *The Consequences of Modernity* (Polity Press, Cambridge, 1990) 30.

everyday notion. Of these, perhaps the most commonly encountered is the realist position which draws upon technical and scientific perspectives and theories of cognitive science. An alternative is the social constructionist approach which considers the social and cultural aspects of risk. Both weak and strong constructionist standpoints can be taken. The weak constructionist approach includes the 'risk society' analysis furthered by Ulrich Beck and Anthony Giddens as well as the 'cultural/symbolic' perspective favoured by anthropologist Mary Douglas. The strong constructionist stance is reflected in governmentality (a neologism for 'government rationality') theory which developed from the ideas of Michel Foucault.[9] Since there is a degree of overlap between these theoretical positions, they should be treated more as a spectrum of viewpoints than as a set of discrete theories, from the realist at one end to the strong constructionist, or relativist, at the other. These different theoretical positions are relevant to the problem of computer misuse, since computer technology is itself a product of late modernity and gives rise to a number of potential risks.

The realist perspective on risk

The realist perspective on risk draws on technical and scientific approaches to measurement and quantification. It considers risk in terms of the scale of its consequences and the likelihood that the risk will occur. From this standpoint, Bradley defines risk as 'the product of the probability and consequences (magnitude and severity) of an adverse event [that is, a hazard]'.[10] The success of such a definition will depend upon the accuracy with which the probability of the hazard has been identified and the scientific modelling of the magnitude and severity of the consequences should they occur.

An example of this perspective is provided by the BSE Inquiry Report[11] which reviewed the history of the emergence and identification of bovine spongiform encephalopathy (BSE) and new variant Creutzfeldt-Jakob disease (CJD) in the United Kingdom and the action taken in response to it. This report demonstrates how risk

9 Baker, T. and Simon, J., 'Embracing risk', in Baker, T. and Simon, J. (eds) *Embracing Risk: The Changing Culture of Insurance and Responsibility* (University of Chicago Press, Chicago, IL, 2002) 16.

10 Bradbury, J., 'The policy implications of differing concepts of risk' (1989) 14 *Science, Technology and Human Values* 380, 382.

11 The BSE Inquiry, *BSE Inquiry Report* HC (1999–2000) 887.

is associated with quantitative scientific techniques for measuring the uncertainty of events:

A risk is not the same as a hazard. A hazard is an intrinsic propensity to cause harm. Natural phenomena, physical substances, human activities will be hazardous if they have an intrinsic propensity to cause harm. A risk is the likelihood that a hazard will result in harm. A risk can usually be evaluated once the nature of the hazard and the degree of exposure to it are identified. Risk evaluation involves considering both the likelihood that a hazard will cause harm and the severity of the harm that is threatened.[12]

In essence, the measurement of likelihood and severity converts a hazard into a risk.

There is a natural tension between the public concern over risks (predominantly health and environmental risks) which result from science, technology and industry and the scientific, technological, industrial and governmental institutions associated both with the production of those risks and the responsibility for managing or responding to them. As Brown suggests, the primary objective of the techno-scientific approach to risk is to provide an objective measurement of risks in order to facilitate understanding and therefore 'to provide a route out of the ever-growing bitterness of clashes between affected publics and the managing institutions.'[13] However, it should be noted that although these scientific or industry bodies do not produce all risks, many of the risks within the prevailing social consciousness are of technical or scientific origin.

Risk and insurance

The quantification and measurement of risk which is inherent in the realist position can be considered in terms of insurance. For Ewald, risk is merely a term that is derived from insurance and that its only precise meaning relates to insurance.[14] Here, the term risk does not

12 Ibid. [162].
13 Brown, J., 'Introduction: approaches, tools and methods', in Brown, J. (ed.) Environmental Threats: Perception, Analysis and Management (Belhaven Press, London, 1989) 2.
14 Ewald, F., 'Insurance and risks', in Burchell, G., Gordon, C. and Miller, P. (eds) The Foucault Effect: Studies in Governmentality (University of Chicago Press, Chicago, IL, 1991) 197.

represent a hazard, but a means by which the occurrence of certain possibilities to certain individuals can be ordered and managed. Actuarial analysis (that is, measurement) of the likelihood of events and the quantification of contingent outcomes is undertaken in order to minimise losses, both emotional and financial, associated with uncertain and undesirable events. In other words, once the measurement of an uncertainty has converted it into a risk, then a budget can be identified and applied to that risk. Individuals and events are placed in 'risk categories'. These categories are further actuarial constructs.

An example of this risk categorisation approach can be found in psychiatry. The focus of debate in relation to patients with severe mental health problems moved during the 1990s from assessing the 'dangerousness' of those patients to calculating the risks that they posed. As Rose states:

[M]any within the criminal justice system argued for a shift from 'clinical' to 'actuarial' methods in the prediction of future conduct.[15]

Here, risk assessment becomes a tool for administrative decision-making rather than providing a strict legal categorisation. The potential level of risk posed by an individual becomes related to the resources which are allocated and deployed in insuring against that risk. The danger posed by 'high-risk' patients may be insured against by a higher level of physical security, the use of particular medication or increased vigilance and intervention by medical staff. 'Low-risk' patients will be managed in a different way. However, the risk categorisation is fluid. The risk posed by an individual is located on a continuum and is constantly fluctuating:

In practice ... all psychiatric patients can and should be allocated to a level of risk, risk assessed and risk re-assessed, risk classified, risk managed, risk monitored: high risk, medium risk, low risk – but rarely no risk.[16]

---

15 Rose, N., 'At risk of madness', in Baker, T. and Simon, J. (eds) *Embracing Risk: The Changing Culture of Insurance and Responsibility* (University of Chicago Press, Chicago, IL, 2002) 209, 212.
16 Ibid., 211.

Statutory assessment of 'dangerousness' is also required under the Criminal Justice Act 2003 (as amended)[17] for all offenders convicted of particular sexual and violent offences.[18] Here a 'dangerous offender' is one who has been convicted of a specified offence[19] and is assessed by the court as posing 'a significant risk to members of the public of serious harm occasioned by the commission … of further such offences'.[20] In cases which involve youth offenders, a structured risk assessment method called *Asset* is used.[21] Although 'significant risk' is not defined in the Act, the Court of Appeal has stated that:

> [Significant risk] is a higher threshold than mere possibility of occurrence and in our view can be taken to mean (as in the Oxford Dictionary) "noteworthy, of considerable amount or importance."[22]

Therefore, in relation to 'dangerousness', risks could not exist independently of classification following measurement. Therefore, in an insurance framework, the creation of risks requires both measurement *and* classification which reflects the realist paradigm of risk as being something amenable to quantification.

For Ewald, insurance creates 'epistemological transformations' leading to a 'philosophy of risk' in which risk is collective.[23] Collective risk represents the *aggregation* of information derived from the application of statistical methods to human affairs rather than individual decisions based on an assessment of probability. Therefore, for Steele, insurance 'contributes more decisively to freedom, because it releases us from fear'.[24] It is only by insuring against risks that the freedom to pursue an activity becomes possible.

---

17 Criminal Justice Act 2003, ss. 224–36, as amended by the Criminal Justice and Immigration Act 2008, s. 17.

18 The 'dangerousness' provisions only apply to offences committed after 4 April 2005.

19 Criminal Justice Act 2003, sch. 15 provides 153 specified violent and sexual offences.

20 Criminal Justice Act 2003, s. 229(1)(b).

21 Asset – Young Offender Assessment Profile <http://www.yjb.gov.uk/en-gb/practitioners/Assessment/Asset.htm> accessed 25 September 2008.

22 *R v. Lang and Others* [2005] EWCA Crim 2864 [17].

23 Steele, J., *Risks and Legal Theory* (Hart, Oxford, 2004) 34.

24 Ibid., 35.

Risk, reinsurance and the welfare state

Of course, the insurers also carry a portfolio of risks which require management. This is achieved by taking reinsurance with other insurers and therefore spreading the risk. Reinsurance may be taken to allow the insurer to assume greater individual risks than its size would otherwise allow and to protect itself by absorbing larger losses and therefore reducing the amount of capital needed to provide coverage. The insurer may also be motivated by arbitrage[25] in purchasing reinsurance coverage at a lower rate than that which they charge the insured for the underlying risk. This network of insurers is therefore one means of dealing with pandemic risk. The reinsurance network becomes the risk-taker of last resort. However, where a risk becomes too great, it will not be accepted by the insurers. For instance, in the aftermath of Hurricane Katrina, the costliest hurricane to hit the United States,[26] some insurance companies stopped insuring homeowners in the affected area.[27]

Ewald further argues that the development of insurance for those who share a common exposure to risk gives rise to solidarity. This solidarity and security are then devices used by the state to guarantee its current existence and to gain support for its continued existence. The development of insurance led to the modern welfare state as a form of social insurance. Therefore, using Ewald's reasoning, the welfare state gave rise to a collective solidarity within society which was reflected in securing the position of the state. In this model, the state becomes the (re)insurer of last resort. However, the UK welfare state which was created to provide lifelong care and to give financial support to the 'sick, the unemployed, the widow and the orphan as well as the aged'[28] has proven to be unsustainable for future generations. As Brans and Rossbach comment:

As 'welfare' is … potentially unlimited, the modern welfare state is at a loss to provide any objective indicators for the

---

25 The practice of taking advantage of a price differential between two or more markets.

26 Knabb, R.D., Rhome, J.R. and Brown, D.P., *Tropical Cyclone Report Hurricane Katrina*, US National Hurricane Centre (10 August 2006) <http://www.nhc.noaa.gov/pdf/TCR-AL122005_Katrina.pdf> accessed 25 September 2008.

27 Miller, M., 'More bad news blows in from Katrina', *CBS News* (Brooklyn, New York, 28 May 2006) <http://www.cbsnews.com/stories/2006/05/28/eveningnews/main1663142.shtml> accessed 25 September 2008.

28 Fraser, D., *The Evolution of the British Welfare State* (2nd edn, Macmillan, Basingstoke, 1984) 162.

boundaries of state activity. As a consequence, the political system is often the creator of the complexity it faces in its continuing operation.[29]

Therefore, increasing public expectation of what the welfare state could, or should, provide proved to be too great a burden, resulting in an unwieldy and inefficient system. The welfare state is returned to later in this chapter in the context of the risk society.

The potential inefficiencies of the welfare state were also examined by Hayek who considered that the costs associated with the welfare state required higher levels of taxation. These higher taxes, in turn, would reduce enterprise, limit freedoms, cripple prosperity and set society on a 'road to serfdom'.[30] For Hayek, the free market economy provided a more efficient and effective means of delivering protection than the welfare state, being more responsive to the needs of large numbers of individuals. This view is in keeping with that of the Chicago School who advocated free market libertarianism over the Keynesian mixed-economy model within which both the state and the private sector have particular roles to play.[31]

As well as identifying operational and economic inefficiencies in the welfare state, Hayek further argued that its advent would result in the decline of the rule of law. He offered two main grounds of contention. First, since the welfare state involves discriminating between the particular needs of different people, this violates the principle of equality before the law. Second, the administrative delivery of the welfare state can only be achieved by the extensive use of delegated discretionary powers which destroys the certainty required by the rule of law:

The important question is whether the individual can foresee the action of the state and make use of this knowledge as a datum in forming his own plans.[32]

However, for Jones, the existence of the welfare state is not incompatible with upholding the rule of law. Instead, the purpose of

29 Brans, M. and Rossbach, M., 'The autopoiesis of administrative systems: Niklas Luhmann on public administration and public policy' (1997) 75 *Public Administration* 417, 430.

30 Hayek, F.A., *The Road to Serfdom* (Routledge, Abingdon, 1944: 2001).

31 Miller, H.L., 'On the "Chicago School of Economics"' (1962) 70 *Journal of Political Economy* 64.

32 Ibid, 81.

the rule of law is in ensuring the fair operation of the welfare state:

> In the welfare state, the private citizen is forever encountering public officials of many kinds ... It is the task of the rule of law to see to it that these multiplied and diverse encounters are as fair, as just, and as free from arbitrariness as are the familiar encounters of the right-asserting private citizen with the judicial officers of the traditional law.[33]

Here Jones is advocating the role of judicial review by which, on the application of an individual, the courts may determine whether a public body has acted lawfully. Hayek concluded that the role of the state properly concerned the provision of a structure within which society can exist rather than acting in direct pursuit of social or welfare goals.[34]

As the welfare state has become unable to fulfil its function as a state insurer, individuals have taken increasing responsibility for their own care provision in the form of private pensions and private healthcare insurance. The responsibility for the management of risk previously handled by the social insurance of the welfare state has shifted to the individual. For Baker and Simon:

> ... private pensions, annuities and life insurance are engaged in a historic shift of investment risk from broad pools (the classic structure of risk spreading through insurance) to individual (middle-class) consumers and employees in return for the possibility of greater return.[35]

The risks that have arisen from the failings of the welfare state, particularly in terms of healthcare and pension provision, have coincided with the state gradually withdrawing its responsibility for individual welfare. Indeed, Powell et al. consider that 'the welfare system as a system of social insurance is beginning to lose its legitimacy with the rise of private health insurance'.[36]

---

33 Jones, H.W., 'The rule of law and the welfare state' (1958) 58 *Columbia Law Review* 143, 156.

34 Hayek, F.A., *The Road to Serfdom* (Routledge, Abingdon, 1944: 2001).

35 Baker, T. and Simon, J., 'Embracing risk', in Baker, T. and Simon, J. (eds) *Embracing Risk: The Changing Culture of Insurance and Responsibility* (University of Chicago Press, Chicago, IL, 2002).

36 Powell, J., Wahidin, A. and Zinn, J., 'Understanding risk and old age in western society' (2007) 27 *International Journal of Sociology and Social Policy* 65, 70.

However, this is not to say that the state no longer intervenes in insuring against certain risks. For instance, in the wake of the collapse of the Northern Rock bank in 2007, the Bank of England and HM Treasury intervened to guarantee all retail savings in its accounts. It is estimated that in early 2008, the bank borrowed approximately £30 billion from the Bank of England[37] 'to win back investor confidence'.[38] This financial guarantee is an example of the state insuring its citizens against a backdrop of rising interest rates and public concern over the economy. The state will also insure against major risks of collective national loss. An example of this is found in the Reinsurance (Acts of Terrorism) Act 1993 which underwrites any reinsurance liabilities entered into by the Secretary of State in respect of loss or damage to property resulting from acts of terrorism,[39] although the Act recognises that 'risk is to be managed rather than soothed away by the Keynsian welfare state or even by the sovereign instruments of security'.[40]

Risk, insurance and moral hazard

The concept of the 'moral hazard' refers to the effect of insurance on incentives,[41] implying that risk is not static but reactive.[42] In other words, the magnitude of a risk can be influenced by the presence of insurance. The effect of insurance can reduce the incentive to take care to avoid a loss and can also reduce the incentive to manage the costs associated with recovering from that loss.

For instance, an individual with fully comprehensive motor insurance may be less troubled by parking their car in an unsafe location, because the negative consequences of an attempt to (say) force the locks are, subject to any policy excess, borne by the insurer. This behaviour is clearly undesirable to the insurer as it increases the burden of risk upon them. The event which is insured therefore becomes more likely precisely because of the presence of the insurance itself. Similarly, some individuals without private health insurance choose to be more careful about maintaining a healthy lifestyle

37 Webster, P. and Seib, C., 'Alistair Darling props up Northern Rock with fresh £30bn debt guarantee', *The Times* (19 January 2008).

38 Northern Rock website <http://northernrock.co.uk> accessed 25 September 2008.

39 Reinsurance (Acts of Terrorism) Act 1993, s. 2(1).

40 Walker, C., 'Political violence and commercial risk' (2003) 56 *Current Legal Problems* 531, 575.

through their own actions because they would otherwise have to bear the full financial cost of healthcare, or rely upon the healthcare provision offered by the state. By implication, those covered by health insurance may take less care with their health, because not only do they not have to cover the costs of healthcare themselves, they are also more likely to be treated privately without recourse to the state. However, the effect of the moral hazard relies upon the personal cost-benefit analysis of the individuals concerned. Where the benefit does not outweigh the cost, there is a greater tendency to take care to avoid risk. Therefore, if an individual considers that the inconvenience of repairing a vandalised car outweighs the benefit of repair at no financial cost, they will park in a well-lit area rather than in a dark alleyway. Equally, it is difficult to imagine a situation in which a person will make a lifestyle choice which adversely impacts upon their health simply because they will receive treatment for the consequences without charge in a private hospital.

However, for Heimer,[43] the reaction to freedom from risk via insurance can be as harmful as the risk that the insurance attempts to prevent. An extreme example of such a moral hazard in action can be found in Vernon, Florida, also known as 'Nub City'. Over fifty people in the town suffered 'accidents' involving the loss of various organs and body parts. Claims of up to US$300,000 had been paid out by insurers. One insurance investigator noted that 'somehow they always shoot off parts they seem to need least'.[44] For the inhabitants of Vernon, the loss of a body part was outweighed by the financial gain offered by insurance. Using Steele's terminology, the prospect of a significant financial settlement released the claimants from the fear of maiming themselves.[45] Moral hazards also affect the welfare state. For example, the provision of incentives for the parents of children born out of wedlock, the unemployed and the poor will encourage some actively to have unwanted children or to refrain from seeking gainful employment. For example, Hull City Council offers the following advice for pregnant teenagers:

---

41 Baker, T., 'On the genealogy of moral hazard' (1996) 75 *Texas Law Review* 237.
42 Heimer, C.A., *Reactive Risk and Rational Action: Managing Moral Hazard in Insurance Contracts* (University of California Press, Berkeley, CA, 1985).
43 Ibid.
44 Dornstein, K., *Accidentally, on Purpose: The Making of a Personal Injury Underworld in America* (St. Martin's Press, New York, 1996) 265.
45 Steele, J., *Risks and Legal Theory* (Hart, Oxford, 2004) 35.

If you decide to keep the baby, you can get help and support on a range of issues, including benefits, childcare, housing, education and employment.[46]

Therefore, a potentially unwanted child can provide the means of access to a range of welfare benefits which would be unavailable to a childless teenager. Similar issues arise in relation to state unemployment benefit. As Wang and Williamson comment:

It is widely recognised that unemployment insurance systems need to be designed with moral hazard in mind. Unemployment insurance provides consumption-smoothing benefits which an unfettered private economy presumably cannot provide, but too much consumption-smoothing can clearly have bad incentive effects.[47]

In essence, where there is insufficient incentive to find work, then many unemployed people will prefer to remain unemployed. Employment is disincentivised through the availability of benefits which negate the economic need to seek paid work. The newly elected Labour government's 1997 budget focused on its 'welfare to work' programme, designed to get unemployed people off state benefits and back into employment by providing financial incentives to employers who recruited from the young or long-term unemployed, as well as offering training schemes to increase the long-term employability and earning potential of those returning to work. The Department for Work and Pensions describes the situation as follows:

We have created Jobcentre Plus as a world leading welfare to work organisation. We have introduced innovative employment programmes such as the New Deal, and we are now helping people on incapacity benefits through Pathways to Work. And we have improved incentives to work by providing greater support through the tax credit system and the introduction of the minimum wage.[48]

---

46 <http://www.hullcc.gov.uk/portal/page?_pageid=221,202942&_dad=portal&_schema=PORTAL> accessed 25 September 2008.

47 Wang, C. and Williamson, S., 'Unemployment insurance with moral hazard in a dynamic economy' (1996) 44 Carnegie-Rochester Conference Series on Public Policy 1.

48 Department for Work and Pensions <http://www.dwp.gov.uk/welfarereform/> accessed 25 September 2008.

The avoidance of moral hazard in relation to unemployment benefit remains a key state initiative.[49]

Heimer[50] proposed that control provides the mechanism by which moral hazard is managed. Where there is no control over loss, there can be no moral hazard. Since the insured cannot influence the chances of incurring or avoiding an insurable loss, then the presence of an insurance incentive will not change the odds of loss. The less the control that the insured has over loss, the more likely that loss is to be insurable and the more complete the insurance can be, since the calculation of risk is more certain and less dependent on the insured's reaction to freedom from risk. However, where the insured has a substantial degree of control over the risk of loss, insurance will often include the insured giving up at least some of that control to the insurer. The insurers require the insured to comply with certain conditions to mitigate against their potential losses through moral hazard. For instance, certain expensive cars will not be insured unless they are fitted with a recognised stolen vehicle recovery system and home insurance may require window locks compliant with a particular safety standard to be fitted. Heimer concludes that insurers require insured parties to retain *some* risks in what she calls a 'community of fate' between insurer and insured.[51] This lessens the incentive to take less care in reaction to insurance. Further mechanisms which are used include policy excesses, where the insured meets part of the financial cost of a claim, the use of neutral third-party loss adjusters to assess whether claimed losses are reasonable and reflexive updating of policies so that the interests of the insured are not significantly changed by a divergence between market value and insured value.

O'Malley considered the regulation imposed by household insurance contracts as a means of governance to minimise moral hazard as follows:

To protect its profits, especially against forms of moral hazard that are not prohibited under criminal law (and thus potentially

---

49 Secretary of State for Work and Pensions, *Ready for Work: Full Employment in Our Generation* (Cm 7290, 2007).

50 Heimer, C.A., *Reactive Risk and Rational Action: Managing Moral Hazard in Insurance Contracts* (University of California Press, Berkeley, CA, 1985).

51 Heimer, C.A., 'Insuring more, ensuring less: the costs and benefits of private regulation through insurance', in Baker, T. and Simon, J. (eds) *Embracing Risk: The Changing Culture of Insurance and Responsibility* (University of Chicago Press, Chicago, IL, 2002) 116, 122.

subject to state policing), the insurance company must establish its own legal order within the framework of the insurance contract. [This] establishes the coercive conditions for the operation of an enforcement network aimed at disciplining householders, in order to minimise the assumed moral hazard.[52]

The conditions imposed within insurance conditions are contractual in nature and are therefore enforceable via the civil law. Insurance contracts become, therefore, a legally enforceable means of regulating behaviour in order both to minimise risk and to mitigate against losses.

Constructionist perspectives on risk

The realist perspective, then, supposes that risk is an objective hazard, threat or danger that 'exists and can be measured independently of social and cultural processes' although it 'may be distorted or biased through social and cultural frameworks of interpretation'.[53] For example, in measuring social or cultural interpretations of risk, cognitive science theory takes the approach in which the 'hazard is taken as the independent variable and people's response to it as dependent'.[54] In other words, the hazard is varied by the experimenter and the response of the subject in relation to that hazard is measured to determine which hazards are subjectively 'riskier'. In this way, psychometric researchers have attempted to identify reactions to risks depending on the nature of the risk itself and the circumstances of the lay subject. For instance, in one study, familiar and voluntary hazards such as those from microwave ovens, food colourings and alcohol were viewed as less risky, while genetic engineering, ozone depletion and nuclear power were viewed as highly risky.[55] While the realist perspective of risk as quantified uncertainty appears to provide a rational, logical and scientific approach to risk management, it can be argued that it overlooks the construction of risks as social fact.

52 O'Malley, P., 'Legal networks and domestic security' (1991) 11 Studies in Law, Politics and Society 171, 172.

53 Lupton, D., Risk (Routledge, Abingdon, 1999) 35.

54 Douglas, M., Risk Acceptability According to the Social Sciences (Russell Sage Foundation, New York, 1985) 25.

55 Marris, C. and Langford, I., 'No cause for alarm', New Scientist (28 September 1996) 36.

There is also an inherent subjectivity in the measurement of risk. Scientific or actuarial opinion may differ as to the likelihood of a particular event, the range of contingent outcomes and the impact of those contingent outcomes. Subjective assumptions can be made which have a bearing in the final risk analysis. Nevertheless, the outcome of these risk measurements are often treated as 'objective facts' or 'absolute truths' in society.[56] The social and cultural influences upon risk have been acknowledged in some psychometric studies of risk[57] which concluded that 'further research was needed'[58] on socio-political factors, such as power, status, political orientation and perception of risk. Subjective perception of risks such as terrorism which pose a vivid and readily imaginable danger is hampered by the cognitive limitations of an emergency which may hinder accurate assessment of the magnitude and probability of certain types of risk. Gross argues that these cognitive limits can result in an over-exaggeration of risk since they 'color our risk assessment in times of crisis and create a strong tilt toward putting undue emphasis on certain potential risks'.[59] This subjective misperception of risk can in turn lead to undue public fear.[60] Sunstein refers to this as 'probability neglect', since 'when intense emotions are engaged, people tend to focus on the adverse outcome, not on its likelihood'.[61]

The distinction between objective and subjective risk is illustrated in the Royal Society report on risk[62] which argues that any situation gives rise to a range of objective risks to which individuals react in subjective ways. The risk itself remains objective and calculated by 'experts', while the judgements and responses of lay people are inevitably mediated through their social or cultural frameworks of interpretation of that risk. As Bradbury had already commented,

56 Bradbury, J., 'The policy implications of differing concepts of risk' (1989) 14 *Science, Technology and Human Values* 380, 382.

57 Flynn, J. and others, 'Gender, race and perception of environmental health risks' (1994) 14 *Risk Analysis* 1101; Graham, J. and Clemente, K., 'Hazards in the news: who believes what?' (1996) 4 *Risk in Perspective* 1.

58 Lupton, D., *Risk* (Routledge, Abingdon, 1999) 24.

59 Gross, O., 'Chaos and rules: should responses to violent crises always be constitutional?' (2003) 112 *Yale Law Review* 1011, 1038.

60 Posner, E.A., 'Fear and the regulatory model of counterterrorism' (2002) 25 *Harvard Journal of Law and Public Policy* 681, 685.

61 Sunstein, C.R., 'Probability neglect: emotions, worst cases and law' (2002) 112 *Yale Law Journal* 61, 63.

62 Royal Society, *Risk: Analysis, Perception and Management* (Royal Society, London, 1992).

individual responses to risk are a 'subjectivist interpretation within a realist paradigm'.[63]

However, reaction to the Royal Society report was mixed, with favour being found in the chapters which aligned risks and risk management with technical and scientific thought (and thus the objectivity of the realist perspective) rather than in the chapters considering the more subjective socio-cultural spheres of politics and economics:

> Four chapters good, two chapters bad (with apologies to George Orwell) appears to have been the orthodoxy's response ... The 'good' four chapters were those written by distinguished engineers, statisticians and natural scientists, which reflected a view of public risk management as properly the domain of science and engineering rather than of politics and economics.[64]

Traditional hard science does not generally consider the symbolic meanings attributed to events or the cultural frameworks through which responses and judgements are mediated. Instead, individuals are represented as self-interested, nuclear and rational. It can therefore be argued that this conception of an individual is unrepresentative of reality and that there is, to a greater or lesser extent, an element of social constructionism in risk. There are various theories which adopt the constructionist position with varying degrees of strength. The weak constructionist position includes the cultural and symbolic perspectives favoured by anthropologist Mary Douglas and the concept of the 'risk society' which draws on the work of Ulrich Beck and Anthony Giddens. There is also the Foucault-inspired strong constructionist governmentality perspective.

Cultural and symbolic perspectives on risk

Douglas is highly critical of the realist perspectives on risk, particularly in relation to the attempts made by cognitive science to measure, and thereby understand, perceptions and responses to risks:

---

63 Bradbury, J., 'The policy implications of differing concepts of risk' (1989) 14 *Science, Technology and Human Values* 380, 384.
64 Hood, C. and Jones, D.K.C. (eds) *Accident and Design* (UCL Press, London, 1996) xi.

The professional discussion of cognition and choice has no sustained theorising about the social influences which select particular risks for attention. Yet it is hard to maintain seriously that perception of risk is private.[65]

One of Douglas's main criticisms is that the cognitive science approach presupposes that individuals are rational and logical in their assessment of, and their reaction to, risk:

Warm-blooded, passionate, inherently social beings though we think we are, humans are presented in this context as hedonic calculators calmly seeking to pursue private interests. We are said to be risk-averse, but, alas, so inefficient in handling information that we are unintentional risk-takers; basically we are fools.[66]

Douglas argues that the realist perspective erroneously assumes that individuals rationally gauge their response to a risk in a detached and objective fashion. Moreover, she considers that, in any case, individuals are ill-equipped to make rational judgements on the basis of scientific data as cultural concerns also influence the ways in which risks are perceived. For Douglas, risk is a 'contemporary western strategy for dealing with danger and Otherness'[67] and is concerned with the reasons why some hazards are identified as risks and others are not.

Engaging in risky behaviour is, for Douglas, not the product of lay deficiency of understanding, but a preference. She contends that 'to account for preferences there is only cultural theory'.[68] Therefore risks are culturally relative and scientific techniques for their measurement do not acknowledge the related cultural issue of whether a risk is to be judged acceptable or not. Indeed, some individuals choose to participate in activities that are considered to be risky to 'escape and resist reality'.[69] Douglas links risk and blame, considering risk to be

65 Douglas, M., *Risk Acceptability According to the Social Sciences* (Russell Sage Foundation, New York, 1985) 3.
66 Douglas, M., *Risk and Blame: Essays in Cultural Theory* (Routledge, Abingdon, 1992) 13.
67 Lupton, D., *Risk* (Routledge, Abingdon, 1999) 36.
68 Douglas, M., *Risk and Blame: Essays in Cultural Theory* (Routledge, Abingdon, 1992) 103.
69 Cohen, S. and Taylor, L., *Escape Attempts: the Theory and Practice of Resistance to Everyday Life* (2nd edn, Routledge, Abingdon 1992).

a political means of attributing blame for a hazard that threatens a particular social group. However, despite the inclusion of cultural factors in her approach to risk, Douglas's perspective represents a weak constructionist position in that she accepts that risks do objectively exist independent of culture:

... the reality of dangers is not at issue. The dangers are only too horribly real, in both cases, modern and pre-modern. This argument is not about the reality of dangers, but about how they are politicised. This point cannot be emphasised too much.[70]

Douglas's early work considers the rituals of pollution and cleanliness across a range of societies and considers how taboos act to protect cultures from potentially destabilising behaviour. Building upon this analysis, Douglas treats the human body as analogous to a community and draws parallels between the boundaries of the human body and the boundaries of society. In this analysis, dirt symbolically represents disorder and cleanliness represents order:

[Dirt] is essentially disorder. There is no such thing as absolute dirt: it exists in the eye of the beholder ... Dirt offends against order. Eliminating it is not a negative movement, but a positive effort to organise the environment.[71]

For Douglas, risk is a cultural response to transgressing a boundary and is used as a political means of blaming an Other who poses a risk to the integrity of the self. In contemporary western culture, the preoccupation with technological and environmental hazards is interpreted against a moral and political cultural framework that inextricably links risk and blame:

In all places at all times the universe is moralised and politicised. Disasters that befoul the air and soil and poison the water are generally turned to political account: someone already unpopular is going to be blamed for it.[72]

70 Ibid, 29.
71 Douglas, M, *Purity and Danger: An Analysis of Concepts of Pollution and Taboo* (Routledge Classics, Routledge & Kegan Paul, London, 1966) 2.
72 Douglas, M, *Risk and Blame: Essays in Cultural Theory* (Routledge, Abingdon, 1992) 5.

Douglas considers that current concerns about risk have emerged as a product of globalisation, which has resulted in 'inter-community discourse and a sense of vulnerability in being part of a world system'.[73] She believes that 'new concern with risk' is part of 'a public backlash against the great corporations'.[74] The public at risk represents the self which demonises and blames the corporations or the state as an Other. Therefore risk is used as a tool of social control to maintain moral and social order. Social structures generate cultural biases toward the world that serve to uphold those social structures.

The grid-group model considers different approaches to risk perception as expressed in these social structures. It proposes that social structures differ along two axes. 'Group' refers to the degree of solidarity between members of the society, that is 'the outside boundary that people have erected between themselves and the outside world'.[75] 'Grid' refers to the extent to which individual behaviours are influenced by social position, that is 'all the other social distinctions and delegations of authority that [people] use to limit how people behave to one another'.[76] Each axis has two categories – high and low – which gives rise to four approaches to risk as shown in Table 5.1

Individualists are entrepreneurial. Their choices are not constrained by social position and they are not closely bound to others within a social group. They trust individuals rather than corporations and support self-regulation of risk. Fatalists are, like individualists, without strong social cohesion but are constrained by their position in the face of an external world which imposes those constraints upon them. They therefore take a passive stance in relation to risk, believing that they have little personal control over it, trusting instead to luck and

Table 5.1   The grid-group model of risk perception

	Low grid	High grid
Low group	Individualist	Fatalist
High group	Egalitarian	Hierarchist

73 Lupton, D., *Risk* (Routledge, Abingdon, 1999) 48.
74 Douglas, M., *Risk and Blame: Essays in Cultural Theory* (Routledge, Abingdon, 1992) 5.
75 Douglas, M. and Wildavsky, A., *Risk and Culture: An Essay on the Selection of Technological and Environmental Dangers* (University of California Press, Berkeley, CA, 1982) 138.
76 Ibid.

fate. Egalitarians have a strong sense of solidarity but little concern with social position. They have a strong sense of group self and blame outsiders for risk. They tend to distrust external constraints and are sensitive to risks with low probability but high consequence and use those risks to forward concerns of an impending apocalyptic outcome. Egalitarians also advocate the precautionary principle, discussed later in this chapter, and are adverse to the risks potentially introduced by new technology. Hierarchists have well-defined roles for each member of society, respect authority, fear social deviance, trust in established organisations and conform to group norms relating to risk.

While providing a readily accessible conceptualisation of socially mediated approaches to risk, the model can be criticised for its rigidity and inflexibility in dealing with individuals who constantly cross between the categories. It also treats the risk as a constant. The response to the risk is predicated on the societal categorisation rather than the nature of the risk itself. However, it can also be argued that it is the world view that determines what is categorised as risk in the first place. In any event, it provides a basis upon which the interplay between risk and culture can be conceptualised.

The cultural and symbolic perspectives on risk adopt a functional structuralist approach to examine the ways in which socio-cultural systems and organisations view and manage risk to maintain social order and deal with deviance from accepted social norms. Alternatively a critical structuralist approach can be adopted which examines the way in which social institutions exercise power over individuals. The 'risk society' theories of Beck and Giddens generally take such a critical structuralist approach.

The 'risk society'

Both Beck and Giddens consider that contemporary western societies are transforming from industrial societies to 'risk societies'. The risk society perspective concerns itself with the ways in which risk interrelates with late modernity. In that sense, it adopts a weak constructionist approach. In common with the realist view, the risk society perspective considers risks to be objective hazards. However, it further considers that risks are inevitably mediated through social and cultural processes and cannot be measured or evaluated in isolation from those processes.

In risk societies, the production of wealth is accompanied by the production of risks, the number of which have grown as a consequence of modernisation. The focus of risk societies has moved from the production and distribution of wealth prevalent in early modernity (and which remains so in contemporary developing countries) to the prevention or limitation of risks. Therefore a risk society is preoccupied with managing risk rather than producing or distributing wealth, since it is risk itself that can inhibit the generation of wealth. In turn, the proliferation of risks has resulted in individuals living in risk societies becoming increasingly risk-aware.

Risk society and the welfare state

Beck's analysis builds on Ewald's notion of the 'provident' state.[77] The provident state makes various forms of insurance available against rationalised calculated uncertainties. The growth of risks in line with wealth production has led to risks permeating many aspects of the day-to-day existence of risk-aware individuals. Consequently, society as a whole becomes a risk group with the state as its insurer. The provident state model is a basis upon which models of the welfare state can be founded. The UK welfare state was introduced by the Labour government of 1945, founded on the principles outlined in the 1942 Beveridge report into the ways that Britain should be rebuilt after the Second World War.[78] Beveridge proposed a system which was designed to counter the five 'giant evils' of illness, ignorance, disease, squalor and want. The report considered the whole question of social insurance, arguing that want could be abolished by a system of social security organised for the individual by the state:

The proposals of the Report mark another step forward to the development of State insurance as a new type of human institution, differing both from the former methods of preventing or alleviating distress and from voluntary insurance. The term 'social insurance' to describe this institution implies both that it is compulsory and that men stand together with their fellows. The term implies a pooling of risks except so far as separation of risks serves a social purpose.[79]

The notion of men standing (compulsorily) together with their fellows echoes Heimer's community of fate, which in this case is between

77 Ewald, F., *L'Etat Providence* (Editions Grasset, Paris, 1986).
78 Fraser, D., *The Evolution of the British Welfare State* (2nd edn, Macmillan, Basingstoke, 1984).
79 Beveridge, W., *Social Insurance and Allied Services* (Cmd 6404, 1942) [25].

the state and its collective society. As Giddens comments, wealth redistribution via the new welfare state became the new solution to counter social ills:

> The welfare state became the left's project in the post 1945-period – it became seen above all as a means of achieving social justice and income redistribution. By and large, however, it did not originate as such. It developed as a security state, a way of protecting against risk, where collective rather than private insurance was necessary.[80]

Beck considers that the welfare state transitions into a risk society where the production of risks becomes so great that it threatens to overload the state insurer's ability to deal with those risks:

> The entry into risk society occurs at the moment when the hazards which are now decided and consequently produced by society undermine and/or cancel the established safety systems of the provident state's existing risk calculations.[81]

It could therefore be argued that the problems encountered by the UK's welfare state (which Brans and Rossbach partially attributed to the 'potentially unlimited' nature of welfare) were symptomatic of a transition to a risk society. In risk society terms, as both the quantity and the public awareness of risks has increased, society has made greater demands of the welfare state to provide more comprehensive insurance against those risks. In doing so, public expectation of the scope of the welfare state's provision also increased, which led to strain upon the system as a whole.

More recently, even the Labour Party have come to accept that the foundations of socialist ideals, such as the welfare state and nationalised industry, have become untenable. The 'Third Way' philosophy of governance is also closely associated with the work of Giddens.[82] It has characterised 'New Labour' from the mid-1990s, mixing both market (capitalist) and interventionist (socialist)

80 Giddens, A., 'Risk society: the context of British politics', in Franklin, J. (ed.) *The Politics of Risk Society* (Polity Press, Cambridge, 1998) 27.
81 Beck U., 'Risk society and the provident state', in Lash, S., Szerszynski, B. and Wynne, B. (eds), *Risk, Environment and Modernity* (Sage, London, 1996) 27, 31.
82 Giddens, A., *The Third Way: Renewal of Social Democracy* (Polity Press, Cambridge, 1998).

philosophies and stressing technological development, education and competition as the vehicles by which to pursue economic progress and state objectives. Within this Third Way, the role of the state is to provide proactive welfare which enables individuals to respond to the risks of globalisation. For Driver and Martell:

[W]here globalisation is bound up with the new digital information and communication technologies and the 'knowledge economy', individuals need the education and training appropriate to these conditions. Public policy should support business in the creation of 'knowledge-rich products and services' which will be the source of future economic growth.[83]

Within the risk society, then, there is a clear link between economic stability and the use of technology.

Risk society and technology

Beck considers that there is a difference between 'a risk itself' and the 'public perception' of that risk. In other words, he differentiates between objective and subjective risk. In reference to the proliferation of risks, he considers that 'it is not clear whether it is the risks that have intensified, or our *view* of them'.[84] However, he continues by arguing that, since risks are 'risks in knowledge', perceptions of risks and risks themselves are actually 'not different things, but one and the same'.[85] Beck is more explicit in terms of the relationship between the social construction of risk and science. Here he argues that risks are 'social constructs which are strategically defined, covered up or dramatised in the public sphere with the help of scientific material supplied for the purpose'.[86] Therefore, for Beck, there is an inherent relationship between risk, technology and social process.

Many risks resulting from technological advances are not spatially or temporally constrained. Risks may arise at any time and within any geographic or jurisdictional boundary. Technological risks may affect vast numbers of individuals. Therefore, as Williams and Carr

---

83 Driver, S. and Martell, L., 'Left, Right and the third way' (2000) 28 *Policy and Politics* 147, 150.
84 Ibid.
85 Beck, U., *Risk Society: Towards a New Modernity* (Sage, London, 1992) 55.
86 Beck, U., 'World risk society as cosmopolitan society? Ecological questions in a framework of manufactured uncertainties' (1996) 13(4) *Theory, Culture and Society* 1.

suggest, the 'old orders which bound time and space have lost meaning or become disembodied'[87] and therefore the ill-defined new 'order' which is consequently more difficult to control is reasonably seen as being inherently less secure. Lenk concurs in no uncertain terms:

> Society therefore has no choice but to defend itself against unknown dangers flowing from our technological achievements. We are at war with our own products and with our overwhelming technological skills. [88]

For Giddens,[89] such disembodied order is a defining characteristic of high modernity. The risks which are caused by technological and scientific advances are complex. In early industrialised society, risks could generally be perceived by the senses whereas many current risks are imperceptible and exist 'in scientific knowledge rather than in everyday experiment'.[90] Beck cites examples of risks 'localised in the sphere of physical and chemical formulas (e.g. toxins in foodstuffs or the nuclear threat)'.[91] This inherent uncertainty brings the conceptualisation of risk back to the pre-modern idea of risks as 'incalculable insecurities'.[92] However, unlike pre-modern risks which could not be imputed to wrongful conduct, contemporary hazards are linked to scientific and technological innovation and therefore carry human responsibility. Technological advances are the result of human endeavour and thus in late modernity have become a product of knowledge. Therefore human knowledge is both a source of risks and a means by which they may be controlled. It follows that contemporary risks arise from decisions in furtherance of techno-economic advantage and utilitarian concerns made by a network of organisations and political groups. For Beck:

87 Williams, K.S. and Carr, I., 'Crime, risk and computers' (2002) 9 *Electronic Communication Law Review* 23, 26.
88 Lenk, K., 'The challenge of cyberspatial forms of human interaction to territorial governance and policing', in Loader, B. (ed.) *The Governance of Cyberspace* (Routledge, Abingdon, 1997) 133.
89 Giddens, A., *The Consequences of Modernity* (Polity Press, Cambridge, 1990).
90 Lupton, D., *Risk* (Routledge, Abingdon, 1999) 64.
91 Beck, U., *Risk Society: Towards a New Modernity* (Sage, London, 1992) 21.
92 Beck, U., *Ecological Politics in the Age of Risk* (Polity Press, Cambridge, 1995) 77.

[I]t is not the number of dead and wounded, but rather a social feature, their industrial self-generation, which makes the hazards of mega-technology a political issue. [93]

Both Beck[94] and Giddens[95] refer to this concept as 'manufactured uncertainty'. The ultimate effect of technological advances is often difficult to assess prior to the introduction and adoption of the new technology. However, technological development requires financial investment. The desire to protect investment may lead technologists to play down or refuse to calculate risks. Economic pressure will then lead politicians to provide reassurance that any such risks are insubstantial. As Beck argues:

[D]angers are being produced by industry, externalised by economics, individualised by the legal system, legitimised by the sciences and made to appear harmless by politics. [96]

This manufactured uncertainly is for Giddens:

... the defining characteristic of what Ulrich Beck calls risk society. A risk society is one in which we increasingly live on a high technological frontier which absolutely no one completely understands and which generates a diversity of possible futures. [97]

A contemporary example of manufactured uncertainty can be found in the social responses to the risk of climate change which has been linked to anthropogenic factors resulting from attempts to improve the standard of living via industrialisation. Here scientists claim that the technological advances associated with the industrial world, in particular the increase in carbon dioxide levels due to emissions from the combustion of fossil fuels, are resulting in an undesirable global climate shift with a range of potential associated risks which will:

---

93 Beck, U., 'From industrial society to risk society: questions of survival, social structure and ecological enlightenment' (1992) 9 *Theory Culture and Society* 98.

94 Beck, U., 'Politics of risk society', in Franklin, J. (ed.) *The Politics of Risk Society* (Polity Press, Cambridge, 1998).

95 Giddens, A., *Beyond Left and Right* (Polity Press, Cambridge, 1994).

96 Beck, U., 'Politics of risk society', in Franklin, J. (ed) *The Politics of Risk Society* (Polity Press, Cambridge, 1998) 16.

97 Giddens, A., 'Risk and responsibility' (1999) 62 *Modern Law Review* 1, 3.

... cause more and more costly damage and disrupt the functioning of our natural environment, which supplies us with food, raw materials and other vital resources. This will negatively affect our economies and could destabilise societies around the globe.[98]

However, scientific responses to combat climate change may yet manufacture their own uncertainties. For example, in a bid to be more energy efficient, the Environment Secretary, Hilary Benn, outlined government plans to phase out the sale of traditional incandescent light bulbs in the UK by 2011[99] in favour of 'low-energy' bulbs. However, these low-energy bulbs, themselves the product of technological advance, have been claimed to exacerbate a range of ailments from migraines[100] to disabling eczema-like reactions and light sensitivities that can lead to skin cancer.[101]

For Furedi, however, a model of the world in which 'the so-called manufactured risks created by humanity are sharply counterposed to the "natural" risks of the past' is 'extremely one-sided'.[102] Although there is some correspondence between risk and technological advance in contemporary western society, Furedi argues that natural risks such as those from famine, flood or lightning are minimised because 'of the high levels of safety assured by scientific and technological advance'.[103] There are not such levels of technology assured security in other parts of the world and further, even in the West, 'traditional' dangers outweigh the risks posed by technology. For Furedi, the technological foundation of manufactured risk 'continually underestimates the social influences of such perceptions' since risks do not transcend society.[104] Instead risks 'affect people in relation to their power and influence'.[105] This is a profoundly Marxist perspective.

---

98 European Commission Climate Change website <http://ec.europa.eu/environment/climat/campaign/what/climatechange_en.htm> accessed 25 September 2008.

99 Naughton, P., 'UK to phase out traditional light bulb by 2011', *The Times* (27 September 2007).

100 Clout, L., 'Energy-saving light bulbs blamed for migraines', *Daily Telegraph* (3 January 2008) <http://www.telegraph.co.uk/earth/main.jhtml?xml=/earth/2008/01/03/eabulb103.xml> accessed 25 September 2008.

101 —, 'Low-energy bulbs "could cause skin cancer"', *Daily Telegraph* (5 January 2008) <http://www.telegraph.co.uk/earth/main.jhtml?xml=/earth/2008/01/05/eabulb105.xml> accessed 25 September 2008.

102 Furedi, F., *Culture of Fear Revisited* (4th edn, Continuum, London, 2006) 64.

103 Ibid.

104 Ibid., 65.

105 Ibid.

Risk society and reflexivity

In the risk society, Beck argues that risk is linked to reflexivity:

[Risks are a] *systematic way of dealing with hazards and insecurities induced and introduced by modernisation itself.* Risks, as opposed to older dangers, are consequences which relate to the threatening force of modernisation and to its globalisation of doubt. They are *politically reflexive.*[106]

This 'globalisation of doubt', or society's awareness of the global nature of risk, influences the development of cooperative international institutions. The management of global risk requires a network of bodies which transcend the traditional boundaries of the nation state to provide a coordinated approach to its management. For Lupton this leads to the 'the boundaries of the political [being] removed, leading to world-wide alliances'.[107] Therefore, the risk society is transformed into a 'world risk society' with corresponding 'global citizenship' focused on the world-wide perspective, generating new alliances in a new and different form of politics beyond traditional hierarchies.[108]

For Beck, reflexive modernisation is a two-stage process. The first stage occurs as part of the transition from industrial society to risk society, which involves the production and proliferation of new risks as a side effect of modernisation. However, at this stage the risks are not in the public concern or subject to political debate. In the second stage, there is a growing realisation of the risks inherent in modernisation. Industrial society then sees itself as a risk society and begins to self-examine and critique its own structures. Beck himself defines reflexive modernisation as:

the combination of reflex and reflections which, as long as the catastrophe itself fails to materialise, can set industrial modernity on the path to self-criticism and self-transformation. Reflexive modernisation contains both elements: the reflex-like threat to industrial society's own foundations through a successful

---

106 Beck, U., *Risk Society: Towards a New Modernity* (Sage, London, 1992) 21.
107 Lupton, D., *Risk* (Routledge, Abingdon, 1999) 66.
108 Beck, U., 'World risk society as cosmopolitan society? Ecological questions in a framework of manufactured uncertainties' (1996) 13(4) *Theory, Culture and Society* 1, 2.

further modernisation which is blind to dangers *and* the growth of awareness, the reflection of this situation.[109]

Therefore, the risk society is characterised by this critical reflection (which Beck calls 'self-confrontation').[110] As risks become reflexive, global and therefore not amenable to control by nation states, the response of the state is often denial. Giddens refers to this in the context of the crisis in the welfare state as 'a crisis of risk management in a society dominated by a new type of risk'.[111] Risk society theory is therefore properly concerned with the distribution and management of risk rather than avoiding or eradicating risk. Politics in the risk society transcends the traditional state-focused hierarchies, requiring wider political debate and new forms of organisation 'for science and business, science and the public sphere, science and politics, *technology and law* and so forth'[112] (emphasis added).

At the time of the Enlightenment, geometric order, rigour and reductionism were seen as the means by which human progress would be achieved. Science represented a source of established knowledge which was considered to be more reliable than the knowledge that had been acquired personally by any single individual. However, in late modernity, lay people have come to question scientific knowledge. The emergence of the global risk society has raised a collective awareness that science may have produced many of the risks that are matters of social concern. Moreover, there is a social awareness that scientific knowledge about risk may be incomplete or contradictory. As Lupton comments:

People must deal, therefore, with constant insecurity and uncertainty: conventional social order seems to be breaking down in the face of the undermining of old certainties.[113]

There is, therefore, a natural tension between the scientists as producers of risks and the lay public as the consumers of risks. This tension is

109 Beck U., 'Risk society and the provident state', in Lash, S., Szerynski, B. and Wynne, B. (eds) *Risk, Environment and Modernity* (Sage, London, 1996) 27, 34
110 Beck, U., 'Politics of risk society', in Franklin, J. (ed.) *The Politics of Risk Society* (Polity Press, Cambridge, 1998) 18.
111 Giddens, A., 'Risk society: the context of British politics', in Franklin, J. (ed.) *The Politics of Risk Society* (Polity Press, Cambridge, 1998) 33.
112 Beck, U., 'From industrial society to risk society: questions of survival, social structure and ecological enlightenment' (1992) 9 *Theory Culture and Society* 98, 119.

manifested in the increasing willingness of the lay public to critique scientific findings based on the increased availability of knowledge. While technological advances brought about through science and engineering have given rise to communications technology that has greatly increased the accessibility and depth of information available to the public, it is also the same information that can be used to cast doubt on new science. For Beck, the process of modernisation and the pace of scientific advance has undermined the basis of rational thought since society 'is placed under permanent pressure to negotiate foundations without a foundation'.[114] The risks themselves become reflexive:

In contrast to early industrial risks, nuclear, chemical, ecological and genetic engineering risks (a) can be limited in terms of neither time nor place, (b) are not accountable according to the established rules of causality, blame and liability and (c) cannot be compensated or insured against.[115]

More risks are generated in response to the scientific or technical means of controlling the initial risk. Beck argues that these global technological risks are immune to control by insurance. For Giddens, this proliferation of risk reveals scientific knowledge to be 'inherently sceptical and mutable'.[116] Science may not be able to solve the problems that it has created. Beck is supportive of the lay person's sceptical response to technical and scientific risk. Rather than dismissing them as ignorant, simply requiring more information about the risk in order to respond appropriately, he argues that their apparent 'irrationality' is actually a highly rational response to the failure of technical and scientific rationality in the context of the proliferation of risks in late modernity.[117] Moreover, for Beck, the pandemic risks of modernisation have an equallising effect, and therefore risk societies are distinct from class societies. Many of these risks affect classes in the same way: 'poverty is hierarchic, smog is democratic'.[118] The

113 Lupton, D., Risk (Routledge, Abingdon, 1999) 67.
114 Beck, U., 'From industrial society to risk society: questions of survival, social structure and ecological enlightenment' (1992) 9 Theory Culture and Society 98, 118.
115 Beck U., 'Risk society and the provident state', in Lash, S., Szersynski, B. and Wynne, B. (eds) Risk, Environment and Modernity (Sage, London, 1996) 27, 31.
116 Giddens, A., 'Risk society: the context of British politics' in Franklin, J. (ed.) The Politics of Risk Society (Polity Press, Cambridge, 1998) 23–4.
117 Beck, U., Risk Society: Towards a New Modernity (Sage, London, 1992) 59.
118 Ibid., 36.

risks affect those who have produced or profited from them and thereby transcend both class and state boundaries; for Beck they possess an inherent tendency towards globalisation.[119] That said, the educated classes have sufficient information to be concerned about risk but insufficient information to be able to reconcile or quell that anxiety.[120]

The role of the state and governmentality

The regulatory role of the state in the management and distribution of risk is linked with the notion of the risk society. Hood *et al.* consider that:

> As well as a 'risk society' we are also said to live in a 'regulatory state' … The idea of the 'regulatory state' is that a new institutional and policy style has emerged in which government's role as regulator advances while its role as a direct employer or property-owner may decline through privatisation and bureaucratic downsizing.[121]

From this viewpoint, the role of the state is to regulate the distribution of risks across society but not to control those risks since they are inherently uncontrollable. This shifts responsibility for risk management from the state to the individual. The idea of individualisation forms part of Beck's view of the risk society[122] and is also a key theme in the governmentality perspective on risk.

The governmentality perspective is similar to that of the risk society in that it interests itself in the ways in which risk operates in late modernity. However, unlike risk society theories which take a weak constructionist position, governmentality theory adopts a strong constructionist position. This position has developed from the work of Foucault. Although Foucault did not consider the topic of risk at great length, his commentary on governmentality and modernity has been drawn upon to extrapolate a socio-cultural analysis of risk.

---

119 Ibid.
120 Ibid., 53.
121 Hood, C., Rothstein, H. and Baldwin, R., *The Government of Risk: Understanding Risk Regulation Regimes* (Oxford University Press, Oxford, 2001) 4.
122 Beck, U., 'The reinvention of politics: towards a theory of reflexive modernisation', in Beck, U., Giddens, A. and Lash, S., *Reflexive Modernisation: Politics, Tradition and Aesthetics in the Modern Social Order* (Polity Press, Cambridge, 1994) 13.

For Foucault, governmentality is the approach to social regulation and control that began to emerge in Europe in the sixteenth century, associated with the breakdown of the feudal system and the development of legitimately ruling administrative states.[123] Contemporary governmentality is, for Foucault, characterised by neo-liberalism which prioritises individual freedom and rights against excessive state intervention. However, part of the remit of governmentality is concerned with risk:

The things with which in this sense government is to be concerned are in fact men, but men in their relations, their links, their imbrication with those other things which are wealth, resources, means of subsistence, the territory with its specific qualities, climate, irrigation, fertility, etc.; men in their relation to the other kind of things, customs, habits, ways of acting and thinking, etc.; lastly men in their relation to that other kind of things, accidents and misfortunes such as famines, epidemics, death, etc.[124]

Like Beck and Giddens, Foucault emphasises the importance of expert scientific knowledge in propagating the late modern subjectivity of risk. However, rather than as a device to catalyse reflexivity, expert knowledge is, for Foucault, the means by which populations are normalised. The technology of surveillance and measurement is used to construct understanding and hence becomes a means of regulation. Lupton summarises Foucault's perspective on risk as

... a governmental strategy of regulatory power by which populations and individuals are monitored and managed through the goals of neo-liberalism. Risk is governed by a heterogeneous network of interactive actors, institutions, knowledges and practices.[125]

This normalising activity problematises risk, thereby rendering it calculable and thence governable. In this sense, Foucault's position is similar to that of Ewald's social actuarialism. For Ewald, risk from

---

123 Foucault, M., 'Governmentality', in Burchell, G., Gordon, C. and Miller, P. (eds) *The Foucault Effect: Studies in Governmentality* (University of Chicago Press, Chicago, IL, 1991) 87.
124 Ibid., 93.
125 Lupton, D., *Risk* (Routledge, Abingdon, 1999) 87.

Foucault's perspective is 'a moral technology. To calculate a risk is to master time, to discipline the future'.[126]

Governmentality includes both direct and indirect strategies to regulate society, relying on voluntary compliance by the autonomous self-regulated individual with state interests and needs as well as coercive and directive regulation. Individuals become participants in governmental discourse and become self-policing in pursuit of their own neo-liberal interests and freedoms.[127] The development of risk through normalisation and aggregation leads to a consensus view of how individuals should then regulate their own conduct. In other words, individuals seek information from scientific experts based on risk analysis in order to apply that expert knowledge to themselves. Lupton uses the example of the pregnant woman in contemporary western society to illustrate this point.[128] Women are surrounded by a broad spectrum of expert and lay advice as to how they should behave both before and during pregnancy in order to minimise the risks to their unborn child. As such, a woman is positioned in a web of surveillance, requiring her to seek out expert advice and act upon it, lest she be found culpable in the event of miscarriage or birth defect. She may actively demand increased surveillance by way of medical examination to alleviate concerns about the risks. Failure to engage in risk-avoidance is a 'failure of the self to take care of itself – a form of irrationality, or simply a lack of skilfulness'.[129] Avoiding risks becomes a moral enterprise, accepting and internalising the objectives of government in what Foucault terms 'practices' or 'technologies of the self'.[130] Risks therefore become products of historical, social and politically contingent viewpoints. It is rationalisation and calculation in an attempt to control uncertainty and disorder that brings risk into being. In the strong constructionist Foucauldian perspective, it is only by categorising something as 'risky' through a process of

---

126 Ewald, F., 'Insurance and risks', in Burchell, G., Gordon, C. and Miller, P. (eds) *The Foucault Effect: Studies in Governmentality* (University of Chicago Press, Chicago, IL, 1991) 197.
127 Gordon, C., 'Governmental rationality', in Burchell, G., Gordon, C. and Miller, P. (eds) *The Foucault Effect: Studies in Governmentality* (University of Chicago Press, Chicago, IL, 1991) 1.
128 Lupton, D., *Risk* (Routledge, Abingdon, 1999) 89–91.
129 Greco, M., 'Psychosomatic subjects and the "duty to be well": personal agency within medical rationality' (1993) 22 *Economy and Society* 357.
130 Foucault, M., 'Technologies of the self', in Martin, L., Gutman, H. and Hutton, P. (eds) *Technologies of the Self: A Seminar with Michel Foucault* (Tavistock, London, 1988) 16.

calculated normalisation that renders it as requiring management. As Ewald put it:

Nothing is a risk in itself; there is no risk in reality. But on the other hand, anything *can* be a risk; it all depends on how one analyses the danger, considers the event.[131]

Therefore, risks only come into social existence when human actors recognise and label them as such.[132]

For Dean, there is more than the risk society perspective of the globalisation of risks that are becoming more difficult to calculate.[133] Rather than behaving as members of a specific society or Ewald's provident state, individuals with a dominant notion of selfhood move between small community- or affiliation-based groups to deal with risk. These groups have limited and dynamic constituencies and interests. Individuals exposed to 'high risk', either as a perpetrator or victim of that risk, take control to prevent that risk through their own actions rather than relying upon state intervention or state insurance. Individuals are imbued with moral and political qualities and are self-interested and responsible. In the same way that the rational choice theory within situational crime analysis presents the criminal as one who weighs up pros and cons, means and ends, costs and benefits, and makes a rational choice to commit an offence,[134] victims become rational choice actors with the responsibility for self-protection by taking action to minimise personal risks and are culpable should they become victims of crime.[135] The use of risk as a technique of social

131 Ewald, F., 'Insurance and risks', in Burchell, G., Gordon, C. and Miller, P. (eds) *The Foucault Effect: Studies in Governmentality* (University of Chicago Press, Chicago, IL, 1991) 197, 199.

132 Fox, N., 'Postmodern reflections on "risks" "hazards" and life choices', in Lupton, D. (ed.) *Risk and Sociocultural Theory: New Directions and Perspectives* (Cambridge University Press, Cambridge, 1999).

133 Dean, M., 'Risk, calculable and incalculable', in Lupton, D. (ed.) *Risk and Sociocultural Theory: New Directions and Perspectives* (Cambridge University Press, Cambridge, 1999).

134 Cornish, D. and Clarke, R. (eds), *The Reasoning Criminal* (Springer-Verlag, New York, 1986); Akers, R., 'Rational choice, deterrence and social learning theory in criminology: the path not taken' (1990) 81 *Journal of Criminal Law and Criminology* 653.

135 O'Malley, P., 'Risk, power and crime prevention' (1992) 21 *Economy and Society* 252.

control has also been explored in relation to tort law and accidents[136] as well as directly to criminal justice and penal policy.[137]

In general, then, the strong constructionist position in relation to the governance of risk places less reliance on social insurance and more on autonomous self-management, self-protection and self-responsibility. This position is in furtherance of the neo-libertarian political ethos which emphasises self-help and minimalises the extent to which the state will intervene in the management of risks.

Governance

There is a common theme, then, within the various analyses of risk, of the withdrawal of the direct intervention of the state in the management and regulation of risks in favour of diffuse networks of risk management actors enabling individuals to take responsibility for themselves within the 'new legal order' offered through insurance. For O'Malley:

> ... these responsibilising processes seemingly *democratise* government through the mobilising of risk and uncertainty. Individuals and communities are made free to choose how they will govern themselves in relation to a host of insecurities.[138]

Therefore, since the potential risks that could result from the creative misuse of emergent technology are by their very nature unforeseen, the question to be considered is how such unforeseen risks should be addressed. This model of risk management by individuals and communities working alongside the state is referred to as 'governance'.

In general terms, governance is synonymous with government. The *Oxford English Dictionary* defines governance as 'the action or manner of governing' or 'the office, function or power of governing'. Governing is in turn defined as ruling 'with authority, especially

---

136 Simon, J., 'The emergence of a risk society: insurance, law and the state' (1987) 95 *Socialist Law Review* 61.

137 Feeley, M. and Simon, J., 'The new penology: notes on the emerging strategy of corrections and its implications' (1992) 30 *Criminology* 449; Feeley, M. and Simon, J., 'Actuarial justice: the emerging new criminal law', in Nelken, D. (ed.) *The Futures of Criminology* (Sage, London, 1994).

138 O'Malley, P., *Risk, Uncertainty and Government* (Glasshouse, London, 2004) 11.

with the authority of a sovereign, to direct and control the actions and affairs of … a state'.[139]

However, the ambit of the term has expanded to encapsulate something distinct from government which includes non-state contributors. For example, Hyden considers that:

Governance is the stewardship of formal and informal political rules of the game. Governance refers to those measures that involve setting the rules for the exercise of power and settling conflicts over such rules.[140]

For Rhodes 'governance … in complex systems'[141] and for Hirst and Thompson 'governance … is a function that can be performed by a wide variety of public and private, state and non-state, national and international, institutions and practices'.[142] Inherent in all these definitions is a recognition of something broader than government which includes informal as well as formal rules, described by Kjær as 'networks of trust and reciprocity crossing the state–society divide'.[143] This notion of some degree of independence from the state is echoed by Rosenau:

Global governance is conceived to include systems of rule at all levels of human activity – from the family to the international organisation – in which the pursuit of goals through the exercise of control has transnational repercussions.[144]

This is consistent with the reducing role of the state and its power in late modernity.[145] As with Hyden, Rosenau's definition of governance also involves the concept of a network: in this instance, a transnational network of states, providing global governance within a framework of international relations. Rhodes provides a complementary perspective:

139 —, *Oxford English Dictionary Online* <www.oed.com> accessed 25 September 2008.
140 Hyden, G., 'Governance and the reconstruction of political order', in Joseph, R. (ed.) *State, Conflict and Democracy in Africa* (Lynne Rienner, Boulder, CO, 1999).
141 Rhodes, R.A.W., 'The hollowing out of the state: the changing nature of the public service in Britain' (1994) 65 *Political Quarterly* 138, 151.
142 Hirst, P. and Thompson, G., 'Globalisation and the future of the nation state' (1995) 24 *Economy and Society* 408, 422.
143 Kjær, A.M., *Governance* (Polity Press, Cambridge, 2004) 4.
144 Rosenau, J.N., 'Governance in the twenty-first century' (1995) 1 *Global Governance* 13.
145 Giddens, A., *The Consequences of Modernity* (Polity Press, Cambridge, 1990).

Governance refers to self-organising, interorganisational networks characterised by interdependence, resource-exchange, rules of the game and significant autonomy from the state.[146]

As Kjær summarises, definitions of governance focus 'on the role of networks in the pursuit of common goals'. These networks may consist of a variety of state and non-state participants active in a particular area of policy. The degree of cohesion will naturally vary from network to network. However, some networks may become sufficiently concerted and cohesive to resist or even to challenge the powers of the state, thereby becoming self-regulatory structures within their policy sector.[147] In this situation, the powerful governance networks regulate more according to the agendas of the individual actors within the network than a consideration of public policy in the collective interest. For Pierre and Peters, such self-organising networks short-circuit the democratic process by separating control and responsibility.[148] The state depends on the specific expertise and the means of interest representation in the network which influences policy although the interests of the network may challenge the interests of the state. From a Marxist standpoint, there is conflict between the state and the governance network who compete for power. The state may require a network to bring non-state participants into the development and governance of a policy area, yet the resulting policies may be obstructed by that network. The position of the network as an autonomous and self-governing body is therefore considerably strengthened. For Kickert:[149]

Government is only one of many actors that influence the course of events in a societal system ... Other social institutions are, to a great extent, autonomous. They are not controlled by any single superordinated actor, not even the government. They control themselves. Autonomy not only implies freedom, it implies self-responsibility ... Deregulation, government withdrawal and

---

146 Rhodes, R.A.W., *Understanding Governance: Policy Networks, Governance, Reflexivity and Accountability* (Open University Press, Buckingham, 1997) 15.
147 Marsh, D. and Rhodes, R.A.W. (eds) *Policy Networks in British Government* (Clarendon Press, Oxford, 1992).
148 Pierre, J. and Peters, B.G., *Governance, Politics and the State* (Macmillan, Basingstoke, 2000) 20.
149 Kickert, W., 'Complexity, governance and dynamics: conceptual explorations of public network management', in Kooiman, J. (ed.) *Modern Governance* (Sage, London, 1993) 275.

steering at a distance ... are all notions of less direct government regulation and control, which lead to more autonomy and self-governance for social institutions.

The network becomes self-organising and self-regulating by reference to negotiated and agreed 'rules of the game'.[150] These rules are based on trust relationships between members of the network, made in furtherance of negotiated shared purposes and with significant autonomy from the state. There is therefore a self-referential relationship between the network and its environment with change being generated from within. As such the governance network could be considered to be an example of an autopoietic system.[151] However, the state may indirectly steer the network towards a desired configuration or common goal: the network does not enjoy complete autonomy. Rhodes attempts to draw these definitional strands together in suggesting that the shared characteristics of governance are interdependence between organisations, continuing interaction between network members, game-like interactions rooted in trust and a significant degree of autonomy from the state.[152]

Although the functionality of these networks is based on trust relationships, Furedi considers that there is a general erosion of legitimacy and authority in contemporary society which is expressed in the loss of public trust in science. This tendency has led to fear about the consequences of technological developments and is one 'of the most visible elements in the growth of risk consciousness itself'.[153] There is therefore a relationship between declining trust and increasing consciousness of risk.[154]

The increasing shift towards a governance approach to certain areas of policy throughout the 1980s and 1990s has been described as the 'hollowing out' of the authority of central government.[155] For Rhodes, this covers four interrelated trends:

(1) Privatisation and limiting the scope and forms of public intervention.

150 Kjaer, A.M., *Governance* (Polity Press, Cambridge, 2004) 7.
151 Morgan, G., *Images of Organisation* (Sage, London, 1986) 235–45.
152 Rhodes, R.A.W., *Understanding Governance: Policy Networks, Governance, Reflexivity and Accountability* (Open University Press, Buckingham, 1997) 53.
153 Furedi, F., *Culture of Fear Revisited* (4th edn, Continuum, London, 2006) 137.
154 Misztal, B., *Trust in Modern Societies* (Polity Press, Cambridge, 1996).
155 Weller, P. and others (eds) *The Hollow Crown: Countervailing Trends in Core Executives* (Macmillan, London 1997).

(2) The loss of functions by central and local government departments to alternative service delivery systems (such as agencies).

(3) The loss of functions by British government to European Union institutions.

(4) Limiting the discretion of public servants through the new public management, with its emphasis on managerial accountability, and clearer political control through a sharper distinction between politics and administration.[156]

Castells considers that nation states are losing their capacity to govern due to the 'globalisation of core economic activities, globalisation of media and electronic communication and globalisation of crime'.[157] This view recognises the decentralised nature of the information technology networks and the corresponding facilitation of trans-jurisdictional criminal activity. Barlow takes the notion of the dwindling capacity for nation states to control global technology networks further still:

... the Internet is too widespread to be easily dominated by any single government. By creating a seamless global economic zone, borderless and unregulatable, the Internet calls into question the very idea of a nation-state.[158]

Reidenberg argues in a similar vein:

The new paradigm must recognise all dimensions of network regulatory power. As a complex mix of rule-makers emerges to replace the simple, state sovereign, model, new policy instruments must appear that are capable of establishing important norms of conduct for networks.[159]

It is common ground, then, that governance blurs the distinction between the state and society with the state becoming a collection of networks with no sovereign actor able to steer or regulate. Forms

---

156 Rhodes, R.A.W., 'The hollowing out of the state: the changing nature of the public service in Britain' (1994) 65 *Political Quarterly* 138.

157 Castells, M., *The Power of Identity (The Information Age: Economy, Society and Culture Volume 2)* (2nd edn, Blackwell, Oxford, 2004) 244.

158 Barlow, J.P., 'Thinking locally, acting globally', *Time* (15 January 1996).

159 Reidenberg, J., 'Governing networks and rule-making in cyberspace' (1996) 45 *Emory Law Journal* 911, 926.

of economic and political organisation are affected.[160] Braithwaite considers that risk management 'decentralises the role of the state' compared with corporations and hybrid public/private regulators.[161] Offe concurs, stating that

the outcomes of administrative action are in many areas not the outcomes of authoritative implementation of pre-established rules, but rather the results of a 'co-production' of the administration and its clients. [162]

Although these governance networks can be seen to be a challenge to traditional democratic accountability by blurring the single point of control inherent in the government there is a counter-viewpoint that the existence of governance networks can empower citizens:

Given a world where governance is increasingly operative without government, where lines of authority are increasingly more informal than formal, where legitimacy is increasingly marked by ambiguity, citizens are increasingly capable of holding their own by knowing when, where and how to engage in collective action.[163]

Similarly, Fox and Miller suggest that by participation as users and governors in networks, citizens may be regaining control of government in the creation of a post-modern public administration:

Networks ... which transcend hierarchical institutions provide a feasible model for public administration. Some policy networks, interagency consortia, and community task forces exhibit potential for discourse. In these nascent forms are found think tank experts, legislative staff, policy analysts, public administrators, interested citizens, process generalists and even

160 Stewart, A., *Theories of Power and Domination: The Politics of Empowerment in Late Modernity* (Sage, London, 2001).

161 Braithwaite, J., 'The new regulatory state and the transformation of criminology' (2000) 40 *British Journal of Criminology* 222, 228–9.

162 Offe, C., *Contradictions of the Welfare State* (Hutchinson, London, 1984) 310.

163 Rosenau, J.N., 'Citizenship in a changing global order', in Rosenau, J.N. and Czempiel, E.-O., *Governance without Government: Order and Change in World Politics* (Cambridge University Press, Cambridge, 1992) 291.

elected officials participating together to work out possibilities for what to do next.[164]

In essence, the state and society are bonded together in the process of creating governance.[165] Lenk considered that the state can no longer control technology by itself and foresaw the potential emergence of a governance approach to its control:

> Taken together, badly designed technology, *misused technology* and unmastered technology concur to put society in a position where it can no longer aspire to regulating and controlling all details through its political institutions. Well-regulated sectors will co-exist with others from where we may expect influences which trigger the emergence of new types of individual and collective behaviour.[166] (emphasis added.)

This viewpoint acknowledges that the state is not impotent in its ability to regulate networked technologies. As Willmore comments, 'Governments are not helpless when it comes to regulation of the Internet'.[167] Hirst and Thompson agree that 'if ... mechanisms of international governance and re-regulation are to be initiated, then the role of nation states is pivotal',[168] although the partnership between society and the state has necessarily limited the scope of state intervention. However, the state does still have a role to play in direct regulation, that is, legislation as a means of control. Public concern regarding threats to society are frequently met by legislative response to political pressure, even where there is little evidence to support the perception of the risk, in other words where social subjectivity outweighs current scientific objectivity. Examples of swift legislative response include the Dangerous Dogs Act 1991 in response to various incidents of serious injury or death resulting from attacks

---

164 Fox, C.J. and Miller, H.T., *Postmodern Public Administration: Towards Discourse* (Sage, London 1995) 149.

165 Pierre, J. and Peters, B.G., *Governance, Politics and the State* (Macmillan, Basingstoke, 2000) 49.

166 Lenk, K., 'The challenge of cyberspatial forms of human interaction to territorial governance and policing', in Loader, B. (ed.) *The Governance of Cyberspace* (Routledge, Abingdon, 1997) 134.

167 Willmore, L., 'Government policies towards information and communication technologies: a historical perspective' (2002) 28 *Journal of Information Science* 89, 95.

168 Hirst, P. and Thompson, G., 'Globalisation and the future of the nation state' (1995) 24 *Economy and Society* 408, 430.

by aggressive and uncontrolled dogs, the firearms ban in the Firearms (Amendment) (No 2) Act 1997 following the Dunblane Massacre in 1996 and the Football (Disorder) Act 2000 extending banning orders in response to football violence following the Euro 2000 match between England and Germany in Charleroi. Such legislative activity links the notions of risk and the regulatory state. For Hood *et al.*

The two ideas of 'risk society' and 'regulatory state' could, indeed, be linked in so far as risk and safety are often held to be one of the major drivers of contemporary regulatory growth, for example in the development of EU regulations.[169]

However, in relation to the Football (Disorder) Act 2000, the Home Secretary, Jack Straw, acknowledged that 'legislation is only part of the answer to the wider problem'.[170] This implies that the wider problem requires a governance response which is in line with the postmodern risk society theories where 'the trajectory of social development is taking us away from the institutions of modernity towards a new and distinct type of social order'.[171]

For Baker and Simon, the preoccupation with embracing risk encompasses a broader idea of 'governing through risk', the core idea of which is 'the use of formal considerations about risk to direct organisational strategy and resources'.[172] Therefore, informed decisions about risk influence the organisational strategies and deployment of resources within the members of the governance network. It follows that legislative strategy as formulated by government as one member of the governance network is influenced by formal considerations of risk. In Simon's view,[173] the role of the criminal law in relation to governance has changed such that advanced industrial societies are increasingly governing themselves through crime. The focus has shifted towards 'shaping the actions of many other individuals in spaces, practices and institutions far beyond the criminal justice

169 Hood, C., Rothstein, H. and Baldwin, R., *The Government of Risk: Understanding Risk Regulation Regimes* (Oxford University Press, Oxford, 2001) 4.

170 Hansard HC vol. 353 col. 172 (4 July 2000).

171 Giddens, A., *The Consequences of Modernity* (Polity Press, Cambridge, 1990) 46.

172 Baker, T. and Simon, J., 'Embracing risk', in Baker, T. and Simon, J. (eds) *Embracing Risk: The Changing Culture of Insurance and Responsibility* (University of Chicago Press, Chicago, IL, 2002) 1, 11.

173 Simon, J., 'Governing through crime', in Friedman, L. and Fisher, G. (eds) *The Crime Conundrum: Essays on Criminal Justice* (Westview Press, Boulder, CO, 1997); Simon, J., 'Managing the monstrous: sex offenders and the new penology' (1998) 4(1) *Psychology, Public Law and Policy* 1.

system'.[174] Although criminal offences are still committed against the state, the impetus for control comes from offering protection to the innocent victim and ensuring the security of the general public. This control is therefore organised in terms of 'an increasingly pervasive "fear of crime"'.[175] For Furedi, fear, and in particular the fear of crime, has become a distinct cultural phenomenon in a society where the 'uncertainties of day-to-day existence' produce anxieties that are echoed in discussions on crime.[176] He argues further that crime is more controlled by informally enforced social rules – in effect peer pressure – than formal policing. However, Ericson and Haggerty consider that policing does have a role to play in governance:

Crime risk, and fear of it, has become the basis for police involvement in governance well beyond crime control itself.[177]

Therefore, for Ericson and Haggerty, risk society is 'characterised by the marketing of [in]security' which gives rise to a reflexive awareness of insecurity by the plethora of security products available which in turn leads to an increased level of fear.[178] The role of 'dangerousness' in relation to the policing of convicted sexual and violent offenders under the Criminal Justice Act 2003[179] has already been discussed. A further example of the interplay between risk and policing can be found in the range of preventative measures against anti-social behaviour, such as anti-social behaviour orders,[180] curfew orders[181] and dispersal orders,[182] which may be employed to manage the risk of crime without proof of a crime having been committed. This philosophy also extends to control orders in relation to terrorism[183] and the recent introduction of serious crime prevention orders.[184]

174 Rose, N., 'At risk of madness', in Baker, T. and Simon, J. (eds), *Embracing Risk: The Changing Culture of Insurance and Responsibility* (University of Chicago Press, Chicago, IL, 2002) 209, 230

175 Ibid.

176 Furedi, F., *Culture of Fear Revisited* (4th edn, Continuum, London, 2006) 5.

177 Ericson, R.V. and Haggerty, K.D., 'The policing of risk', in Baker, T. and Simon, J. (eds) *Embracing Risk: The Changing Culture of Insurance and Responsibility* (University of Chicago Press, Chicago, IL, 2002) 238, 257

178 Ibid. 269.

179 Criminal Justice Act 2003, ss. 224–36.

180 Crime and Disorder Act 1998, s. 1(1).

181 Crime and Disorder Act 1998, s. 14.

182 Anti-social Behaviour Act 2003, s. 30.

183 Terrorism Act 2005, s. 1(1).

184 Serious Crime Act 2007, s. 1(1).

The precautionary principle

The precautionary principle is simply to 'avoid steps that will create a risk of harm'.[185] It is traditionally associated with failures of the assimilative capacity approach to environmental risk which considers the extent to which the environment can accommodate or tolerate pollutants. For Hey, this approach is 'based on certain assumptions regarding the relationship between environment, science, technology and economics'.[186] The approach fails where scientific proof of potential harm resulting from particular activities or substances has come too late to prevent the realisation of that harm and such failures have led to a re-prioritisation 'in favour of a bias towards safety and caution'.[187] As Hey comments:

[The precautionary] concept requires that policy-makers adopt an approach which ensures that errors are made on the side of excess environmental protection ... [It] may require preventative action before scientific proof of harm has been submitted.[188]

This precautionary approach recognises the limitations of science to make accurate predictions about future consequences of particular activities. It has been claimed that the precautionary principle is becoming established in customary international law:

Opinion remains divided as to whether the precautionary principle may have crystallised into a binding norm of customary international law. However, the prevalence of the principle in recent environmental treaties, declarations and resolutions ... suggests that it may indeed have attained this status.[189]

---

185 Sunstein, C.R., 'Beyond the precautionary principle' (2003) 151 *University of Pennsylvania Law Review* 1003.

186 Hey, E., 'The precautionary concept in environmental policy and law: institutionalising caution' (1992) 4 *Georgetown International Environmental Law Review* 303, 308.

187 Freestone, D., 'The road to Rio: international environmental law after the Earth Summit' (1996) 6 *Journal of Environmental Law* 193, 211.

188 Hey, E., 'The precautionary concept in environmental policy and law: institutionalising caution' (1992) 4 *Georgetown International Environmental Law Review* 303, 307.

189 McIntyre, O. and Mosedale, T., 'The precautionary principle as a norm of customary international law' (1997) 9 *Journal of Environmental Law* 221, 235.

The principle has certainly been reflected within various international documents, such as the United Nations World Charter for Nature,[190] the Rio Declaration on Environment and Development[191] and the Treaty on European Union which states that:

Community policy on the environment shall … be based on the precautionary principle and on the principles that preventive action should be taken, that environmental damage should as a priority be rectified at source and that the polluter should pay.[192]

However, although the Treaty does not offer a definition of the principle, the European Commission considered that its scope is 'much wider' than the environment and should be used:

specifically where preliminary objective scientific evaluation indicates that there are reasonable grounds for concern that the potentially dangerous effects on the *environment, human, animal or plant health* may be inconsistent with the high level of protection chosen for the Community.[193] (emphasis added.)

The principle therefore concerns itself with potentially dangerous effects within a structured analysis of risk assessment, risk communication and, most significantly, risk management. In essence, the precautionary principle places a burden of proof on the producers of a product or proponents of an activity to demonstrate that their product or activity is 'safe'. An example of this can be found in the law relating to defective consumer products. The Consumer Protection Act 1987 establishes strict liability in tort on any supplier of defective goods which cause damage as a result of the defect.[194] There are limited statutory defences to this tort, although potential defendants may escape liability if they can prove that the state of scientific or technical knowledge was such that the defect was

---

190 United Nations, *World Charter for Nature*, UN Doc A A/RES/37/7 (1982).
191 United Nations, *Rio Declaration on Environment and Development*, UN Doc A/Conf. 151/5/Rev. 1 (1992).
192 Art. 174(2) EC.
193 Commission (EC), *Communication from the Commission on the Precautionary Principle*, COM (2000) 1 final, 2 February 2000.
194 Consumer Protection Act 1987, s. 2(1).

unknown and unforeseeable when the product was circulated.[195] This allows suppliers to use manufactured uncertainty as a defence.

The essence of the precautionary principle, then, is that activities which create a risk of harm should be approached cautiously until safety is proven through clear scientific evidence. Precaution also applies the idea of substitution. Where 'safer' alternatives are available these should be promoted over the risky activity. This creates reasonable suspicion of the riskier option and an impetus for the safer alternative.

In terms of governance and regulation, the state needs to make itself aware of the extent of the uncertainty within the available scientific information and determine an acceptable level of risk for society. This determination is an inherently political exercise, requiring consideration of the risk itself, scientific doubt and public concern. The public concern element is amplified in situations which evoke strong emotional responses, such as terrorism. This leads to 'probability neglect' where public response to risk tends to overlook its likelihood in favour of fearing its outcome.[196] Moreover, responses to risks vary across societies. As Wiener comments in comparing the responses of the United States and Europe to use of the precautionary principle:

Viewed across the array of risks, both the United States and Europe are precautionary about many risks (and both resist precaution regarding other risks), but they repeatedly differ as to which risks to worry about and regulate most or earliest.[197]

The reflection of cultural factors in the adoption of the precautionary principle demonstrates that it is related to social constructions of risk as well as to governance. As previously discussed, the correspondence between precaution and social constructions of risk is particularly marked for egalitarians who are especially sensitive to risks of low probability but high consequence. The precautionary principle does not, therefore 'resolve the problems associated with uncertainty

---

195 Consumer Protection Act 1987, s. 4(1)(e); *A and Others v. National Blood Authority and Others* [2001] 3 All ER 289 (DC).

196 Sunstein, C.R., 'Essay: on the divergent American reactions to terrorism and climate change' (2007) 107 *Columbia Law Review* 503, 540.

197 Wiener, J.B., 'Whose precaution after all? A comment on the comparison and evolution of risk regulatory systems' (2003) 13 *Duke Journal of Comparative and International Law* 207, 262.

because in some senses it merely draws attention to them'.[198] Once attention has been drawn to a risk, it still does not necessarily follow that a legal response is required to mitigate against that risk. There is a continuum of regulatory responses from commissioning further research, issuing guidelines or making recommendations to the binding use of the law.

Sunstein argues that, in many ways, the precautionary principle seems 'quite sensible, even appealing,'[199] considering that:

People buy smoke alarms and insurance. They wear seatbelts and motorcycle helmets, even if they are unlikely to be involved in an accident. Should rational regulators not follow the same approach as well?[200]

He describes the principle as a 'plea for a kind of regulatory insurance'[201] and acknowledges, as does Steele, that the principle demands that neglected problems receive attention. However, he argues that the over-adherence to the principle will be 'paralyzing, forbidding every imaginable step, including no step at all'.[202]

As far as technological or scientific advances are concerned, there are many examples of the precautionary principle at work. For instance, in relation to mobile telephones, the report of the Independent Expert Group on Mobile Phones chaired by Sir William Stewart in 2000 concluded that, despite the fact that the balance of evidence to date did not suggest that emissions from mobile telephones and base stations put the health of the UK population at risk:

... we recommend that a precautionary approach to the use of mobile phone technologies be adopted until much more detailed and scientifically robust information on any health effects becomes available.[203]

The Social Issues Research Centre encapsulated this reasoning as 'just because there is no evidence of harm, that does not mean that

---

198 Steele, J., *Risks and Legal Theory* (Hart, Oxford, 2004) 194.
199 Sunstein, C.R., 'Beyond the precautionary principle' (2003) 151 *University of Pennsylvania Law Review* 1003, 1007.
200 Sunstein, C.R., 'The paralyzing principle', *Regulation* (Winter 2002–3) 32.
201 Sunstein, C.R., 'Beyond the precautionary principle' (2003) 151 *University of Pennsylvania Law Review* 1003, 1007.
202 Ibid., 1008.

something is not harmful'[204] before concurring with Sunstein that it represents a 'serious obstacle to rational discussion'.[205] The SIRC article considers that the precautionary principle works to prevent, rather than encourage, scientific debate since the burden of proof is placed upon a scientific community which is often powerless to respond rationally and logically to those who make 'unjustified and whimsical claims'.[206] Therefore, even though there was no hard scientific evidence that mobile telephones were unsafe, there was some doubt that they might be and the Stewart Report recommended that:

... national and local government, industry and the consumer should all become actively involved in addressing concerns about possible health effects of mobile phones.[207]

In doing so, they advocated a networked approach to addressing the risk posed by the problem which is in line with the idea of a cooperative and collaborative approach to governance. From this, it is possible to conclude that the precautionary principle is 'essentially linked with a participatory and pluralistic approach to governing'.[208] However, the precautionary principle could also be linked to Furedi's notion of 'governing through fear' and unnecessary regulation in the face of limited scientific evidence of risk. In some instances, it has been argued that the official precautionary reaction to an event can prove far more damaging than the event itself. For example, following the outbreak of foot-and-mouth disease in the UK in 2001, the European Commission banned all British milk, meat and livestock exports. Six million animals were slaughtered in response to 2,030 confirmed cases of the disease which resulted in an estimated overall cost to the UK economy of around £5 billion.[209] Despite this criticism, the UK government appears to be committed to the use of the precautionary principle. The United Kingdom Interdepartmental

---

203 Independent Expert Group on Mobile Phones, *Mobile Phones and Health* (2000) [1.20] <http://www.iegmp.org.uk/report/text.htm> accessed 25 September 2008.
204 Social Issues Research Centre, *Beware the Precautionary Principle* <http://www.sirc.org/articles/beware.html> accessed 25 September 2008.
205 Ibid.
206 Ibid.
207 Independent Expert Group on Mobile Phones, *Mobile Phones and Health* (2000) [1.24] <http://www.iegmp.org.uk/report/text.htm> accessed 25 September 2008.
208 Steele, J., *Risks and Legal Theory* (Hart, Oxford, 2004) 195.
209 Royal Society, *Infectious Diseases in Livestock* (Royal Society, London, 2002).

Liaison Group on Risk Assessment (UK-ILGRA) considered that the purpose of the precautionary principle is 'to create an impetus to take a decision notwithstanding scientific uncertainty about the nature and extent of the risk' and stated that 'although there is no universally accepted definition, the Government is committed to using the precautionary principle'.[210] A recent example of this can be found in the UK Parliamentary report on harmful content on the Internet and in video games.[211] This report concluded that:

> ... there is still no clear evidence of a causal link [between exposure to violent content and violent behaviour]; but incontrovertible evidence of harm is not necessarily required in order to justify a restriction of access to certain types of content in any medium, and ... any approach to the protection of children from online dangers should be based on the probability of risk.[212]

This demonstrates the application of the precautionary principle in a technological environment.

Risk, computer misuse and the domestic criminal law

The first part of this book concluded that the problems posed by computer misuse cannot readily be encapsulated within the parameters of the domestic criminal law due to a number of incompatibilities between their respective natures. Moreover, Chapters 2 and 3 identified a number of potential risks which arise as a result of computer misuse. Many of these risks were also identified within the debates prior to the enactment of the Computer Misuse Act 1990 and the amendments to the Act introduced by the Police and Justice Act 2006. The risks considered during the legislative passage included the financial risk to the economy, the data integrity risks posed by computer hacking, the service availability risks arising from denial-of-service attacks and the security of state systems such as the

---

210 United Kingdom Interdepartmental Liaison Group on Risk Assessment, *The Precautionary Principle: Policy and Application* (2002) <http://www.hse.gov.uk/aboutus/meetings/ilgra/pppa.htm> accessed 25 September 2008.

211 Culture, Media and Sport Committee, *Harmful Content on the Internet and in Video Games*, HC (2007–8) 353-I.

212 Ibid., 3.

proposed national identity register, police DNA databases and the critical national infrastructure.

There is a range of potential responses to risks. Where it is feasible to do so, the risk may be terminated by refraining from the risky activity. Countermeasures may be introduced which prevent the risk from occurring or resilience may be 'built in' to prevent the realised risk from having any detrimental impact. The risk may be reduced by taking action which either reduces the probability of the risk occurring (target hardening) or limiting its impact to an acceptable level. The management of the risk may be transferred to a third party via insurance. The risk may also be tolerated if its likelihood or consequences are at an acceptable level or that measures to prevent or reduce it are impracticable or prohibitively expensive. Contingency plans may be developed which are executed if the risk occurs.

From the realist perspective, risk is considered in terms of probability and consequences. The greater the severity and likelihood of an adverse event, the riskier that event becomes. Events may then be placed in risk categories against which insurance may be taken. However, the domestic criminal law does not always sit easily with the notion of insurance, although it could be argued to at least offer some protection against the behaviour associated with computer misuse. For instance, the criminalisation of unauthorised access to computer systems,[213] for instance, represents an attempt at state intervention to protect against the associated financial and data integrity risk on society's behalf. Similarly, the more recent offence relating to impairing the performance of a computer system[214] can be viewed as offering some protection against risks to service availability. As Policy-Maker 1 commented:

We have to ensure that our key businesses function in the current technological climate. I think that the law is trying to protect commerce here.

However, the use of the domestic criminal law in response to risk does not necessarily protect individuals from the consequences of that risk. For example, the domestic criminal law does not usually provide financial restoration or the ability to substitute new resources. Even if the domestic criminal law is constructed as some form of collective social insurance in protecting against the risks associated

---

213 Computer Misuse Act 1990, s. 1.
214 Police and Justice Act 2006, s. 36.

with computer misuse, it has been demonstrated by the decline of the welfare state and the increased use of private insurance, particularly in relation to healthcare and pension provision, that the state is gradually withdrawing its responsibility for individual welfare. The interests of the domestic criminal law are predominantly public rather than private. With regard to the management of risk related to computer misuse, this is in line with the role of the domestic criminal law being particularly apposite where there is a risk of collective public harm, such as a threat to national security, but less so where separate individuals require protection. Moreover, there is little to suggest that the domestic criminal law offers a significant deterrent against computer misuse. As previously discussed, computer misuse often comprises *de minimis* harms and is not considered to be especially immoral. Low-impact consequences of questionable wrongness are not traditional candidates for criminalisation. Computer misuse suffers further from the reluctance of most individual and some corporate victims to report it. These factors combine to present problems for the domestic criminal law. Its presence will not deter those from behaving in ways which cause little harm, are of dubious immorality and are unlikely to attract the interests of the criminal justice system. The domestic criminal law, then, is in keeping with the state's role as offering some sort of protection as the reinsurer of last resort against significant risk but is of less utility to the protection of individuals. It is therefore highly questionable whether the domestic criminal law is an appropriate means of managing risks to individuals, or, as with the welfare state, the individual should take a less passive approach to ensuring their own security. The active assumption of personal responsibility was clearly shown across the spectrum of interview participants:

Because we're not set up properly to deal with computer crime, people have to take steps to protect themselves. Surely it's common sense. You wouldn't go out and leave your windows open. Crime prevention is the key.[215]

IT security is key across our whole enterprise. We spend a small fortune on keeping ourselves protected. No-one else is going to.[216]

215 Police Officer 4.
216 User 2.

We have to build software and systems that are secure. There's a lot of R&D going on in that area, just to try and keep one step ahead – of the criminals, as well as our competitors.[217]

Even if the domestic criminal law is considered to provide some sort of limited protection against major computer misuse risk, computer misuse does not present a significant moral hazard. The existence of the criminal law does not significantly reduce the incentive for the computer user to take care to avoid loss. Although the prospect of a criminal conviction may provide some satisfaction to a victim of computer misuse, it must be remembered that the criminal law suffers from low conviction rates. Moreover, even where a conviction is secured, it is by no means guaranteed that a compensation order would be granted to offset some or all of the financial cost of recovery. This was seen in *Lennon*, where the defendant's actions caused significant financial loss but no compensation was awarded. The absence of moral hazard, as far as domestic criminal law is concerned, is evidenced by the range of security hardware and software that is available to both the business and consumer markets. Individuals take personal responsibility for computer security *despite* the presence of the domestic criminal law:

The law doesn't offer enough protection. Not to businesses or users. The trouble is, is that I'm not sure whether it could. I'm certainly sure that I don't know how it could. If you think that you don't have to protect yourself because the law will, then you deserve all you get.[218]

From the cultural and symbolic constructionist perspective, the role of the domestic criminal law as a response to risk will vary depending on the viewpoint of the individual. Using the grid-group model, individualists (low grid/low group) will support the use of self-regulation and thence self-management of risk. They will not consider that there is a significant role for state regulation of any form in general, or the use of the domestic criminal law in particular. Fatalists (high grid/low group) will adopt a passive stance. Believing that they have little personal control over risk, the presence, absence, efficacy or inadequacy of the domestic criminal law will not trouble them. For the egalitarian (low grid/high group), there will be a general distrust

---

217 Technician 4.
218 User 5.

of the external constraint imposed by the domestic criminal law, although their sensitivity to high-consequence risks would suggest that they will find favour with criminal laws targeted at computer misuse which impacts upon national security. The hierarchists (high grid/high group) will consider that the domestic criminal law has a definite role to play, not just in relation to computer misuse, but in terms of creating a well-defined and ordered society. Although this functional structuralist approach is necessarily somewhat artificial, given the blurring between categorisations that naturally occurs in society, it can be seen that the role of the domestic criminal law in relation to computer misuse is predominantly either marginal or restricted to high-consequence events. It is only unequivocally desirable to those who would consider the domestic criminal law to be an appropriate hierarchical response to *any* form of risk which threatened disorder.

Within the critically structuralist risk society, the production of computer misuse risks associated with technological advances has undermined the domestic criminal law as an established means of social control which regulates behaviour by delineating the boundaries of acceptable conduct. In risk society, the quantity and public awareness of risks have combined to require a greater level of state protection than has proven to be sustainable. In relation to computer technology, the increase in its power and accessibility has led to a proliferation of risks which, in turn, have come more into the public consciousness by virtue (at least in part) of the very same technologies that produced those risks in the first place. State protection against such widely known and increasing risks in the form of the domestic criminal law is therefore also unsustainable. Moreover, the risks associated with computer misuse exist within a disembodied order which transcends geographic and jurisdictional boundaries, rendering the domestic criminal law an inadequate means of control. Equally, in the risk society, technological advances can control, as well as produce risks. However, it has been demonstrated in the first part of this book that technological advances are largely decoupled from legal advances and therefore it is arguable that in the risk society, domestic criminal law has a limited role to play. Even the counter-viewpoint of Furedi, who considers that the risks posed by technology are not as significant as they are portrayed in the risk society, acknowledges that technology can provide high levels of safety. Therefore it follows that there is a potential role for technology itself in managing the risks associated with computer misuse. This notion of technological control is returned to in Chapter 7.

However, in the risk society, technical responses to technical risk generate more risks themselves. This reflexivity gives rise to global technological risks which are immune to complete control by the local mechanism of the domestic criminal law. These pandemic reflexive risks inherently tend towards globalisation. Again, therefore, a domestic means of control will be incomplete. This is recognised within the concept of the regulatory state which serves to manage the distribution of risks rather than the control of risks. Therefore the role of the law is one of management and guidance rather than one of control. The domestic criminal law is capable of guiding as well as controlling conduct and therefore may have some role within a regulatory state framework.

The governmentality viewpoint advocates neo-libertarianism. Although this subjugates excessive state intervention, it includes both direct and indirect strategies of control, combining both autonomous individual responsibility and coercive regulation. Moreover, governmentality manages risk via a network of state and private actors, institutions, knowledge and practice. In relation to computer misuse risk, the technology itself drives understanding as both a facilitator and a means of regulation. This understanding may be used to provide both a means of technological control and to inform the discourse of legal reform. There is therefore a role within the governmentality framework for the domestic criminal law as a means of direct and coercive regulation, shaped and informed by knowledge and as part of a broader control network. However, it must be stressed that governmentality emphasises autonomous self-management, self-protection and self-responsibility and that the role of the domestic criminal law as a form of state intervention has less prominence.

Overall, then, regardless of epistemological position, there is a common theme which indicates the withdrawal of the state, to a greater or lesser extent, from the management of risk. It is therefore possible to conclude that, from a risk perspective, the use of the domestic criminal law as a tool of the state cannot provide a complete solution to the problems associated with computer misuse. The first part of this book concluded in similar terms, albeit from an analysis of the nature of computer misuse and the nature of the criminal law. That is not to say that the role of the domestic criminal law is to be dismissed altogether. It still has a role to play as *part* of a controlling network which facilitates protection against computer misuse risks.

Governance theory proposes a means of controlling complex systems within a broader framework than can be provided by the state alone.

Governance encompasses both public and private institutions and practices. This is particularly noteworthy since computer misuse is generally viewed as a private, rather than a public, wrong. Moreover, since the threats or risks arising from computer misuse often come from individuals or sub-national groups which cannot be readily or easily controlled by nation states and are equally often directed against an infrastructure which might not belong to the state,[219] then it follows that the means of governance should come from private organisations as much as from the state, since bodies with a legal duty to prepare for and respond to emergencies are often private-sector organisations. For instance, there is a statutory duty imposed upon transport and utility companies to cooperate with state emergency services in response to emergencies.[220] It follows that private control mechanisms may be appropriate in the management of computer misuse risk, although the state does retain its capacity to regulate matters of public or national safety by direct use of the domestic criminal law. Extra-legal considerations will be considered in Chapter 7.

The domestic criminal law does not appear to have been deployed in any sort of precautionary sense. This is evidenced by the fact that the Computer Misuse Act 1990 was not updated for 16 years and even then was reactively changed in response to new forms of mischief and to fulfil the UK's European obligations. From a risk society perspective, the potential risks emerging from technological advance are unseen and unforeseeable. Therefore it becomes impossible to legislate for that which is, at present, unknown, since new domestic criminal legislation will be drafted either too narrowly or too broadly. This problem of technology-neutral drafting has already been seen in relation to the amendments within the Police and Justice Act 2006. Against a backdrop of precaution, it is therefore necessary to reconsider whether there is sufficient evidence to suggest that computer misuse poses a risk with the substantially harmful consequences required to warrant a precautionary approach. Although it could be argued that society has been overwhelmed by a construction of computer misuse which emphasises its negative aspects in order to create a climate of fear, the state does not generally consider computer misuse to be a prime area of responsibility. This has been reflected in the lack

---

219 For instance, the UK Critical National Infrastructure comprises many private as well as state organisations.
220 Civil Contingencies Act 2004, s. 2.

of legislative impetus in its regulation. However, computer misuse does indisputably give rise to certain risks and it can therefore be argued that the precautionary principle does, at the very least, draw attention to these issues.

Computer technology is generally a creature of private enterprise and its misuse is generally considered to be a private concern. In its early days, when firmly within the realm of the scientific, technical and military experts, it was considered that its unfettered use gave rise to the greatest benefits. However, as technology has evolved, it has created some associated risks which warrant some form of control. The domestic criminal law, as a public mechanism, has some part to play in that control. However, it will not provide a complete solution. The domestic criminal law is prescriptive, not network-cooperative. In relation to computer misuse, it is unsuitable as a precautionary tool of prevention. Although it does carry a symbolic deterrent effect, with the exception of acts that are 'more than merely preparatory' to the commission of an offence,[221] it comes into operation *ex post* rather than *ex ante*.

While the various theoretical perspectives explain the limitations of the domestic criminal law in the context of computer misuse, they also open up a wide field within which alternative network-reliant control strategies may be explored. These include alternative tiers of legal governance at supranational and international levels, as well as additional tiers of extra-legal governance. The domestic criminal law is therefore best placed within a broader framework of governance in relation to the control of computer misuse risks as a tool of management and guidance as well as a tool of direct coercion. The next chapter will broaden the discussion from the domestic criminal law to consider the role of alternative tiers of legal governance within this framework while Chapter 7 will examine a range of potential extra-legal alternatives.

---

221 Criminal Attempts Act 1981, s. 1(1); *R v. Griffin* [1993] Crim LR 515 (CA); *R v. Geddes* [1996] Crim LR 894 (CA).

Chapter 6

The legal governance of computer misuse: beyond the domestic criminal law

Law is order and good law is good order.

Aristotle (384 BC – 322 BC)

The previous chapter considered the application of risk and governance theories to the domestic criminal law in the context of computer misuse. It explored whether the domestic criminal law offered a feasible solution to the risks arising from computer misuse which were identified in the first part of this book. In doing so, it established that the domestic criminal law has some part to play within a broader framework of governance, albeit a non-exclusive part. This chapter will broaden the discussion beyond the domestic criminal law to consider the role of the law in general within this governance framework. It will introduce new tiers of legal governance at the European Union, Council of Europe, Commonwealth, United Nations and Group of Eight (G8) levels and explore the impact of these upon the UK in the light of their effects on national sovereign powers. It will examine the proposition that there may be advantages in moving beyond the domestic criminal law by examining these alternative approaches within the context of governing transborder risks and transborder technology networks.

European Union initiatives

The domestic criminal law is a vehicle for the exercise of sovereign powers through legislation. However, the European Union also

187

represents an important tier of governance in the regulation of commerce and social affairs, exercising power, authority and influence which transcends national boundaries, governments and institutions. The enactment of the European Communities Act 1972 gave effect within the UK to all directly applicable European law (that is Treaty Articles and Regulations)[1] without the need for further domestic legislation.[2] In doing so, the UK joined a community which (in the opinion of the Court of Justice of the European Communities) represented 'a new legal order ... for whose benefit the [Member] States have limited their sovereign rights'[3] and the rules of which the House of Lords has held to be supreme over domestic law.[4] The primary aim of the Treaty of Rome[5] which gave birth to the European Economic Community (as it then was) was to create a common market and an economic and monetary union by implementing common policies and activities[6] to promote employment and social protection, to raise standards of living and to facilitate economic and social cohesion.[7] This focus on economic and social well-being traditionally meant that the European Community did not interfere with the criminal law of Member States. However, Community law can overrule national law (including national criminal law) where there is incompatibility between the two.[8] Moreover, the doctrine of equivalence which requires Member States to protect rights under Community law in a way no less favourable than those relating to national law may require Member States to give effect to Community law by providing criminal sanctions.[9]

---

1 Treaty establishing the European Community (as amended) (EC Treaty) [2002] OJ C325/33, art. 249EC.
2 European Communities Act 1972, s. 2(1).
3 *Van Gend en Loos v. Nederlandse Administratie der Belastingen* [1963] ECR 1 (CJEC).
4 *R v. Secretary of State for Transport, ex parte Factortame (No. 2)* [1991] 1 AC 603 (HL).
5 Treaty establishing the European Economic Community (Treaty of Rome) 1957/ CEE 1.
6 Outlined in EC Treaty, arts 3 and 4.
7 EC Treaty, art. 2.
8 *Criminal Proceedings against Donatella Calfa* (Case C-348/96) [1999] ECR I-11 (CJEC).
9 *Commission v. Greece* (Case C-68/88) [1989] ECR 2965 (CJEC).

The criminal law competence of the European Community and the European Union

The Treaty on European Union[10] founded the European Union upon the Communities[11] 'supplemented by the policies and forms of cooperation established by [the] Treaty'.[12] The European Union currently consists of three 'pillars'. The First Pillar is comprised of the European Communities; the Second Pillar is Common Foreign and Security Policy (CFSP);[13] the Third Pillar is Police and Judicial Cooperation in Criminal Matters (PJCC), formerly known as Cooperation in the Fields of Justice and Home Affairs (JHA).[14] The Second and Third Pillars therefore supplement the traditional Community structure now residing within the First Pillar. They are essentially inter-governmental in nature; that is, they are not run by the EC institutions such as the Commission, but by collaboration between the governments of the Member States. The Third Pillar, then, is primarily concerned with cooperation between national police forces, customs authorities and judicial authorities and is implemented via agencies set up by the European Union, namely: Eurojust, responsible for countering serious crime through closer judicial cooperation; Europol, responsible for improving cooperation between the police and customs authorities of the Member States; and the European Judicial Network (EJN).[15] This cooperation includes the development of mechanisms for the mutual recognition of judicial decisions in criminal matters and the approximation of rules, where necessary, on certain 'criminal matters' in the Member States,[16] that is:

[P]rogressively adopting measures establishing minimum rules relating to the constituent elements of criminal acts and to

10 Treaty on European Union (as amended) [2002] OJ C325/5.
11 Comprising the European Community and the only other surviving European Community, the European Atomic Energy Community (EURATOM), the European Coal and Steel Community (ECSC) having been absorbed into the European Community on the expiry of the 1951 Treaty of Paris in July 2002.
12 Treaty on European Union, art 1 (ex art. A(3)).
13 Treaty on European Union, Title V.
14 Treaty on European Union, Title VI.
15 There is an EJN in criminal matters responsible for facilitating mutual judicial assistance in the fight against transnational crime; there is also an EJN in civil and commercial matters.
16 Treaty on European Union, art. 29.

penalties in the fields of organised crime, terrorism and illicit drug trafficking.[17]

The criminal matters referred to here are undeniably matters of significant public concern with the potential to cause serious harm.

The concept of cooperation in European criminal matters is not new. For example, in 1977 the French government reintroduced a plan via the European Council for the 'European judicial space' in response to increased terrorist activity in Europe throughout the 1970s. This plan was first mooted in 1975 to simplify extradition proceedings and improve mutual assistance between States in criminal matters via the harmonisation of criminal laws. However, as Vermeulen comments, the plan proved to be 'premature and unrealistic' since criminal justice and law enforcement systems of the Member States 'are based entirely on the principle of sovereignty'.[18]

The distinction between the criminal competence of the EU and the EC is constitutionally significant, since criminal law in particular varies between Member States, reflecting their fundamental differences and therefore becoming a closely guarded aspect of their national sovereignty. As a vehicle for approximation of laws in certain policy areas, European law has the ability to establish a common ground which can bind Member States and shape the laws beyond sovereign boundaries in a way that domestic law cannot, notwithstanding the extraterritorial legislative competence of the UK inherent in Parliamentary sovereignty.[19]

It was, however, common ground until September 2005 that the EC Treaty itself conferred no power to define criminal offences or prescribe criminal sanctions. The distribution of competencies between the First and Third Pillars of the EU was then examined in *Commission v. Council* (Case C-176/03).[20] The issue at hand had no precedent and the importance of the case was reflected by the court sitting as a Grand Chamber to hear observations from eleven Member States. The Commission also issued a Communication on the

---

17 Treaty on European Union, art. 31(e).
18 Vermeulen, G., 'Pre-judicial (preventative) structuring of international police action in Europe' (1996) <http://www.ncjrs.gov/policing/pre75.htm> accessed 25 September 2008.
19 *Edinburgh & Dalkeith Railway Co. v. Wauchope* (1842) 8 ER 810 (HL); *Mortensen v. Peters* (1906) 14 SLT 227 (High Court of Justiciary).
20 *Commission v. Council* (Case C-176/03) [2005] ECR I-7879 (CJEC).

implications of the Court's judgement,[21] such communications being reserved for important cases such as *Cassis de Dijon*[22] and *Kalanke*.[23]

In case C-176/03, the Court considered a Council Framework Decision[24] which laid down a number of environmental offences in respect of which the Member States were required to prescribe criminal penalties. The Commission asked the Court to annul the Framework Decision on the grounds that the imposition of this obligation to prescribe sanctions based upon art. 29 *et seq.* of the Treaty on European Union (that is, a Third Pillar basis) was incorrect. The Commission argued that the correct legal basis for criminal sanctions was article 175(1) of the EC Treaty (that is, a First Pillar basis) upon which it had presented a proposal for an environmental protection Directive. The Court stated that 'as a general rule, neither criminal law nor the rules of criminal procedure fall within the Community's competence', citing *Casati*[25] and *Lemmens*[26] as examples of cases in which it was held that, in principle, criminal legislation and the rules of criminal procedure are matters for which the Member States are responsible. However, as Tobler argues, this is no more than a general rule which 'does not mean that Community law is irrelevant for the purposes of national criminal law. The question is rather one of degree'.[27] She argues further that:

[S]ince *von Colson and Kamann*[28] it has been clear that the Member States' duty to provide for effective, proportionate and dissuasive sanctions in the event of infringements of Community law may

21 Commission (EC), 'Communication from the Commission to the European Parliament and the Council on the implications of the Court's judgement of 13 September 2005 (Case C-176/03, *Commission v. Council*)' COM (2005) 583 final, 24 November 2005.

22 *Rewe-Zentrale AG v. Bundesmonopolverwaltung für Branntwein (sub nom. Cassis de Dijon)* (Case 120/78) [1979] ECR 649 (CJEC) concerning measures equivalent to quantitative restriction on imports.

23 *Eckhard Kalanke v. Freie Hansestadt Bremen* (Case C-450/93) [1995] ECR I-3051 (CJEC) concerning positive discrimination.

24 Council Framework Decision (EU) 2003/80/JHA of 17 January 2003 on the protection of the environment through criminal law [2003] OJ L29/55.

25 *Casati* (Case 203/80) [1981] ECR 2595 (CJEC) [27].

26 *Lemmens* (Case C-226/97) [1998] ECR I-3711 (CJEC) [19].

27 Tobler, C., 'Annotation: Case C-176/03, Commission v. Council, judgement of the Grand Chamber of 13 September 2005' (2006) 43 *Common Market Law Review* 835, 846.

28 *Von Colson and Kamann v. Land Nordrhein-Westfalen* (Case 14/83) [1984] ECR 1891 (CJEC).

include the duty to impose criminal sanctions even where there is no explicit written Community law on the matter.[29]

Indeed, in case C-176/03 *Commission v. Council* the Court explicitly stated that there is nothing in this general rule which prevents the Community from requiring competent national authorities to impose 'effective, proportionate and dissuasive criminal penalties' where they are an 'essential measure'.[30] The Court held that since articles 174 to 176 of the EC Treaty establish general environmental policy as an essential Community objective then the measures within the Third Pillar Framework Decision could have been properly adopted on the First Pillar basis of article 175 of the EC Treaty.

The situation following case C-176/03 is that any criminal law required for the effective implementation of Community policy is a matter for the EC Treaty (First Pillar) whereas horizontal criminal law provisions to facilitate police and judicial cooperation fall within Title VI of the Treaty on European Union (Third Pillar). Peers commented that:

Given that the Member States argued that this was not what they wanted to give to the Community as competence, it is surprising that the Court felt that it was. Nevertheless … there are reasonable grounds to support the Court's conclusion that the Community has some sort of criminal law competence.[31]

White further considers that the adoption of criminal law under the First Pillar 'may still prove difficult' within the Treaty structure, pointing out that 'the Council was supported in its argument against this approach by 11 out of 15 Member States'.[32] For Greatorex and Peter, the decision strengthens the EU as an institution by demonstrating the Court's willingness to 'strike down any attempt by Member States, even where acting unanimously, to legislate on matters which are properly within the competence of the Community

---

29 Tobler, C., 'Annotation: Case C-176/03, *Commission v. Council*, judgement of the Grand Chamber of 13 September 2005' (2006) 43 *Common Market Law Review* 835, 846.

30 *Commission v. Council* (Case C-176/03) [2005] ECR I-7879 (CJEC) [48].

31 European Union Committee, 'The Criminal Law Competence of the European Community: Report with Evidence' HL (2005–06) 227 [Q47].

32 White, S., 'Harmonisation of criminal law under the First Pillar' (2006) 31 *European Law Review* 81, 92.

legislature'.[33] However, Renouf considers that the decision 'takes nothing away from the powers of the Member States' concluding that 'Brussels cannot imprison Britons'.[34] In its report on the criminal law competence of the European Community, the House of Lords, while accepting that there was a possibility of Community legislation defining offences 'with some degree of particularity', considered that this would lead to 'problems of definition and drafting resulting in part from the different approaches taken by Member States' criminal laws and rules of evidence and procedure'.[35]

The decision in *Commission v. Council* (C-176/03) was further considered in *Commission v. Council* (C-440/05).[36] Here, the main issue was whether or not the earlier ruling applied to EC policy areas other than environmental protection. In case C-440/05, which concerned the criminal law relating to ship-source pollution, the Commission sought annulment of a Third Pillar Council Framework Decision[37] in favour of a First Pillar Directive.[38] The Commission, supported by the European Parliament, argued that the subject matter concerned fell within the Community competence of transport policy. The Council was backed by twenty Member States, highlighting the predominantly held viewpoint among the Member States that criminal law fell within their national sovereign competencies. The court held that the Framework Decision encroached on the competence given to the Community by article 80(2) of the EC Treaty[39] and therefore infringed article 47 of the EU Treaty[40] and therefore 'being indivisible, must be annulled in its entirety'.[41]

Therefore the Community can enact First Pillar measures in respect of some criminal law matters insofar as they impinge on the environment, trade or other core areas of Community policy.

---

33 Greatorex, P. and Peter, N., 'Gloves off: *Commission v. Council*' (2005) 155 *New Law Journal* 1706.

34 Renouf, M., 'The Euro battle to legislate' (2005) 102 *Law Society Gazette* 15.

35 European Union Committee, 'The Criminal Law Competence of the European Community: Report with Evidence' HL (2005–06) 227 [61].

36 *Commission v. Council* (Case C-440/05) [2008] 1 CMLR 22 (CJEC).

37 Council Framework Decision (EU) 2005/667/JHA of 12 July 2005 to strengthen the criminal law framework for the enforcement of the law against ship-source pollution [2005] OJ L255/164.

38 Council Directive (EC) 2005/35 of 7 September 2005 on ship-source pollution and on the introduction of penalties for infringements [2005] OJ L255/11.

39 To make 'appropriate provisions' for sea transport.

40 That nothing in the Treaty on European Union shall affect the Treaties establishing the European Community.

41 *Commission v. Council* (Case C-440/05) [2008] 1 CMLR 22 (CJEC) [74].

However, criminal law is not, of itself, a core Community policy area, since Community intervention in criminal matters is only permissible on a specific legal basis and only then where there is a clear need.

Treaty on European Union, article 42: the passerelle provision

Article 42 of the EU Treaty introduces a *passerelle* (bridge) provision which may also be of relevance. It provides that:

The Council, acting unanimously on the initiative of the Commission or a Member State, and after consulting the European Parliament, may decide that action in areas referred to in article 29 shall fall under Title IV of the Treaty establishing the European Community, and at the same time determine the relevant voting conditions relating to it. It shall recommend the Member States to adopt that decision in accordance with their respective constitutional requirements.[42]

In effect, this provision would move action on police and judicial cooperation in criminal matters from Third Pillar Framework Decisions to First Pillar Community Regulations or Directives. These would be made under Title IV of the EC Treaty which gives the Council the ability to 'adopt measures ... aimed at a high level of security by preventing and combating crime within the Union'.[43] While cases C-176/03 and C-440/05 established that there is certainly *some* criminal competence under the First Pillar, there are other areas of police and judicial cooperation which could move under the First Pillar via a *passerelle* decision.

The *passerelle* therefore allows the movement of a policy issue from intergovernmentalism to the 'Community method', that is from unanimity to supranational qualified majority voting, without an Intergovernmental Conference. It follows that First Pillar measures in relation to criminal law both potentially weaken the position of a Member State to exercise its veto as well as subjugating jurisdiction for interpretation (and enforcement in the event of non-implementation) to the Court of Justice. As the House of Lords comments, use of the *passerelle* would:

---

42   Treaty on European Union, art. 42.
43   Treaty establishing the European Community, art. 61(e).

prima facie increase the roles of the European Parliament and the Court. [Qualified majority voting] could replace unanimity in the Council. At stake, therefore, are national vetoes and national control over certain policing and criminal law matters.[44]

However, in relation to the veto, it should be noted that the UK has an 'opt-in' to matters under Title IV EC, such that it can decide (within three months from the presentation of a proposal to the Council) whether it 'wishes to take part in the adoption and application of any such proposed measure'.[45] The House of Lords considers that there is 'a good argument'[46] that this opt-in will survive the *passerelle* and apply to an enlarged Title IV and, as such, the loss of the national veto within the Third Pillar would be of less consequence than it might have been without retention of the opt-in. If the voting requirements within the *passerelle* included an 'emergency brake' procedure[47] (by which a Member State may refer a draft Directive to the Council if it considers that it would affect fundamental aspects of its criminal justice system) then the UK would be in a very strong position. Peers commented that:

We could opt out at the beginning or we can opt in and then pull the emergency brake, having decided we do not like the way the discussions have gone, and then they would go ahead without us, and so you still have two bites at opting out.[48]

The House of Lords concluded that the proposal to use the *passerelle* deserves 'careful examination and cautioned against any knee-jerk reaction resulting from media coverage'[49] urging the UK government to engage itself 'in a detailed examination of the issues which use of the *passerelle* raises for the Union and the UK'.[50] In common with

---

44 European Union Committee, 'The Criminal Law Competence of the European Community: Report with Evidence' HL (2005–06) 227 [12].

45 Treaty of Amsterdam amending the Treaty on European Union, the Treaties Establishing the European Communities and Related Acts (Treaty of Amsterdam) [1997] OJ C340/1, Protocol on the position of the UK and Ireland, art. 3.

46 European Union Committee, 'The Criminal Law Competence of the European Community: Report with Evidence' HL (2005–06) 227 [152].

47 As outlined in art. III-271(3) of the Treaty establishing a Constitution for Europe [2004] OJ C310/1; now superseded by art. 69A(3) of the Treaty of Lisbon.

48 European Union Committee, 'The Criminal Law Competence of the European Community: Report with Evidence' HL (2005–06) 227 [153].

49 Ibid. [172].

50 Ibid. [180].

many Member States, the UK was not enthusiastic about the proposal to use the *passerelle* in respect of criminal matters, although it wished to maintain a flexible and pragmatic approach:

[W]e think that the current debate [on the *passerelle*] is effectively over. We should instead focus our energy on delivering practical measures.[51]

Somewhat more controversially, Michael Connarty MP, a member of the House of Commons EU Scrutiny Committee, was reported as saying:

Once you go off the end of the *passerelle*, you give away the power to the Commission … so it is like a gangplank more than a bridge. Once you plunge off it, it is difficult to get back onto.[52]

The debate on the *passerelle* may indeed be over with the overhaul of the pillar structure and review of EU competencies proposed within the Treaty of Lisbon.

The Treaty of Lisbon

The Treaty of Lisbon[53] was intended to come into force on 1 January 2009, subject to ratification by all Member States. However, following a referendum on 12 June 2008, the Irish electorate voted against its ratification by 53 per cent to 47 per cent[54] and, as such, the Treaty cannot come into force in its current form. It is, however, anticipated that Ireland will call a second referendum in late 2009 after securing concessions on particular policies, including abortion, taxation and military neutrality. The Treaty of Lisbon therefore remains of relevance. The remainder of this section will consider its key provisions which are unlikely to be substantially changed despite the Irish position.

The Treaty of Lisbon will replace the three-pillar structure of the EU. Instead the EU will divide its policy areas into three categories:

---

51 Hansard HC vol. 453 col. 1256 (30 November 2006).

52 —, 'MEPs in row with UK parliament over "gangplank" report', *EU Observer* (7 December 2006) <http://euobserver.com/?aid=23045> accessed 25 September 2008.

53 Treaty of Lisbon amending the Treaty on European Union and the Treaty establishing the European Community (Treaty of Lisbon) ([2007] OJ C306/1).

54 <http://www.referendum.ie/home/> accessed 25 September 2008.

exclusive competence, shared competence (with the Member St.. and supporting competence (where the EU supports, coordinate supplements the actions of the Member States). Within this model, the EU will also seek to increase its competence within the areas formerly covered by the Second and Third Pillars and more definitively into the realm of the criminal law. Article 69B(1) of the Treaty of Lisbon provides that:

The European Parliament and the Council may, by means of Directives adopted in accordance with the ordinary legislative procedure, establish minimum rules concerning the definition of criminal offences and sanctions in the areas of particularly serious crime with a cross-border dimension resulting from the nature or impact of such offences or from a special need to combat them on a common basis.

These areas of crime are the following: terrorism, trafficking in human beings and sexual exploitation of women and children, illicit drug trafficking, illicit arms trafficking, money laundering, corruption, counterfeiting of means of payment, *computer crime* and organised crime. [55] (emphasis added.)

This provision is self-evidently relevant to computer misuse. Since computer crime is specifically mentioned in the list of criminal activities, the EU is granting itself power to direct Member States to adopt a minimum level of criminalisation and sanction in response. The transnational nature of computer misuse gives it both a cross-border dimension and a need to combat it on a common basis. The examples of other 'particularly serious' crimes demonstrate the EU's perception of the problem of computer crime as being potentially as significant as that of trafficking in drugs, arms or people. Moreover, article 69B(2) gives the EU power to impose the approximation of criminal law where essential to fulfil Union policy via Directives which may establish 'minimum rules with regard to the definition of criminal offences and sanctions in the area concerned'.[56]

The UK opposed the extension of supranational powers in these areas to avoid a national referendum in respect of an unpopular political issue. It has also opted out from the change from unanimity to qualified majority voting in the area of Justice and Home Affairs. This is not the only area in which the UK has opted out of what

---

55 Treaty of Lisbon, art. 69B(1).
56 Treaty of Lisbon, art. 69B(2).

it considers to be unnecessary European interference in its national affairs. The Schengen *acquis*[57] concerned *inter alia* extradition, mutual criminal assistance, cross-border surveillance by police officers and a database including persons wanted for extradition and questioning in connection with criminal offences between Member States (the 'Schengen Information System' or 'SIS'). In theory, this would ease the way to a borderless internal super-state. The Schengen *acquis* was implemented[58] via a 'flexible incorporation'[59] partly in the First Pillar and partly in the Third Pillar.[60] However, the UK did not sign the 1990 Convention implementing the original Schengen agreement and reserved an opt-out within the Treaty of Amsterdam.[61] Therefore the new EU legislative competence within the Schengen policy areas did not automatically extend to the UK. The UK may, however, apply to opt *in* to legislation made under Schengen in whole or in part. It has done so in relation to some information-sharing initiatives[62] but has

---

57 The 1985 Agreement between the Governments of the States of the Benelux Economic Union, the Federal Republic of Germany and the French Republic on the gradual abolition of checks at their common borders ([2000] OJ L239/13) and the 1990 Convention implementing the Schengen Agreement of 14 June 1985 between the Governments of the States of the Benelux Economic Union, the Federal Republic of Germany and the French Republic on the gradual abolition of checks at their common borders ([2000] OJ L239/19) plus the Accession Protocols and Agreements and Decisions and Declarations adopted by the Executive Committee established by the 1990 Implementation Convention and its delegated authorities; see Annex: Schengen *Acquis* to the Protocol Integrating the Schengen *Acquis* into the Framework of the European Union annexed to the Treaty on European Union and the Treaty establishing the European Community (the 'Schengen Protocol').

58 Treaty of Amsterdam, art. 2(15).

59 Select Committee on European Communities, 'Incorporating the Schengen *acquis* into the European Union' HL (1997–98) 139 [53].

60 Council Decision (EC) 1999/435 concerning the definition of the Schengen *acquis* for the purpose of determining, in conformity with the relevant provisions of the Treaty establishing the European Community and the Treaty on European Union, the legal basis for each of the provisions or decisions which constitute the *acquis* [1999] OJ L176/1; Council Decision (EC) 1999/436 determining, in conformity with the relevant provisions of the Treaty establishing the European Community and the Treaty on European Union, the legal basis for each of the provisions or decisions which constitute the Schengen *acquis* [1999] OJ L176/17.

61 Schengen Protocol, arts 3, 4 and 6; Protocol on the position of the United Kingdom and Ireland, annexed to the Treaty on European Union and the Treaty establishing the European Community.

62 Council Decision (EC) 2000/365 of 29 May 2000 concerning the request of the United Kingdom of Great Britain and Northern Ireland to take part in some of the provisions of the Schengen *acquis* [2000] OJ L131/42; Council Decision (EC)

not removed border controls. Therefore the UK has allowed European interference with sovereignty and territoriality but only to the extent that it considers acceptable. The UK's position on opting in and out of European initiatives was also demonstrated in respect of the Social Chapter[63] from which the UK opted out at Maastricht in 1991 and back in five years later following a change of government.[64]

A key difficulty in extending the European system to criminal law is that there are bigger differences between the domestic criminal laws of Member States than between their respective civil laws. These differences lie in procedural aspects as well as the construction of individual offences. Concerns have been expressed that the Treaty of Lisbon gives rise to 'classic instances of EU "state-building"[65] particularly in relation to judicial and police cooperation.[66] The EU is creating more bodies and agencies (such as Europol and Eurojust) to act on a Union-wide basis, with administrative[67] and operational[68] cooperation being centrally organised by the EU. Bunyan commented that:

Overall we are witnessing the extension, and cementing, of the European state with potentially weak democratic intervention on policy-making and no scrutiny mechanisms in place on implementation and practice.[69]

This tension between national and EU competence may also mean that measures taken at the EU level may become problematic to enforce, notwithstanding the EU's urgency for cooperation in criminal matters.

The legislative vehicle intended to incorporate the provisions of the Treaty of Lisbon within the UK is the European Union (Amendment)

---

63 2004/926 of 22 December 2004 on the putting into effect of parts of the Schengen *acquis* by the United Kingdom of Great Britain and Northern Ireland [2004] OJ L395/70.

64 Protocol 14 of the EC Treaty on Social Policy and the Agreement on Social Policy.

65 Barnard, C., 'The United Kingdom, the "Social Chapter" and the Amsterdam Treaty' (1997) 26 *Industrial Law Journal* 275.

66 Bunyan, T., 'EU: Cementing the European state – new emphasis on internal security and operational cooperation at EU level' (2007) 17 *Statewatch Bulletin* 3.

67 Treaty of Lisbon, art. 63 concerning freedom, security and justice.

68 Treaty of Lisbon, art. 67 covering the whole of Title IV.

69 For example, Treaty of Lisbon, art. 69(1), (i) in the matter of police cooperation. Bunyan, T., 'EU: Cementing the European state – new emphasis on internal security and operational co-operation at EU level' (2007) 17 *Statewatch Bulletin* 3.

Bill.[70] During the House of Lords' debate on the Bill, Lord Giddens countered the argument that the Treaty of Lisbon further erodes national sovereignty by conceptualising 'sovereignty plus'[71] as 'the capability of a country to shape its own future and to influence the wider world around it'.[72] For Giddens, these influences are 'much stronger as members of the European Union than they would be outside'[73] and would enable the UK to counter 'massive dynamic forces which no nation could adequately confront on its own'.[74] He dismissed the notion of the super-state as dead, considering it to have been replaced by a Europe which not only acknowledges but also actively supports national identity and diversity. He further argued that the Treaty of Lisbon gives the UK what it desired from Europe: openness, flexibility and enlargement.[75] Giddens's notion of 'sovereignty plus' is in line with earlier arguments put forward by MacCormick who considered that although absolute or unitary legal and political sovereignty is absent from the European Community, sovereignty has not been lost in the sense that 'no state or other entity outside the Union has any greater power over member states individually or jointly than before'.[76] The divided sovereignty of the Member States has been combined within the Community to enhance their individual positions, it being preferable in global society to exercise power through the EU rather than losing it to the EU and thus moving the UK 'beyond the sovereign state'.[77]

Specific initiatives relating to computer misuse

At its Brussels meeting in 1993, the European Council sought advice on the 'specific measures to be taken into consideration by the Community and the Member States for the infrastructures in the sphere of information'.[78] The resulting report, generally referred to as the Bangemann Report, considered that the exploitation of the new

70 European Union (Amendment) HC Bill (2007–08) [48].
71 Hansard HL vol. 700 col. 957 (1 April 2008).
72 Ibid.
73 Ibid.
74 Ibid.
75 Ibid.
76 MacCormick, N., *Questioning Sovereignty: Law, State and Nation in the European Commonwealth* (Oxford University Press, Oxford, 1999) 132.
77 MacCormick, N., 'Beyond the sovereign state' (1993) 53 *Modern Law Review* 1.
78 Bangemann, M. and others, *Europe and the Global Information Society* (The Bangemann Report) (1994) <http://ec.europa.eu/archives/ISPO/infosoc/backg/bangeman.html> accessed 25 September 2008.

technologies required to participate in 'the new industrial revolution' would require 'partnership between individuals, employers, unions and governments dedicated to managing change'.[79] This partnership would mean 'developing a common regulatory approach'[80] and thus reflected the European policy objectives of flexibility, legal certainty, harmonisation and technological neutrality.

Creating a safer information society

The European Commission produced a report in 2001 entitled *Creating a Safer Information Society by Improving the Security of Information Infrastructures and Combating Computer-Related Crime*.[81] This report echoed the economic risks associated with computer misuse that were raised in the debates leading to the enactment of the Computer Misuse Act 1990 some ten years previously:

> ... there is little doubt that these offences constitute a threat to industry investment and assets, and to safety and confidence in the information society. Some recent examples of denial-of-service and virus attacks have been reported to have caused extensive financial damage.[82]

The report further considered that the legal responses to computer crime are predominantly effected by use of national criminal laws, although there is little consensus between states on the manner in which these criminal laws are implemented:

> In most countries, reactions to computer crime focus on national law (especially criminal law), neglecting alternative preventive measures ... various national laws world-wide show remarkable differences, especially with respect to the criminal law provisions on hacking, trade secret protection and illegal content.[83]

The Commission went on explicitly to acknowledge that there are potential extra-legal means of governance which have a role to play alongside legal regulation, proposing a number of non-legislative

---

79 Ibid., 5.
80 Ibid., 4.
81 Commission (EC), 'Creating a safer information society by improving the security of information infrastructures and combating computer-related crime' COM (2000) 890, 26 January 2001.
82 Ibid., 2.
83 Ibid., 7.

actions that will be further considered in the next chapter. However, that is not to say that national criminal laws are redundant. The nation states at the very least remain as the local representatives of the supranational governance initiatives. As Hirst and Thompson comment:

If ... mechanisms of international governance and re-regulation are to be initiated, then the role of nation states is pivotal.[84]

The European Commission continued to set out its guiding principles for national criminal laws:

National substantive criminal laws should be sufficiently comprehensive and effective in criminalising serious computer-related abuses and provide for dissuasive sanctions, helping to overcome dual criminality problems and facilitating international cooperation.[85]

In doing so, it recognised that national criminal laws were required in order to protect against computer misuse, although it stressed that international cooperation was key at the supranational level to facilitate a harmonised approach between Member States. However, it recommended that it was necessary:

... to further approximate substantive criminal law in the area of high-tech crime. This will include offences related to hacking and denial-of-service attacks.[86]

Although this report was not binding on States, its proposals were furthered by the CoE Convention on Cybercrime and will be discussed in detail later in this chapter. These proposals also ultimately underpin the amendments to the Computer Misuse Act 1990 made by the Police and Justice Act 2006.

84 Hirst, P. and Thompson, G., 'Globalisation and the future of the nation state' (1995) 24 *Economy and Society* 408, 430.
85 Commission (EC), 'Creating a safer information society by improving the security of information infrastructures and combating computer-related crime' COM (2000) 890, 26 January 2001, 30.
86 Ibid., 31.

EU Council Framework Decision on attacks against information systems

In 2005, the Council of the European Union issued a Framework Decision on attacks against information systems.[87] As a Framework Decision, it is binding upon the Member States as to the result to be achieved, but leaves form and method of implementation to each Member State.[88]

The Framework Decision identifies the threats arising from attacks against information systems as 'organised crime' and the 'potential of terrorist attacks against information systems which form part of the critical infrastructure of the Member States'.[89] The nature of these threats is distinct from the economic concerns raised in the Bangemann Report. However, the Framework Decision does reiterate the desire to approximate the criminal law in an attempt to transcend jurisdictional difficulties between States in the interests of:

... the greatest possible police and judicial cooperation in the area of criminal offences ... and to contribute to the fight against organised crime and terrorism.[90]

Interestingly, the Framework Decision also implies that there should be a *de minimis* exception to less harmful manifestations of computer misuse by stating that:

There is a need to avoid over-criminalisation, particularly of minor cases, as well as a need to avoid criminalising right-holders and authorised persons.[91]

Therefore the backdrop against which the Framework Decision is set appears to be emphasising the protection of public interests rather than the interests of private individuals. This was made explicit in the earlier proposal for the Framework Decision which considered the nature of the primary threat was that to communication network operators, service providers, e-commerce companies, manufacturing industries, service industries, hospitals, public sector organisations and governments themselves before acknowledging that there can be

---

87 Council Framework Decision (EU) 2005/222/JHA of 24 February 2005 on attacks against information systems [2005] OJ L69/67.
88 Treaty on European Union, art. 34(2)(b).
89 Ibid., recitals [2].
90 Ibid., recitals [8].
91 Ibid., recitals [13].

'direct, serious and damaging effects on individuals as well'.[92] The Council also drew reference again to the 'considerable' economic burden associated with such threats.[93]

The Framework Decision introduces three main areas in which measures are to be taken concerning illegal access and interference with systems or data. Article 2(1) requires Member States to ensure that the 'intentional access without right to the whole or any part of an information system is punishable as a criminal offence, at least for cases which are not minor'. The Member States may choose to criminalise this conduct 'only where the offence is committed by infringing a security measure'.[94] Article 3 requires Member States to ensure that:

... the intentional serious hindering or interruption of the functioning of an information system by inputting, transmitting, damaging, deleting, deteriorating, suppressing or rendering inaccessible computer data is punishable as a criminal offence when committed without right, at least for cases which are not minor.

Finally, article 4 requires Member States to ensure that:

... the intentional deletion, damaging, deterioration, alteration, suppression or rendering inaccessible of computer data on an information system is punishable as a criminal offence when committed without right, at least for cases which are not minor.

In the use of the wording 'at least for cases which are not minor', each of these provisions reflects the *de minimis* exception referred to in the recitals to the Framework Decision. In doing so, the Framework Decision reinforces the use of the criminal law as an instrument which is predominantly concerned with public wrong and substantial harm.[95] Minor cases involving transient or trifling harm are not mandatory candidates for criminalisation.

---

92 Commission (EC), 'Proposal for a Council Framework Decision on attacks against information systems' COM (2002) 173 final, 19 April 2002, 3.
93 Ibid.
94 Council Framework Decision (EU) 2005/222/JHA of 24 February 2005 on attacks against information systems [2005] OJ L69/67, art. 2(2).
95 See Chapter 4.

The Framework Decision goes on to require the criminalisation of aiding, abetting[96] or attempting[97] these offences, although it allows each Member State the option of not criminalising attempted illegal access to information systems.[98] It further stipulates penalties of at least between one and three years' imprisonment[99] for the system and data interference offences, rising to a minimum of between two and five years if the act has been committed by a criminal organisation[100] or caused serious damages or affected essential interests.[101] The minimum tariff of two to five years also applies to the illegal access offence if a security measure has been infringed in the commission of the offence.[102]

With regard to jurisdiction, each Member State is directed to establish its jurisdiction where the offence has been committed within its territory (in whole or in part),[103] by one of its nationals,[104] or for the benefit of a legal person with its head office within the Member State's territory.[105] This includes cases where the offence is committed when physically present within the territory regardless of the location of the target information system[106] or, conversely, where the target system is on its territory regardless of the territorial location of the offender.[107]

These measures were required to be implemented by 16 March 2007 and were one of the driving factors behind the amendments proposed to the Computer Misuse Act 1990 by the Police and Justice Act 2006 discussed in Chapter 3. As a Third Pillar measure, it could potentially be annulled in favour of a corresponding Directive, or legislative competence in this area could be transferred to the EC via a *passerelle* decision, but there is currently no EC legislative offering in this area. It is therefore likely that the Framework Decision will survive unaffected should the Treaty of Lisbon come into force. From the UK perspective, the implementing criminal law provisions are in

---

96 Council Framework Decision (EU) 2005/222/JHA of 24 February 2005 on attacks against information systems [2005] OJ L69/67, art. 5(1).
97 Ibid., art. 5(2).
98 Ibid., art. 5(3).
99 Ibid., art. 6(2).
100 Ibid., art. 7(1).
101 Ibid., art. 7(2).
102 Ibid., art. 7(1).
103 Ibid., art. 10(1)(a).
104 Ibid., art. 10(1)(b).
105 Ibid., art. 10(1)(c).
106 Ibid., art. 10(2)(a).
107 Ibid., art. 10(2)(b).

place. The relevant provisions of the Police and Justice Act 2006 were brought into force in Scotland on 1 October 2007[108] and in England and Wales on 1 October 2008.[109]

Current European Commission policy initiatives on cybercrime

In the wake of the Council Framework Decision on attacks against information systems, the European Commission issued a further Communication 'towards a general policy on the fight against cyber-crime'.[110] Commission Communications contain legislative proposals and as such are not binding on Member States. This Communication identified a growing sophisticated, internationalised and organised element to criminal activity, juxtaposed with a static number of European prosecutions on the basis of cross-border law enforcement cooperation.[111] It considered that there is an 'urgent need to take action'[112] at the national, European and international level, although the legal response is geared towards enforcement and international cooperation rather than the use of particular provisions of criminal law. In particular, the Communication conceded that:

> General harmonisation of crime definitions and national penal laws ... is not yet appropriate due to the variety of types of offences covered by this notion. Since effective cooperation between law enforcement authorities often depends on having at least partly harmonised crime definitions, it remains a long-term objective to continue harmonising Member States' legislation.[113]

This statement illustrates that little practical benefit had been achieved in the preceding six years, since harmonisation was also a long-term objective of the 2001 Communication. The Communication makes a number of extra-legal recommendations which the Commission will take forward, assess progress and report to the Council and Parliament. These will be returned to in Chapter 7. In terms of *legal* recommendation, the Commission encourages Member States and relevant third countries to ratify the Council of Europe Convention on

---

108 Police and Justice Act 2006 (Commencement) (Scotland) Order 2007 SI 2007/434.
109 Police and Justice Act 2006 (Commencement No. 9) Order 2008 SI 2008/2503.
110 Commission (EC), 'Communication from the Commission to the European Parliament, the Council and the Committee of the Regions towards a general policy on the fight against cybercrime' COM (2007) 267 final, 22 May 2007.
111 Ibid. [1.2.1].
112 Ibid. [1.3].
113 Ibid. [3.3].

Cybercrime which is described as 'arguably the predominant European and international instrument in this field'.[114] This Convention will be further discussed later in this chapter.

Conclusion

By virtue of the UK's membership of the EU, it is obliged to implement both Community Directives made under the First Pillar and Union Framework Decisions made under the Third Pillar. In that respect, the route by which European measures are implemented is immaterial: the UK must comply. A key distinction, however, lies in the extent of the UK's power during the legislative passage. First Pillar measures are often adopted through qualified majority voting whereas Third Pillar Framework Decisions require unanimity between the Member States. In this sense, while both routes involve a relaxation of national sovereignty, it could be considered that the national position is weaker under the First Pillar than under the Third due to the lack of veto. The potential use of the *passerelle* provision by which matters of police and judicial cooperation in criminal matters could be transferred from Third to First Pillar could therefore be seen as a further erosion of the UK's sovereign power. However, the existence of the 'opt-in' to Title IV measures could still operate as a limited veto, in that the UK could not veto a disagreeable proposal but could still choose not to opt in so that it would not be bound by it. The Treaty of Lisbon would, if in force, restructure the competencies of the EU and would further strengthen its criminal competence to direct Member States to adopt a minimum level of criminalisation and sanction in relation to computer crime.

However, there is a tension between the opposition to the extension of EU powers into traditional areas of national sovereignty and the potential 'sovereignty plus' benefits put forward by Giddens and MacCormick deriving from membership of the EU, allowing Member States to confront international issues more effectively in unity rather than individually. This tension may lead to fragmentation between the EU Member States and prove to be a significant obstacle to any future EU-led harmonisation initiative.

It could also be considered that the UK has used its political influence to shape the initiatives coming from Europe. The exercise of the UK's influence at the EU level is routine and unexceptional.

---

114 Ibid [2.2].

It remains a significant international player capable of both initiating and blocking proposals at a high level. It has one of only five seats on the UN Security Council. The UK has enjoyed some successes in imposing its own agenda on the rest of Europe, for instance in the indefinite postponing of the requirement for metric units on draft beer, cider, bottled milk and road signs[115] and the maintenance of dual metric and imperial labelling on other foodstuffs.[116] The UK had enacted computer misuse legislation in the form of the Computer Misuse Act 1990 long before any binding European initiatives were in place. It has long recognised the economic and positive social impact of new technology and has been desirous of regulation which it is unable to achieve beyond its own borders with its domestic law but can influence via the EU, the Council of Europe, the Commonwealth, the G8 or the UN. In essence, the UK is capable of moving its strategy of domestic control onto a wider international playing field. However, with the exception of the Framework Decision on attacks against information systems, there has been little EU legislative activity specifically in relation to computer misuse. Indeed, the most recent Commission Communication encourages Member States to adopt the Council of Europe Convention on Cybercrime.

Council of Europe initiatives

The Council of Europe (CoE) comprises 47 Member States and, notably, four non-European 'observer' countries: the United States, Canada, Japan and Mexico. It is therefore broader in reach than the European Union which comprises 27 Member States, all of which are also members of the CoE. Aside from the observer countries, the most significant non-EU inclusion in the CoE is the Russian Federation. It can, therefore, achieve greater global effect than the EU. It has the ability to include the United States and Russia as signatories to its Treaties, although their accession is voluntary. Therefore the European Commission's Communication encouraging ratification of the CoE Convention on Cybercrime would achieve a wider

---

115 Council Directive (EC) 80/181/EEC of 20 December 1979 on the approximation of the laws of the Member States relating to units of measurement and on the repeal of Directive 71/354/EEC [1980] OJ L39/40.

116 *Thoburn v. Sunderland City Council* [2003] QB 151 (DC); European Commission, 'Your pint safe in EU hands', 11 September 2007 <http://ec.europa.eu/unitedkingdom/press/frontpage/11092007_en.htm> accessed 25 September 2008.

geographic implementation than that which could be achieved via the EU alone. The Convention also contains a provision that allows the CoE to open it up to a much broader membership by invitation to any non-Member State which has not participated in the elaboration of the Convention.[117] Moreover, given the traditional stance of the EU to refrain from interference with domestic criminal law, even in the light of the *passerelle* and the Treaty of Lisbon, then the CoE Convention may prove to be a more politically acceptable vehicle for the implementation or harmonisation of criminal law. However, CoE Conventions are not statutory acts; they owe their legal existence simply to the will of those States that may become parties to them via signature and ratification. It is therefore open to CoE Member States to choose not to sign or ratify any particular Convention, unlike EU initiatives which are binding on Member States regardless of whether they are expressed by EC Directives or Regulations under the First Pillar or Council Framework Decisions under the Third Pillar. It follows, then, that CoE initiatives are broader in scope than those of the EU, but are softer in terms of compulsion on the respective Member States. However, given the European Commission's steering of EU Member States towards the CoE Convention on Cybercrime and the extent of its geographic reach, it is necessary to examine its provisions in greater detail.

Council of Europe Convention on Cybercrime

Prior to the adoption of the Convention on Cybercrime, the Council of Europe had reported on various aspects of computer-related crime[118] and issued Recommendations relating to both substantive offences[119] and procedural law.[120] However, such Recommendations do not bind Member States and therefore, not unsurprisingly, had limited effect. Therefore, in 1997, building on the principles developed in the earlier Recommendations, the Council of Europe established a Committee of Experts on Crime in Cyberspace (PC-CY) to begin work on drafting

---

117 Council of Europe Convention on Cybercrime (signed 23 November 2001) ETS 185, art. 37.
118 Council of Europe Committee on Crime Problems, *Computer-Related Crime* (Council of Europe, Strasbourg, 1990).
119 Council of Europe Committee of Ministers Recommendation R(89) 9 'On Computer-Related Crime', 13 September 1989.
120 Council of Europe Committee of Ministers Recommendation R(95) 13 'Concerning Problems of Criminal Procedural Law Connected with Information Technology', 11 September 1995.

a Convention to which the largest possible number of Member States would become parties.[121]

The resultant CoE Convention on Cybercrime[122] attempts to provide a solution to the problems posed by cybercrime by the use of 'international law, necessitating the adoption of adequate international legal instruments'.[123] Its principal aims are the harmonisation of domestic criminal laws in relation to cybercrime, the provision of procedural law for the investigation and prosecution of cybercrime offences and establishing effective mechanisms of international cooperation.[124] Section 1 of Chapter II of the Convention[125] sets up four categories of offences: those against the confidentiality, integrity and availability of computer data and systems; computer-related offences (forgery and fraud); content-related offences (child pornography); and offences relating to and infringement of copyright and related rights. It also addresses inchoate liability in respect of attempts, aiding or abetting and issues of corporate liability. Section 2 of Chapter II[126] considers relevant procedural provisions. Section 3[127] addresses jurisdictional issues.

Offences against the confidentiality, integrity and availability of computer data and systems

Article 2 of the Convention requires criminalisation of the intentional access to the whole or any part of a computer system without right. Article 3 establishes the offence of the interception without right of 'non-public transmissions of computer data to, from or within a computer system, including electromagnetic emissions from a computer system carrying such computer data' made by technical means. Article 4(1) prohibits the 'damaging, deletion, deterioration, alteration or suppression of computer data without right', although parties to the Convention may require that the interference with data results in 'serious harm'.[128] Article 5 concerns intentional serious

---

121 Decision CM/Del/Dec(97)583.
122 Council of Europe Convention on Cybercrime (signed 23 November 2001) ETS 185.
123 Council of Europe Explanatory Report to the Convention on Cybercrime ETS 185 [6].
124 Ibid. [16].
125 Council of Europe Convention on Cybercrime (signed 23 November 2001) ETS 185, arts 2–19.
126 Ibid., arts 14–21.
127 Ibid., art. 22.
128 Ibid., art. 4(2).

hindering without right of the functioning of a computer system by inputting, transmitting, damaging, deleting, deteriorating, altering or suppressing computer data. These articles were reflected in the EU Council Framework Decision on attacks against information systems as discussed previously.

Article 6 introduced the new concept of criminalising articles used in the commission of the aforementioned offences which ultimately posed the difficulties in implementation for the Police and Justice Act 2006:

Each Party shall ... establish as criminal offences under its domestic law, when committed intentionally and without right:

a   the production, sale, procurement for use, import, distribution or otherwise making available of:

i   a device, including a computer program, designed or adapted primarily for the purpose of committing any of the offences established in accordance with articles 2 through 5;

ii   a computer password, access code, or similar data by which the whole or any part of a computer system is capable of being accessed,

with intent that it be used for the purpose of committing any of the offences established in articles 2 through 5; and

b   the possession of an item referred to in paragraphs a.i or ii above, with intent that it be used for the purpose of committing any of the offences established in articles 2 through 5. A Party may require by law that a number of such items be possessed before criminal liability attaches.

As is stands, article 6(1) suffers from the same limitations in respect of 'dual use' tools as the Police and Justice Act 2006. However, it is interesting to note that the Convention deals with this situation explicitly in article 6(2):

This article shall not be interpreted as imposing criminal liability where the production, sale, procurement for use, import, distribution or otherwise making available or possession referred to in paragraph 1 of this article is not for the purpose of committing an offence established in accordance with articles 2 through 5 of this Convention, such as for the authorised testing or protection of a computer system.

Article 6(2), then, establishes that tools created for the authorised testing or protection of systems, such as penetration test software and network analysis tools, are specifically excluded from the imposition of criminal liability. The Explanatory Report reconciles this by stating that such test tools are produced for legitimate purposes and their use would therefore be considered to be 'with right'.[129] This approach was not explicitly taken in the Police and Justice Act 2006.

Computer-related offences

Article 7 criminalises intentional computer-related forgery and article 8 computer-related fraud, that is manipulation of data or interference with a computer system with the fraudulent or dishonest intent of procuring an economic benefit. While these offences may be covered by existing national criminal legislation, the Council of Europe specifically included them within the Convention in acknowledgement of the fact that 'in many countries certain traditional legal interests are not sufficiently protected against new forms of interference and attacks'.[130]

Content-related offences

Article 9 concerns the production, distribution, procurement or possession of child pornography via computer systems, including 'realistic' images representing a minor engaged in sexually explicit conduct.

Offences related to infringements of copyright and related rights

Article 10 criminalises the infringement of copyright and related rights where committed 'wilfully, on a commercial scale and by means of a computer system'.

Adoption of the Convention

The Convention on Cybercrime was adopted by the Committee of Ministers and opened for signature in November 2001. It has been

---

129 Council of Europe Explanatory Report to the Convention on Cybercrime ETS 185 [77].
130 Ibid. [80].

signed by 45 of the members and observers and ratified by 23 of them.[131] The United States ratified the Convention in September 2006 and brought it into force in January 2007. This leaves 22 states who are signatories to the Convention without having ratified it: notably this includes the UK. However, the Convention has caused little stir within the UK. The All Party Internet Group inquiry into revising the Computer Misuse Act 1990 reported that it 'received very few comments on the implications for the CMA of ratifying the Convention on Cybercrime, suggesting that this is not widely seen to be a contentious issue'.[132] There has also been little Parliamentary time spent on discussing the Convention outside the debates leading to the enactment of the Police and Justice Act 2006 which were covered in Chapter 3. Although most had heard of it, there was limited appreciation in the Convention among the interview participants. The response of User 4 was typical:

I can see why Europe is trying to bring everything into line, but until it affects me directly, I'm not going to waste too much time finding out what it's all about. I suppose, like most of my colleagues, I'm fairly apathetic. I can't see that it's that big a deal.

There is also little concern regarding infringement of individual rights and liberties. The government considered that a 'proper balance between the interests of law enforcement and respect for fundamental human rights' had been achieved in its drafting.[133] Despite the considerable lapse of time since signature, the UK government 'fully support[s] the Council of Europe Convention'[134] and is 'fully committed'[135] to its ratification, stating that the Police and Justice Act 2006 reforms will 'ensure that the Computer Misuse Act 1990 is fully compliant with the Convention'.[136]

---

131 At 25 September 2008; <http://conventions.coe.int/Treaty/Commun/ChercheSig.asp?NT=185&CM=&DF=&CL=ENG>.

132 All-Party Internet Group, 'Revision of the Computer Misuse Act: Report of an Inquiry by the All Party Internet Group', June 2004 <http://www.apcomms.org.uk/apig/archive/activities-2004/computer-misuse-inquiry/CMAReportFinalVersion1.pdf> [82] accessed 25 September 2008.

133 Hansard HL vol. 620 col. 59 (20 December 2000 WA).

134 Hansard HL vol. 695 col. 6 (7 November 2007 WA).

135 Ibid.

136 Hansard HL vol. 694 col. 240 (12 July 2007 WA).

The Council of Europe considers the relatively slow adoption and ratification of the Convention to be a continued challenge to its desire for international harmonisation across both substantive and procedural national criminal laws:

The challenges [to establishing a framework for international cooperation] include:

- Increasing the number of parties to the Convention and the additional Protocol. In particular, States having already signed these treaties should speed up the ratification process.

- Promoting the Convention at a global level ... other States should be encouraged to seek accession.[137]

However, as Walden comments, the 'comprehensive nature of the Convention, as well as the geographical spread of its signatories, means it is likely to remain the most significant legal instrument in the field for the foreseeable future'.[138] The CoE has also initiated a 'Project Against Cybercrime', partly funded by Microsoft, aiming to have 40 countries (including eight non-European) as ratifying parties to the Convention by February 2009.[139] It has reported that reforms 'based on Convention guidelines' are in progress in Argentina, Brazil, Egypt, India, Nigeria, Pakistan and the Philippines.[140] This demonstrates the expansion of the CoE-style approach beyond its Member States as well as the cooperation between public and private bodies inherent in theories of governance.

---

137 Council of Europe, 'Octopus Interface conference on co-operation against cybercrime, Strasbourg, France (11–12 June 2007): Conference Summary', 3. <http://www.coe.int/t/e/legal_affairs/legal_co-operation/combating_economic_crime/3_technical_co-operation/cyber/567%20IF%20IF%202007-d-sumconclusions1g%2 0Provisional.pdf> accessed 25 September 2008.

138 Walden, I., *Computer Crimes and Digital Investigations* (Oxford University Press, Oxford, 2007) 332.

139 Council of Europe, 'Project against cybercrime: Summary and workplan 2007–2008' <http://www.coe.int/t/e/legal_affairs/legal_co-operation/combating_economic_crime/3_technical_co-operation/cyber/567-d-summary%20and%20w orkplan%202007-2008%20_20%20May%2007_WEB.pdf> accessed 25 September 2008.

140 Council of Europe, 'Countries worldwide turn to Council of Europe Cybercrime Convention', Press Release 413(2007), Strasbourg, 13 June 2007 <https://wcd.coe.int/ViewDoc.jsp?id=1150107> accessed 25 September 2008.

Additional Protocol criminalising acts of a racist and xenophobic nature

During the drafting of the Convention, the PC-CY Committee discussed the possibility of including other content-related offences than those child pornography offences defined in article 9, such as the distribution of racist propaganda through computer systems. This notion was supported by several Member States, but was dropped when the United States resisted. As a result, the PC-CY Committee recommended drawing up an additional Protocol to the Convention as soon as practicable. This approach unblocked the path for the United States to sign the Convention while allowing them (and others) to choose not to sign the Protocol. The additional Protocol was introduced in January 2003[141] and required the criminalisation of various acts in relation to racist and xenophobic material, which it defined as:

> ... any written material, any image or any other representation of ideas or theories, which advocates, promotes or incites hatred, discrimination or violence, against any individual or group of individuals, based on race, colour, descent or national or ethnic origin, as well as religion if used as a pretext for any of these factors.[142]

These acts include dissemination of such material through computer systems,[143] threats[144] and insults[145] motivated by racism and xenophobia and the denial of genocide and crimes against humanity.[146] It has been signed by 31 of the CoE Member States and observers and ratified by 11 of them.[147] It came into force following the fifth ratification in March 2006. However, unlike the Convention itself, the Protocol has not been signed by either the UK or the United States.

The position of the United States is not surprising, given its refusal to support the inclusion of similar provisions in the Convention itself.

---

141 Council of Europe Additional Protocol to the Convention on Cybercrime, concerning the criminalisation of acts of a racist and xenophobic nature committed through computer systems (signed 28 January 2003) ETS 189 (the Additional Protocol).

142 Ibid., art. 2(1).

143 Ibid., art. 3.

144 Ibid., art. 4.

145 Ibid., art. 5.

146 Ibid., art. 6.

147 At 25 September 2008; <http://conventions.coe.int/Treaty/Commun/ChercheSig. asp?NT=189&CM=1&DF=3/13/2008&CL=ENG>.

It considers the Protocol to be incompatible with the guarantee to freedom of speech provided by the First Amendment to the United States Constitution:

Congress shall make no law respecting an establishment of religion, or prohibiting the free exercise thereof; or abridging the freedom of speech or of the press; or the right of the people peaceably to assemble, and to petition the Government for a redress of grievances.[148]

This stance is in line with the Supreme Court decision in *Reno v. American Civil Liberties Union*[149] regarding the regulation of materials distributed via the Internet. Here the anti-obscenity provisions of the Communications Decency Act[150] were struck down for violating the freedom of speech provisions of the First Amendment. Justice Stevens, in delivering the judgement concluded that:

As a matter of constitutional tradition, in the absence of evidence to the contrary, we presume that governmental regulation of the content of speech is more likely to interfere with the free exchange of ideas than to encourage it.[151]

However, the United States had no objection to ratifying the child pornography provisions within the main Convention. This follows *New York v. Ferber*[152] in which the Supreme Court held that the First Amendment right to freedom of speech did not prevent states from banning the sale of child pornography. It reasoned that although, following *Miller v. California*,[153] pornography can only be banned if it is obscene, pornography depicting actual children can be proscribed regardless of obscenity to protect the exploitation of children in the production process. *Virtual* child pornography, that is, material produced by using young-looking adults or by digital manipulation, was also banned within the Child Pornography Prevention Act 1996.[154]

---

148 Constitution of the United States of America (as amended) (25 July 2007) <http://frwebgate.access.gpo.gov/cgi-bin/getdoc.cgi?dbname=110_cong_documents&docid=f:hd050.pdf> accessed 25 September 2008.
149 521 US 844 (1997).
150 47 USC §§223(a)(1)(B), 223(a)(2), 223(d).
151 521 US 844 (1997) 885 [IX].
152 458 US 747 (1982).
153 413 US 15 (1972).
154 18 USC §§2256(8)(B), 2256(8)(D).

However, in *Ashcroft* v. *Free Speech Coalition*[155] the Supreme Court considered that the Act banned material that was neither obscene under *Miller* nor produced by exploiting real children under *Ferber*. It concluded that the prohibitions were substantially overbroad, in violation of the First Amendment and therefore unconstitutional.

The US Department of Justice makes its constitutional position on the additional Protocol very clear:

The United States does not believe that the final version of the protocol is consistent with its Constitutional guarantees. For that reason, the U.S. has informed the Council of Europe that it will not become a Party to the protocol. It is important to note that the protocol is separate from the main Convention. That is, a country that signed and ratified the main Convention, but not the protocol, would not be bound by the terms of the protocol. Thus, its authorities would not be required to assist other countries in investigating activity prohibited by the protocol.[156]

Therefore, not only will the United States not sign the Protocol but it will not assist other countries in investigating activities criminalised by it. This refusal to engage with the additional Protocol immediately establishes the US as a potential safe haven for race-related computer misuse. For Van Blarcum, this safe haven would be created by the visibility of 'pre-established American sites in Europe and America's status as an attractive home for European sites escaping the restrictions on speech present in Europe'.[157]

The UK has also made it quite clear that it will not ratify the Protocol. In January 2008, Vernon Coaker MP, Under-Secretary of State in the Home Office, stated in a written answer to the question of whether the additional Protocol was to be implemented:

The Government believe that our current law effectively deals with incitement to racial hatred, and strikes the right balance between the need to protect individuals from violence and hatred and the need to protect freedom of expression. We will therefore

155 535 US 234 (2002).
156 United States Department of Justice, Computer Crime and Intellectual Property Section, 'Council of Europe Convention on Cybercrime Frequently Asked Questions and Answers' (11 November 2003) <http://www.usdoj.gov/criminal/cybercrime/COEFAQs.htm> accessed 25 September 2008.
157 Van Blarcum, D., 'Internet hate speech: the European Framework and the emerging American haven' (2005) 62 *Washington and Lee Law Review* 781, 829.

not ratify the protocol as it does not allow us to maintain our criminal threshold for this sort of offence.[158]

The UK is therefore using the same argument as the US regarding freedom of expression as a determining factor in refusing to ratify the Protocol, although it has a different threshold of tolerance for interference with that freedom. For instance, the Criminal Justice and Immigration Act 2008[159] expands the meaning of 'photograph' in relation to the Protection of Children Act 1978 to include images derived from photographs or pseudo-photographs as well as electronic data capable of being converted into such an image. This criminalises virtual child pornography in the UK, although it is protected in the US via the First Amendment.

The Public Order Act 1986 criminalised the display of any written material which is threatening, abusive or insulting with intent to stir up racial hatred, or which is likely to stir up such hatred.[160] These offences were extended to religious hatred by the Racial and Religious Hatred Act 2006.[161] The domestic criminal law therefore seems to cover the offences required by articles 3–5 of the additional Protocol. Indeed, in relation to religious hatred, the domestic offence offers greater protection than that required by the Protocol. The Protocol includes religion only if used as a pretext for racial hatred,[162] whereas the Racial and Religious Hatred Act 2006 criminalises hatred against persons defined by reference to their religious belief (or lack thereof) *regardless* of race. Religious hatred therefore becomes distinct from racial hatred. Although certain religious groups such as Sikhs[163] and Jews[164] have been held to be racial groups for the purposes of the Race Relations Act 1976,[165] other less ethnically homogenous religious groups including Muslims[166] and Rastafarians[167] have fallen outside its protection. As Lord Denning MR commented in *Mandla v. Dowell Lee*

---

158 Hansard HC vol. 470 col. 290W (29 January 2008).
159 Criminal Justice and Immigration Act 2008, s. 69(3).
160 Public Order Act 1986, ss. 18–23.
161 Racial and Religious Hatred Act 2006, s. 1; this inserts, *inter alia*, new ss. 29A–29F into the Public Order Act 1986.
162 Additional Protocol, art. 2(1).
163 *Mandla v. Dowell Lee* [1983] 2 AC 548 (HL).
164 *Seide v. Gillette Industries* [1980] IRLR 427 (EAT).
165 See s. 3(1) which defines 'racial group' as 'a group of persons defined by reference to colour, race, nationality or ethnic or national origins'.
166 *Tariq v. Young* (1989) 247738/88 (Birmingham Industrial Tribunal).
167 *Dawkins v. Department of the Environment* [1993] IRLR 284 (CA).

in the Court of Appeal, the Race Relations Act 1976 'does not include religion or politics or culture', giving examples of Roman Catholics, Communists and hippies as groups who can be discriminated for or against 'as much as you like without being in breach of the law'.[168] Racial hatred or religious hatred is therefore not criminalised per se. To fall within the criminal law, the hatred must carry some public disorder connotations. For racial hatred offences, it is sufficient that 'having regard to all the circumstances racial hatred is likely to be stirred up'.[169] Religious hatred offences[170] require direct intention to stir up religious hatred, mere likelihood being insufficient. The public order element required to make out an offence is therefore more pronounced in relation to religious hatred.[171]

Section 1(2) of the Terrorism Act 2006 criminalises the publication of statements with the intention[172] that members of the public are directly or indirectly encouraged or otherwise induced to commit, prepare or instigate acts of terrorism or Convention offences.[173] This offence does not, however, correspond with the criminalisation of the denial, gross minimisation, approval or justification of crimes against humanity as required by art. 6 of the additional Protocol. Such statements are those of glorification or those from which the public could reasonably be expected to infer that the glorification is of conduct that 'should be emulated by them in existing circumstances'.[174] Therefore statements glorifying genocide, for instance, would be unlikely to fall within section 1 of the Terrorism Act 2006, since right-thinking members of the public would not reasonably infer that they should emulate genocide as a result. The Explanatory Note gives an example of conduct which would fall within the Act:

---

168 *Mandla* v. *Dowell Lee* [1983] QB 1, 8 (CA).

169 Public Order Act 1986, ss. 18–22.

170 Public Order Act 1986, ss. 29B–29F.

171 For other national approaches to racist content, see Akdeniz, Y., 'Governing racist content on the Internet: national and international responses' (2007) 56 *University of New Brunswick Law Journal* 103.

172 Or recklessness: Terrorism Act 2006, s. 1(2)(b)(ii).

173 Terrorism Act 2006, Sch. 1. These offences are categorised as explosives offences, biological weapons, offences against internationally protected persons, hostage-taking, hijacking or other offences against aircraft, offences involving nuclear material, chemical or nuclear weapons, directing terrorist organisations, offences related to terrorist funds and offences under the Aviation and Maritime Security Act 1990. Inchoate liability is included. They are not to be confused with infringements of the European Convention on Human Rights.

174 Terrorism Act 2006, s. 1(3).

[I]f it was reasonable to expect members of the public to infer from a statement glorifying the bomb attacks on the London Underground on 7 July 2005 that what should be emulated is action causing severe disruption to London's transport network, this will be caught.[175]

Therefore, since views on historical events do not generally encourage their repetition, they cannot constitute the glorification of terrorism or crimes against humanity.

The Terrorism Act 2006 also specifically considers the use of the Internet in the encouragement of terrorism and the dissemination of terrorist publications.[176] Section 3 of the Act allows the police to issue a summary 'notice and take-down' advice to 'anyone involved in the provision or use of electronic services'[177] used in connection with such encouragement or dissemination activities. Service of the notice does not require the authority of a court; in theory such a notice may be initiated by any constable. In practice, it will be initiated by a counter-terrorist officer and should be authorised by a police officer of the rank of superintendent or above. It is also recognised that take-down notices will only be used if the offending material is not removed voluntarily. The Home Office guidance illustrates that this could include content providers or aggregators, hosting ISPs, webmasters, forum moderators and bulletin board hosts. The advice is not binding on the service provider. However, if the provider ignores the advice, then they will be deemed to have endorsed the offending content and therefore, if subsequently prosecuted under sections 1 or 2, will be unable to avail themselves of the statutory defences.[178] The advice cannot be served on ISPs who act as 'mere conduit'; that is, an ISP who does no more than provide network access or facilitate the transmission of information.[179] However, concerns have been expressed that the framework established in the Terrorism Act 2006

---

175 Terrorism Act 2006, Explanatory Note [24].
176 Terrorism Act 2006, s. 2.
177 Home Office, 'Guidance on notices issued under section 3 of the Terrorism Act 2006' (9 October 2006) <http://security.homeoffice.gov.uk/news-and-publications1/publication-search/legislation-publications/guidance-notices-section3-t1.pdf> accessed 25 September 2008.
178 Terrorism Act 2006, ss. 1(6), 2(9).
179 Home Office, 'Guidance on notices issued under section 3 of the Terrorism Act 2006' (9 October 2006) [34] <http://security.homeoffice.gov.uk/news-and-publications1/publication-search/legislation-publications/guidance-notices-section3-t1.pdf> accessed 25 September 2008.

will 'have an inhibiting effect on legitimate freedom of expression and will therefore lead to disproportionate interferences with free speech'.[180] Such provisions in relation to proscribed content are of potentially broader application than terrorism. The idea of 'notice and take-down' is consistent with the framework established by the EC e-commerce Directive,[181] which requires that:

... the provider of an information society service, consisting of the storage of information, upon obtaining actual knowledge or awareness of illegal activities has to act expeditiously to remove or to disable access to the information concerned.[182]

However, this more general procedure is more generally encountered in terms of private regulation rather than via police intervention in relation to specified content.

The additional Protocol illustrates the difficulties in harmonisation initiatives where there are fundamental constitutional barriers to adoption or pre-existing domestic legislation which goes beyond that required. Both these situations can be considered in terms of the State giving primacy to its sovereign affairs rather than acceding to an international agreement that it considers to be incompatible or unnecessary. As Whine comments, in relation to the issue of online hate content 'future success depends on the determination of governments themselves'.[183]

Criticisms of the Convention

Although the Convention is undoubtedly legally significant, it has been criticised for a variety of reasons, particularly in the US. The American Civil Liberties Union (ACLU) considered that it was drafted 'in a closed and secretive manner'[184] and that it is lacking in protection for privacy and civil liberties. However, for Marler, there

---

180 Joint Committee on Human Rights, 'The Council of Europe Convention on the Prevention of Terrorism' HL (2006–07) 26; HC (2006–07) 247 [47].

181 Directive (EC) 2000/31 of 8 June 2000 on certain legal aspects of information society services, in particular electronic commerce, in the Internal Market (e-commerce Directive) [2000] OJ L178/1.

182 Ibid., art. 46.

183 Whine, M., 'Cyberhate, anti-semitism and counterlegislation' (2006) 11 *Communications Law* 124, 131.

184 American Civil Liberties Union, 'The Seven Reasons why the Senate should reject the International Cybercrime Treaty', 18 December 2003 <http://www.aclu.org/privacy/internet/14861res2003218.html> accessed 25 September 2008.

is 'no support for the argument that the Convention directly violates the right to privacy'[185] since the Convention specifically addresses human rights and privacy, concluding that:

The right to privacy is a fundamental right. Human rights must be accorded the highest respect, but the potential threat to them is not definite enough to continue allowing cyber-criminals to violate the innocence of children, or to steal money from our businesses, government, and taxpayers.[186]

In response to the mutual assistance provisions, the ACLU stated that:

Ratification of the Council of Europe's Cybercrime Convention will put the United States in the morally repugnant position of supporting the actions of politically corrupt regimes.[187]

It cited Ukraine, Azerbaijan and Romania as particular problematic examples before concluding that ratification would require the United States to 'use extraordinary powers to do the dirty work of other nations'.[188] On the contrary, prior to its opening for signature, the independent EU advisory body on data protection and privacy had stressed that the Convention should pay 'particular attention to the protection of fundamental rights and freedoms, especially the right to privacy and personal data protection'.[189] Concerns have also been expressed by communications service providers over the requirements imposed upon them to assist law enforcement agencies. As Downing comments:

Interception of communications generally is regarded as an intrusive investigative technique. Unrestricted interception can

---

185 Marler, S.L., 'The Convention on Cybercrime: should the United States ratify?' (2002) 37 *New England Law Review* 183, 218.

186 Ibid, 219.

187 American Civil Liberties Union, 'ACLU Memo on the Council of Europe Convention on Cybercrime', 16 June 2004 <http://www.aclu.org/news/NewsPrint.cfm?ID=15954&c=39> accessed 25 September 2008.

188 Ibid.

189 Article 29 Data Protection Working Party Opinion 4/2001 'On the Council of Europe's Draft Convention on Cybercrime', 22 March 2001 <http://ec.europa.eu/justice_home/fsj/privacy/docs/wpdocs/2001/wp41en.pdf> accessed 25 September 2008.

constitute a grave privacy violation as it allows access to the most private communications and has the potential to inhibit freedom of speech and association.[190]

In terms of enforcement, the Convention does not go so far as to allow investigators to conduct inquiries in a foreign state; it preserves the exclusive national jurisdictions of the investigation authorities within Member States, introducing 'procedural measures, but only at national level and to enable States to respond to the requests for mutual assistance that will continue to be submitted'.[191]

Broad implementation of the Convention may also be time-consuming. As Brenner and Clark comment, since it incorporates substantive and procedural law that may not be routine in some Member States then:

> ... it means implementing the Convention will be a complicated process for many countries, one that will take time. Consequently, even if the Convention proves to be a viable means of improving law enforcement's ability to react to transnational cybercrime, we are unlikely to see any marked improvement in the near future.[192]

This view is echoed by Flanagan who further considers delay resulting from the prospect of constitutional difficulties, the propensity of individual legislatures to 'do things their own way' and the 'workings of special interest groups to ensure their input into national implementations all around the world'.[193]

Lewis[194] criticises the effectiveness of the Convention (in common with all international initiatives) on a number of grounds. He considers that there is a lack of incentive for many countries

---

190 Downing, R.W., 'Shoring up the weakest link: what lawmakers around the world need to consider in developing comprehensive laws to combat cybercrime' (2005) 43 *Columbia Journal of Transnational Law* 705, 749.

191 Cangemi, D., 'Procedural law provisions of the Council of Europe Convention on Cybercrime' (2004) 18 *International Review of Law, Computers and Technology* 165, 167.

192 Brenner, S.W. and Clarke, L.L., 'Distributed security: preventing cybercrime' (2005) 23 *John Marshall Journal of Computer and Information Law* 659, 671.

193 Flanagan, A., 'The law and computer crime: reading the script of reform' (2005) 13 *International Journal of Law and Information Technology* 98, 117.

194 Lewis, B.C., 'Prevention of computer crime amidst international anarchy' (2004) 41 *American Criminal Law Review* 1353.

to participate, particularly in those developing countries where computer crime is not yet a significant concern. He further argues that there will be problems with effectiveness even where countries do participate, citing a list of obstacles including the speed at which new technologies are developed, differences in certain substantive values between States, different standards for conviction, the imposition of different punishments upon conviction, the failure of many countries to commit adequate resources to fighting computer crime and the lack of any viable international body to coordinate national agencies and enforce international agreement. However, the International Criminal Police Organisation (INTERPOL), which exists to facilitate cross-border police cooperation between 186 member countries, does collect, store, analyse and share information on electronic crime. It has also established regional working parties and developed a training and operational standard initiative to provide enhanced investigative support to its members.[195] Lewis argues that opposition from civil liberties groups (such as the ACLU) to increased government power might also hinder progress.

Keyser raises a potential economic drawback in relation to the costs to ISPs and other related businesses of retaining and preserving data in case they are called upon for assistance by an investigating agency. He argues that associated compliance costs will be passed on to consumers via increased subscription and service costs, concluding that:

> ... it is ultimately the consumer that will need to weigh the importance of policing cybercrime with the increased cost associated with Internet access when deciding whether to support the Convention.[196]

Weber[197] also highlights the potential flaws within the Convention, arguing that it will fail without universal participation and will take 'years' to ratify. Lack of worldwide participation could lead to safe havens beyond the Convention's reach, meaning that States will still need to take unilateral action against individuals in countries that fail to join, ratify, implement or enforce the treaty. For Goldsmith,

---

195 INTERPOL, 'Fact Sheet "Cyber-crime"' COM/FS/2007-09/FHT-02 <http://www.interpol.int/Public/ICPO/FactSheets/FHT02.pdf> accessed 25 September 2008.

196 Keyser, M., 'The Council of Europe Convention on Cybercrime' (2003) 12 *Journal of Transnational Law and Policy* 287, 325.

197 Weber, A.M., 'The Council of Europe's Convention on Cybercrime' (2003) 18 *Berkeley Technology Law Journal* 425, 444-5.

such unilateral assertions of power might encourage accession to the Convention and facilitate global adoption.[198] Weber proposes an alternative in the form of a model criminal code rather than 'the widespread adoption of a treaty codifying the current law of the hegemony'.[199] This model code, she argues, would be more easily adapted in the light of developing technologies and would also enable States to maintain consistency between their national laws and the model code. However, such a code would still be slow to create, would be likely to overlap considerably with the Convention and would still require mechanisms to facilitate cross-border investigation.

Conclusion

The CoE Convention on Cybercrime is perhaps the most complete international legislative instrument in the area of computer misuse in effect at present. It is capable of reaching significantly more States that any EU initiative could, notably the United States and Russia. The Convention is legally binding, but, crucially, only upon those Member States which sign and subsequently ratify it. It does not therefore represent a mandatory minimum framework of criminal law required of each of its Member States. Moreover, where politically sensitive rights are concerned, there is less likelihood of adoption by States that will be reluctant to allow a harmonised CoE view to be imposed to the detriment of their national sovereignty. A prime example of this is found in the refusal of the United States to sign the additional Protocol on racist and xenophobic acts on a fundamental constitutional basis and that of the UK on the basis that current domestic law is more than adequate to strike an appropriate balance between freedom of expression and protection from hatred. Concerns have been expressed about the Convention: from its impact on the right to expression and the time and cost that it could take to implement to the adequacy of investigative resources and the difficulties inherent in cross-border investigation. These difficulties are particularly striking where (as is the case with the United States and the additional Protocol) one State will refuse to cooperate in the investigation of an offence which it has not implemented within its own domestic legislation.

---

198 Goldsmith, J.L., 'The Internet and the legitimacy of remote cross-border searches' (2001) 1 *University of Chicago Legal Forum* 103, 117.

199 Weber, A.M., 'The Council of Europe's Convention on Cybercrime' (2003) 18 *Berkeley Technology Law Journal* 425, 445.

Commonwealth initiatives

The Commonwealth is an association of 53 independent States[200] which developed out of the British Empire. Most of its Member States are former British colonies. It provides an international forum for both developed and developing nations to seek agreement on particular matters by consensus. Unlike the Council of Europe, its reach extends into many African, Caribbean and South Pacific States. The Commonwealth issued a Computer and Computer-related Crimes Bill which was recommended for endorsement by Law Ministers in October 2002.[201] This Bill was developed on the basis of the draft CoE Convention on Cybercrime and aimed to:

> … protect the integrity of computer systems and the confidentiality, integrity and availability of data, prevent abuse of such systems and facilitate the gathering and use of electronic evidence.[202]

Its provisions are focused at computer integrity offences: illegal access,[203] interfering with data[204] or computer systems[205] and illegal interception of data.[206] It also proposes criminalising the production or possession (with requisite intent) of devices for the use of committing a computer integrity offence.[207] Its only content offence is restricted to child pornography.[208] In common with the CoE Convention, the Commonwealth model contains mutual assistance recommendations. These recommendations amend the Harare Scheme on Mutual Assistance in Criminal Matters to include the preservation of stored computer data to assist in a criminal investigation.[209]

---

200 <http://www.thecommonwealth.org/Internal/142227/members/> accessed 25 September 2008.

201 Commonwealth, 'Model Law on Computer and Computer-related Crime' LMM(02) 17 October 2002 <http://www.thecommonwealth.org/shared_asp_files/uploadedfiles/%7BDA109CD2-5204-4FAB-AA77-86970A639B05%7D_Computer%20Crime.pdf> accessed 25 September 2008.

202 Ibid., s. 2.
203 Ibid., s. 5.
204 Ibid., s. 6.
205 Ibid., s. 7.
206 Ibid., s. 8.
207 Ibid., s. 9.
208 Ibid., s. 10.
209 Commonwealth, 'Scheme relating to mutual assistance in criminal matters within the Commonwealth including amendments made by Law Ministers in

As Walden comments, computer misuse 'may not figure high on the reform agenda of developing nations'.[210] However, the similarities between the Commonwealth model and the CoE Convention could smooth the way to broader harmonisation beyond that within the CoE's immediate reach, although, as Bourne points out, the mutual assistance approach is voluntary and lacks the binding force of a treaty.[211] Moreover, adoption of a model law does not necessarily mean that every Member State is bound to reproduce it without amendment. Its aim is to reduce the effort for drafters, particularly in small states, reinforcing 'a world of common law in which precedents from one country's court are quoted in another's'.[212] Therefore Commonwealth states are left to enjoy a non-binding head-start on drafting a domestic criminal law that is broadly compatible with the CoE Convention. That is not to say that the developed world does not have an interest in good enforcement elsewhere: for example, Advance Fee Fraud, which involves requests to help move large sums of money with the promise of a substantial share of the cash in return, originates predominantly in Nigeria and was estimated to have caused losses of around US$4.3 billion in 2007.[213]

Therefore the Commonwealth offers the opportunity for a 'CoE Convention style' model criminal law to be implemented in a largely different set of both developed and developing states. However, the Commonwealth model criminal law is merely recommended for adoption by Law Ministers. While it might prove to be convenient for the legislative drafters in developing countries, it is also open to each Member State to adapt the law to suit their own view (and hence preserve their national sovereignty) or indeed to choose not to implement it at all. Moreover, the Commonwealth mutual assistance provisions within the Harare Scheme are voluntary and therefore without binding force.

---

210 Walden, I., *Computer Crimes and Digital Investigations* (Oxford University Press, Oxford, 2007) 337.

211 Bourne, R., '2002 Commonwealth Law Ministers' Meeting: Policy Brief', Commonwealth Policy Studies Unit, Institute of Commonwealth Studies <http://www.cpsu.org.uk/downloads/2002CLMM.pdf> accessed 25 September 2008.

212 Ibid.

213 Ultrascan, '419 fraud stats and trends for 2007', 19 February 2008 <http://www.ultrascan.nl/assets/applets/2007_Stats_on_419_AFF_feb_19_2008_version_1.7.pdf> accessed 25 September 2008.

April 1990, November 2002 and October 2005' <http://www.thecommonwealth.org/shared_asp_files/uploadedfiles/2C167ECF-0FDE-481B-B552-E9BA23857CE3_HARARESCHEMERELATINGTOMUTUALASSISTANCE2005.pdf> accessed 25 September 2008.

United Nations initiatives

The United Nations (UN) is an international body comprising virtually all internationally recognised independent States: 192 Member States in total.[214] It has broad purposes in the arena of international relations; the most relevant purpose in relation to computer misuse is to be 'a centre for harmonizing the actions of nations'.[215] Like the EU and the CoE, the UN has the capability to bind Member States by Treaty and could offer an almost global reach to the approximation of law.

The UN General Assembly issued an endorsement of a general resolution on computer-related crimes[216] from the Eighth United Nations Congress on the Prevention of Crime and the Treatment of Offenders as early as 1990.[217] In 1994, the UN published a manual on the prevention and control of computer-related crime[218] which identified a 'need for global action'[219] in the areas of substantive[220] and procedural law,[221] data security as a preventative measure[222] and international cooperation.[223] In particular, it recommended criminalisation of the alteration of computer data or computer programs without right, computer espionage, the unauthorised use of a computer and the unauthorised use of a protected computer program (that is, use of an unauthorised copy of a computer program protected by law).[224] It also suggested that Member States consider criminalisation of misuse such as trafficking in wrongfully obtained computer passwords and other information about means of obtaining unauthorised access

---

214 United Nations Member States <http://www.un.org/members/list.shtml> accessed 25 September 2008.

215 United Nations Organisation <http://www.un.org/aboutun/basicfacts/unorg.htm> accessed 25 September 2008.

216 United Nations General Assembly Resolution A/RES/45/121 (14 December 1990).

217 United Nations, Eighth United Nations Congress on the Prevention of Crime and the Treatment of Offenders, Havana (27 August – 7 September 1990)' UN Doc E/91/IV/2, ch. 1, s. C, res. 9.

218 United Nations, 'Manual on the prevention and control of computer-related crime' (1994) 43–44 International Review of Criminal Policy UN Doc E/94/IV/5 <http://www.uncjin.org/Documents/EighthCongress.html> accessed 25 September 2008.

219 Ibid., Part I, section C.

220 Ibid., Parts II and III.

221 Ibid., Part IV.

222 Ibid., Part V.

223 Ibid., Part VI.

224 Ibid., Part II, Section C [122].

to computer systems, and the distribution of viruses or similar programs. It also considered that 'special attention should be given to the use of criminal norms that penalise recklessness or the creation of dangerous risks and to practical problems of enforcement'.[225] This approach is again broadly similar to the direction taken by the CoE Convention.

In 2001, the General Assembly adopted a second resolution on 'Combating the Criminal Misuse of Information Technologies'.[226] This resolution made a series of very general recommendations concerning the elimination of safe havens, cooperation between States in enforcement, investigation and prosecution and adequate training of law enforcement personnel, before inviting States to takes its measures into account in their efforts to deal with the issues. Such resolutions are, as the word 'invites' suggests, simply recommendations and consequently have no binding effect on Member States. At the Eleventh UN Congress on Crime Prevention and Criminal Justice in 2005, there was some discussion surrounding the creation of a UN Convention on Cybercrime, building on the CoE Convention, while attempting to deal with some of its deficiencies 'regarding the effective protection of human rights, the protection of customer privacy and the high cost of co-operating with law enforcement investigators'.[227] However, in a later press release, the Congress concluded that:

While there was a wide consensus on the need for a combined approach, and better mechanisms of international cooperation, participants felt that a United Nations Convention on Cybercrime would be premature at this stage, and it was more critical to provide technical assistance to Member States, in order to provide a level playing field.[228]

The UN's focus on technical assistance is complementary to the CoE's Project Against Cybercrime which is focused on facilitating accession and implementation of its Convention or the additional

---

225 Ibid., Part II, Section C [125].
226 United Nations General Assembly Resolution A/RES/55/63 (22 January 2001).
227 United Nations, 'Congress Discussion Guide', UN Doc A/CONF/203/PM/1 (11 February 2005) [190].
228 United Nations, '"Around the clock" capability needed to successfully fight cybercrime, workshop told', UN Doc SOC/CP/334 (25 April 2005).

Protocol rather than instilling technical capability.[229] The UN has not yet resurrected the notion of its own cybercrime convention.

The United Nations has the broadest reach of the intergovernmental bodies discussed in this chapter, covering virtually all recognised states. It has adopted broad resolutions in the areas of computer crime; these are recommendations and compel no action on the part of Member States. Legislative action in the form of a UN Cybercrime Convention to build and improve upon the CoE offering is still considered premature. The UN is instead focusing on providing technical (rather than legal) assistance to Member States thereby harmonising technical capability rather than legal regulation.

This approach of providing technical assistance is similar to the that adopted by the UN in relation to terrorism. Following the attacks on the US of 11 September 2001, the UN introduced a two-fold mechanism to facilitate global adoption of effective laws against the financing of terrorist activity.[230] The problem that the UN faced was that States such as Yemen, for example, were disinclined to take action since such action was inconvenient, not a national priority and difficult to implement for lack of technical expertise. The UN therefore established the Counter Terrorism Committee to which all States were called upon to report on the steps taken to implement its proposals (many of which required legislative action). As well as acting as a focal point for the UN efforts, this Committee also facilitates the provision of 'assistance of appropriate expertise'[231] to States in furtherance of the objectives set out in the Resolution. Therefore the UN takes a role of coordination and assistance rather than direct coercion. However, this arrangement was only brought into being as a result of the political impetus following 11 September 2001. It is therefore reasonable to assume that a similar coordinated international approach to computer misuse would require an event of similar gravity to precipitate it. However, the conceptual idea of coordinated international technical assistance remains at least theoretically attractive. The idea of technical assistance as a extra-legal means of governance will be further explored in Chapter 7.

---

229 Council of Europe, 'Project against cybercrime: Summary and workplan 2007–2008' <http://www.coe.int/t/e/legal_affairs/legal_co-operation/combating_economic_crime/3_technical_co-operation/cyber/567-d-summary%20and%20workplan%202007-2008%20_20%20May%2007_WEB.pdf> accessed 25 September 2008.

230 United Nations Security Council Resolution 1373 (28 September 2001).
231 Ibid., art. 6.

Group of Eight initiatives

The Group of Eight (G8) is an international forum for the governments of the leading industrial nations: the UK, the United States, Canada, France, Germany, Russia, Italy and Japan. Although it is an informal assembly by comparison to the Council of Europe and the European Union, it undertakes policy research which culminates in an annual summit meeting attended by the heads of government of each of the G8 States. The European Commission is also represented at the G8 summit. By virtue of its membership, the G8 is influential in the formation of international policy in areas as diverse as health, economic and social development, energy, environment, foreign affairs, terrorism and justice and law enforcement.

After the 1995 Summit in Halifax, Nova Scotia, a group of experts was brought together to look for better ways to fight international crime. This group (which became known as the 'Lyon Group') produced 40 recommendations aimed at increasing the efficiency of collective government responses to organised crime.[232] These recommendations were endorsed at the G8 Lyon Summit and emphasised the importance of a coordinated response to high-tech crime. As a consequence of these recommendations the Lyon Group's 'High-Tech Crime Subgroup' was established.

At the Denver Summit in June 1997, the G8 issued a Communiqué stating that its areas of concern included the 'investigation, prosecution, and punishment of high-tech criminals, such as those tampering with computer and telecommunications technology, across national borders' and a 'system to provide all governments with the technical and legal capabilities to respond to high-tech crimes, regardless of where the criminals may be located'.[233] An accompanying Foreign Ministers' Report considered that the response to computer crime required more than simply legal regulation:

The significant growth in computer and telecommunications technologies brings with it new challenges: global networks require new legal *and technical* mechanisms that allow for a

---

232 These were updated in May 2002 as the G8 Recommendations on Transnational Crime <http://canada/justice.gc.ca/en/news/g8/doc1.html> accessed 25 September 2008.

233 G8, 'Denver Summit of the Eight: Communiqué' (22 June 1997) [40] <http://www.g8.utoronto.ca/summit/1997denver/g8final.htm> accessed 25 September 2008.

timely and effective international law enforcement response to computer-related crimes.[234] (emphasis added.)

In December 1998, the G8 Justice and Interior Ministers issued a further Communiqué 'to meet the challenges of the information age'[235] in relation to high-tech crime. In doing so they considered three 'distinct components' of a common approach to the 'unique borderless nature of global networks'. The first component was that the domestic criminal law should ensure appropriate criminalisation of computer misuse and facilitate the collection and preservation of computer evidence, backed up by sufficient technically conversant policing resources. This was followed by the proposal that there should be a 'new level' of international cooperation consistent with the 'principles of sovereignty and the protection of human rights, freedoms and privacy'. The final observation was that there should be an 'unprecedented' level of cooperation between government and industry to develop secure systems which should be accompanied by the best computer and personnel security practices.[236] This approach was to be underpinned by ten principles and a ten-point Action Plan. Most of the principles concern international cooperation and policing. In relation to computer misuse, the most pertinent principles are the first and fourth. The first principle requires that there must be no safe havens for those who 'abuse information technologies'. The fourth deals with substantive criminal offences:

IV. Legal systems must protect the confidentiality, integrity and availability of data and systems from unauthorised impairment and ensure that serious abuse is penalised.[237]

This requirement to legislate in the areas of data confidentiality, integrity and availability is supported by the third point of the Action Plan directing Member States to review their domestic legal systems to ensure that such abuses are 'appropriately' criminalised.[238]

---

234 G8, 'Denver Summit of the Eight: Foreign Ministers' Progress Report' (21 June 1997) [25] <http://www.g8.utoronto.ca/summit/1997denver/formin.htm> accessed 25 September 2008.

235 G8, 'Meeting of Justice and Interior Ministers of the Eight: Communiqué' (10 December 1997) <http://www.usdoj.gov/criminal/cybercrime/g82004/97Communique.pdf> 3 accessed 25 September 2008.

236 Ibid., 2, 3.

237 Ibid., 6.

238 Ibid., 7.

The networked response is reinforced by point 7 of the Action Plan:

7. Work jointly with industry to ensure that new technologies facilitate our effort to combat high-tech crime by preserving and collecting critical evidence.[239]

On the face of it, this point could be taken simply to require the development of secure systems. However, taken in conjunction with the ninth principle, which requires systems to 'facilitate the tracing of criminals and the collection of evidence', it could be considered to imply, as Walden comments:

… law enforcement involvement in the development of new technologies and the standards upon which they operate … meddling with existing … private sector processes.[240]

In essence, the G8 principles and Action Plan strengthen the interplay between the criminal law and technology in the response to computer misuse. Regulation through technology is considered further in Chapter 7.

At its 2000 summit in Japan, the G8 issued the Okinawa Charter on the Global Information Society[241] which considered that computer misuse issues 'such as hacking and viruses … require effective policy responses' developed by engaging 'industry and other stakeholders' as well as by implementing 'effective measures, as set out in the Organisation for Economic Cooperation and Development (OECD) Guidelines for Security of Information Systems'.[242] The dialogue between the public and private sectors had been initiated prior to the summit[243] which produced a set of guiding principles to be taken into account when developing responses to computer misuse:

---

239 Ibid.
240 Walden, I., *Computer Crimes and Digital Investigations* (Oxford: Oxford University Press, 2007) 334.
241 G8, 'Okinawa Charter on Global Information Society' (July 2000) <http://www.mofa.go.jp/policy/economy/summit/2000/documents/charter.html> accessed 25 September 2008.
242 Ibid. [8].
243 G8, 'A Government/Industry Dialogue on Safety and Confidence in Cyberspace' (May 2000) <www.mofa.jp/policy/economy/summit/2000/crime.html> accessed 25 September 2008.

1. ensuring protection of individual freedoms and private life
2. preserving governments' ability to fight high-tech crime
3. facilitating appropriate training for all involved
4. defining a clear and transparent framework for addressing cybercriminality
5. ensuring free and fair economic activities, the sound development of industry, and supporting effective industry-initiated voluntary codes of conduct and standards
6. assessing effectiveness and consequences.[244]

The G8 Justice and Interior Ministers again considered computer misuse as part of their 2002 'Recommendations on Transnational Crime' which was an update to the Lyon Group's 40 recommendations.[245] The section covering 'high-tech and computer-related crimes'[246] reinforces the view that computer misuse should be 'adequately criminalised'.[247] It also directs states to be 'guided' by earlier G8 policies as well as the CoE Convention on Cybercrime in reviewing its national criminal law.[248] The G8 nations also stated their intention to become parties to the Convention and urged other states to do so if entitled or, if not, to approximate the measures called for in the Convention within their own legal frameworks.[249] In practical terms, this meant that Russia intended to become a party to the Convention, since the other seven States had already done so on the date that it opened for signature. Six years later,[250] Russia has still neither signed nor ratified the Convention. The Recommendations further stress the use of extra-legal as well as legal management of the problem such as cooperating with private industry to ensure systems security and to develop contingency plans in the event that those systems are attacked.[251] This style of arrangement has been considered in relation to civil contingency plans and the critical national infrastructure. Unlike the UN position, the G8 Recommendations make no specific mention of technical assistance. The Council of Europe is also aiming

---

244 Ibid., s. 2 [2].

245 G8, 'Recommendations on Transnational Crime' (May 2002) <http://canada/justice.gc.ca/en/news/g8/doc1.html> accessed 25 September 2008.

246 Ibid., Part IV, Section D.

247 Ibid. [1].

248 Ibid. [2].

249 Ibid. [3].

250 As at 1 February 2008.

251 G8, 'Recommendations on Transnational Crime' (May 2002) Part IV, Section D [4] <http://canada/justice.gc.ca/en/news/g8/doc1.html> accessed 25 September 2008.

to facilitate close cooperation between the G8 High-Tech Crime Subgroup and the network of contact points established by the States which are parties to the Convention.[252]

The G8 has blurred the distinction between law and technology (and the public and private domain) as tiers of governance. While its Action Plan is mostly concerned with international cooperation and policing, it does recommend there be a collaborative effort between state and industry to ensure that new technologies are 'policeable': that is, that they facilitate the investigation of computer misuse via the collection and preservation of robust evidence. The role of technology as an extra-legal tier of governance in its own right will be considered in Chapter 7. Moreover, the G8 stresses the involvement of industry in the development of secure systems and participation and cooperation in civil contingency planning. The G8 Action Plan is not binding upon its Members. Instead, it follows the approach of the European Commission in encouraging the G8 Members to ratify the CoE Convention, all of which (with the notable exception of Russia) have done so. This highlights the inherent problem with non-binding legal instruments: states cannot be compelled to sign or ratify.

Computer misuse and legal governance

The previous chapter introduced the idea of governance as a means of controlling complex systems and considered the limitations of the application of domestic criminal law to computer misuse in the light of governance theory. Governance encompasses both public and private institutions and practices. The potential tiers of legal governance in relation to computer misuse examined by this chapter remain within the public sphere, recommending or requiring legislative responses. Extra-legal responses within the private domain will be considered in the next chapter. However, this chapter has broadened the scope beyond the domestic criminal law to encompass initiatives beyond the boundaries of the nation state.

These initiatives lie on a continuum of compulsion from those which *must* be implemented by the UK to those which offer broad guidance and suggested steps. The European Union measures lie at the hard end of the scale, through to less binding offerings from the

---

252 Council of Europe, 'Cybercrime: closer co-operation between law enforcement and internet service providers,' Press Release 160(2008), Strasbourg, 5 March 2008 <https://wcd.coe.int/ViewDoc.jsp?id=1258339> accessed 25 September 2008.

Commonwealth, UN and G8 via the CoE Convention on Cybercrime which is binding on states which choose to ratify it.

There is a role for legal initiatives beyond the domestic criminal law in the control of computer misuse. However, these initiatives are politically charged since they inevitably come, to some extent, at the expense of national sovereignty. This political sensitivity is particularly evident in initiatives which impinge on domestic criminal law. Where States have similar national values then legal harmonisation is more likely to succeed: where there are fundamental conflicts or where computer misuse is not a major national concern, then it is not. In terms of the impact of initiatives beyond the domestic criminal law on the individual, the more remote the instigating organisation then the less is its individual impact. Even where there is an impact on the individual, it is achieved indirectly via intergovernmental policy networks rather than directly via the domestic criminal law or the forms of extra-legal governance which will be introduced in the next chapter. If a European initiative is implemented via a Directive under the First Pillar or a Framework Decision under the Third Pillar, it will be binding on governments, not individuals. States become obliged to address the agenda, yet the consequences of non-compliance or defective implementation do not generally offer protection to the individual. Framework Decisions do not give rise to direct effect,[253] though the Court of Justice has held that the principle of indirect effect applies.[254] For Directives, individuals are left to rely upon direct effect[255] (against the state[256] or an emanation of the state),[257] the indirect effect of a presumption of compliance in interpretation of any domestic law,[258] or a claim in state liability following defective or non-implementation.[259] This situation therefore offers less protection to the individual than the domestic law.

253 Treaty on European Union, art. 34(2)(b).
254 *Criminal Proceedings against Maria Pupino* (Case C-105/03) (16 June 2005) (CJEC).
255 Provided that the wording of the provision is clear, precise and unconditional and allows no room for discretion in implementation: *Van Gend en Loos v. Nederlandse Administratie der Belastingen* (Case 26/62) [1963] ECR 1 (CJEC). The implementation date for the Directive must have passed: *Pubblico Ministerio v. Ratti* (Case 148/78) [1979] ECR 1629 (CJEC).
256 *Marshall v. Southampton and South West Hampshire Area Health Authority (No. 1)* (Case 152/84) [1986] ECR 723 (CJEC).
257 *Foster v. British Gas* (Case C-188/89) [1990] ECR I-3313 (CJEC).
258 *Von Colson and Kamann v. Land Nordrhein-Westfalen* (Case 14/83) [1984] ECR 1891 (CJEC).
259 *Francovich and Others v. Italian Republic* (joined Cases C-6/90 and C-9/90) [1991] ECR I-5357 (CJEC).

Attempts at legal harmonisation have value in the promotion of broadly shared good principles and the need for cross-border networked cooperation in response to networked risk. Whine's assertion that 'future success depends on the determination of governments themselves'[260] could therefore be applied to all forms of international legal response, not just that to online hatred or Holocaust denial. The uniform adoption of a global minimum framework of criminal laws within each nation state with clearly defined cross-border cooperation, investigation and assistance provisions is a panacea. Absent this, the current piecemeal adoption of the CoE Convention (and the encouragement of other organisations for its members to adopt it) represents at least *some* international governance. The Convention is, however, hardly a nimble instrument which must lead to a consideration of whether extra-legal and private mechanisms also have a role to play within a governance framework. Not only may such mechanisms be less threatening to national sovereignty but they are also consistent with the withdrawal of direct state intervention in the management of complex, networked and global risk. Unlike intergovernmental approaches, the extra-legal and private initiatives are capable of addressing individuals directly rather than indirectly. Many of the intergovernmental organisations referred to in this chapter have made recommendations and observations concerning extra-legal responses. The next chapter will therefore broaden the discussion further beyond legal governance to consider these extra-legal responses to computer misuse.

260 Whine, M., 'Cyberhate, anti-semitism and counterlegislation' (2006) 11 *Communications Law* 124, 131.

Chapter 7

The extra-legal governance of computer misuse

In my experience, only third-rate intelligence is sent to Legislatures to make laws, because the first-rate article will not leave important private interests to go unwatched ...

Mark Twain (1835–1910)

The previous chapter considered the broad role of the law in the governance of computer misuse. It established that there is a role for legal harmonisation initiatives beyond the domestic criminal law in the control of computer misuse and that these prove to be a useful adjunct to national law as part of an overall governance network. However, such intergovernmental initiatives recognise themselves that they still do not provide a complete means of addressing the issues. Indeed many such initiatives come with recommendations or observations concerning extra-legal action as a complementary part of their response. This chapter will therefore broaden the discussion further from legal governance to explore potential extra-legal approaches. It will consider the emergence of networks of private sector regulation and the extent to which these private networks interact with the state.

In order to perform a meaningful survey of the extra-legal proposals, it is first necessary to attempt to identify a framework (or frameworks) within which each individual proposal can be located.

Frameworks for extra-legal governance

This section will consider the whole range of regulatory initiatives from two alternative perspectives. The first perspective will consider these initiatives in terms of the balance between public and private interests in relation to each. The second perspective will involve the extrapolation of a broad typology of extra-legal proposals from the initiatives proposed by the various intergovernmental organisations and the activities they are seeking to impact upon.

A *public/private framework of governance*

'Digital realism' advocates that technology naturally becomes self-regulating:

> [The] digital realism of cybercrime is such that the more a behaviour is mediated by new technology, the more it can be governed by that same technology.[1]

This draws upon the work of Lessig[2] and Greenleaf.[3] Lessig draws a distinction between 'East Coast Code' and 'West Coast Code'.[4] East Coast Code refers to the legislation that is enacted by the US Congress.[5] This legislative code uses legislative commands to control behaviour. West Coast Code is a technical code. It is a sequence of statements written in a human-readable computer programming language, the instructions embedded within the software and hardware that makes computer technology work.[6] Lessig argues (in what he refers to as the 'New Chicago School')[7] that 'code is law'. West Coast Code becomes a newly salient regulator beyond the traditional lawyer's scope of laws, regulations and norms. The coded instructions within

---

1 Wall, D.S., *Cybercrime: The Transformation of Crime in the Digital Age* (Polity Press, Cambridge, 2007) 3–4.
2 Lessig, L., *Code and Other Laws of Cyberspace* (Basic Books, New York, 1999).
3 Greenleaf, G., 'An endnote on regulating cyberspace: architecture vs law?' (1998) 21 *University of New South Wales Law Journal* 52.
4 Lessig, L., *Code and Other Laws of Cyberspace* (Basic Books, New York, 1999) 53–4.
5 In Washington, DC on the east coast of the United States, hence 'East Coast Code'.
6 The heart of the US software industry is located on the west coast in Silicon Valley and Redmond (although it also a key industry in the Boston area).
7 Lessig, L., 'The New Chicago School' (1998) 27 *Journal of Legal Studies* 661.

the technology also serve to regulate that technology.[8] However, code is not, in itself, the ultimate regulator of technology. In other words, 'traditional' law retains the capability to influence not only the environment which produces the technical code, but also social norms of behaviour in relation to that technology and the economic incentives and disincentives which help to shape both behaviour and the commercial development and adoption of new technology.

Lessig therefore proposes a framework within which four 'modalities of regulation' apply to the regulation of behaviour in cyberspace. These are law, social norms, market or economic forces and (West Coast) code.[9] These modalities are equally applicable to the regulation of computer misuse as they are to the more general arena of cyberspace and are naturally interrelated.

The relationship between law and social norms is of fundamental importance. Organic development of the law is important if the equilibrium between it and society is to be maintained. The law must lead in some instances. Examples include the Abortion Act 1967 which legalised abortion by registered medical practitioners and the Sexual Offences Act 1967 which partially decriminalised homosexuality. Equally the law can also follow prevailing social opinion. For instance, as gender reassignment has become more socially acceptable, the legal status of persons who have undergone or intend to undergo gender reassignment has shifted from virtual non-recognition to full recognition via the Gender Recognition Act 2004.[10] However, the relationship is, and should be, symbiotic, with society developing in response to the law and the law being both flexible and reflexive to take account of social developments.

Law can impose or remove free market constraints on certain behaviours by way of taxes and subsidies. For instance, the ownership of vehicles which emit higher levels of carbon dioxide is financially penalised by increased levels of taxation. A Treasury minister commented that changes to rates of vehicle excise duty are primarily aimed at changing motorists' behaviour:

---

8 Lessig, L., *Code and Other Laws of Cyberspace* (Basic Books, New York, 1999) 6.

9 Ibid., 88.

10 Council Directive (EC) 76/207/EEC of 9 February 1976 on the implementation of the principle of equal treatment for men and women as regards access to employment, vocational training and promotion, and working conditions [1976] OJ L39/40; *P v. S and Cornwall County Council* (Case C-13/94) [1996] ECR I-2143 (CJEC); *Chessington World of Adventures v. Reed* [1997] IRLR 556 (EAT); Sex Discrimination (Gender Reassignment) Regulations 1999 SI 1999/1102.

Owners of those cars will have to make decisions about whether they want to continue in ownership of those cars or whether they want to trade down.[11]

Conversely, use of public transport is encouraged by the subsidisation of bus companies.[12] In relation to technology, economic forces empower the law to intervene as an instrument of regulation. As Lessig comments:

When software was the product of hackers and individuals located outside of any institution of effective control, East Coast Code could do little to control West Coast Code. But as code has become the product of companies, then code can be controlled, because commercial entities can be controlled. Thus the power of East over West increases as West Coast Code becomes increasingly commercial.[13]

Regulation, for Lessig, is therefore achieved via an axis between commerce and the state.[14] This is supported by Lemley and McGowan who propose that technology itself is heavily influenced by economic 'network externalities' which can in turn promote 'winner-takes-all' markets.[15] However, this position has been criticised. Post challenges Lessig's view that the increased commercialisation of code will aid the ability to regulate it. Reflecting upon Lessig's argument, he comments:

As code writing becomes commercial, it becomes the product of 'a smaller number of large companies'? Why is that? Lessig writes of this concentration of economic power as if it were somehow foreordained, an inevitable consequence of commercialisation ... That's a rather strong premise, it seems to me ...[16]

---

11 Kirkup, J., 'Nine million face "green" road tax increases', *The Telegraph* (London, 9 July 2008) <http://www.telegraph.co.uk/earth/main.jhtml?xml=/earth/2008/07/09/earoadtax109.xml> accessed 25 September 2008.

12 Department for Transport, *Local Bus Service Support – Options for Reform* (March 2008).

13 Lessig, L., *Code and Other Laws of Cyberspace* (Basic Books, New York, 1999) 53.

14 Ibid, 6.

15 Lemley, M. and McGowan, D., 'Legal implication of network economic effects' (1998) 86 *California Law Review* 479.

16 Post, D., 'What Larry doesn't get: code, law and liberty in cyberspace' (2000) 52 *Stanford Law Review* 1439, 1452–3.

For Post, the inexorable journey towards a single technical architecture proposed by Lessig is not inevitable and different technical architectures will persist. As such, this will hinder the ability to regulate a single technology model through market forces alone:

> ... if there are many different architectures, then there is choice about whether to obey these controls ... Lessig's notion that the invisible hand of commerce somehow drives towards uniformity may be correct, but it is surely not self-evidently correct ... the one thing that [the invisible hand does best] ... is to place before members of the public a diverse set of offerings in response to the diverse needs and preferences of that public.[17]

Law may also regulate architecture in the physical world. For instance, reasonable adjustments must be made to facilitate access to public places by disabled persons.[18] However, the law has been used to mandate technical developments, particularly in the United States. These laws were introduced to 'protect the interests of US industry'[19] as well as (in some instances) to protect against socially undesirable behaviour. Lessig[20] and Wall[21] both cite the example of the 'V-chip'. The US Telecommunications Act 1996[22] required this to be developed and implemented by television manufacturers to facilitate the blocking of broadcasts with a particular rating.[23] This was a response to the increasing levels of sexual content and violence on television which, in turn, was considered harmful to children. However, the V-chip has been criticised on a number of grounds. The Federal Communications Commission (FCC) reports that V-chip technology is not widely used, partly since many users are simply unaware of its existence and others lack the ability to programme it correctly. The Parents Television Council called the V-chip education campaign 'a failure'.[24] Moreover,

---

17 Ibid., 1454.
18 Disability Discrimination Act 1995, s. 19(3)(a).
19 Reno, J., 'Law enforcement in cyberspace' (address to Commonwealth Club of California, San Francisco, 14 June 1996), in Wall, D.S., *Cybercrime: The Transformation of Crime in the Digital Age* (Polity Press, Cambridge, 2007) 191.
20 Lessig, L., *Code and Other Laws of Cyberspace* (Basic Books, New York, 1999) 47.
21 Wall, D.S., *Cybercrime: The Transformation of Crime in the Digital Age* (Polity Press, Cambridge, 2007) 191.
22 Telecommunications Act 1996 USC §551.
23 Similar parental controls are available on UK satellite transmissions but the adoption of the technology is not mandated by statute.
24 Federal Complaints Commission, 'In the matter of violent television programming

it has been claimed that the blocking of transmissions is a violation of the US First Amendment constitutional right to free speech since it should be the responsibility of parents and guardians to exercise their personal discretion to determine what is appropriate for children to view. According to the American Civil Liberties Union:

> These FCC recommendations are political pandering. The government should not replace parents as decision makers in America's living rooms. There are some things that the government does well, but deciding what is aired and when on television is not one of them.[25]

While the V-chip is essentially a hardware constraint, it does require a certain level of programming in order to operate effectively. As the FCC acknowledges, the lack of user ability to operate the chip has been a limitation on its success as a regulator. Moreover, it also requires its target audience to take responsibility for regulating the content to which children under their care are exposed. As such it has some parallels with technological responses to computer misuse, since their adoption is primarily a matter of individual (or corporate) responsibility which further requires a combination of installation, configuration or programming expertise on the part of the user. This serves to highlight a potential weakness of extra-legal regulation via technology, which often requires a level of skill its users may not possess. Moreover, it requires a willingness to assume responsibility which may be met with reluctance or opposition. The domestic law, however, is not a regulator to which individuals or corporations may opt in or opt out. It exists independently of technological expertise or inclination as to its use.

East Coast Code and West Coast Code are not equivalent. Indeed, they are fundamentally different. Lessig's East Coast Code stops at the boundaries of the United States. West Coast Code is global. Moreover, software is a medium that, unlike law, is predicated on invention. Such invention may be focused through large international corporations that are subject to the influence and control of the law while being offered its protection via the law of intellectual property.

---

25 Labaton, S., 'FCC moves to restrict TV violence', *New York Times* (26 April 2007) <http://www.nytimes.com/2007/04/26/business/media/26fcc.html> accessed 25 September 2008.

and its effect on children' FCC 07-50 (25 April 2007) <http://hraunfoss.fcc.gov/edocs_public/attachmatch/FCC-07-50A1.pdf> accessed 25 September 2008.

However, open source software makes its code available under a copyright licence (or via the public domain) that permits it to be used, changed and redistributed in both modified and unmodified forms. It is often developed in a public, collaborative manner that is inherently resistant to commercial ownership. Indeed, a 2008 report estimates that the adoption of open source software loses the proprietary software industry about US$60 billion per year in potential revenues.[26] The most familiar example of open source software is the Linux operating system which has ultimately become supported by most of the mainstream commercial technology manufacturers. This demonstrates a synergy between commercial interests and those of the open development community.

East Coast Code did prevail over that of the West Coast in relation to file-sharing software such as Napster and Grokster. As well as facilitating legitimate file-sharing applications, these also enabled the distribution of music files. However, they were eventually shut down for enabling the copying of copyright-protected material.[27] A further example of the disparity between East Coast and West Coast Code can be found in online gambling. The United States attempted to curtail online gambling within its own jurisdiction via the Unlawful Internet Gambling Enforcement Act of 2006 which criminalised the acceptance of funds from bettors by operators of most online gambling websites. However, this has not deterred providers of online gambling services from continuing to operate from outside US territory and accepting bets from within it.[28]

A similar interplay between law, culture and norms to that proposed by Lessig in relation to cyberspace has been considered within the sphere of business. Here, Teubner talks of a regulatory trilemma: a law which goes against business culture risks irrelevance; a law that crushes the naturally emerging normative systems in business can destroy virtue; a law that allows business norms to take it over

26 Standish Group, *Trends in Open Source* (April 2008).
27 *A&M Records Inc. v. Napster Inc.* 239 F.3d 1004 (9th Cir. 2001); *MGM Studios v. Grokster* 545 US 913 (2005); Orbach, B., 'Indirect free riding on the wheels of commerce: dual-use technologies and copyright liability' (2008) 57 *Emory Law Journal* 409.
28 Costigan, C., 'Ladbrokes prepared to accept US poker bets says managing director', *Gambling 911* (8 July 2008) <http://www.gambling911.com/gambling-news/ladbrokes-prepared-accept-us-poker-bets-says-managing-director-080708. html> accessed 25 September 2008.

can destroy its own virtues.[29] For both Teubner and Braithwaite,[30] this trilemma can be avoided through the 'structural coupling' of reflexively related systems or nodes of networked governance. In other words, legal and extra-legal regulatory mechanisms must work together in order to achieve stability.

Braithwaite further argues that these legal and extra-legal nodes require sufficient autonomy so as to avoid domination by other nodes.[31] However, when coupled, these semi-autonomous nodes enhance each other's capability to respond to human needs or societal trends.[32] In Selznick's terminology, such nodes have integrity.[33] In this model, then, an extra-legal regulatory node can derive integrity by interacting with a legal node in order to build the learning capacity of a system as a whole to address potential risks. The role of the law here is to act as an indirect enabler rather than as a direct prescriptive set of principles. As Lessig comments, law as a direct regulator tells individuals how to behave and threatens punishment if there is deviation from that behaviour. As an indirect regulator, the law aims to modify one of the other structures of constraint. However, as Lessig comments it is desirable that indirect regulation should maintain transparency as a constraint on the exercise of state power.[34] Post approaches this from an alternative libertarian stance:

Just as Lessig recognises the need for constraints on collective power, the conscientious libertarian recognises that there are times when collective action is required to promote the common welfare, that the government, while not always the answer, is

---

29 Teubner, G., 'After legal instrumentalism: strategic models of post-regulatory law', in Teubner, G. (ed.), *Dilemmas of Law in the Welfare State* (Walter de Gruyter, Berlin, 1986).

30 Braithwaite, J., *Markets in Vice, Markets in Virtue* (Oxford University Press, 2005).

31 Braithwaite, J., 'Responsive regulation and developing economies' (2006) 34 *World Development* 884, 885; Ayres, I. and Braithwaite, J., *Responsive Regulation: Transcending the Deregulation Debate* (Oxford University Press, Oxford, 1992).

32 Teubner, G., 'After legal instrumentalism: strategic models of post-regulatory law', in Teubner, G. (ed.), *Dilemmas of Law in the Welfare State* (Walter de Gruyter, Berlin, 1986) 316.

33 Selznick, P., *The Moral Commonwealth: Social Theory and the Promise of Community* (University of California Press, Berkeley, CA, 1992).

34 Lessig, L., *Code and Other Laws of Cyberspace* (Basic Books, New York, 1999) 95, 98.

not always the enemy, and that deliberation need not always be de-liberating. [35]

The attractiveness of law as an indirect regulator is in line with the theory proposed by Habermas for whom law as a 'medium' colonising a 'lifeworld' (that is, a society as lived or experienced) is dangerous. However, law acting as a 'constitution' enables that lifeworld more effectively to deliberate responsive solutions to problems. [36]

The indirect role of the law, then, facilitates the operation of a regulatory framework which enables responses to problems. Each problem carries with it a range of potential risks and therefore the regulatory framework of legal and extra-legal nodes may be conceptualised as a *risk-based* framework. For Black, such risk-based frameworks provide their own 'technology of regulation', that is:

a set of understandings of the world and of regulatory practices which abstracts from the complexities of individual organisations and provides a framework for rational action which accords with actors' need to believe that the task of governing and controlling is one which they can achieve. [37]

Black considers that, in an ideal form, such frameworks enable the rationalisation, order, management and control of challenging and complex regulatory need. Within this framework, Scott considers dispersed or fragmented resources exercising regulatory capacity which are not 'restricted to formal, state authority derived from legislation or contracts, but also include information, wealth and organisational capacities'. [38]

However, these frameworks carry their own risks in implementation, design and culture. This accords with the concept of manufactured uncertainty put forward by Beck[39] and Giddens.[40] The risk-based

---

35 Post, D., 'What Larry doesn't get: code, law and liberty in cyberspace' (2000) 52 *Stanford Law Review* 1439, 1459.

36 Habermas, J., *The Theory of Communicative Action – Volume 2: Lifeworld and System: A Critique of Functionalist Reason* (Beacon Press, Boston, MA, 1987).

37 Black, J., 'The emergence of risk-based regulation and the new public risk management in the United Kingdom' [2005] *Public Law* 512, 542.

38 Scott, C., 'Analysing regulatory space: fragmented resources and institutional design' [2001] *Public Law* 329, 330.

39 Beck, U., 'Politics of risk society', in Franklin, J. (ed.), *The Politics of Risk Society* (Polity Press, Cambridge, 1998).

40 Giddens, A., *Beyond Left and Right* (Polity Press, Cambridge, 1994).

framework is therefore both (following Black's terminology) a technology in itself and a source of new risk. Moreover, Baldwin cites the dangers of extra-legal regulation as leading to controls which are 'lacking in legitimacy, prove unfair and that are exclusive and inefficient'.[41] For Ogus, the key variables in any regulatory model are the degrees of legislative constraint, outsider participation in relation to rule formation or enforcement (or both) and external control and accountability.[42] This accords with Lessig's desire for transparency in the exercise of indirect legislative power by the state:

The state has no right to hide its agenda. In a constitutional democracy its regulations should be public ... Should the state be permitted to use nontransparent means when transparent means are available?[43]

Within this networked regulatory model, technological and commercial regulators are enabled and backed by the rule of law, although this necessarily involves the devolution of control to distributed sources of authority. For Lessig:

The challenge of our generation is to reconcile these two forces. How do we protect liberty when the architectures of control are managed as much by government as by the private sector? How do we assure privacy when the ether perpetually spies? How do we guarantee free thought when the push is to propertise every idea? How do we guarantee self-determination when the architectures of control are perpetually determined elsewhere?[44]

However, Katyal considers that the lack of transparency in code is the reason why the government 'should regulate architecture and why such regulation is not as dire a solution as Lessig portrays'.[45] As Wall comments, government regulation, for Katyal, is 'the lesser of the two evils because it works within more transparent frameworks

41 Baldwin, R., 'The new punitive regulation' (2004) 67 *Modern Law Review* 351, 351.
42 Ogus, A., 'Rethinking self-regulation' (1995) 15 *Oxford Journal of Legal Studies* 97, 100.
43 Lessig, L., *Code and Other Laws of Cyberspace* (Basic Books, New York, 1999) 98.
44 Ibid., x–xi.
45 Katyal, N.K., 'Digital architecture as crime control' (2003) 112 *Yale Law Journal* 2261, 2261.

of accountability'.[46] Indeed, any state initiative should be consistent with the accepted norms of regulatory intervention: proportionality, accountability, consistency, transparency and targeting.[47]

This spectrum of regulatory initiatives can be therefore be viewed as existing along a continuum from those originating from state agencies or bodies at one extreme to those originating from private functions at the other. The state institutions favour 'top-down' regulation. Private institutions, which are self-tasked, originate regulation from the 'bottom-up'. At the two extremes of this continuum are state legislation regulating from the 'top-down' and open source software itself as the ultimate 'bottom-up' regulator.

A typology of extra-legal governance initiatives

Chapter 6 surveyed a range of new tiers of legal governance at the European Union, Council of Europe, Commonwealth, United Nations and G8 levels. Many of these responses promoted extra-legal initiatives as well as proposing legal action.

The 2001 European Commission report *Creating a Safer Information Society by Improving the Security of Information Infrastructures and Combating Computer-Related Crime*[48] proposed four main areas. The first of these was the establishment of a European Union forum to 'enhance co-operation' between law enforcement, Internet service providers, network operators, consumer groups and data protection authorities. This forum would aim to raise public awareness of risks, promote best practice, develop counter-crime tools and procedures, and encourage the development of early warning and crisis management mechanisms. Such a forum would represent a dynamic networked approach to computer misuse which would be significantly more flexible and responsive than any potential legislative response. The second was the continued promotion of 'security and trust' through products and services with 'appropriate' levels of security and more liberalised use of 'strong' encryption techniques. The third was increased training of law enforcement staff and further

46 Wall, D.S., *Cybercrime: The Transformation of Crime in the Digital Age* (Polity Press, Cambridge, 2007) 202–3.

47 Better Regulation Task Force, *Better Regulation – From Design to Delivery* (London, 2005) <http://archive.cabinetoffice.gov.uk/brc/publications/designdelivery.html> accessed 25 September 2008.

48 Commission (EC), 'Creating a Safer Information Society by Improving the Security of Information Infrastructures and Combating Computer-Related Crime' COM (2000) 890, 26 January 2001.

research in forensic computing. The final area was a study to 'obtain a better picture of the nature and extent of computer-related crime in the Member States.'[49] Similarly, the European Commission's later Communication 'towards a general policy on the fight against cyber crime'[50] reinforced the need for further training of law-enforcement personnel, further research, the development of technical measures to counter 'traditional' crime (such as fraud) in electronic networks and private–public cooperation in the exchange of information and the raising of public awareness.

The United Nations considered that priority should be given to the provision of technical assistance to Member States, in order to provide a 'level playing field'[51] thereby harmonising technical capability rather than legal regulation.

The G8 Action Plan[52] recommended that there should be a collaborative effort between state and industry to ensure that new technologies are 'policeable': that is, they facilitate the investigation of computer misuse via the collection and preservation of robust evidence. This introduces technological design as an additional potential tier of governance. Moreover, the G8 stresses the involvement of industry in the development of secure systems and participation and cooperation in civil contingency planning.

The OECD produced a set of guidelines for the security of information systems and networks.[53] This provided a set of com-plementary principles for 'participants'. 'Participants' is a broadly defined term encompassing 'governments, businesses, other organi-sations and individual users who develop, own, manage, service and use information systems and networks'.[54] The principles to which the participants are expected to adhere are awareness, responsibility, response, ethics, democracy, risk assessment, security design and implementation, security management and reassessment.

49 Ibid., 31–2.
50 Commission (EC), 'Communication from the Commission to the European Parliament, the Council and the Committee of the Regions towards a general policy on the fight against cyber crime' COM (2007) 267 final, 22 May 2007.
51 United Nations, "Around the clock" capability needed to successfully fight cybercrime, workshop told' UN Doc SOC/CP/334 (25 April 2005).
52 G8, 'Meeting of Justice and Interior Ministers of the Eight: Communiqué' (10 December 1997) <http://www.usdoj.gov/criminal/cybercrime/g82004/97Communique.pdf> 3 accessed 25 September 2008.
53 OECD, Guidelines for the Security of Information Systems and Networks: Towards a Culture of Security (OECD, Paris, 2002) <http://www.oecd.org/dataoecd/16/22/15582260.pdf> accessed 25 September 2008.
54 Ibid., 7.

The resulting 'culture of security' is one in which these participants take responsibility for their own safety while remaining flexible and cooperative in prevention, detection and response to incidents and respecting the legitimate interests of others. Risk assessments enable the 'selection of appropriate controls' which underpins the security management of systems containing components for which security has been an 'integral part of system design and architecture'. This culture is reflexive, undergoing a constant process of review, reassessment and modification.

There is clearly an overlap between many of the areas proposed by the various organisations. These fall into a number of broad categories: warning and response systems, education and public engagement, and technical design. The initiatives are founded on cooperation, information-sharing, reflexivity and responsiveness.

Warning and response systems

The first functional category of extra-legal response is that of warning and response systems. These can be further subdivided into Computer Emergency Response Teams (CERTs) and Warning, Advice and Reporting Points (WARPs).

CERTs

In general terms, a CERT is an organisation that studies computer and network security in order to provide incident response services to victims of attacks, to publish alerts concerning vulnerabilities and threats, and to offer other information to help improve computer and network security.[55]

The CERT model derives originally from the US Computer Emergency Response Team which is a publicly funded research and development centre hosted within the Software Engineering Institute at Carnegie Mellon University.[56] It was set up in 1988 under the direction of the Defense Advanced Research Projects Agency (DARPA) following the unleashing of the Morris worm which infected around

55 ENISA, 'Inventory of CERT activities in Europe' (September 2007) <http://enisa. europa.eu/cert_inventory/downloads/Enisa_CERT_inventory.pdf> accessed 25 September 2008.

56 <http://www.cert.org> accessed 25 September 2008.

10 per cent of Internet systems.[57] It now largely concentrates on the study of Internet security vulnerabilities and associated education and training. In 2003, the US Computer Emergency *Readiness* Team (US-CERT)[58] was formed as a partnership between the Department of Homeland Security and the public and private sectors to 'co-ordinate defense against, and responses to, cyber attacks on the nation'.[59] The US is also home to the National Cyber Forensic Training Alliance (NCFTA)[60] which presents itself as 'a neutral collaborative venue where critical confidential information about cyber incidents can be shared discreetly, and where resources can be shared among industry, academia and law enforcement'.[61] This also, then, fosters and encourages interplay between public and private stakeholders. It offers an automated global incident reporting, tracking and response system and is funded jointly by industry, the FBI and the US government.

For Van Wyk and Forno, a CERT exists 'to minimise the impact of an incident on a company and allow it to get back to work as quickly as possible'[62] whereas for Killcrece it should act as a 'focal point for preventing, receiving and responding to computer security incidents'.[63] Wiik refers to the 'new emerging survivability paradigm'[64] which proposes that no matter how much security is built into a system, it will never be totally secure,[65] replacing the traditional notion of a fortress providing full protection against malicious attack.[66] This is reflected in the historic reactive nature of CERTs. Over time, however,

57 Spafford, E., *The Internet Worm Program: An Analysis*, Purdue Technical Report CSD-TR-823, 29 November 1988 <http://homes.cerias.purdue.edu/~spaf/tech-reps/823.pdf> accessed 2 April 2008.
58 <http://www.us-cert.gov> accessed 25 September 2008.
59 Ibid.
60 <http://www.ncfta.net> accessed 25 September 2008.
61 Ibid.
62 Van Wyk, K.R. and Forno, R., *Incident Response* (O'Reilly & Associates, Sebastopol, CA, 2001) 21.
63 Killcrece, G. and others, *State of the Practice of Computer Security Incident Response Teams* (Carnegie Mellon University, Pittsburgh, PA, 2003).
64 Wiik, J., Gonzalez, K.K. and Kossakowski, K-P., 'Limits to effectiveness in Computer Security Incident Response Teams' (Twenty-third International Conference of the System Dynamics Society, Boston, 2005).
65 Lipson, H. and Fisher, D.A., 'Survivability – a new technical and business perspective on security' (Proceedings of the 1999 New Security Paradigms Workshop, Association for Computing Machinery, Caledon Hills, 1999).
66 Blakley, R., 'The Emperor's Old Armor' (Proceedings of the 1996 New Security Paradigms Workshop, Association for Computing Machinery, Arrowhead, 1996).

such CERTs widened the scope of their services from purely reactive emergency response towards the more proactive provision of security services including preventive services such as issuing alerts and advisories and providing training on incident management capability, performance standards, best practices, tools and methods. In the late 1990s the term 'Computer Security Incident Response Team' (CSIRT) arose to reflect this broadened scope. Both terms (CERT and CSIRT) are synonymous in current usage. A further definition of CSIRT has been offered by West-Brown:

For a team to be considered as a CSIRT, it must provide one or more of the incident handling services: incident analysis, incident response on site, incident response support or incident response coordination.[67]

Although this emphasises the largely reactive nature of a CSIRT and recognises that such impact-mitigation services will always be required, there is a growing realisation that some level of proactive service ought to be offered as well.[68] CERTs therefore address different types of risk on a spectrum from serious electronic attacks on the public infrastructure, government departments or the financial services industry, through online fraud and identity theft to less serious (but more prevalent) harms involving general online nuisance.

The constituency (that is, the set of potential users) of a CERT can include national, governmental or private organisations. Equally, although some CERTs may be ostensibly linked to particular national interests, some are effectively global, such as the NCFTA, whereas others focus on particular industry sectors, such as the Financial Services Information Sharing and Analysis Centre (FSISAC).[69] By way of illustration, the UK currently has 19 CERTs with differing constituencies: these include large commercial organisations,[70] former

67 West-Brown, M.J. and others, *Handbook of Computer Security Incident Response Teams* (2nd edn, Carnegie Mellon University, Pittsburgh, PA, 2003) 23.
68 Killcrece, G. and others, *State of the Practice of Computer Security Incident Response Teams* (Carnegie Mellon University, Pittsburgh, PA, 2003).
69 <http://www.fsisac.com> accessed 25 September 2008.
70 BP DSCA (British Petroleum); Cisco PSIRT (Cisco); CITIGROUP (UK) (Citi Group); DCSIRT (Diageo); E-CERT (Energis); MLCERT (UK) (Merrill Lynch); RBSG-ISIRT (Royal Bank of Scotland Group); Sky-CERT (Skype).

nationalised industries,[71] academic institutions,[72] academic networks[73] and government organisations.[74] Within Europe there are 111 CERTs at institutional and national level.[75] The CERT model has also been adopted in Asia and Australasia.

Each of these CERTs therefore acts as an independent node, collecting, processing and disseminating information relating to risk, although the differences in their constituencies may mean that the relative prioritisation of risks differs between CERTs. Assuming that each CERT has some data of interest to others, it follows that connecting CERTs which represent both public (state) and private (commercial and individual) interests could produce, in Kjær's terms, a 'network ... of trust and reciprocity crossing the state-society divide'[76] in the pursuit of shared goals or, in Rhodes's words, an 'interorganisational network ... characterised by interdependence, resource-exchange, rules of the game and significant autonomy from the state'.[77] In other words, interconnected CERTs could provide a response or readiness network consistent with theoretical conceptualisations of governance discussed in Chapter 5.

In terms of a networked response to a networked problem, it is necessary to examine the nature and extent of inter-CERT collaboration to establish whether information sharing alone is an adequate response or whether CERTs should build relationships with other bodies and assist with collaborative responses to the problems arising from the misuse of computer technology.

Collaboration between CERTs

Inter-CERT collaboration will be explored at both the domestic and regional/international levels.

71 BT CERTCC and BTGS (British Telecommunications); RM CSIRT (Royal Mail Group); Q-CIRT (QinetiQ).

72 EUCS-IRT (University of Edinburgh); OxCERT (University of Oxford).

73 JANET CSIRT (Joint Academic Network); DAN-CERT (GÉANT pan-European research network).

74 GovCertUK (UK government community; public sector); CPNI (UK Centre for the Protection of National Infrastructure); MODCERT (UK Ministry of Defence).

75 As at September 2007. ENISA, 'Inventory of CERT activities in Europe' (September 2007) <http://enisa.europa.eu/cert_inventory/downloads/Enisa_CERT_inventory.pdf> accessed 25 September 2008.

76 Kjær, A.M., *Governance* (Polity Press, Cambridge, 2004) 4.

77 Rhodes, R.A.W., *Understanding Governance: Policy Networks, Governance, Reflexivity and Accountability* (Open University Press, Buckingham, 1997) 15.

UKCERTs

UKCERTs is an informal forum of domestic CSIRTs including government, academic and commercial teams, again designed to encourage cooperation and information-sharing between the participants. It also invites UK WARPs to its forum meetings. The role of WARPs is considered in greater detail later in this chapter. There are similar forms of national cooperation operating in Austria,[78] Germany,[79] the Netherlands[80] and Poland.[81]

European Network and Information Security Agency

The European Network and Information Security Agency (ENISA) was established in 2004 by Regulation (EC) 460/2004.[82] ENISA is a European Community Agency, that is a body set up by the EU to carry out a very specific technical, scientific or management task within the Community domain (the First Pillar) of the EU. ENISA's purpose, as defined in its establishing Regulation, is that of:

Ensuring a high and effective level of network and information security within the Community and [to] develop a culture of network and information security for the benefit of citizens, consumers, enterprises and public sector organisations of the European Union.[83]

It does, however, acknowledge that its objectives are without prejudice to non-First Pillar competencies of Member States (such as police and judicial cooperation in criminal matters) and the activities of the States in areas of criminal law.[84] It is specifically charged to 'provide assistance and deliver advice'[85] to the Commission and Member States in relation to information security and to use its expertise to 'stimulate broad co-operation between actors from the public and private sectors'.[86] Part of ENISA's work is in facilitating cooperation between CERTs. It also supports the Member States in setting up

78 CIRCA (Computer Incident Response Co-ordination Austria).
79 CERT-Verbund.
80 O-IRT-O.
81 Polish Abuse Forum.
82 Council Regulation (EC) 460/2004 of 10 March 2004 establishing the European Network and Information Security Agency [2004] OJ L 77/1.
83 Regulation (EC) 460/2004, art. 1(1).
84 Ibid., art. 1(3).
85 Ibid., art. 2(2).
86 Ibid., art. 2(3).

their own national or organisational CERTs and provides technical support to close the gaps between the Network Information Security competencies of individual EU Member States. Its 2008 work plan includes an initiative to facilitate cooperation between Member States to set up new governmental or national CERTs, acting as a 'good practice knowledge-base and contact broker'.[87]

European Government CSIRTs group

The European Government CSIRTs (EGC) group is an informal organisation of governmental CSIRTs[88] that is 'developing effective co-operation on incident response matters between its members, building upon the similarity in constituencies and problem sets between governmental CSIRTs in Europe'.[89] It works to develop measures to deal with large-scale network security incidents, facilitating the sharing of information and specialist knowledge and instigating collaborative research in areas of mutual interest specifically related to the operational work of governmental CSIRTs. It differs from ENISA in its more limited membership: ENISA is concerned with facilitating communication between all European CERTs whereas the EGC focuses only on governmental CSIRTs.

Other inter-CERT collaborations

The Task Force of Computer Security and Incident Response Teams (TF-CSIRT) exists to promote collaboration between European CSIRTs with a research and education constituency.[90] It was established as part of the technical programme within the Trans-European Research and Education Networking Association (TERENA). It has similar aims to the EGC in promoting collaboration, promulgating common standards and procedures for responding to security incidents and providing training for new CSIRT staff. The Trusted Introducer (TI) programme was also established under the auspices of TERENA.[91] It recognises the nature of the trust relationship which is a necessary condition for collaboration between nodes within a governance network.

---

87 ENISA, 'ENISA Work Programme 2008' 24 <http://www.enisa.europa.eu/doc/pdf/management_board/decisions/enisa_wp_desig_ver_2008.pdf> accessed 25 September 2008.

88 France, Germany, Finland, the Netherlands, Sweden, UK, Norway and Switzerland.

89 <http://www.egc-group.org> accessed 25 September 2008.

90 <http://www.terena.nl/tech/task-forces/tf-csirt/> accessed 25 September 2008.

91 <http://www.trusted-introducer.nl/> accessed 25 September 2008.

While the inter-CSIRT trust network was originally based upon personal recommendation between members of the particular CSIRTs involved, as the number of CSIRTs proliferated and staff moved on, this personal recommendation method became unwieldy at best. TI therefore exists to facilitate trust between European response teams by formally accrediting CSIRTs who wish to join its community. On a similar regional basis, APCERT was established by CSIRTs within the Asia Pacific region, aiming to improve cooperation, response and information-sharing among CSIRTs in the region. APCERT consists of 20 CSIRTs from 14 economies.

Following the foundation of the US CERT, the number of incident response teams grew. The interaction between these teams experienced difficulties due to differences in language, time zone and international standards or conventions. In October 1989, a major incident called the 'WANK[92] worm'[93] highlighted the need for better communication and coordination between teams. The Forum of Incident Response and Security Teams (FIRST) was formed in 1990 in response to this problem. Since that time, it has continued to grow and evolve in response to the changing needs of the incident response and security teams and their constituencies. The FIRST membership consists of teams from a wide variety of organisations including educational, commercial, vendor, government and military.

Finally, the Central and Eastern European Networking Association (CEENet) comprises 23 national research and education CERTs. It is primarily a knowledge network which shares information regarding computer network security.

Effectiveness of CERTs

The effectiveness of CERTs can be considered at two levels. The first of these is the internal effectiveness of the CERT itself: the ability of the CERT to deal with its workload and service its constituents as a reflection of its technical, financial, organisational and management capability. The second is the effectiveness of inter-CERT communication. If the networked response offered by CERTs is to be valuable, it follows that the propagation of pertinent information between CERTs is key to avoid them existing only as silos of information accessible only to the particular constituency of each individual CERT.

---

92 Worms Against Nuclear Killers.
93 CERT, 'WANK Worm On SPAN Network', Advisory CA-1989-04 (17 October 1989) <http://www.cert.org/advisories/CA-1989-04.html> accessed 25 September 2008.

In terms of internal effectiveness, the main challenges are described by West-Brown:

To ensure successful operation, a CSIRT must have the ability to adapt to changing needs of the environment and exhibit the flexibility to deal with the unexpected. In addition, a CSIRT must simultaneously address funding issues and organisational changes that can affect its ability to either adapt to the needs or provide the service itself.[94]

Therefore internal challenges are two-fold: adroitness (both technological and organisational) and availability of resources. In terms of resources, as Salomon and Elsa comment, information security is often viewed as a drain since it is a support service rather than a core business activity:

Safeguarding the enterprise itself is a fairly unglamorous task, costs money and is difficult to justify to managers unfamiliar with the potential consequences of not having a strong commitment to IT security.[95]

The tension between business and technological priorities was clearly expressed in interview. User 1 commented:

The IT folk are always after money for their security stuff. I don't understand why they need so much ... Surely it's only a question of making sure that the firewalls are all up to date.

By contrast, Technician 5 offered a diametrically opposing view:

[Senior management] don't realise that without us, the whole enterprise could come falling down about their ears. One major breach and we're all toast. Fair enough, we don't make money ourselves, but we're safeguarding everything we do.

Overstretched resources are a common issue within many CSIRTs. As early as 1994, only six years after the establishment of the US CERT at Carnegie Mellon, Smith commented that:

94 West-Brown, M.J. and others, *Handbook of Computer Security Incident Response Teams* (2nd edn, Carnegie Mellon University, Pittsburgh, PA, 2003) 177.
95 Salomon, J.M. and Elsa, P., 'Computer security incident response grows up' (2004) 11 *Computer Fraud and Security* 5.

About the only common attributes between existing Incident Response Teams are that they are under-funded, under-staffed and over-worked.[96]

Moreover, according to Lipson:

Although the sophistication of Internet attacks has increased over time, the technical knowledge of the average attacker is declining, in the same manner that the technical knowledge of the average user has declined.[97]

Therefore more people have the capability to launch attacks and the scope, frequency and volume of attacks (and hence the need for CERT services) is continuously increasing.[98] As Technician 4 commented:

There's more [incidents requiring some form of action] coming in all the time. What with investigations, analysis, countermeasures, fixing and trying to educate those who don't understand or won't take notice, there aren't enough hours in the day.[99]

A further complication arises in respect of the scope of 'IT security'. It spans a wide range of activity within which security-related tasks may fall to groups which are not immediately concerned with security as a core function, such as architecture, network operations, IT strategy or server support.[100] Even where adequately funded and resourced, CERTs must be able to respond swiftly to new forms of technological risk. By comparison with the problems faced by the domestic and international legal responses to computer misuse discussed in Chapters 4 and 6 respectively, a CERT organisation should be able to adapt to technological advances relatively quickly. However, the speed of response required in order to be effective is increasing. As Salomon and Elsa comment:

96 Smith, D., 'Forming an Incident Response Team' (Proceedings of the FIRST Annual Conference, University of Queensland, Brisbane, 1994).
97 Lipson, H., *Tracking and Tracing Cyber-Attacks: Technical Challenges and Global Policy Issues* (Carnegie Mellon University, Pittsburgh, PA, 2002) 9.
98 Killcrece, G. and others, *State of the Practice of Computer Security Incident Response Teams* (Carnegie Mellon University, Pittsburgh, PA 2003).
99 Participant T4.
100 Salomon, J.M. and Elsa, P., 'Computer security incident response grows up' (2004) 11 *Computer Fraud and Security* 5.

The 'flash-to-bang' time between the discovery of new vulnerabilities (or configuration errors) and the exploit thereof on a wide scale has narrowed considerably ... Even assuming efficient processes and good communication, the sheer scale of many corporate security organisations makes effective and timely countermeasures difficult.[101]

Communication between CERTs also poses a number of potential problems. As EURIM commented,[102] those running CERTs differ in 'cultural values' and approaches to security. These range from those who only engage with trusted organisations to those which purport to provide open services to all. Moreover, some are more open to communication with peer organisations than others and some exist to protect the commercial interests and intellectual property rights of themselves and their customers. Police Officer 4 offered an interesting illustration of the importance of the routine administrative matters which underpin CERT-to-CERT communication:

Through our WARP, we got wind of a DDOS attack that was being routed through a country in Eastern Europe. So the obvious thing to do was get in touch with the relevant CERT in that country. Would have been fine – except it turns out that the CERT in question had changed their phone number three years ago and hadn't thought to tell anyone. Certainly would have limited the amount of incoming information they would have got – so, you see, without some sort of proper day-to-day coordination and action then all these bodies are next to useless.

There are also legal concerns affecting CERTs. Graux comments that CERTs require their own legal expertise in order to develop and apply internal policies as well as to determine whether or not a particular incident requires the involvement of the criminal or civil law. He concludes that the need for international legal cooperation and coordination is paramount, requiring the 'pragmatic availability' of legal channels of communication.[103] There is, therefore, a role for

---

101 Ibid.
102 EURIM, 'Cyber-crime Reporting and Intelligence' ('Tackling Crime and Achieving Confidence in the On-line World, Parliament and the Internet Conference, London, 2007).
103 Graux, H., 'Promoting good practices in establishing and running CSIRTs – a legal perspective' (ENISA Workshop, 13–14 December 2005).

the law to govern and inform the internal framework of the extra-legal response mechanism of the CERT.

Conclusion: CERTs

CERTs have two principal functions. The first is proactively to disseminate information regarding the prevention of technical vulnerabilities and threats. The second is reactively to provide assistance in response to particular instances of computer misuse. CERTs exist to serve both public and private interests across a range of constituencies. They may therefore operate from both 'top-down' (governmental) and 'bottom-up' (private) perspectives. However, in isolation, an inwardly focused CERT will operate as an information silo; that is, it will not exchange relevant information with other CERTs. Indeed, many CERTs have a closed constituency and may not even desire to participate in such information-sharing. This lack of reciprocity is fundamentally at odds with the networked approach required within governance theory, even though the individual CERTs themselves may represent both public and private concerns. Facilitating communication and information-sharing between CERTs should therefore lead to a structure more aligned with the governance approach. This has been achieved to a certain extent at both national and international levels through various forums of varying degrees of formality, membership and geographic reach. In essence, there is a state-led imperative for cooperation between institutions which often exists only to serve private interests. Provided that there is at least some cooperation, however reluctant, it follows that CERTs should have a part to play within an overall governance network on the basis that even limited information-sharing is better than none at all.

However, in order to achieve a meaningful role within this network, CERTs need to be effective, both internally in their capacity to cope with the nature and extent of their workload and externally in the efficiency of their information exchange. Historically, CERTs have been characterised by constrained resources and increasing workload. Moreover, despite the existence of the diverse umbrella coordinating bodies, communications between CERTs are inconsistent, depending upon the cultural values and individual priorities of each CERT.

Even though an ideal CERT network seems well-suited as an extra-legal response to the problem of computer misuse, it must be recognised that CERTs cannot exist in a legal vacuum. The law still has the role of governing and informing the internal framework within which the CERT operates. However, CERTs do offer the advantage of an alternative response beyond that of the law in isolation and bring private concerns and day-to-day technical incidents into the response network.

Warning, Advice and Reporting Points

Warning, Advice and Reporting Points (WARPs)[104] are part of the information-sharing strategy of the UK Centre for the Protection of the National Infrastructure (CPNI).[105] They are therefore primarily a domestic initiative, although two international WARPs have been registered[106] but are yet to be operational. There are 18 WARPs registered in total, covering the public service, local government, business and voluntary sectors, 13 of which are operational.[107] Examples include the National Health Service (Connecting for Health) Information Governance WARP, which provides centralised distribution of warnings and advisories, good practice advice brokering and trusted sharing of electronic-related security problems and solutions, and PENWARP which serves the journalist community.

The model is not new or restricted only to the sphere of computer technology. For instance, the Radio Amateurs Emergency Network (RAYNET)[108] is a national voluntary communications service for major civil emergencies or related exercises and local community events provided by licensed radio amateurs. It liaises with emergency services, local authorities and other voluntary agencies who could be involved in the integrated management response to major civil emergencies.[109] The Environment Agency also operates an advisory and response service for flood risk.[110]

WARPs are predominantly a 'bottom-up' initiative, although their increasing importance in the area of contingency planning and management of the critical national infrastructure means that they are strategically part of the 'top-down' agenda of the CPNI.

---

104 <http://www.warp.gov.uk> accessed 25 September 2008.
105 <http://www.cpni.gov.uk> accessed 25 September 2008.
106 HIWARP (serving Hitachi in Japan) and IE1WARP (serving small and medium businesses in the Republic of Ireland).
107 As at 1 June 2008 <http://www.warp.gov.uk/Index/WARPRegister/indexcurrentwarps.htm> accessed 25 September 2008.
108 <http://www.raynet-uk.net/> accessed 25 September 2008.
109 RAYNET now has an associated WARP (RAYWARP).
110 <http://www.environment-agency.gov.uk/subjects/flood/> accessed 25 September 2008.

Unlike CERTs which generally focus on broader constituencies, a WARP (according to the CPNI) is a 'community based service where members can receive and share up-to-date advice on information about security threats, incidents and solutions'.[111] Therefore WARPs essentially operate as small-scale CERTs serving a community which may be within a smaller organisation or acting as a hub to particular organisations or individuals. UKERNA[112] proposed a model within which WARPs reduce incidents by providing preventative advice and CSIRTs respond to those incidents which do, in fact, occur.[113]

WARPs generally have a greater emphasis on sharing than many CERTs. As Technician 1 commented:

As a security manager, I spend a great deal of time networking outside my company. It's probably one of the most important things I do. We need to draw on outside knowledge and skills to identify new threats, share best practice ... or just to swap ideas and ask each other's point of view on things. Trust is important – you never know when you might need help from your friends. That's where [the WARP] helps.

Therefore the idea of personal networking is added to that of the technical networking propagated through CERTs.

WARPs have three core elements: filtered warnings, advice brokering and trusted sharing (reporting). These services are based upon software developed by Microsoft and the CPNI which is only available to registered WARPs (that is, those approved by the CPNI). The filtered warning service takes alert information from a variety of sources, including CERTs themselves and major industry members such as Microsoft, Symantec and Cisco, and enables WARP members to select the categories of warning most pertinent to their operation. Advice brokering consists of a bulletin-board service restricted to WARP members. Trusted sharing involves the publication of anonymised reports to facilitate a trusted environment in which sensitive information concerning incidents or problems may be shared.

There is little regulatory constraint to concern WARPs other than a short Code of Practice which requires little from new WARPs other

---

111 Ibid.
112 Now JANET(UK).
113 UKERNA, 'CSIRTs and WARPs: Improving Security Together' (March 2005) <http://www.warp.gov.uk/Marketing/WARPCSIRT%20handout.pdf> accessed 25 September 2008.

than a willingness to cooperate and share information, to maintain effectiveness and not to bring the WARP model into disrepute.[114] Agreement to this Code is a prerequisite for registration with the CPNI.

WARPs therefore are lightly-regulated 'mini-CERTs' serving similar needs to a more restricted community. As with CERTs, the trust relationship between WARP members is important and one which is stressed by the CPNI as being crucial to their effectiveness. However, given the smaller scale of WARPs as compared to CERTs, it might be expected that there would be considerably more of the former than the latter in operation, although there actually remains a larger number of CERTs than WARPs in the UK at present. Despite this limited adoption, the role of WARPs within the overall framework of governance responses seems theoretically attractive, extending the reach of the extra-legal response network to parties that may not, of themselves, fall within a CERT's constituency or have the capacity or desire to establish a CERT of their own. However, the very existence of WARPs does not seem to be particularly widespread knowledge. Few industry participants (both industrial and technical) had encountered WARPs, although those that had were generally supportive. Policy-maker 1 commented on WARPs in relation to risk:

Most security risks [to the critical national infrastructure] are scattered across hundreds of smaller public and private organisations. We have to extend our security capability; if we don't then the country will be more at risk. WARPs are one way of doing that. We need more of them.

For the CPNI, the desire to increase the prevalence of WARPs is clear. It believes that WARPs should become 'endemic' in the future, wherever a need is identified, while remaining sustainable, cooperative, flexible and versatile. It further envisages linkage between some WARPs and existing CERTs, with some potentially evolving into full CERTs themselves, before concluding that 'the future of WARPs is bright'.[115]

There is limited material available in relation to the overall effectiveness of WARPs. This is probably due to their having been

114 —, 'WARP Code of Practice v.2.0' (August 2004) <http://www.warp.gov.uk/BusinessCase/CodeofPracticeV2.0.pdf> accessed 25 September 2008.

115 —, 'The future of WARPs' <http://www.warp.gov.uk/Index/indexfutureofwarps.htm> accessed 25 September 2008.

in existence a comparatively short time and being few in number. However, given the similarities between WARPs and CERTs in many respects, it seems reasonable to assume that they may both suffer from similar limitations in terms of capacity and inter-WARP communication. The latter may be less significant, since WARPs are focused on domestic concerns and registered WARPs may use a common communications infrastructure provided by the CPNI.

Given the smaller reach of WARPs, they may be considered to be the computer misuse equivalent of a Neighbourhood Watch scheme. Whereas Neighbourhood Watch creates a partnership between the local community, the police and the local authority in the interests of protecting public safety, WARPs endeavour to create networks of trust and information between technology users for their protection. However, there is no formal link to policing through a WARP. Such a link could work in a similar fashion to that between a Neighbourhood Watch scheme and a local Crime Prevention Officer or Police Community Support Officer. While this might seem attractive, the Home Office reported in 2001 that Neighbourhood Watch schemes tend to be most active in areas where there are relatively low crime rates. Moreover, owner-occupied households and those with an annual income over £30,000 were most likely to be members of a scheme.[116] Schemes are therefore more difficult to establish and maintain in the areas which need them most.[117] Similarly, WARPs currently tend to serve communities which already have an awareness of computer misuse issues combined with the resources and inclination to form themselves into a group. This pattern then leaves those who are either unaware of the risks or insufficiently technologically adept to mitigate against them (that is, are more vulnerable to computer misuse) without a WARP to support them, just as those who are more vulnerable to burglary are less likely to enjoy the vigilance offered by Neighbourhood Watch. The police encourage Neighbourhood Watch schemes to be established in areas of need in the same way that the CPNI encourages the promulgation of WARPS. While there is some element of proactive promotion of WARPs from the CPNI, the protection of individuals from computer misuse is not core to its purpose which is properly concerned with the protection of critical

---

116 Sims, L., *Neighbourhood Watch: Findings from the 2000 British Crime Survey* (Home Office, London, 2001).

117 Rosenbaum, D., 'The theory and research behind neighbourhood watch' (1987) 33 *Crime and Delinquency* 103; Bennett, T., 'Factors related to participation in neighbourhood watch schemes' (1989) 29 *British Journal of Criminology* 207.

national resources from terrorist or other attacks. Finally, it can be argued that successful schemes require a certain level of crime in order to be successful. If the scheme operates as a successful deterrent of crime, then recruitment of new members to the scheme will fall, since potential participants will tend to consider that they are not needed. The scheme will decline, crime rates will rise and the scheme will recommence. This dependency on some crime for the success of a Neighbourhood Watch scheme suggests that an optimal crime reduction policy may aim at a tolerably low level of crime rather than total prevention.[118]

A further analogy can be drawn between a WARP and a Citizens' Advice Bureau. The Citizens' Advice service provides free information and advice in response to particular problems just as WARPs are a means of disseminating definitive information as to risk to particular communities within a trusted environment. However, the Citizens' Advice service is accessible, widespread, well-known and well-established. WARPs remain low in number and relatively unknown.

Education and public engagement

Education has been identified as one of the functions of both CSIRTs and WARPs, which provide advisory services to their constituents. However, in terms of Lessig's modalities of constraint, education is also a means by which the law can change social norms. As Marshall commented:

> Education is not the teaching of the three Rs. Education is the teaching of the overall citizenship, to learn to live together with fellow citizens and above all to learn to obey the law.[119]

Education is therefore a means by which certain social norms may be reinforced and the content of which (particularly in state schools) is regulated by law via the National Curriculum.[120] The state can specifically exclude certain topics. For instance, section 28 of the Local Government Act 1988 provided that:

---

118 Huck, S. and Kosfield, M., 'The dynamics of neighbourhood watch and norm enforcement' (2007) 117 *The Economic Journal* 270, 281.
119 Thurgood Marshall, oral argument on behalf of respondents; *Cooper v. Aaron* 358 US 1 (1958) (no. 1).
120 Education Act 1996, s. 351.

A local authority shall not –

(a) intentionally promote homosexuality or publish material with the intention of promoting homosexuality;

(b) promote the teaching in any maintained school of the acceptability of homosexuality as a pretended family relationship.[121]

It is therefore readily conceivable that the law could intervene to compel a certain level of education in schools relating to the issues surrounding protection from the misuse of computer technology. However, it would take a generation before this knowledge could spread through the nation as a whole. Moreover, state-led education initiatives in schools would not circumvent the problem arising from the continued pace of technological advance. Knowledge acquired at, say, the age of 16 would still rapidly become out of date. As discussed in Chapter 2, one of the key drivers behind the emergence and growth of computer misuse was the collective diminution in general computing skill levels as technology became more accessible to the non-expert user. The exploitation of this knowledge gap became a facilitator of susceptibility to computer misuse.

Therefore an ongoing programme of public engagement is key to addressing this gap. In Lessig's terms this would modify social norms such that 'safe' computer usage would become commonplace and individuals and businesses would become equipped with sufficient knowledge to take their own precautions against computer misuse. The predominant UK initiative is Get Safe Online,[122] involving government, the Serious Organised Crime Agency and private sector sponsors from technology, retail and finance.[123] It is the first national Internet-based computer security awareness campaign for the general public and small businesses. Its website has 13,000 websites linked to it. It provides information to individuals on how to protect themselves, their families or their business from online threats. It has been operational since October 2005. However, the Parliamentary Office of

---

121 Section 28 of the Local Government Act 1988 inserted a new s. 2A into the Local Government Act 1986. The new s. 2A was repealed in Scotland by the Ethical Standards in Public Life etc. (Scotland) Act 2000, s. 34 and later repealed in England and Wales by the Local Government Act 2003, s. 122.

122 Get Safe Online, <http://www.getsafeonline.org> accessed 25 September 2008.

123 Including BT, Dell, eBay, HSBC, LloydsTSB, Microsoft, MessageLabs, securetrading. com and Yell.com.

Science and Technology reports that there is 'limited' awareness of computer security among home as well as business users. Research from Get Safe Online shows that users tend to assume they know how to remain safe online, but they do not demonstrate adequate skills when tested. Respondents to the Get Safe Online survey rated computer security as a high priority but over half admitted to little or no knowledge of safe practices. Although 75 per cent had a firewall, 86 per cent did not follow recommendations to update their security software.[124]

Many of the participants interviewed during the course of the research for this book were more security aware by virtue of their professional position. However, there was a consistent theme that education of itself would not significantly address the knowledge gap. Technician 3 commented specifically that:

It [Get Safe Online] seems like a good idea on the face of it. But how many average users know that it exists? And, even assuming that they all do, they can read as many horror stories as they want and realise that they need to do something to protect their computers ... but when they get to PC World they won't have a clue where to start. They just don't have the hands-on skills. Generic advice raises awareness – but even in these days of commodity computing, everyone's system is slightly different. Making changes to suit their own set-ups might well be beyond them.

Policy-Maker 2 commented further that:

Education and awareness campaigns cannot help those who don't think that it is their personal responsibility to protect themselves from the ill effects of computer misuse.

This then raises the issue of who should carry the responsibility of protecting individuals and commercial concerns from computer misuse. A survey of the general public commissioned by Get Safe Online found that 15 per cent of people believe that it is their own responsibility to protect themselves, 49 per cent believe that it should be the responsibility of 'big business' and 11 per cent think that it

124 <http://www.getsafeonline.org/nqcontent.cfm?a_id=1432#_edn1> accessed 25 September 2008.

should be a government responsibility.[125] It follows that, given these findings, education and awareness campaigns will not be effective for those 85 per cent who think that responsibility for their protection lies with someone else.

However, the view of IT users in industry is somewhat different. User 2 commented that:

Of course we are responsible for our own protection. We have to survey the market and make sensible decisions as to what to buy and how to implement it so that we are safe. No one else is going to tell us how to do it. We'd rather not tell anyone else how we did it either.

A similar view was shared by User 4:

We put locks on the doors and locks on our systems. Simple as that.

The IT industry seemed ready, to a certain extent, to accept some of the responsibility that the general public expected it to. For Technician 8:

The [security] products that we make absolutely have to be usable by the general public. Otherwise our market share will vanish.

However, this comment seems to be driven as much by market constraints as the desire for taking responsibility for the general public. Clearly, if the public views the IT industry as being responsible for its protection, then the industry will accept that responsibility, but only if the price is right. Moreover, the industry itself is not generally responsible for offering redress, investigating security breaches (unless compelled to do so by contract) or imposing sanctions on offenders. The Computer Misuse Act 1990 draws strong analogies between burglary in the physical world and unauthorised access to computer systems. In relation to burglary, it is an accepted social norm that individuals take steps to secure their own private property. If a burglary occurs, then the violation of private property rights gives rise to an expectation that the police will investigate and take steps to apprehend the burglar backed by the criminal law. However, while

---

125 Ibid.

the physical computer which is the target of outside computer misuse exists as a piece of private property located within a particular office or dwelling, its networked existence gives it a quasi-public presence within which it becomes more susceptible to attack. It is generally considered that individuals are afforded some degree of protection while in public, via policing or other forms of surveillance. This is backed up by the criminal sanction imposed should the protection fail and the individual come to harm. However, for computer misuse there is no analogous blanket public protection. Moreover, as already seen in Chapter 3, there is a general reluctance to investigate and prosecute. This is where the analogy fails. Perhaps a more useful role for education and awareness would be to ensure that users recognise that *without* taking steps to protect themselves (albeit in concert with the commercial providers of the technology that will enable them to do so) then they will be exposed to a greater level of risk than they might otherwise have appreciated.

Technical regulation

The governance initiatives covered in Chapter 6 also proposed various technical regulatory mechanisms. The European Commission promoted the development of secure products and more liberalised use of encryption technology and other technical measures aimed at preventing crime. The UN prioritised technical capability among its Member States to provide a minimal level of technical expertise to facilitate cross-border investigation and enforcement. The G8 advocated a collaboration between state and industry to ensure that technologies are policeable. The OECD considered that security should become an integral part of system design and architecture.

The role of code as regulator is central to Lessig's theory as previously mentioned in this chapter. For Lessig, the ability of a technology architecture to regulate depends on the code which brings that technology into being. For Lessig:

Some architectures ... are more regulable that others; some architectures enable better control than others. Thus, whether a [technology] can be regulated turns on the nature of its code.[126]

126 Lessig, L., *Code and Other Laws of Cyberspace* (Basic Books, New York, 1999) 20.

It follows then that if ability to regulate is the aim of the state and some architectures are more amenable to regulation than others, then the state will favour some technical architectures more than others. This is in line with the aim of the G8 to design technologies that are more policeable. A preferred set of technical architectures would also assist the UN in any initiative to provide cross-border technical assistance.

Katyal argues that such policeable solutions must exploit the characteristics of networked technology, particularly its potential for natural surveillance (via means such as access control logs and supervisor monitoring).[127] As Wall comments, these inherent technological capabilities can generate a range of 'automated active policing tools that seek to identify wrongdoing'.[128] An example can be found in 'honeynets'.[129] These honeynets contain a number of 'honeypots' which are traps set to detect attempts at unauthorised access. The honeypots generally consist of a computer, data or site that appears to be part of a legitimate network and which seems to contain information or a resource that would be of value to attackers. However, these honeypots are isolated, deliberately unprotected and monitored. They socially engineer users to access them and pass through various levels of security, indicating their assent and willingness to proceed at each stage. Eventually, their details are recorded and, where appropriate, investigated. For Wall:

Their purpose is to acquire intelligence about criminality, but also simultaneously to create a preventative 'chilling effect' which, through the awareness of being surveilled, tempers the actions of consumers of child pornography, fraudsters, spammers and hackers.[130]

However, technological responses to computer misuse must balance policeability and security with fundamental rights such as privacy. For example, the 'Clipper chip' was developed and promoted by the US government as an encryption device to be adopted by telecommunications companies for voice transmission. However, the

---

127 Katyal, N.K., 'Digital architecture as crime control' (2003) 112 *Yale Law Journal* 2261, 2268.
128 Wall, D.S., *Cybercrime: The Transformation of Crime in the Digital Age* (Polity Press, Cambridge, 2007) 190.
129 The Honeynet Project <http://www.honeynet.org> accessed 25 September 2008.
130 Ibid.

nature of encryption is such that the same technology enables both confidentiality and surveillance. The Clipper chip simultaneously encrypted communications while permitting government to un-scramble them 'through a back door'.[131] The chip transmitted a 128-bit 'Law Enforcement Access Field' that contained the information necessary to recover the encryption key provided that government agencies had established their authority to listen to a particular communication. In this instance, technological policeability created the electronic panopticon.[132]

However, encryption technology provides many advantages of privacy and security to users.[133] While encryption technology has many legitimate purposes,[134] it can also circumvent the legal powers of interception afforded to the state.[135] As Akdeniz and Walker comment, such technology 'can be so effective against oversight that law enforcement agencies have begun to voice concerns about the viability of future crime detection in cyberspace'.[136] For Baker and Hurst:

> ... cryptography surely is the best of technologies and the worst of technologies. It will stop crimes, and it will create new crimes. It will undermine dictatorships, and it will drive them to new excesses. It will make us all anonymous, and will track our every transaction.[137]

It has been suggested that, on balance, state access to encryption keys would hinder the development of electronic commerce and infringe

---

131 Post, D., 'Encryption vs. The Alligator Clip: the Feds worry that encoded messages are immune to wiretaps', *American Lawyer* (January/February 1995) 111.

132 Lyon, D., *The Electronic Eye: The Rise of Surveillance Society* (University of Minnesota Press, Minneapolis, MN, 1994); Foucault, M., *Discipline and Punish: The Birth of the Prison* (Allen Lane, London, 1977).

133 Denning, D., *Information Warfare and Security* (Addison-Wesley, Reading, 1998) Part III.

134 Bok, S., *Secrets: On the Ethics of Concealment and Revelation* (Oxford University Press, Oxford, 1982).

135 See *Malone v. United Kingdom* (App. no. 8691/79) (1984) Series A no. 82, (1984) 7 EHRR 14 (ECtHR) [81]; Interception of Communications Act 1985; Intelligence Services Act 1994; Police Act 1997; Regulation of Investigatory Powers Act 2000.

136 Akdeniz, Y. and Walker, C., 'Whisper who dares: encryption, privacy rights and the new world disorder', in Akdeniz, Y., Walker, C. and Wall, D.S., *The Internet, Law and Society* (Pearson, Harlow, 2000) 317, 319.

137 Baker, S. and Hurst, P., *The Limits of Trust* (Kluwer, The Hague, 1998) xv.

the individual rights of privacy and freedom of speech. Indeed, for Akdeniz and Walker:

> ... there is no compelling state interest in such an invasion of privacy, as the perpetrators [in cases of Internet 'misuse'] have been detected and evidence gathered without any new powers to survey or search.[138]

Even though it would not be prohibitively costly or technologically complex, encryption technology is not routinely embedded within software. However, Pretty Good Privacy (PGP) software which provides public-key cryptography and authentication is freely available and has proved problematic to law enforcement. In *Re Boucher*,[139] US customs authorities seized a laptop computer containing encrypted files which allegedly contained child pornography images. The state was unable to access the files and subpoenaed the defendant to provide the key. The Vermont District Court held that forcing the defendant to reveal his PGP key would violate his right not to incriminate himself under the Fifth Amendment and quashed the subpoena accordingly. The decision is currently under further appeal brought by the prosecution.

Although the routine use of encryption technology would help to protect the law-abiding majority and promote safer electronic commerce, an inevitable tension between private and public interests will remain. The investigative and surveillance desires of the state will try to resist more widespread use of encryption technology even though it has been argued that the state does not require any such new surveillance powers to achieve its aims. Here, in Lessig's terminology, West Coast Code may be used to thwart (or at least provide a check on) East Coast Code.

A further potential means of regulation through technology can be found in software development standards. These originated within military applications,[140] but are now of increasing importance in

---

138 Akdeniz, Y. and Walker, C., 'Whisper who dares: encryption, privacy rights and the new world disorder', in Akdeniz, Y., Walker, C. and Wall, D.S., *The Internet, Law and Society* (Pearson, Harlow, 2000) 317, 347.

139 *In re Grand Jury Subpoena to Sebastien Boucher* No. 2:06-mj-91, 2007 WL 4246473 (D. Vt. 29 November 2007).

140 UK Ministry of Defence Def. Stan. 00-55 deals with standards for safety-related software in defence applications; US MIL-STD 498 was designed to establish uniform requirements for software development and documentation (combining and replacing DOD-STD-2167A, DOD-STD-7935A and DOD-STD-2168).

commercial development.[141] The predominant international standard is ISO/IEC 12207, introduced in 1995 and revised in 2008, which:

> ... establishes a common framework for software life cycle processes, with well-defined terminology, that can be referenced by the software industry. It contains processes, activities, and tasks that are to be applied during the acquisition of a software product or service and during the supply, development, operation, maintenance and disposal of software products.[142]

The United States has its own adaptation of the 'international standard'[143] which it developed in collaboration with the Department of Defense to include more rigorous extended compliance requirements. The UK and Swedish software industries support the TickIT[144] scheme which is based upon the generic quality standard of ISO 9001[145] applied to the processes of software development. The use of such standards is not mandatory, although it may be a contractual requirement, particularly in public procurement exercises. For example, the core pre-qualification questionnaire produced by the Office of Government Contracts for evaluation of competitive tender responses asks *any* potential supplier to provide evidence of 'ISO 9000[146] or equivalent'[147] or an explanation as to why it is unable to do so.

International standards are voluntary and market-driven. The requirements are fed into the International Standards Organisation through national member bodies. In the case of the UK, this is the British Standards Institution, which works with manufacturing and service industries, businesses, governments and consumers to facilitate the production of British, European and international standards. It also has a 'close working relationship with the UK government, primarily through the Department for Innovation, University and

---

141 The US civil standard IEE J-STD-016 developed from MIL-STD 498 and has now been incorporated into IEEE/EIA 12207.

142 International Standards Organisation, 'Systems and software engineering – software lifecycle processes', ISO 12207:2008 (18 March 2008) <http://www.iso.org/iso/catalogue_detail?csnumber=43447 accessed 25 September 2008.

143 IEEE/EIA 12207.

144 <http://www.tickit.org/index.htm> accessed 25 September 2008.

145 Developed from British Standard BS5750.

146 Now ISO 9001:2008.

147 <http://www.ogc.gov.uk/documents/core_questionnaire.pdf> accessed 25 September 2008.

Skills'.[148] Government therefore has a role to play in setting domestic and international standards, albeit as part of what is essentially a governance network taking both public and private interests into account. As part of the overall regulatory response to computer misuse, standard setting becomes a network within a network.

Microsoft could also be considered to be exercising forms of technical governance. Since Microsoft has over 90 per cent of the global operating system market share,[149] it can pursue its own technological agenda. Many of its software updates are to address security vulnerabilities and, for many 'average' users, the system of updates works well provided that it is activated and configured accordingly. Given Microsoft's market dominance, its software updates could be viewed as a means of universal governance rather than purely as a customer service activity. Microsoft's governance derives its power from commercial (rather then political) origins, but may still be considered as a top-down means of governance.

In summary, top-down development of code can provide a means of control over technology. However, from the bottom-up, open code provides a check on state or monopolistic power to regulate through code. As Lessig argues, even if open code does not disable government power to regulate, it changes that power:

[Open code] is an important – some might say an essential – check on the power of government … Regulability is conditional on the character of the code and open code changes that character. It is a limit on government's power to regulate – not necessarily defeating the power to regulate, but changing it.[150]

Regulation through code, then, becomes a further extra-legal mode of governance. Within the functional regulatory framework, it can be initiated from the top down in furtherance of state-led or industry-led initiatives (via closed code or embedded software within hardware devices) or from the bottom up via decentralised emerging norms that are, to a certain extent, resistant to state control.[151]

148 BSI, 'About BSI British Standards' <http://www.bsi-global.com/en/Standards-and-Publications/About-BSI-British-Standards/> accessed 25 September 2008.
149 Mendel, T., *Enterprise Desktop and Web 2.0/SaaS Platform Trends, 2007* (Forrester Research, Cambridge, 2008).
150 Lessig, L., *Code and Other Laws of Cyberspace* (Basic Books, New York, 1999) 108.
151 Johnson, D. and Post, D., 'And how shall the net be governed? A meditation on the relative virtues of decentralised, emergent law', in Kahin, B. and Keller, J.H. (eds), *Co-ordinating the Internet* (MIT Press, Cambridge, MA, 1997) 62.

Conclusion

There are several advantages inherent in extra-legal governance. In particular, extra-legal measures have a flexibility and responsiveness that is generally lacking from the slower-moving legislative response. From the perspective of the general end-user, extra-legal mechanisms are less confrontational than the direct use of the law. As such, they tend to encourage and cajole participation rather than mandating it. Extra-legal responses may also act as a voice to the individual, explaining the issues and providing advice in a language that is more readily understood. Technical solutions may simply work quietly in the background providing protection without the user being aware of their existence until a threat is uncovered.

There is, of course, the prospect of the state indirectly influencing the steering of the overall governance network towards its own ends. This is not necessarily undesirable. Indeed, it is a general principle of governance theory that an effective networked regulatory response will cross the divide between public and private. However, where the hand of the state pushes the network in a direction that has the potential for interfering with private rights then it is crucial in the interests of legitimacy and accountability that this is done in a proportionate and transparent manner.

Extra-legal responses to computer misuse are viable, but their success is dependent upon the extent to which private organisations and individuals engage with them. There is currently a general lack of awareness of many extra-legal initiatives which naturally limits their impact. It is only by more active participation that their potential will be realised. This participation requires an assumption of self-reliance and self-responsibility, that is a conscious acknowledgement that state-led legal responses alone are insufficient and that potential victims of computer misuse must therefore take steps to protect themselves. In turn, many of these steps require a level of technical competence that may be beyond most likely victims, that is the naive end-users.

This problem is compounded by the speed at which technology advances. While the relatively informal nature of discussion forums and information-sharing mechanisms can deal well with this dynamic, the most vulnerable targets of computer misuse are usually outside their reach and continue computing in ignorance. By way of analogy, the public realises that the existence of section 9 of the Theft Act 1968 will not prevent their homes from being burgled. Despite the existence of a very clear piece of law, individuals take responsibility for the protection of their own property, tacitly acknowledging that the legal

275

response is insufficient and fitting locks to their doors. The difference here is that door locks have been the mechanism for preventing unwanted access for generations.[152] Although locks themselves might have become more sophisticated pieces of engineering, their premise remains the same and is readily understood. Their operation is also largely the same. Even though it is perfectly technically possible to engineer potentially more secure locks at accessible pricing, such electronic key pads or biometrically operated mechanisms are not in widespread public use. Their unfamiliarity arouses suspicion and insecurity compared to the more familiar key. With computing, the forms of protection required are relatively new (certainly when compared with physical locks) and change on a very frequent basis. In order to assume responsibility for its own protection against computer misuse, the general public would be required to assume the skills of an expert locksmith with daily refresher training. Of course, this frequent and periodic update may be facilitated through software, but such software still needs to be installed and configured which requires a certain level of technical competence and inclination on the part of the user.

Extra-legal responses may be further criticised for their lack of enforcement capability (in the criminal justice and policing sense) and their lack of uniformity, neither of which are problematic for legislative responses. This does not, however, fatally undermine their value.

Regulatory approaches are not new. As Walker comments in relation to a regulatory approach to governance of the physical security of the critical national infrastructure:

Regulatory approaches, which are built on networks of governance and are sensitive to the interests and cost burdens of the private sector, have long been established and have been applied, for example, to the design of cities and buildings, to airport security and to commercial insurance against terrorism.[153]

Similar rounded regulatory approaches have also been taken in respect of certain technologies and industries. For instance,

---

152 Certainly from Biblical times: the workers repairing the gates of Jerusalem 'laid the beams thereof, and set up the doors thereof, the locks thereof, and the bars thereof' (Nehemiah 3:3 (KJV)).

153 Walker, C., 'Governance of the Critical National Infrastructure' [2008] *Public Law* 323, 351.

the Information Commissioner exists as an independent official appointed by the Crown and reporting annually to Parliament to oversee the operation of the Data Protection Act 1998, the Freedom of Information Act 2000 and the Environmental Information Regulations 2004. The Commissioner's decisions are subject to the supervision of the courts and the Information Tribunal. Similarly, Ofcom exists as an independent regulator for the UK communications industries, with responsibilities across television, radio, telecommunications and wireless communications services. The Financial Services Authority (FSA) is an independent non-governmental body that regulates the financial services industry in the UK, holding a wide range of rule-making, investigatory and enforcement powers. These bodies each have various enforcement powers: failure to comply with notices served by the Information Commissioner may be dealt with as though the public authority concerned had committed contempt of court, Ofcom may impose enforceable penalties[154] and the FSA can discipline authorised firms and people, impose penalties for market abuse, apply to the court for injunction and restitution orders and prosecute various offences.[155] Each of them may also make recommendations for issues that may require criminal legislation. Networked responses have also been proposed for policing online behaviour.[156] However, each of these regulatory structures operates within a framework of law while maintaining a degree of autonomy and flexibility.

In summary, there is a role for extra-legal functions and institutions within the governance networked response to computer misuse. These functions and institutions are primarily of private rather than state origin. They therefore require an assumption of self-reliance and responsibility from individuals and may need further technical capability in order to realise their potential. However, they are flexible, responsive and reflexive and may transcend national borders. They are a complement to legal responses, requiring a certain degree of legal guidance in order to maximise their efficacy.

---

154 Communications Act 2003, s. 392.
155 Financial Services and Markets Act 2000.
156 Nhan, J. and Huey, L., 'Policing through nodes, clusters and bandwidth', in Leman-Langlois, S. (ed.), *Technocrime: Technology, Crime and Social Control* (Willan, Cullompton, 2008)

Part 3

Examining the solution

Chapter 8

The constellation of control

None of us is as smart as all of us.
Phil Condit, Chairman of Boeing (1941–)

This chapter will offer some critical reflection on the previous chapters, summarising the findings of the preceding chapters and providing a final evaluation of the central hypothesis as a whole.

Principal research findings

This book set out to answer six principal research questions, each of which was considered in a separate chapter.

What is meant by computer misuse and did it present a problem for the domestic law? If so, how did the law respond?

Chapter 2 considered the history of the domestic criminal law in relation to the history of computing. From the very earliest calculating machines to the late 1980s, the principal technological advancements were in capacity (both storage and processing power), user-friendliness (and hence accessibility) and networking (both the technological networks of interconnected computers and the social networks of user communities). Computer technology moved from the realm of the specialist and the scientist into private industry and the home. It consequently became part of the wider public consciousness. As a result of the increasing accessibility of the technology, in terms of both enhanced usability and decreased cost of acquisition, the technical capability of the average computer user has diminished. This collective diminution in general computing skill levels gave rise to a knowledge gap between the expert and non-expert user, the exploitation of which acted as a facilitator and driver of computer misuse. Moreover, even the more technologically aware user became vulnerable. By 1990, computing had become relatively routine and relied upon and technology was often being used by experts without adequate thought for their own protection. The banal nature of high-powered computing rendered an extra vulnerability – or, in other words, familiarity bred contempt.

The unauthorised use of this new technology grew in parallel with the advances in the technology itself. In particular, with the growth in networking capability and the consequent ability for computers to be accessed remotely, malicious hackers and virus writers emerged throughout the 1980s. These risks prompted a level of increased public concern. The domestic criminal law was able to deal with some of the problems resulting from computer misuse before the Computer Misuse Act 1990, primarily through (often creative) use of the law relating to criminal damage. However, the failure of the Forgery and Counterfeiting Act 1981 in relation to the unauthorised access to the BT Prestel system by Gold and Schifreen and the findings of both the Scottish Law Commission and the Law Commission of England and Wales led to the enactment of the Computer Misuse Act 1990. This created three new offences: unauthorised access to computer material, unauthorised access to computer material with the intent to commit or facilitate further offences and unauthorised modification of computer material.

Although computer misuse may be framed in terms of unauthorised or unethical use of technology, this definition remains both technologically and socially relative. That is, what is unauthorised or unethical depends on the nature and capability of the technology itself as well as the collective viewpoint of its users. As technology advances in complexity and sophistication, then the ambit of its potential misuse will also change. This may also bring it outside the scope of the criminal law itself, as seen in *Gold and Schifreen*. The options for the law were to continue to stretch the interpretation of the existing criminal law in order to catch previously unforeseen circumstances or to draft a new statute to deal with the issue. It follows that:

Computer misuse, which is a fluid term encapsulating the unauthorised or unethical use of technology, presented problems for the domestic law prior to 1990. The law responded via the enactment of the Computer Misuse Act 1990 which created three new criminal offences aimed at malicious hackers and virus writers.

Was the Computer Misuse Act 1990 an effective response to computer misuse and has it stood the test of time?

Chapter 3 continued the discussion of computer technology and computer misuse begun in Chapter 2 from 1990 to the present day and examined the practical operation of the 1990 Act. It demonstrated that the 1990 Act has produced relatively low prosecution rates while the instances of computer misuse have risen significantly. It seems that the Act itself has been exercised relatively lightly in comparison to the expansion of the problem. However, it is often the case that alternative means of redress are used against perpetrators of computer misuse. For computer misuse committed by insiders, many commercial organisations believe that they would not benefit from bringing a prosecution under the 1990 Act, relying instead on internal disciplinary measures as a private sanction. There is no prospect of restitutionary damages or compensation for loss in a criminal prosecution under the Act which may dissuade victims from invoking the criminal law over private action which has the added advantage of not publicising breaches of security. A further problem lies in the fact that, for many victims, there is a general perception that no law has been broken and therefore the case goes unreported. The 1990 Act also suffers as a result of relatively limited expert resources within the criminal justice system. Since computer misuse can be problematic to investigate or prosecute then victims are also less inclined to report.

The 1990 Act has also given rise to some curious interpretational difficulties particularly in relation to newer examples of computer misuse which were unforeseen at the time of its enactment. Its application to denial-of-service attacks in *Lennon* and the unauthorised access in *Cuthbert* seemed inconsistent and contrary to the intention of the Act. That is not to say that the 1990 Act is devoid of merit. It may have had a deterrent effect which is unquantifiable. However, the low prosecution rates and interpretational difficulties suggest that there may be other legal avenues which are pursued in situations where the 1990 Act might have been applied. There is a range of possibilities here both in statute and at common law.

The common law offence of misconduct in public office is an apposite choice for prosecutors in cases where public servants (in particular police officers) have accessed computer systems without authorisation. As a common law offence, it carries a penalty of up to life imprisonment and is therefore more attractive in the more serious cases where the conduct merits a penalty well in excess of that available under the 1990 Act. It also avoids many of the definitional problems within the 1990 Act. There are a number of potential statutory alternatives which can be found in the Theft Act 1968, Data Protection Act 1998, Regulation of Investigatory Powers Act 2000, Malicious Communications Act 1988 (as amended), Communications Act 2003, Terrorism Act 2000 (as amended) and the Fraud Act 2006. The law in this area is somewhat fragmented and overlapping.

The Police and Justice Act 2006 introduced three amendments to the 1990 Act, largely driven by the uncertainty in relation to denial-of-service attacks and the UK's obligations under the EU Council Framework Decision on attacks against information systems and as a signatory to the Council of Europe Convention on Cybercrime. First, the unauthorised access offence is broadened and attracts an increased tariff. The unauthorised modification offence is replaced by a new provision concerning unauthorised acts with intent to impair the operation of a computer. Finally, a new offence is introduced to criminalise the production, supply or acquisition of articles for use in computer misuse offences. However, these new provisions have been criticised on the basis that they are drafted in such a way that they might criminalise desirable activity, such as software penetration testing. There are currently no cases on the potentially contentious points.

It may be doubted, given the history of the 1990 Act, whether the new provisions which have recently come into force will have a significant effect. This is not because of problematic drafting or that the Act misses the point of the problem. It may be that computer misuse is not amenable to governance by the domestic criminal law alone. Therefore:

The Computer Misuse Act 1990 has produced relatively low prosecution rates, as well as instances of inconsistent application and the use of alternative bases for prosecution. That is not to say that it has been ineffective, but it is undoubtedly true that computer misuse remains a current issue. The 1990 Act has stood the test of time reasonably well, although new instances of misuse culminated in its amendment 16 years on. It may be that computer misuse is not amenable to governance by the domestic criminal law alone.

Does the effective regulation of computer misuse require more than just a response in domestic criminal law?

Chapter 4 reflected upon the characteristics and purpose of the criminal law from a range of perspectives and its application to computer misuse in particular. In many cases, computer misuse is not generally perceived as causing significant harm. Computer misuse often comprises so-called *de minimis* harm which may be transient, inconvenient, trifling, secret, latent or hidden. This does not sit easily with the instrumentalist construction of the criminal law in which the criminal law exists to protect a set of interests from substantial harm. Equally, from a consensus perspective where criminal behaviour is determined by reference to a set of commonly agreed social norms, computer misuse would not be a candidate for criminalisation unless it crossed the threshold of seriousness that rendered it harmful to others or society. However, these constructions would justify the use of the domestic criminal law for those instances of computer misuse which posed a threat to public safety or national security. Such instances would naturally fall within the remit of criminal legislation other than the Computer Misuse Act 1990. For example, the anti-terrorism legislation would be more likely to be employed in these cases since it is accompanied by enhanced police powers of investigation and greater limits on sentencing.

Computer misuse is also problematic from a moralistic standpoint, since society in general does not consider the behaviour of the misusers to be particularly immoral. This viewpoint may arise from the relationship between (mis)users and the technology, in which conventional moral rules and norms do not always apply. However, there is some support for the criminalisation of computer misuse from a structural conflict point of view which protects both political and economic power. The economic cost associated with computer misuse was a key political driver behind the enactment of the 1990 Act and was reiterated in the debates leading to its amendment via the Police and Justice Act 2006. However, while many businesses choose to protect their interests via alternatives to the criminal law, it must be questioned why the criminal law has not done more to protect those interests. As such, structural conflict theory alone does not provide a complete explanation. Interactionist theory suggests that moral entrepreneurs constructed computer misuse (which was initially considered to be harmless at worst and positively beneficial at best) as a sufficient risk in the late 1980s to justify the passage of the 1990 Act. Social pressure was brought to bear by actors with less overtly political positions to protect, although for the conflict theorists, this would be an exercise in the protection of political capitalism.

Each theoretical standpoint suffers to a greater or lesser extent from inadequacies. It is therefore difficult to propose a single coherent theoretical basis for the criminalisation of computer misuse. However, the domestic criminal law is still considered to be an appropriate vehicle for the regulation of computer misuse, although, as has already been discussed, it is not exercised particularly vigorously.

The criminal law demands certainty. It follows, then, that the criminal law might have especial difficulty in dealing with uncertain subject matter. Since it has already been established that computer misuse suffers from an inherent fluidity and ill-definition which results from its technological relativity, then it is reasonable to conclude that it may be problematic for the criminal law to provide effective regulation by itself. Moreover, save for the serious instances already mentioned, computer misuse is generally constructed as a private rather than a public wrong. Victims are more likely to seek private remedies than to pursue criminal charges, even if the police were amenable to proceeding. Jurisdiction presents a further issue. The criminal law is traditionally associated with sovereignty and states have traditionally not taken interest in criminal activities beyond national borders. Since computer misuse often originates outside the UK, this renders the use of the domestic criminal law cumbersome and unattractive as a means of control, except, as before, where there is a threat to national security for which extradition proceedings are employed.

In summary, the domestic criminal law is an appropriate response to computer misuse which has the potential to cause serious harm or loss or a threat to national security. It may also be useful where the computer misuse is entirely within national boundaries, although this is an increasingly uncommon circumstance. This is consistent with the role of the criminal law dealing with significant issues of public concern within the domestic jurisdiction. However, computer misuse is uncertain in definition, fluid in nature and generally viewed as a private wrong. It often causes bulk *de minimis* harm and is not generally considered to be immoral. These aspects of its nature are inconsistent with the desire of the criminal law for certainty and its traditional concerns for upholding public morality and protecting against substantial harm and public wrongdoing. Hence:

There are a number of incompatibilities between the nature of computer misuse and the nature of the domestic criminal law. Therefore the effective regulation of computer misuse may require more than just the domestic criminal law alone.

How do theories of risk and governance apply to computer misuse and the domestic criminal law?

Chapter 5 considered theories relating to risk from various theoretical perspectives. There are a range of possible responses to risk. These include introducing countermeasures which minimise the probability of the risk occurring or the severity of its consequences. Alternatively, management of the risk may be transferred to a third party via insurance. In some cases, no action may be taken if the risk is unlikely and its consequences are prohibitive. From a realist perspective, risk is considered in terms of probability and consequences and insurance may be taken against those risks. The deterrent effect of domestic criminal law could be considered to act as some form of collective social insurance against the risks associated with computer misuse. However, the criminal law does not protect individuals from the consequences of the materialised risk nor does it usually provide financial restoration or the ability to substitute new resources. In any event, the state is increasingly withdrawing its responsibility for individual welfare, focusing instead on predominantly public interests. The domestic criminal law is readily useful as a tool to protect such interests, in keeping with the state's role as an insurer of last resort, but it is of less utility to the protection of individuals. Individuals therefore need to take a more active approach to ensuring their own security. The domestic criminal law does not significantly reduce the incentive for the computer user to take care to avoid loss. As such it does not represent a significant moral hazard. This is evidenced by the range of security hardware and software which is available. Individuals take personal responsibility for computer security despite the presence of the domestic criminal law. Moreover, from the cultural and symbolic constructionist perspective, the domestic criminal law is either predominantly marginal or restricted to instances of computer misuse which carry severe consequences. It is only unequivocally desirable to those who consider the domestic criminal law to be an appropriate response to any form of risk which threatens disorder or harm.

In the critical structuralist risk society, the domestic criminal law is an established safety system used by the state to define the boundaries of acceptable conduct and to regulate behaviour by reference to those boundaries. However, the proliferation of technology-related risks and the increased public awareness of those risks has created a level of state protection which is unsustainable. Therefore technology itself may be deployed in managing the risks associated with computer misuse. However, in the risk society, technological responses to technical risk reflexively generate more risks, ultimately propagating pandemic risks which inherently tend towards globalisation. As such, a domestic response to these risks will necessarily be incomplete. The regulatory state approach manages the distribution of such risks rather than their control. Within this the role of the domestic criminal law is one of management and guidance rather than one of direct control.

From the governmentality standpoint, both direct and indirect strategies of control may be employed, combining autonomous individual responsibility and coercive state control. Governmentality approaches manage risk via a combination of state and private actors, emphasising autonomous self-management, self-protection and self-responsibility. Here the domestic criminal law as a tool of state intervention has less prominence. Therefore, regardless of epistemological position, the withdrawal of the state in the management of risk leads to a conclusion that the use of the domestic criminal law cannot provide a complete solution to computer misuse risk. This is in accord with the analysis performed on the basis of the nature of computer misuse and the nature of the criminal law. Again, however, this does not mean that the domestic criminal law has no part to play in response to these technological risks. It may be used as part of a network of control.

Governance theory is concerned with the control of complex systems within a framework including both state and private institutions and practices. Since computer misuse is often construed as a private wrong then it follows that private control measures might be appropriate in the management of associated risk. Although the state retains its capacity to legislate directly in matters of public concern by the use of the domestic criminal law in such a framework, it does not appear to have been deployed in a precautionary sense. As such the state does not generally consider computer misuse to be a prime area of responsibility. Moreover, the domestic criminal law is prescriptive rather than network-cooperative, and is unsuitable as a precautionary tool save for its deterrent effect. With the exception of attempted offences, it also comes into operation *ex post* rather than *ex ante*. In summary:

> *Theories of risk and governance can be applied to explain the limitations of the domestic criminal law in the context of computer misuse. However, they also open up the potential for alternative network-reliant strategies of control to be explored and exploited. The domestic criminal law is therefore best placed within a broader framework of governance in relation to the control of computer misuse risks as a tool of management and guidance as well as a tool of direct coercion.*

What is the role of the law in the governance of computer misuse?

Chapter 6 examined the role of the law in general within the governance framework introduced in Chapter 5. Governance approaches encompass both public and private institutions and practices. The law falls into the public part of the governance framework, requiring or recommending legislative (state) responses. The role of the domestic criminal law within this governance framework was examined in Chapter 5. However, there are also a number of legal initiatives originating from beyond the boundaries of the nation state. The extent to which these measures are binding upon the UK is variable, ranging from the mandatory obligations imposed by the European Union, through the Council of Europe Convention on Cybercrime which binds states which choose to ratify it, to recommendations from the Commonwealth, the UN and the G8.

Legal harmonisation initiatives beyond the domestic criminal law are attractive in promoting broadly shared good principles and facilitating cross-border networked cooperation in response to networked risks. However, these initiatives come at the expense of some degree of national sovereignty and, as such, become politicised. Harmonisation will be more successful between states with similar values and will experience difficulty where there are fundamental conflicts or where one state is not especially concerned about computer misuse. Therefore the uniform adoption of a minimum framework of criminal laws with defined mechanisms of international cooperation in investigation and prosecution is highly unlikely. The problem of achieving international harmony is highlighted in the piecemeal adoption of the Council of Europe Convention on Cybercrime. However, this is not to say that such intergovernmental systems cannot be effective. In the context of terrorism, for instance, the global desire to achieve effective laws against the financing of terrorist activity was achieved through a two-fold mechanism. This mechanism involves overseeing by the Counter Terrorism Committee, to which all countries report and which facilitates counter-terrorism technical assistance from richer to poorer countries. It is feasible that a similar model could be applied to computer misuse with the establishment of a coordinating body coupled with the provision of technical assistance. However, the anti-terrorism initiative only gained the political impetus to bring it into being following the terrorist attacks of 11 September 2001. It is therefore unlikely that such a coordinated international approach to computer misuse would be precipitated without an event of similar magnitude. The notion of international technical aid facilitated by a coordinating international body remains attractive.

A limitation of international legal initiatives lies in their impact upon the individual. Any impact is brought to bear via indirect intergovernmental policy networks rather than by the direct use of domestic criminal law and, as such, these initiatives offer less direct protection to individuals. However, there is still value in the various international legal responses to computer misuse. While these responses might not be the most nimble or reflexive, they do offer a legislative framework which assists in the overall response network, but, as with the domestic criminal law, cannot offer a complete solution. Indeed, many of the originating institutions have offered extra-legal proposals by way of response. There are also other private and technological strategies which must be considered. These extra-legal mechanisms do not conflict with national sovereignty in the way that the law does. They are also consistent with the trend of reducing state intervention in managing complex or networked risks. They are also more likely to be able to address individuals directly. Therefore:

Legal initiatives beyond the domestic criminal law also have a role to play in the control of computer misuse. They offer a certain degree of harmonisation and help to enable the international cooperation required in response to computer misuse risks transcending national boundaries. However, they are problematic in terms of sovereignty and have limited direct impact on the individual. Moreover, they are not especially flexible or reflexive and their adoption is not always mandatory. The role of the law in the governance of computer misuse is therefore to facilitate cooperation and enforcement between nation states within the public part of the overall governance framework. This may extend to the provision of technical assistance.

Can extra-legal approaches provide an effective response to computer misuse?

Chapter 7 broadened the discussion followed in Chapter 6 from the role of the law in response to computer misuse to include extra-legal responses. Extra-legal responses have several advantages. They are generally more flexible and responsive than their legal counterparts, are less confrontational and can act as a voice to the individual. As such, they can provide a viable and potentially effective response to computer misuse. However, they are dependent upon the extent to which private organisations and individuals engage with them. A lack of awareness of their very existence will also limit their success. Therefore their success is predicated on an assumption of self-reliance and self-responsibility from the users of the technology itself. This will require an acknowledgement that legal responses, whether domestic or international, cannot provide a complete solution by themselves. It will also need a level of technical competence sufficient to take countermeasures or to understand and act on warnings and advisory notices.

Against a backdrop of rapid technological change, new risks are promulgated just as rapidly. Informal discussion forums and information-sharing mechanisms can deal with dynamically changing and complex technological environments, although the most vulnerable targets are often outside of these discussion communities. The existence of discussion and advisory groups is nothing new. There were discussion networks established between experts and enthusiasts in the very early days of computing. However, at that time, those outside the group did not need to know or understand what the group was discussing since they were not personally involved with or at risk from the technology. Nowadays, computing is widespread and the technology is in the care of the unaware. A level of awareness, technological education and training is therefore necessary to maximise the reach (and hence the effectiveness) of many extra-legal responses. Regulation through technology currently requires a certain level of competence and inclination on the part of the user. However, the technology itself could evolve in such a way that its protection becomes increasingly transparent to the user, thereby minimising the need for action or technical knowledge. This is seen to a certain extent in the provision of automatic updates from the key vendors, Microsoft and Apple, as well as frequent updates to the wide variety of protection software suites that are commercially available. While these still require some set-up on the part of the user, the level of skill needed is decreasing and may ultimately tend towards self-configuring, self-diagnosing, self-protecting systems facilitated by the very same networking technology that rendered them more vulnerable to attack in the first instance.

Extra-legal responses may be further criticised for a lack of enforcement capability and a lack of uniformity in application, accessibility and coverage. Although none of these criticisms presents problems for legal responses, technological responses have the capability to be uniformly available and will enforce the extra-legal rules contained within them. In summary:

Extra-legal functions and institutions form a further part of the networked governance response to computer misuse. These represent predominantly private, rather than state, interests. As such, they require an assumption of self-reliance and may require a certain level of technical ability to maximise their effectiveness. Although they may be limited in terms of enforcement, uniformity and accessibility, they have the key advantages of flexibility and responsiveness while transcending national borders. They do, however, require a certain level of interaction with legal responses to realise their full potential.

Conclusion

As computer technology and computer misuse evolved, certain forms of behaviour presented problems for the law in England and Wales. These problems arose from the difficulty in encapsulating new forms of wrongdoing within the parameters of the existing criminal law. By way of response, the Computer Misuse Act 1990 was introduced which has remained (with some recent amendment) the predominant piece of domestic criminal law dealing with criminal computer misuse. The 1990 Act has, however, produced relatively low prosecution rates, been inconsistent in application and has not always been used as a basis for prosecution where it might have been possible to do so. Computer misuse remains a current problem. Therefore it must be questioned whether the domestic criminal law alone is a suitable tool of regulation. Indeed, many of the characteristics of computer misuse are incompatible with those of the domestic criminal law. In particular, computer misuse can be trans-jurisdictional. It often causes only transient or trifling harm and is not generally considered to be especially immoral or a matter of public concern. Its definition is uncertain and fluid. By contrast, the domestic criminal law focuses on the domestic landscape, is concerned with preventing substantial harm and public wrong and with upholding morality, and demands certainty.

A broader perspective of risk and governance can be applied to the problems associated with computer misuse. Within this governance framework, the domestic criminal law still has limitations but is not redundant. It has a role to play in protecting those interests within its ambit, as a symbolic tool of deterrence and as a practical tool of management and guidance. The governance framework opens up alternative network-reliant means of control. From a legal standpoint, international harmonisation initiatives fit within the governance framework to facilitate international cooperation and enforcement. However, nation states are not uniformly compelled to adopt such measures. They present problems of competing sovereignty, have limited direct impact on the individual and are resistant to swift reflexive change. Extra-legal initiatives complement the legal initiatives, upholding private interests while retaining the flexibility required to respond to rapid change. However, they are not uniformly available and require the assumption of personal responsibility and a certain degree of technical capability.

It is clear that no single response mechanism will provide an entire solution to the problems posed by the misuse of computer technology. Each mechanism comes with its own limitations. However, each mechanism also offers benefits that the others do not. The governance network enables the domestic criminal law, the broader law and extra-legal responses to work together and as such they form a holistic response to computer misuse: the constellation of control. The role of the law within this network is to enable and facilitate the framework within which non-legal nodes of governance operate while balancing the needs of the individual and the state. The framework thus requires certain statutory provisions to operate but cannot rely wholly on the direct use of the law. Instead, the non-legal nodes must be allowed to develop and propagate flexible responses to new problems while the state remains accountable for the steering of the network as a whole.

The response to computer misuse is gestalt. It is greater than the sum of its parts and is not defined in terms of a rigid legal template, a problem-independent set of instructions or a collection of overriding private interests. It emerges instead from the complex interplay

293

between the natural tensions within law, society and technology. Just as computers have moved from being stand-alone discrete systems to complex networked systems, then the response to computer misuse has also moved from the use of the domestic law to a diffuse model of governance within which the domestic law is but one regulatory node. There is, however, a role for a central authority to marshal and coordinate the various regulators so that their reach and effectiveness is maximised without compromising individual agendas.

In conclusion:

There are a number of incompatibilities between the nature of computer misuse and the nature of the criminal law. This means that computer misuse cannot be regulated effectively by the criminal law alone. Such regulation requires a reflexive and cohesive approach which is only viable in a global networked society by a networked response combining nodes of both legal and extra-legal governance: the constellation of control.

Appendix

Outline research methodology

The main narrative of this study draws upon a range of different sources and is founded on documentary research supported by findings from fieldwork which was designed to provide an insight into the views of experts on the efficacy of various forms of regulation and their practices and attitudes towards the issue of computer misuse. As such, it was decided that the research should take the form of qualitative interviews (rather than any form of quantitative approach) for two principal reasons. First, the knowledge, views, understandings, interpretations and experiences of the participants were considered to be meaningful properties of the social responses to computer misuse which this research was designed to explore. This required an interview methodology which was reflexive, open and flexible and which gave primacy to the participant.[1] Second, it was considered that interaction with the participants by way of conversation was a valid means to gather data on these ontological properties.[2] This was a pragmatic decision in that there was no feasible alternative to talking and listening to the participants to ascertain the research data sought. Qualitative interviews are based in conversation[3] and emphasise researchers asking questions, listening

1   Sarantakos, S., *Social Research* (3rd edn, Palgrave Macmillan, Basingstoke, 2005) 270.

2   Mason, J., *Qualitative Researching* (Sage, London, 1996) 39–40.

3   Kvale, S., *InterViews: An Introduction to Qualitative Research Interviewing* (Sage, London, 1996).

and reflecting and respondents answering.[4] They are characterised by a relatively informal style, a thematic approach and the assumption that the data will be generated via the interaction.[5]

Since much of the potential value in the qualitative research data derives from the expert viewpoints of the participants, the fieldwork could be considered to be a form of 'elite' study, that is one in which the participants are more powerful members of society such as senior police officers, industry figures or policy-makers.[6] It is recognised that the semi-structured interview is a suitable methodology in such an elite study.[7]

Semi-structured interviews are appropriate where depth of study is of foremost concern and in situations exploring the ways in which complex phenomena have developed over time.[8] This was suitable for this book since it is primarily concerned with responses to complex technological evolution and its potential for misuse. Such interviews recognise the special nature of each interviewee's contribution and consist of a list of information required from each participant but allowing variation in the phrasing and order of questions.[9]

Since the objective of this study was to gather broad views from a sample of knowledgeable individuals in order to explore and develop the central thesis rather than to produce meaningful statistical data, a non-random sampling approach was adopted. Many research studies focus on very specific groups of the population for whom sampling frames are not readily available and often only have sufficient resources to study a small number of participants. When considering the high levels of specialist expertise needed to provide meaningful insight into the issues raised in the field of computer misuse, the population of potential participants was, in any case, relatively narrow. Such focused purposive studies remain valid provided that the constraints on interpretation which arise are noted

4   Rubin, H. and Rubin, I., *Qualitative Interviewing: The Art of Hearing Data* (2nd edn, Sage, London, 2005).
5   Mason, J., *Qualitative Researching* (Sage, London, 1996) 38.
6   Moyser, G. and Wagstaffe, M. (eds), *Research Methods for Elite Studies* (Allen & Unwin, London, 1987).
7   Odendahl, T. and Shaw, A., 'Interviewing elites', in Gubrium, J. and Holstein, J. (eds), *Handbook of Interview Research: Context and Method* (Sage, London, 2001) 299, 310.
8   Crow, I. and Semmens, N., *Researching Criminology* (Open University Press, Maidenhead, 2008) 119.
9   Ibid., 118.

clearly and honestly.[10] While there are obvious dangers in seeking to extrapolate findings from such a small-scale study, it was not the aim of this research to draw purportedly generalisable conclusions from the interviews. The contribution of the participants was to supplement and enhance the findings of the documentary research. The participants were experts who provided valuable information and were not merely a source of data. Moreover, the complexity of the potential range of responses to computer misuse required an understanding of the depth and complexity of participants' accounts and experiences rather than a more superficial quantitative analysis of limited accounts from a larger sample.

Having established the parameters of a small-scale focused study, it was then necessary to identify the categories from which the participants would be indentified. In qualitative research, theoretical representativeness requires a decision as to which categories of respondent would best suit the overall experimental hypothesis.[11] In order to explore the particular issues associated with computer misuse, it was decided to sample from the field of high-level information technology users and policy-makers. The categories into which this field was theoretically sampled were representatives from state and organisational policing bodies (at both local and national level); representatives of the IT industry, such as software engineers and security professionals; representatives of IT users within industry (that is, commercial enterprises which use IT but are not part of the IT industry itself); and policy-makers, influencers and representatives of professional bodies such as the British Computer Society (BCS), the European Information Society Group (EURIM) and the Information Technologists' Company (ITC), whose membership also intersects with the previous categories.

The number of interviews performed in each category is shown in Table A.1. Each participant is referred to throughout this study by the corresponding label.

This distribution was selected to give primacy to those who operate within the industry or use its products or services while encompassing complementary perspectives from those responsible for making and influencing policy and those responsible for its enforcement.

Given the small sample size, no quantitative analysis was undertaken. The findings from the interviews are spread pervasively

---

10 Ibid, 62–3.
11 Gomm, R., *Social Research Methodology: A Critical Introduction* (Palgrave Macmillan, Basingstoke, 2004) 235.

Table A.1 Categorisation of research participants

Category	Label	Number of interviews
Policing (local)	Police Officer 1, 2	2
Policing (national)	Police Officer 3, 4	2
IT industry	Technician 1–8	8
IT users in industry	User 1–8	8
Policy-makers and professional bodies	Policy-maker 1–4	4
Total		**24**

throughout the book where appropriate. Quotes have been used throughout the main narrative where they have been representative of the kinds of responses gathered or have provided an interesting counterpoint.

Since the research interviews were relatively non-contentious, the main areas requiring ethical consideration concerned informed consent and confidentiality and data protection. The participants were fully informed in meaningful terms as to the purpose of the research, who was undertaking and financing it, how and why it was being undertaken and how any research findings were to be disseminated, and gave their consent. The interview process involved the collection of personal information that could identify the participants in the research, including names, addresses, telephone numbers and e-mail addresses. There were also certain linking indicators within responses that related to an individual's job or position. All data collected were anonymised during analysis so that the research participants could not be identified.[12] The storage and use of data was compliant with the Data Protection Act 1998 and the ethical guidelines of both the British Society of Criminology and the Socio-Legal Studies Association.

---

12 Boruch, R. and Cecil, J., *Assuring the Confidentiality of Social Research Data* (University of Pennsylvania Press, Philadelphia, PA, 1979).

Bibliography

——, 'WARP Code of Practice v.2.0' (August 2004) <http://www.warp.gov.uk/BusinessCase/CodeofPracticeV2.0.pdf>.

——, 'MEPs in row with UK parliament over "gangplank" report', *EU Observer* (7 December 2006) <http://euobserver.com/?aid=23045>.

——, 'The future of WARPs' <http://www.warp.gov.uk/Index/indexfutureofwarps.htm>.

Akdeniz, Y., 'Section 3 of the Computer Misuse Act 1990: an antidote for computer viruses!' [1996] 3 *Web Journal of Current Legal Issues* <http://webjcli.ncl.ac.uk/1996/issue3/akdeniz3.html>.

Akdeniz, Y., 'CyberCrime', in Stokes, S. and Carolina, R. (eds), *E-Commerce Law and Regulation Encyclopedia* (Sweet & Maxwell, London, 2003).

Akdeniz, Y., 'Governing racist content on the Internet: national and international responses' (2007) 56 *University of New Brunswick Law Journal* 103.

Akdeniz, Y. and Walker, C., 'Whisper who dares: encryption, privacy rights and the new world disorder', in Akdeniz, Y., Walker, C. and Wall, D.S., *The Internet, Law and Society* (Pearson, Harlow, 2000) 317.

Akers, R., 'Rational choice, deterrence and social learning theory in criminology: the path not taken' (1990) 81 *Journal of Criminal Law and Criminology* 653.

All Party Internet Group, *Revision of the Computer Misuse Act: Report of an Inquiry by the All Party Internet Group* (June 2004).

American Civil Liberties Union, 'The Seven Reasons why the Senate should reject the International Cybercrime Treaty', 18 December 2003 <http://www.aclu.org/privacy/internet/14861res20031218.html>.

American Civil Liberties Union, 'ACLU Memo on the Council of Europe Convention on Cybercrime', 16 June 2004 <http://www.aclu.org/news/NewsPrint.cfm?ID=15954&c=39>.

299

Arber, S., 'Designing samples', in Gilbert, N., *Researching Social Life* (2nd edn, Sage, London, 2001).

Article 29 Data Protection Working Party, Opinion 4/2001, 'On the Council of Europe's Draft Convention on Cybercrime', 22 March 2001.

Auger, C., *Information Sources in Grey Literature* (4th edn, Bowker-Saur, London, 1998).

Austin, J., *The Providence of Jurisprudence Determined* (1831), reprinted as *The Providence of Jurisprudence Determined and The Uses of the Study of Jurisprudence* (Weidenfeld & Nicolson, London, 1954).

Austrian, G.D., *Herman Hollerith: The Forgotten Giant of Information Processing* (Columbia University Press, New York, 1982).

Ayres, I. and Braithwaite, J., *Responsive Regulation: Transcending the Deregulation Debate* (Oxford University Press, Oxford, 1992).

Bainbridge, D., 'Hacking – the unauthorised access of computer systems: the legal implications' (1989) 52 *Modern Law Review* 236.

Baker, T., 'On the genealogy of moral hazard' (1996) 75 *Texas Law Review* 237.

Baker, T. and Simon, J. (eds), *Embracing Risk: The Changing Culture of Insurance and Responsibility* (University of Chicago Press, Chicago, IL, 2002).

Baldwin, R., 'The new punitive regulation' (2004) 67 *Modern Law Review* 351.

Bangemann, M. and others, *Europe and the Global Information Society* (1994) <http://ec.europa.eu/archives/ISPO/infosoc/backg/bangeman.html>.

Barlow, J.P., 'Thinking locally, acting globally', *Time* (15 January 1996).

Barnard, C., 'The United Kingdom, the "Social Chapter" and the Amsterdam Treaty' (1997) 26 *Industrial Law Journal* 275.

Beck, U., 'From industrial society to risk society: questions of survival, social structure and ecological enlightenment' (1992) 9 *Theory Culture and Society* 98.

Beck, U., *Risk Society: Towards a New Modernity* (Sage, London, 1992).

Beck, U., *Ecological Politics in the Age of Risk* (Polity Press, Cambridge, 1995).

Beck, U., 'World risk society as cosmopolitan society? Ecological questions in a framework of manufactured uncertainties' (1996) 13(4) *Theory, Culture and Society* 1.

Beck, U., 'Politics of risk society', in Franklin, J. (ed.), *The Politics of Risk Society* (Polity Press, Cambridge, 1998).

Beck, U., Giddens, A. and Lash, S., *Reflexive Modernisation: Politics, Tradition and Aesthetics in the Modern Social Order* (Polity Press, Cambridge, 1994).

Becker, H., *Outsiders: Studies in the Sociology of Deviance* (Free Press, New York, 1963).

Bell, C., Mudge, J. and McNamara, E., *Computer Engineering: A DEC View of Hardware Systems Design* (Digital, Bedford, 1979).

Bennett, T., 'Factors related to participation in neighbourhood watch schemes' (1989) 29 *British Journal of Criminology* 207.

Bergstein, H., 'An interview with Eckert and Mauchly' [1962] *Datamation* 25.

Berners-Lee, T., 'WWW: past, present and future' (1996) 29 *IEE Computer* 69.

Better Regulation Task Force, *Better Regulation – From Design to Delivery* (London, 2005).

Bijker, W.E., Hughes, T.P. and Pinch, T.J. (eds), *The Social Construction of Technological Systems: New Directions in the Sociology and History of Technology* (MIT Press, Cambridge, MA, 1987).

Black, J., 'The emergence of risk-based regulation and the new public risk management in the United Kingdom' [2005] *Public Law* 512.

Blakley, R., 'The Emperor's Old Armor' (Proceedings of the 1996 New Security Paradigms Workshop, Association for Computing Machinery, Arrowhead, 1996).

Bok, S., *Secrets: On the Ethics of Concealment and Revelation* (Oxford University Press, Oxford, 1982).

Bonger, W., *Criminality and Economic Conditions* (reissued edn, Indiana University Press, Bloomington, IN, 1969).

Boruch, R. and Cecil, J., *Assuring the Confidentiality of Social Research Data* (University of Pennsylvania Press, Philadelphia, PA, 1979).

Boyle, J., *Shamans, Software, and Spleens: Law and the Construction of the Information Society* (Harvard University Press, Cambridge, MA, 1996).

Boyle, J., 'Foucault in cyberspace: surveillance, sovereignty, and hard-wired censors' (1997) <http://www.law.duke.edu/boylesite/foucault.htm>.

Bradbury, J., 'The policy implications of differing concepts of risk' (1989) 14 *Science, Technology and Human Values* 380.

Braithwaite, J., 'Responsive regulation and developing economies' (2006) 34 *World Development* 884.

Brans, M. and Rossbach, M., 'The autopoiesis of administrative systems: Niklas Luhmann on public administration and public policy' (1997) 75 *Public Administration* 417.

Braithwaite, J., 'The new regulatory state and the transformation of criminology' (2000) 40 *British Journal of Criminology* 222.

Braithwaite, J., *Markets in Vice, Markets in Virtue* (Oxford University Press, Oxford, 2005).

Brenner, S.W. and Clarke, L.L., 'Distributed security: preventing cybercrime' (2005) 23 *John Marshall Journal of Computer and Information Law* 659.

Brown, J. (ed.), *Environmental Threats: Perception, Analysis and Management* (Belhaven Press, London, 1989).

Buchsbaum, H., 'Revenge of the nerds', *Scholastic Update* (2 September 1994) 14.

Bulmer, N., 'The ethics of social research', in Gilbert, N., *Researching Social Life* (2nd edn, Sage, London, 2001).

Bunyan, T., 'EU: cementing the European state – new emphasis on internal security and operational cooperation at EU level' (2007) 17 *Statewatch Bulletin* 3.

Burchell, G., Gordon, C. and Miller, P. (eds), *The Foucault Effect: Studies in Governmentality* (University of Chicago Press, Chicago, IL, 1991).

Burchell, G., Gordon, C. and Miller, P. (eds), *The Politics of Everyday Fear* (University of Minnesota Press, Minneapolis, MN, 1993).

Burgess, R., *In the Field: An Introduction to Field Research* (Allen & Unwin, London, 1984).

Burgess, R., 'Sponsors, gatekeepers, members and friends: access in educational settings', in Shaffir, W. and Stebbins, R., *Experiencing Fieldwork: An Inside View of Qualitative Research* (Sage, London, 1991).

Butcher, D., *Official Publications in Britain* (Bingley, London, 1991).

Cangemi, D., 'Procedural law provisions of the Council of Europe Convention on Cybercrime' (2004) 18 *International Review of Law, Computers and Technology* 165.

Castells, M., *The Power of Identity (The Information Age: Economy, Society and Culture Volume 2)* (2nd edn, Blackwell, Oxford, 2004).

CERT, 'WANK worm on SPAN Network', Advisory CA-1989-04 (17 October 1989) <http://www.cert.org/advisories/CA-1989-04.html>.

Ceruzzi, P., *A History of Modern Computing* (2nd edn, MIT Press, Cambridge, MA, 2003).

Chandler, D., 'Technological or Media Determinism' <http://www.aber.ac.uk/media/Documents/tecdet/tecdet.html>.

Charlesworth, A., 'Addiction and hacking' (1993) 143 *New Law Journal* 540.

Clough, B. and Mungo, P., *Approaching Zero: Data Crime and the Criminal Underworld* (Faber & Faber, London, 1992).

Clout, L., 'Energy-saving light bulbs blamed for migraines', *Daily Telegraph* (3 January 2008) <http://www.telegraph.co.uk/earth/main.jhtml?xml=/earth/2008/01/03/eabulb103.xml>.

Cohen, M.R., 'Moral aspects of the criminal law' (1940) 49 *The Yale Law Journal* 987.

Cohen, S. and Taylor, L., *Escape Attempts: The Theory and Practice of Resistance to Everyday Life* (2nd edn, Routledge, London 1992).

Coleman, C. and Moynihan, J., *Understanding Crime Data: Haunted by the Dark Figure* (Open University Press, Maidenhead, 1996).

Committee on Homosexual Offences and Prostitution, *Report of the Committee on Homosexual Offences and Prostitution* (HMSO, London, 1957).

Commonwealth, 'Model Law on Computer and Computer-related Crime' LMM(02) 17 October 2002.

Commonwealth, 'Scheme relating to mutual assistance in criminal matters within the Commonwealth including amendments made by Law Ministers in April 1990, November 2002 and October 2005' <http://www.thecommonwealth.org/shared_asp_files/uploadedfiles/2C167ECF-0FDE-481B-B552-E9BA23857CE3_HARARESCHEMERELATINGTOMUTUALASSISTANCE2005.pdf>.

Cooley, C.H., *Sociological Theory and Social Research* (Henry Holt, New York, 1930).

Copeland, B.J., *Colossus: The Secrets of Bletchley Park's Code-breaking Computers* (Oxford University Press, Oxford, 2006).

Cornish, D. and Clarke, R. (eds), *The Reasoning Criminal* (Springer-Verlag, New York, 1986).

Cornwall, H., *The Hacker's Handbook* (Century, London, 1985).

Costigan, C., 'Ladbrokes prepared to accept US poker bets says managing director', *Gambling 911* (8 July 2008).

Council of Europe, 'Countries worldwide turn to Council of Europe Cybercrime Convention', Press release 413(2007), Strasbourg, 13 June 2007 <https://wcd.coe.int/ViewDoc.jsp?id=1150107>.

Council of Europe, 'Cybercrime: closer co-operation between law enforcement and internet service providers', Press release 160(2008), Strasbourg, 5 March 2008 <https://wcd.coe.int/ViewDoc.jsp?id=1258339>.

Council of Europe, 'Octopus Interface conference on cooperation against cybercrime, Strasbourg, France (11–12 June 2007): Conference Summary' <http://www.coe.int/t/e/legal_affairs/legal_co-operation/combating-economic_crime/3_technical_cooperation/cyber/567%20F%202007-d-sum conclusions1g%20Provisional.pdf>.

Council of Europe, 'Project against cybercrime: Summary and workplan 2007–2008' <http://www.coe.int/t/e/legal_affairs/legal_co-operation/combating_economic_crime/3_technical_cooperation/cyber/567-d-summary%20and%20workplan%202007-2008%20_20%20May%2007_WEB.pdf>.

Council of Europe Committee on Crime Problems, *Computer-related Crime* (Council of Europe, Strasbourg, 1990).

Cretney, S. and Davis, G., 'Prosecuting "domestic" assault' [1996] *Criminal Law Review* 162.

Croall, H., *Crime and Society in Britain* (Longman, Harlow, 1998).

Crow, I. and Semmens, N., *Researching Criminology* (Open University Press, Maidenhead, 2008).

Crown Prosecution Service, 'Computer Misuse Act 1990' <http://www.cps.gov.uk/legal/section12/chapter_s.html>.

Crown Prosecution Service Inspectorate, *The Inspectorate's Report on Cases Involving Domestic Violence* (Crown Prosecution Service Inspectorate, London, 1998).

Dahrendorf, R., *Class and Class Conflict in Industrial Society* (Stanford University Press, Stanford, CA, 1959).

Dale, R., *The Sinclair Story* (Duckworth, London, 1985).

de Bruxelles, S., 'Hackers force mass website closures', *The Times* (6 December 2007).

Denby, K., 'Dissident websites crippled by Burma on anniversary of revolt', *The Times* (22 September 2008).

Denning, D., *Information Warfare and Security* (Addison-Wesley, Harlow, 1998).

Denzin, N., *The Research Act: A Theoretical Introduction to Sociological Methods* (2nd edn, McGraw-Hill, Columbus, OH, 1978).

Department for Constitutional Affairs, *Increasing Penalties for Deliberate and Wilful Misuse of Personal Data*, Consultation Paper CP 9/06 (24 July 2006).

Department for Transport, *Local Bus Service Support – Options for Reform* (March 2008).

Devlin, P., *The Enforcement of Morals* (Oxford University Press, Oxford, 1965).

Dornstein, K., *Accidentally, on Purpose: The Making of a Personal Injury Underworld in America* (St. Martin's Press, New York, 1996).

Douglas, M., *Purity and Danger: An Analysis of Concepts of Pollution and Taboo* (Routledge Classics, Routledge & Kegan Paul, London, 1966).

Douglas, M., *Risk Acceptability According to the Social Sciences* (Russell Sage Foundation, New York, 1985).

Douglas, M., *Risk and Blame: Essays in Cultural Theory* (Routledge, London, 1992).

Douglas, M. and Wildavsky, A., *Risk and Culture: An Essay on the Selection of Technological and Environmental Dangers* (University of California Press, Berkeley, CA, 1982).

Downing, R.W., 'Shoring up the weakest link: what lawmakers around the world need to consider in developing comprehensive laws to combat cybercrime' (2005) 43 *Columbia Journal of Transnational Law* 705.

Driver, S. and Martell, L., 'Left, Right and the third way' (2000) 28 *Policy and Politics* 147.

DTI, *Information Security Breaches Survey 2004* <http://www.pwc.com/images/gx/eng/about/svcs/grms/2004Technical_Report.pdf>.

Duff, R.A., 'Theories of criminal law', *Stanford Encyclopedia of Philosophy* <http://plato.stanford.edu/entries/criminal-law/>.

Duff, R.A., 'Theorizing criminal law: a 25th anniversary essay' (2005) 25 *Oxford Journal of Legal Studies* 353.

Dworkin, R., *Law's Empire* (Belknap Press, Cambridge, 1986).

Dworkin, R., *Taking Rights Seriously* (Harvard University Press, Cambridge, MA, 2005).

Edwards, S., *Sex and Gender in the Legal Process* (Blackstone, London, 1996).

Ellison, L., 'Prosecuting domestic violence without victim participation' (2002) 65 *Modern Law Review* 834.

ENISA, 'Inventory of CERT activities in Europe' (September 2007) <http://enisa.europa.eu/cert_inventory/downloads/Enisa_CERT_inventory.pdf>.

ENISA, 'ENISA Work Programme 2008' <http://www.enisa.europa.eu/doc/pdf/management_board/decisions/enisa_wp_desig_ver_2008.pdf>.

Espiner, T., 'Lord vows to fight cybercrime laws' (25 May 2006) <http://news.zdnet.co.uk/security/0,100000189,39271086,00.htm>.

EURIM, Newsletter (March 2006).

EURIM, 'Cyber-crime Reporting and Intelligence' ('Tackling Crime and Achieving Confidence in the On-line World, Parliament and the Internet Conference, London, 2007).

European Commission, 'Your pint safe in EU hands', 11 September 2007 <http://ec.europa.eu/unitedkingdom/press/frontpage/11092007_en.htm>.

Evans, E., 'Personal data of 600,000 on lost laptop', The Times (19 January 2008).

Ewald, F., L'Etat Providence (Editions Grasset, Paris, 1986).

Fafinski, S., 'Access denied: computer misuse in an era of technological change' (2006) 70 Journal of Criminal Law 424.

Fafinski, S., 'Computer misuse: denial-of-service attacks' (2006) 70 Journal of Criminal Law 474.

Fafinski, S., 'Computer misuse: the implications of the Police and Justice Act 2006' (2008) 72 Journal of Criminal Law 53.

Federal Complaints Commission, 'In the matter of violent television programming and its effect on children', FCC 07-50 (25 April 2007).

Feeley, M. and Simon, J., 'The new penology: notes on the emerging strategy of corrections and its implications' (1992) 30 Criminology 449.

Fielding, N. and Thomas, H., 'Qualitative interviewing', in Gilbert, N. (ed.), Researching Social Life (2nd edn, Sage, London, 2001).

Finch, E., The Criminalisation of Stalking: Constructing the Problem and Evaluating the Solution (Cavendish, London, 2001).

Fites, P., Johnston, P. and Kratz, M., The Computer Virus Crisis (Van Nostrand Reinhold, New York, 1989).

Flanagan, A., 'The law and computer crime: reading the script of reform' (2005) 13 International Journal of Law and Information Technology 98.

Flynn, J. and others, 'Gender, race and perception of environmental health risks' (1994) 14 Risk Analysis 1101.

Forester, T. and Morrison, P., Computer Ethics: Cautionary Tales and Ethical Dilemmas in Computing (MIT Press, London, 1990).

Foucault, M., Discipline and Punish: the Birth of the Prison (Allen Lane, London, 1977).

Fox, C.J. and Miller, H.T., Postmodern Public Administration: Towards Discourse (Sage, London, 1995).

Franklin, J. (ed.), The Politics of Risk Society (Polity Press, Cambridge, 1998).

Freestone, D., 'The road to Rio: international environmental law after the Earth Summit' (1996) 6 Journal of Environmental Law 193.

Freiberger, P. and Swaine, M., Fire in the Valley: The Making of the Personal Computer (McGraw-Hill, New York, 2000).

Friedman, L. and Fisher, G. (eds), *The Crime Conundrum: Essays on Criminal Justice* (Westview Press, Boulder, CO, 1997).

Frith, H., 'Stowaway computer virus sent into orbit', *The Times* (28 August 2008).

Fuller, L.L., *The Morality of Law* (Yale University Press, New Haven, CT, 1964).

Furedi, F., *Culture of Fear Revisited* (4th edn, Continuum, London, 2006).

G8, 'Denver Summit of the Eight: Communiqué' (22 June 1997) <http://www.g8.utoronto.ca/summit/1997denver/g8final.htm>.

G8, 'Denver Summit of the Eight: Foreign Ministers' Progress Report' (21 June 1997) <http://www.g8.utoronto.ca/summit/1997denver/formin.htm>.

G8, 'Meeting of Justice and Interior Ministers of the Eight: Communiqué' (10 December 1997) <http://www.usdoj.gov/criminal/cybercrime/g82004/97Communique.pdf>.

G8, 'A Government/Industry Dialogue on Safety and Confidence in Cyberspace' (May 2000) <www.mofa.jp/policy/economy/summit/2000/crime.html>.

G8, 'Okinawa Charter on Global Information Society' (July 2000) <http://www.mofa.go.jp/policy/economy/summit/2000/documents/charter.html>.

G8, 'Recommendations on Transnational Crime' (May 2002) <http://canada/justice.gc.ca/en/news/g8/doc1.html>.

Gibson, W., 'Burning chrome', *Omni Magazine* (July 1982).

Gibson, W., *Neuromancer* (Harper Collins, London, 1984).

Gibson, W., *Burning Chrome* (Arbor, New York, 1986).

Giddens, A., *Capitalism and Modern Social Theory: An Analysis of the Writings of Marx, Durkheim and Max Weber* (Cambridge University Press, Cambridge, 1973).

Giddens, A., *A Contemporary Critique of Historical Materialism. Vol. 2. The Nation State and Violence* (Polity Press, Cambridge, 1985).

Giddens, A., *The Consequences of Modernity* (Polity Press, Cambridge, 1990).

Giddens, A., *Modernity and Self-Identity* (Polity Press, Cambridge, 1991).

Giddens, A., *Beyond Left and Right* (Polity Press, Cambridge, 1994).

Giddens, A., *The Third Way: Renewal of Social Democracy* (Polity Press, Cambridge, 1998).

Giddens, A., 'Risk and responsibility' (1999) 62 *Modern Law Review* 1.

Goldsmith, J.L., 'The Internet and the legitimacy of remote cross-border searches' (2001) 1 *University of Chicago Legal Forum* 103.

Gomm, R., *Social Research Methodology: A Critical Introduction* (Palgrave Macmillan, Basingstoke, 2004).

Goodwin, W., 'Computer Misuse Act amendment could criminalise tools used by IT professionals', *Computer Weekly* (21 February 2006).

Graham, J. and Clemente, K., 'Hazards in the news: who believes what?' (1996) 4(4) *Risk in Perspective* 1.

Graux, H., 'Promoting good practices in establishing and running CSIRTs – a legal perspective' (ENISA Workshop, 13–14 December 2005).

Greatorex, P. and Peter, N., 'Gloves off: *Commission v. Council* (2005) 155 *New Law Journal* 1706.

Greco, M., 'Psychosomatic subjects and the "duty to be well": personal agency within medical rationality' (1993) 22 *Economy and Society* 357.

Greenleaf, G., 'An endnote on regulating cyberspace: architecture vs law?' (1998) 21 *University of New South Wales Law Journal* 52.

Gross, O., 'Chaos and rules: should responses to violent crises always be constitutional?' (2003) 112 *Yale Law Review* 1011.

Habermas, J., *The Theory of Communicative Action – Volume 2: Lifeworld and System: A Critique of Functionalist Reason* (Beacon Press, Boston, MA, 1987).

Hacking, I., *The Taming of Chance* (Cambridge, Cambridge University Press, 1990).

Hafner, K. and Markoff, J., *CYBERPUNK: Outlaws and Hackers on the Computer Frontier* (Touchstone, New York, 1995).

Hart, C., *Doing a Literature Search* (Sage, London, 2004).

Hart, H.L.A., *The Concept of Law* (Oxford University Press, Oxford, 1961).

Hart, H.L.A., *Law, Liberty and Morality* (Oxford University Press, Oxford, 1963).

Hart, H.L.A., 'Book review of *The Morality of Law*' (1965) 78 *Harvard Law Review* 1281.

Harvey, M. and Henderson, M., 'Hackers claim there's a black hole in the atom smashers' computer network', *The Times* (13 September 2008).

Hayek, F.A., *The Road to Serfdom* (Routledge, London, 1944/2001).

Heidensohn, F., *Crime and Society* (Macmillan, Basingstoke, 1989).

Heimer, C.A., *Reactive Risk and Rational Action: Managing Moral Hazard in Insurance Contracts* (University of California Press, Berkeley, CA, 1985).

Hey, E., 'The precautionary concept in environmental policy and law: institutionalising caution' (1992) 4 *Georgetown International Environmental Law Review* 303.

Higney, F., 'Interview: Robert Schifreen', *Legal IT Forum Bulletin* (16 October 2003).

Hines, N., 'Philip Thompson admits he is child porn "librarian"', *The Times* (18 August 2008).

Hirst, P. and Thompson, G., 'Globalisation and the future of the nation state' (1995) 24 *Economy and Society* 408.

Holder, C., 'Staying one step ahead of the criminals' (2002) 10(3) *IT Law Today* 17.

Home Office, 'Guidance on notices issued under section 3 of the Terrorism Act 2006' (9 October 2006) <http://security.homeoffice.gov.uk/news-

and-publications1/publication-search/legislation-publications/guidance-notices-section3-t1.pdf>.

Hood, C. and Jones, D.K.C. (eds), *Accident and Design* (UCL Press, London, 1996).

Hood, C., Rothstein, H. and Baldwin, R., *The Government of Risk: Understanding Risk Regulation Regimes* (Oxford University Press, Oxford, 2001).

Hruska, J., *Computer Viruses and Anti-Virus Warfare* (Ellis Horwood, Chichester, 1990).

Huck, S. and Kosfield, M., 'The dynamics of neighbourhood watch and norm enforcement' (2007) 117 *The Economic Journal* 270.

Hughes, T.P., 'Technological momentum', in Teich, A. (ed.), *Technology and the Future* (8th edn, Bedford/St. Martins, New York, 2000).

Hume, D., *A Treatise of Human Nature* (1777), in Freeman, M.D.A., *Lloyd's Introduction to Jurisprudence* (6th edn, Sweet & Maxwell, London, 1994).

Husak, D.N., *Philosophy of Criminal Law* (Rowman & Littlefield, Totowa, NJ, 1987).

Hyman, H., *Interviewing in Social Research* (University of Chicago Press, Chicago, IL, 1954).

Ifrah, G., *The Universal History of Computing: From the Abacus to the Quantum Computer* (Wiley, New York, 2007).

Independent Expert Group on Mobile Phones, 'Mobile Phones and Health' (2000) <http://www.iegmp.org.uk/report/text.htm>.

Information Commissioner, *What Price Privacy? The Unlawful Trade in Confidential Personal Information* (The Stationery Office, London, 10 May 2006).

Ingraham, D., 'On charging computer crime' (1980) 2 *Computer and Law Journal* 429.

International Standards Organisation, *Systems and Software Engineering – Software Lifecycle Processes*, ISO 12207:2008 (18 March 2008).

INTERPOL, 'Fact Sheet "Cyber-crime"' COM/FS/2007-09/FHT-02 <http://www.interpol.int/Public/ICPO/FactSheets/FHT02.pdf>.

Johnson, D. and Post, D., 'Law and borders: the rise of law in cyberspace' (1996) 48 *Stanford Law Review* 1367.

Johnson, D. and Post, D., 'And how shall the net be governed? A meditation on the relative virtues of decentralised, emergent law', in Kahin, B. and Keller, J.H. (eds), *Co-ordinating the Internet* (MIT Press, Cambridge, MA, 1997) 62.

Jones, H.W., 'The rule of law and the welfare state' (1958) 58 *Columbia Law Review* 143.

Joseph, R. (ed.), *State, Conflict and Democracy in Africa* (Lynne Rienner, Boulder, CO, 1999).

Kant, I., *Critique of Pure Reason* (1781), trans. Kemp Smith, N., <http://www.hkbu.edu.hk/~ppp/cpr/toc.html>.

Katyal, N.K., 'Digital architecture as crime control' (2003) 112 *Yale Law Journal* 2261.

Keller, S., *Beyond the Ruling Class* (Random House, New York, 1963).

Keyser, M., 'The Council of Europe Convention on Cybercrime' (2003) 12 *Journal of Transnational Law and Policy* 287.

Killcrece, G. and others, *State of the Practice of Computer Security Incident Response Teams* (Carnegie Mellon University, Pittsburgh, PA, 2003).

Kirkup, J., 'Nine million face "green" road tax increases', *The Telegraph* (London 9 July 2008).

Kjaer, A.M., *Governance* (Polity Press, Cambridge, 2004).

Knabb, R.D., Rhome, J.R. and Brown, D.P., 'Tropical Cyclone Report Hurricane Katrina', US National Hurricane Centre (10 August 2006) <http://www.nhc.noaa.gov/pdf/TCR-AL122005_Katrina.pdf>.

Kooiman, J. (ed.), *Modern Governance* (Sage, London, 1993).

Kutz, R., 'Computer crime in Virginia' (1986) 27 *William and Mary Law Review* 783.

Kvale, S., *InterViews: An Introduction to Qualitative Research Interviewing* (Sage, London, 1996).

Labaton, S., 'FCC moves to restrict TV violence', *New York Times* (26 April 2007).

Lacey, N., 'Contingency and criminalisation', in Loveland, I. (ed.), *Frontiers of Criminality* (Sweet & Maxwell, London, 1995).

Lacey, N., Wells, C. and Meure, D., *Reconstructing Criminal Law: Critical Social Perspectives on Crime and the Criminal Process* (Weidenfield & Nicolson, London, 1990).

Lash, S., Szersynski, B. and Wynne, B. (eds), *Risk, Environment and Modernity* (Sage, London, 1996) 27.

Law Commission, *Computer Misuse* (Working Paper No. 110, 1988).

Law Commission, *Criminal Code for England and Wales* (Law Com. No. 177, Cm 299, 1989).

Law Commission, *Computer Misuse* (Law Com. No. 186, Cm 819, 1989).

Lemley, M. and McGowan, D., 'Legal implication of network economic effects' (1998) 86 *California Law Review* 479.

Lessig, L., 'The New Chicago School' (1998) 27 *Journal of Legal Studies* 661.

Lessig, L., 'The law of the horse: what cyberlaw might teach' (1999) 113 *Harvard Law Review* 501.

Lessig, L., *Code and Other Laws of Cyberspace* (Basic Books, New York, 1999).

Levi, M. and Pithouse, A., 'Victims of fraud', in Downes, D. (ed.), *Unravelling Criminal Justice* (Macmillan, London, 1992).

Levy, S., *Hackers* (Anchor Doubleday, New York, 1984).

Lewis, B.C., 'Prevention of computer crime amidst international anarchy' (2004) 41 *American Criminal Law Review* 1353.

Linzmayer, O., *Apple Confidential 2.0: The Real Story of Apple Computer, Inc.* (2nd edn, No Starch Press, San Francisco, CA, 2004).

Lipson, H., *Tracking and Tracing Cyber-Attacks: Technical Challenges and Global Policy Issues* (Carnegie Mellon University, Pittsburgh, PA, 2002).

Lipson, H. and Fisher, D.A., 'Survivability – a new technical and business perspective on security' (Proceedings of the 1999 New Security Paradigms Workshop, Association for Computing Machinery, Caledon Hills, 1999).

Lloyd, I., 'Computer abuse and the law' (1988) 104 *Law Quarterly Review* 202.

Loader, B. (ed.), *The Governance of Cyberspace* (Routledge, London, 1997).

Lofland, J. and Lofland, L., *Analyzing Social Settings* (Wadsworth, Belmont, CA, 1994).

Luhmann, N., *Risk: A Sociological Theory* (Aldine de Gruyter, New York, 1993).

Lupton, D. (ed.), *Risk and Sociocultural Theory: New Directions and Perspectives* (Cambridge University Press, Cambridge, 1999).

Lupton, D., *Risk* (Routledge, Abingdon, 1999).

Lyon, D., *The Electronic Eye: The Rise of Surveillance Society* (University of Minnesota Press, Minneapolis, MN, 1994).

MacCormick, N., 'Beyond the sovereign state' (1993) 53 *Modern Law Review* 1.

MacCormick, N., *Questioning Sovereignty: Law, State and Nation in the European Commonwealth* (Oxford University Press, Oxford, 1999).

McIntyre, O. and Mosedale, T., 'The precautionary principle as a norm of customary international law' (1997) 9 *Journal of Environmental Law* 221.

MacKinnon, R., 'Virtual rape' (1997) 2(4) *Journal of Computer Mediated Communication* <http://jcmc.indiana.edu/vol2/issue4/mackinnon.html>.

Mandell, S., *Computers, Data Processing and the Law* (West Publishing, St Paul, MN, 1984).

Marler, S.L., 'The Convention on Cybercrime: should the United States ratify?' (2002) 37 *New England Law Review* 183.

Marris, C. and Langford, I., 'No cause for alarm', *New Scientist* (28 September 1996).

Marsh, D. and Rhodes, R.A.W. (eds), *Policy Networks in British Government* (Clarendon Press, Oxford, 1992).

Marshall, S.E. and Duff, R.A., 'Criminalisation and sharing wrongs' (1998) 11 *Canadian Journal of Law and Jurisprudence* 7.

Martin, L., Gutman, H. and Hutton, P. (eds), *Technologies of the Self: A Seminar with Michel Foucault* (Tavistock, London, 1988).

Marx, K., *A Contribution to the Critique of Political Economy* (trans., Progress, Moscow, 1970).

Mason, J., *Qualitative Researching* (Sage, London, 1996).

Mead, G., *Mind, Self and Society* (University of Chicago Press, Chicago, IL, 1934).

Michael, J. and Adler, M., *Crime, Law and Social Science* (Harcourt Brace Jovanovich, New York, 1933) 5.

Mill, J.S., *On Liberty and Other Essays* (revd edn, Oxford University Press, Oxford, 1991).

Miller, M., 'More bad news blows in from Katrina', *CBS News* (Brooklyn, New York, 28 May 2006) <http://www.cbsnews.com/stories/2006/05/28/eveningnews/main1663142.shtml>.

Mills, C., *The Power Elite* (Oxford University Press, Oxford, 1956).

Milton, P., 'David Hume and the eighteenth-century conception of natural law' [1982] *Legal Studies* 14.

Miniwatts Marketing Group, 'World Internet Usage Statistics' <http://www.internetworldstats.com/stats.htm>.

Misztal, B., *Trust in Modern Societies* (Polity Press, Cambridge, 1996).

Mitchell, B., *Law, Morality and Religion in a Secular Society* (Oxford University Press, London, 1967).

Moore, G.E., *Principia Ethica* (Cambridge University Press, Cambridge, 1903).

Moore, M.S., *Placing Blame: A Theory of Criminal Law* (Oxford University Press, Oxford, 1997).

Morgan, G., *Images of Organisation* (Sage, London, 1986).

Moyser, G. and Wagstaffe, M. (eds), *Research Methods for Elite Studies* (Allen & Unwin, London, 1987).

Nadel, S., 'The concept of social elites' (1956) 8 *International Social Science Bulletin* 413.

National Statistics, 'Internet access: households and individuals' (23 August 2006).

Neal, D., 'Judge says law allows denial-of-service attacks', *IT Week* (7 November 2005).

Nelken, D. (ed.), *The Futures of Criminology* (Sage, London, 1994).

Neuman, W.L., *Basics of Social Research* (Pearson, Harlow, 2004).

Nhan, J. and Huey, L., 'Policing through nodes, clusters and bandwidth', in Leman-Langlois, S. (ed.), *Technocrime: Technology, Crime and Social Control* (Willan, Cullompton, 2008).

Nimmer, R., *The Law of Computer Technology* (Wiley, New York, 1985).

Noakes, L. and Wincup, E., *Criminological Research* (Sage, London, 2004).

O'Malley, P., 'Legal networks and domestic security' (1991) 11 *Studies in Law, Politics and Society* 171.

O'Malley, P., 'Risk, power and crime prevention' (1992) 21 *Economy and Society* 252.

O'Malley, P., *Risk, Uncertainty and Government* (Glasshouse, London, 2004).

O'Neill, S. and Ford, R. 'Thousands of criminal files lost in data fiasco', *The Times* (22 August 2008).

Odendahl, T. and Shaw, A., 'Interviewing elites', in Gubrium, J. and Holstein, J. (eds), *Handbook of Interview Research: Context and Method* (Sage, London, 2001).

OECD, *Guidelines for the Security of Information Systems and Networks: Towards a Culture of Security* (OECD, Paris, 2002).

Offe, C., *Contradictions of the Welfare State* (Hutchinson, London, 1984).

Ogus, A., 'Rethinking self-regulation' (1995) 15 *Oxford Journal of Legal Studies* 97.

Oppenheim, A., *Questionnaire Design, Interviewing and Attitude Management* (Continuum, London, 1992).

Orbach, B., 'Indirect free riding on the wheels of commerce: dual-use technologies and copyright liability' (2008) 57 *Emory Law Journal* 409.

Ormerod, D., *Smith and Hogan Criminal Law* (11th edn, Oxford University Press, Oxford, 2004).

Osborn, R.F., 'GE and UNIVAC: harnessing the high-speed computer' [1954] *Harvard Business Review* 99.

Packer, H.L., *The Limits of the Criminal Sanction* (Stanford University Press, Stanford, CA, 1968).

Parke Hughes, T., *Networks of Power: Electrification in Western Society 1880–1930* (Johns Hopkins University Press, Baltimore, MD, 1983).

Pierre, J. and Peters, B.G., *Governance, Politics and the State* (Macmillan, Basingstoke, 2000).

Pinch, T.J. and Bijker, W.E., 'The social construction of facts and artefacts: or how the sociology of science and the sociology of technology might benefit each other' (1984) 14 *Social Studies of Science* 399.

Platt, A.M., *The Child Savers: The Invention of Delinquency* (University of Chicago Press, Chicago, IL, 1969).

Plummer, K., *Sexual Stigma* (Routledge & Kegan Paul, London, 1975).

Posner, E.A., 'Fear and the regulatory model of counterterrorism' (2002) 25 *Harvard Journal of Law and Public Policy* 681.

Post, D., 'Encryption vs The Alligator Clip: the Feds worry that encoded messages are immune to wiretaps', *American Lawyer* (January/February 1995) 111.

Post, D., 'What Larry doesn't get: code, law and liberty in cyberspace' (2000) 52 *Stanford Law Review* 1439.

Powell, J., Wahidin, A. and Zinn, J., 'Understanding risk and old age in western society' (2007) 27 *International Journal of Sociology and Social Policy* 65.

Poynter, K., *Review of Information Security at HM Revenue and Customs: Final Report* (HMSO, London, 2008).

Pugh, E., *Building IBM: Shaping an Industry and Its Technology* (MIT Press, Boston, MA, 1995).

Quinney, R., *The Social Reality of Crime* Boston (Little, Brown, Boston, MA, 1970).

Raymond, E., *A Brief History of Hackerdom* (May 2000) <http://catb.org/~esr/writings/hacker-history/hacker-history.html>.

Reidenberg, J., 'Governing networks and rule-making in cyberspace' (1996) 45 *Emory Law Journal* 911.

Reidenberg, J., 'Lex informatica' (1998) 76 *Texas Law Review* 553.

Reno, J., 'Law enforcement in cyberspace' (address to Commonwealth Club of California, San Francisco, CA, 14 June 1996).

Renouf, M., 'The Euro battle to legislate' (2005) 102 *Law Society Gazette* 15.

Rheingold, H., *The Virtual Community: Homesteading on the Electronic Frontier* (MIT Press, London, 2000).

Rhodes, R.A.W., 'The hollowing out of the state: the changing nature of the public service in Britain' (1994) 65 *Political Quarterly* 138.

Rhodes, R.A.W., *Understanding Governance: Policy Networks, Governance, Reflexivity and Accountability* (Open University Press, Buckingham, 1997).

Richards, J., 'Georgia accuses Russia of waging "cyber-war"', *The Times* (11 August 2008).

Richards, J., 'Thousands of cyber attacks each day on key utilities', *The Times* (23 August 2008).

Richards, L., *Handling Qualitative Data: A Practical Guide* (Sage, London, 2005).

Rosenau, J.N., 'Governance in the twenty-first century' (1995) 1 *Global Governance* 13.

Rosenau, J.N. and Czempiel, E.-O., *Governance without Government: Order and Change in World Politics* (Cambridge University Press, Cambridge, 1992).

Rosenbaum, D., 'The theory and research behind neighbourhood watch' (1987) 33 *Crime and Delinquency* 103.

Royal Society, *Risk: Analysis, Perception and Management* (Royal Society, London, 1992).

Royal Society, *Infectious Diseases in Livestock* (Royal Society, London, 2002).

Rubin, H. and Rubin, I., *Qualitative Interviewing: The Art of Hearing Data* (2nd edn, Sage, London, 2005).

Salomon, J.M. and Elsa, P., 'Computer security incident response grows up' (2004) 11 *Computer Fraud and Security* 5.

Salus, P. (ed.), *The ARPANET Sourcebook: The Unpublished Foundations of the Internet* (Peer-to-Peer Communications, Charlottesville, VA, 2008).

Sarantakos, S., *Social Research* (3rd edn, Palgrave Macmillan, Basingstoke, 2005).

Scott, C., 'Analysing regulatory space: fragmented resources and institutional design' [2001] *Public Law* 329.

Scottish Law Commission, *Computer Crime* (Consultative Memorandum No. 68, 1986).

Scottish Law Commission, *Report on Computer Crime* (Cm 174, July 1987).

Sellin, T., *Culture, Conflict and Crime* (Social Research Council, New York, 1938).

Selznick, P., *The Moral Commonwealth: Social Theory and the Promise of Community* (University of California Press, Berkeley, CA, 1992).

Shaw, I., 'Ethics in qualitative research and evaluation' (2003) 33 *British Journal of Social Work* 107.

Simon, J., 'The emergence of a risk society: insurance, law and the state' (1987) 95 *Socialist Law Review* 61.

Simon, J., 'Managing the monstrous: sex offenders and the new penology' (1998) 4(1) *Psychology, Public Law and Policy* 1.

Smith, D., 'Forming an Incident Response Team' (Proceedings of the FIRST Annual Conference, University of Queensland, Brisbane, 1994).

Smith, J.C., '*R v. Bow Street Metropolitan Stipendiary Magistrate and Allison, ex parte Government of the United States of America*' (case note) [1999] Criminal Law Review 970.

Social Issues Research Centre, 'Beware the Precautionary Principle' <http://www.sirc.org/articles/beware.html>.

Sommer, P., 'Computer Misuse Prosecutions' (Society for Computers and Law 2005) <http://www.scl.org.uk/services/default.asp?p=154&c=9999&cID=1140001017&ctID=12>.

Spafford, E., 'Are hacker break-ins ethical?', in Ermann, M., Williams, M. and Shauf, M. (eds), *Computers, Ethics, and Society* (Oxford University Press, New York, 1997).

Spafford, E., *The Internet Worm Program: An Analysis*, Purdue Technical Report CSD-TR-823 (29 November 1988) <http://homes.cerias.purdue.edu/~spaf/tech-reps/823.pdf>.

Spurgeon, C., *Ethernet: The Definitive Guide* (O'Reilly, Sebastopol, CA, 2000).

Standish Group, *Trends in Open Source* (April 2008).

Statement by Joan Ryan MP (Letter to Lord Grenfell 26 April 2007) <http://www.parliament.uk/documents/upload/LetGovResSISRpt26040 7w.pdf>.

Steele, J., *Risks and Legal Theory* (Hart, Oxford, 2004).

Stein, K., '"Unauthorised access" and the UK Computer Misuse Act 1990: House of Lords "leaves no room" for ambiguity' (2000) 6 *Computer and Telecommunications Law Review* 63.

Stephen, J.F., *Liberty, Equality, Fraternity* (1873), reprinted in White, J. (ed.), *Liberty, Equality, Fraternity* (Cambridge University Press, Cambridge, 1967).

Sterling, B., *The Hacker Crackdown* (Bantam Books, New York, 1992).

Stewart, A., *Theories of Power and Domination: The Politics of Empowerment in Late Modernity* (Sage, London, 2001).

Stewart, T.A., *Intellectual Capital: The New Wealth of Organizations* (Currency/Doubleday, New York, 1999).

Stoll, C., *The Cuckoo's Egg: Tracking a Spy Through the Maze of Computer Espionage* (Pocket Books, New York, 1990).

Strauss, A. and Corbin, J., *Basics of Qualitative Research: Techniques and Procedures for Developing Grounded Theory* (3rd edn, Sage, London, 2008).

Sudman, S. and Bradburn, N., *Response Effects in Surveys* (Aldine, Chicago, IL, 1974).

Suler, J., *The Psychology of Cyberspace* <http://www.rider.edu/~suler/psycyber/psycyber.html>.

Sullivan, D., *Qualitative Research: Theory, Method and Practice* (2nd edn, Sage, London, 2004).

Sunstein, C.R., 'Probability neglect: emotions, worst cases and law' (2002) 112 *Yale Law Journal* 61.

Sunstein, C.R., 'The paralyzing principle', *Regulation* (Winter 2002–03) 32.

Sunstein, C.R., 'Beyond the precautionary principle' (2003) 151 *University of Pennsylvania Law Review* 1003.

Sunstein, C.R., 'Essay: on the divergent American reactions to terrorism and climate change' (2007) 107 *Columbia Law Review* 503.

Tappan, P.W., 'Who is the criminal?' (1947) 12 *American Sociological Review* 96.

Tapper, C., 'Computer crime: Scotch mist?' [1987] *Criminal Law Review* 4.

Teichner, F., 'Regulating cyberspace', 15th BILETA Conference (14 April 2000) <http://www.bileta.ac.uk/Document%20Library/1/Regulating%20Cyberspace.pdf>.

Teubner, G., 'After legal instrumentalism: strategic models of post-regulatory law', in Teubner, G. (ed.), *Dilemmas of Law in the Welfare State* (Walter de Gruyter, Berlin, 1986).

Thomas, D., 'Home Office seeks to increase jail terms for hackers', *Computing* (20 July 2005).

Thomas, D., 'Clamping down on the cyber criminals', *Computing* (2 February 2006).

Thomas, W.I. and Thomas, D.S., *The Child in America: Behavior Problems and Programs* (Knopf, New York, 1928).

Tierney, K., 'The battered women movement and the creation of the wife-beating problem' [1982] 2 *Social Problems* 207.

Tobler, C., 'Annotation: Case C-176/03, *Commission v. Council*, judgment of the Grand Chamber of 13 September 2005' (2006) 43 *Common Market Law Review* 835.

Tompkins, J. and Mar, L., 'The 1984 Federal Computer Crime Statute: a partial answer to a pervasive problem' (1985) 6 *Computer and Law Journal* 459.

Turk, A.T., *Criminality and the Social Order* (Rand-McNally, Chicago, IL, 1969).

UKERNA, 'CSIRTs and WARPs: Improving Security Together' (March 2005) <http://www.warp.gov.uk/Marketing/WARPCSIRT%20handout.pdf>.

Ultrascan, '419 fraud stats and trends for 2007' (19 February 2008) <http://www.ultrascan.nl/assets/applets/2007_Stats_on_419_AFF_feb_19_2008_version_1.7.pdf>.

United Kingdom Interdepartmental Liaison Group on Risk Assessment, *The Precautionary Principle: Policy and Application* (2002) <http://www.hse.gov.uk/aboutus/meetings/ilgra/pppa.htm>.

United Nations, 'World Charter for Nature', UN Doc A A/RES/37/7 (1982).

United Nations, 'Eighth United Nations Congress on the Prevention of Crime and the Treatment of Offenders, Havana (27 August – 7 September 1990)', UN Doc E/91/IV/2.

United Nations, 'Rio Declaration on Environment and Development', UN Doc A/Conf. 151/5/Rev. 1 (1992).

United Nations, 'Manual on the prevention and control of computer-related crime' (1994) 43–44 International Review of Criminal Policy, UN Doc E/94/IV/5.

United States Department of Justice, Computer Crime and Intellectual Property Section, 'Council of Europe Convention on Cybercrime Frequently Asked Questions and Answers' (11 November 2003) <http://www.usdoj.gov/criminal/cybercrime/COEFAQs.htm>

United Nations, 'Congress Discussion Guide', UN Doc A/CONF/203/PM/1 (11 February 2005).

United Nations, '"Around the clock" capability needed to successfully fight cybercrime, workshop told', UN Doc SOC/CP/334 (25 April 2005).

Van Blarcum, D., 'Internet hate speech: the European Framework and the emerging American haven' (2005) 62 *Washington and Lee Law Review* 781.

Van Wyk, K.R. and Forno, R., *Incident Response* (O'Reilly & Associates, Sebastopol, CA, 2001).

Vermeulen, G., 'Pre-judicial (preventative) structuring of international police action in Europe' (1996) <http://www.ncjrs.gov/policing/pre75.htm>.

Vold, G., *Theoretical Criminology* (Oxford University Press, Oxford, 1958).

Wagner, R.P., 'Information wants to be free: intellectual property and the mythologies of control' (2003) 103 *Columbia Law Review* 995.

Walden, I., *Computer Crimes and Digital Investigations* (Oxford University Press, Oxford, 2007).

Walker, C., 'Political violence and commercial risk' (2003) 56 *Current Legal Problems* 531.

Walker, C., 'Cyber-terrorism: legal principle and law in the United Kingdom' (2006) 110 *Penn State Law Review* 625.

Walker, C., 'Governance of the Critical National Infrastructure' [2008] *Public Law* 323.

Walker, C. and Broderick, J., *The Civil Contingencies Act 2004: Risk, Resilience and the Law in the United Kingdom* (Oxford University Press, Oxford, 2006).

Wall, D.S., *Cybercrime: The Transformation of Crime in the Digital Age* (Polity Press, Cambridge, 2007).

Wang, C. and Williamson, S., 'Unemployment insurance with moral hazard in a dynamic economy' (1996) 44 *Carnegie-Rochester Conference Series on Public Policy* 1.

Warren, C., 'Qualitative interviewing', in Gubrium, J. and Holstein, J. (eds), *Handbook of Interview Research: Context and Method* (Sage, London, 2001).

Wasik, M., 'Criminal damage and the computerised saw' (1986) 136 *New Law Journal* 763.

Wasik, M., *Crime and the Computer* (Clarendon Press, Oxford, 1991).

Wasik, M., *The Role of the Criminal Law in the Control of Misuse of Information Technology* (University of Manchester Working Paper No. 8, July 1991).

Wasik, M., 'Dealing in the information market: procuring, selling and offering to sell personal data' (1995) 9 *International Yearbook of Law, Computers and Technology* 193.

Wasik, M., 'Hacking, viruses and fraud', in Akdeniz, Y., Walker, C. and Wall, D.S. (eds), *The Internet, Law and Society* (Pearson Education, Harlow, 2000).

Wasik, M., 'Computer misuse and misconduct in public office' (2008) 22 *International Review of Law, Computers and Technology* 135.

Weber, A.M., 'The Council of Europe's Convention on Cybercrime' (2003) 18 *Berkeley Technology Law Journal* 425.

Webster, P., 'Millions more ID records go missing', *The Times* (18 December 2007).

Webster, P. and Seib, C., 'Alistair Darling props up Northern Rock with fresh £30bn debt guarantee', *The Times* (19 January 2008).

Webster, P., O'Neill, S. and Blakely, R., '25 million exposed to risk of ID fraud', *The Times* (21 November 2007).

Weller, P. and others (eds), *The Hollow Crown: Countervailing Trends in Core Executives* (Macmillan, London 1997).

West-Brown, M.J. and others, *Handbook of Computer Security Incident Response Teams* (2nd edn, Carnegie Mellon University, Pittsburgh, PA, 2003).

Whine, M., 'Cyberhate, anti-semitism and counterlegislation' (2006) 11 *Communications Law* 124.

White, S., 'Harmonisation of criminal law under the First Pillar' (2006) 31 *European Law Review* 81.

Wiener, J.B., 'Whose precaution after all? A comment on the comparison and evolution of risk regulatory systems' (2003) 13 *Duke Journal of Comparative and International Law* 207.

Wiik, J., Gonzalez, K.K. and Kossakowski, K.-P., 'Limits to Effectiveness in Computer Security Incident Response Teams' (Twenty-third International Conference of the System Dynamics Society, Boston, 2005).

Williams, K.S. and Carr, I., 'Crime, risk and computers' (2002) 9 *Electronic Communication Law Review* 23.

Computer Misuse

Williams, M., *Virtually Criminal* (Routledge, Abingdon, 2006).

Willmore, L., 'Government policies towards information and communication technologies: a historical perspective' (2002) 28 *Journal of Information Science* 89.

Wilson, D. and others, *Fraud and Technology Crimes: Findings from the 2003/04 British Crime Survey, the 2004 Offending, Crime and Justice Survey and Administrative Sources*, Home Office Online Report 09/06 <www.homeoffice.gov.uk/rds/pdfs06/rdsolr0906.pdf>.

Young, J., *The Exclusive Society* (Sage, London, 1999).

Zedner, L., *Criminal Justice* (Oxford University Press, Oxford, 2004).

Command papers

Beveridge, W., *Social Insurance and Allied Services* (Cmd 6404, 1942).

HM Treasury, *Investing in Britain's Potential: Building Our Long-term Future* (Cm 6984, 2006).

Secretary of State for Work and Pensions, *Ready for Work: Full Employment in Our Generation* (Cm 7290, 2007).

Parliamentary reports

The BSE Inquiry, 'BSE Inquiry Report' HC (1999–00) 887.

European Union Committee, 'The Criminal Law Competence of the European Community: Report with Evidence' HL (2005–06) 227.

European Union Committee, 'Schengen Information System II (SIS II)' HL (2006–07) 49.

Joint Committee on Human Rights, 'The Council of Europe Convention on the Prevention of Terrorism' HL (2006–07) 26; HC (2006–07) 247.

Select Committee on European Communities, 'Incorporating the Schengen *Acquis* into the European Union' HL (1997–98) 139.

Standing Committee C, 'Computer Misuse Bill' HC (1989–90).

Index